READING
THE GRAIN

Through an analysis of a wide array of contemporary Chinese literature from inside and outside of China, this volume considers some of the ways in which China and Chineseness are understood and imagined.

Using the central theme of the way in which literature has the potential to both reinforce and to undermine a national imaginary, the volume contains chapters offering new perspectives on well-known authors, from Jin Yucheng to Nobel Prize winning Mo Yan, as well as chapters focusing on authors rarely included in discussions of contemporary Chinese literature, such as the expatriate authors Larissa Lai and Xiaolu Guo. The volume is complemented by chapters covering more marginalized literary figures throughout history, such as Macau-born poet Yiling, the Malaysian-born novelist Zhang Guixing, and the ethnically Korean author Kim Hak-ch'ŏl. Invested in issues ranging from identity and representation, to translation and grammar, it is one of the few publications of its kind devoting comparable attention to authors from Mainland China, authors from Manchuria, Macau, and Taiwan, and throughout the global Chinese diaspora.

Reading China Against the Grain: Imagining Communities is a rich resource of literary criticism for students and scholars of Chinese studies, sinophone studies, and comparative literature.

Carlos Rojas is Professor of Chinese Cultural Studies; Genders, Sexuality, and Feminist Studies; and Arts of the Moving Image at Duke University. He is the author, editor, and translator of numerous books on global Chinese literature and culture.

Mei-hwa Sung received her PhD in English from Brown University in 1983 and has taught at National Taiwan University, Tamkang University, and Beijing Normal University-Hong Kong Baptist University United International College (UIC). She has a long record of professional service, including the editorship of *Chung-Wai Literary Monthly* and *Tamkang Review*. She has published essays and books on eighteenth-century English literature, gender studies, and Taiwan fiction.

READING CHINA AGAINST THE GRAIN

Imagining Communities

Edited by Carlos Rojas and Mei-hwa Sung

Routledge
Taylor & Francis Group

LONDON AND NEW YORK

First published 2021
by Routledge
2 Park Square, Milton Park, Abingdon, Oxon OX14 4RN

and by Routledge
52 Vanderbilt Avenue, New York, NY 10017

Routledge is an imprint of the Taylor & Francis Group, an informa business

British Library Cataloguing-in-Publication Data
A catalogue record for this book is available from the British Library

Library of Congress Cataloging-in-Publication Data
Names: Rojas, Carlos, 1970– editor. | Sung, Mei-hwa, editor.
Title: Reading China against the grain : imagining communities / edited by Carlos Rojas and Mei-hwa Sung.
Description: Abingdon, Oxon ; New York : Routledge, 2021. | Includes bibliographical references and index.
Identifiers: LCCN 2020025077 | ISBN 9780367406653 (hardback) | ISBN 9780367415495 (paperback) | ISBN 9781000216516 (adobe pdf) | ISBN 9781000216615 (epub) | ISBN 9781000216561 (mobi)
Subjects: LCSH: Chinese literature—Foreign countries—History and criticism. | Chinese literature—20th century—History and criticism. | Chinese literature—21st century—History and criticism. | Chinese diaspora in literature. | Chinese in literature. | China—In literature.
Classification: LCC PL3033 .R43 2021 | DDC 895.109—dc23
LC record available at https://lccn.loc.gov/2020025077

ISBN: 978-0-367-40665-3 (hbk)
ISBN: 978-0-367-41549-5 (pbk)
ISBN: 978-0-367-81515-8 (ebk)

Typeset in Bembo
by Apex CoVantage, LLC

CONTENTS

ILLUSTRATIONS

CONTRIBUTORS

Rosa Vieira de Almeida is Lecturer in International Studies at Leiden University. She completed her doctorate in Chinese Literature (2018) with a thesis on Macau literature during the period of decolonization. She is interested in the themes of diaspora, (post)colonialism, and literary marginality.

Mary Goodwin is Professor of English at National Taiwan Normal University in Taipei. Her research interests include the modern American novel, crime fiction, and Anglophone Asian literature, with an emphasis on writing from Taiwan.

Wen Jin is Professor of Comparative Literature at East China Normal University, China. Her book, *Pluralist Universalism: An Asian Americanist Critique of U.S. and Chinese Multiculturalisms* (Ohio State UP, 2012), provides comparative readings of American, Chinese, and Chinese American fiction. Her current projects deal with English novels and patterns of emotion in the eighteenth century, and with comparisons of Anglo-American, Chinese, and European novel traditions. She has published numerous essays in journals and edited volumes, and she is on the editorial board of *The International Journal of Cultural Studies*.

Lucas Klein (PhD Yale) is a father, writer, and translator. His scholarship and criticism have appeared in the monograph *The Organization of Distance: Poetry, Translation, Chineseness* (2018), as well as in *Comparative Literature Studies*, *LARB*, *Jacket*, *CLEAR*, *PMLA*, and other venues. His translations of the poetry of Duo Duo, forthcoming from Yale University Press, won a PEN/Heim Translation Fund grant, and he co-edited *Chinese Poetry and Translation: Rights and Wrongs* (2019). He is currently an associate professor in the School of Chinese at the University of Hong Kong; as of 2021, he will be teaching at Arizona State University.

Belinda Kong is Associate Professor of Asian Studies and English at Bowdoin College. Her research focuses on contemporary literature by Chinese diaspora and Asian American writers. Her current book project, *What Lived Through SARS: Chronicles of Pandemic Resilience*, explores cultural expressions of epidemic life at the epicenters of the 2003 SARS outbreak.

Charles Lowe is Associate Professor and Associate Dean at Beijing Normal University-Hong Kong Baptist University United International College (UIC). His work has been included in *China and the Human(e/i)ties At the Crossroads of Humanities* and *Friend, Follow, Text: #Storiesfromlivingonline*. It has also appeared in *The International Journal of the Humanities, Hardy Review, AGNI, Prairie Schooner*, and *J Journal: New Writing on Justice*.

MEI Chia-ling is Distinguished Professor of Chinese Literature and Chair of the Chinese Department at National Taiwan University. Her expertise includes modern and contemporary Chinese literature, Taiwan literature, and Six Dynasties Literature.

Carlos Rojas is Professor of Chinese Cultural Studies; Genders, Sexuality, and Feminist Studies; and Arts of the Moving Image at Duke University. He is the author, editor, and translator of numerous books on global Chinese literature and culture.

Mei-hwa Sung received her PhD in English from Brown University in 1983 and has taught at National Taiwan University, Tamkang University, and Beijing Normal University-Hong Kong Baptist University United International College (UIC). She has a long record of professional service, including the editorship of *Chung-Wai Literary Monthly* and *Tamkang Review*. She has published essays and books on eighteenth-century English literature, gender studies, and Taiwan fiction.

Q. S. Tong is formally University Professor of English in the College of Liberal Arts and English Department, Sun Yat-sen University, China. Before he joined Sun Yat-sen University in 2015, he had worked and taught at the University of Hong Kong for over two decades. He has published extensively, in both English and Chinese, on issues of critical significance in literary and cultural studies, criticism and theory, with special attention to the historical interactions between China and the West. He has served as advisory editor for a number of international journals.

XU Xi is Assistant Professor in the English Language and Literature Studies Program, Beijing Normal University-Hong Kong Baptist University United International College (UIC). He received his BA in English language and literature from Peking University and his PhD in Cross-cultural Studies in English from the University of Hong Kong. His research interests include global modernism, travel writing, children's literature, and comparative literature.

Miya Qiong Xie is Assistant Professor of Chinese in the Asian Societies, Cultures and Languages Program at Dartmouth College, specializing in comparative East Asian literatures. She is currently working on her first book manuscript about Chinese, Korean, and Japanese literatures from the northeastern Asian borderland of Manchuria, and her second book project on Ethnic Korean literature in China.

PREFACE: IMAGINING CHINA

Carlos Rojas

In *Imagined Communities*, Benedict Anderson famously proposes that modern nations function as imagined constructs whose members are bound together more by projected affiliations than by tangible communities. Unlike smaller communities, in which it is possible for most members to know one another directly, nations are vast conglomerates of individuals who, for the most part, will never meet in a meaningful way. Despite their inherent heterogeneity, however, national communities are perceived as being anchored by a set of deep commonalities, and it is this perception that has permitted nationality to emerge as one of the key loci of collective identity in the modern age.

Anderson emphasizes the role of what he called print capitalism in helping consolidate nationalist sentiment, arguing that the spread of print capitalism in the eighteenth and nineteenth centuries was an important catalyst for the global emergence of modern nationalism during that same period. However, while considerable attention has been given to Anderson's discussion of how the modern perception of homogenous time is reinforced by newspapers and other periodicals – specifically, their ability to permit readers positioned throughout a broad geographic area to simultaneously access the same news – equally important is his emphasis on the role of the novel in helping to structure this sort of national imaginary. Not only do novels feature a diegetic space, like a nation, in which different individuals may be imagined to be simultaneously engaged in a variety of unrelated activities; they also are important in consolidating and reinforcing the sorts of shared values and cultural attributes with which national identities tend to be inextricably intertwined.

In this volume we adopt a similar approach, though in reverse. Taking as our starting point the inherently constructed and contingent nature of national formations, we examine some of the ways literature may help constitute not only these sorts of national formations but also the fault lines that run through them.

We give particular attention to novels, but also consider poetry and other modes of literary production.

Our focus is on modern China, which provides a particularly useful prism for examining questions of national identity through a literary lens. On one hand, China is often perceived as having a continuous linguistic and cultural tradition that dates back for millennia and as having enjoyed a continuous civilization for two, three, or even five millennia. These claims of civilizational coherence and continuity are often greatly exaggerated, though historically this sort of rhetorical appeal has played an important role in helping shape the way that the Chinese nation and its antecedents are imagined. On the other hand, modern China also features a number of peculiarities that bring into stark relief the sorts of contingencies on which all modern nations are grounded.

To begin with, when the People's Republic of China (PRC) was founded in 1949, the government in Beijing only held sovereignty over a subset of the geographic region that was theoretically covered by the term "China." At the time, Tibet was an autonomous state, Hong Kong was a British colony, Macau was a Portuguese colony, and Taiwan was functionally a newly established nation-state controlled by the Nationalists and known as the Republic of China (ROC), though the PRC government in Beijing and the ROC government in Taipei each supported the political fiction that they retained sovereignty over the entirety of China. Even today, the Chinese nation continues to be a patchwork of different political arrangements. Taiwan remains, for all practical purposes, an autonomous nation-state, even as the PRC has worked to solidify economic and cultural ties between Taiwan and the mainland, while also going to considerable effort to limit international recognition of Taiwan's identity as a nation-state. Meanwhile, Hong Kong and Macau both have been returned to Chinese control but continue to be categorized as semiautonomous "special administrative regions"; Tibet is now also under Chinese control, but – like Inner Mongolia, Ningxia, Xinjiang, and Guangxi – it is recognized not as a province but rather as an "autonomous region." Moreover, modern China officially comprises fifty-six distinct ethnicities including the majority Han ethnicity, which makes up over 90 percent of the population, and another fifty-five ethnic groups, many of whom are concentrated along the nation's inland border regions, particularly Inner Mongolia, Xinjiang, Tibet, Sichuan, and Yunnan. The Chinese term for ethnic group is *minzu* 民族, for which the official PRC translation is "nationality." Accordingly, if we reverse-translate the common characterization that the PRC is a *"duominzu guojia"* 多民族国家 into English, we are left with the curiously paradoxical formulation that China is a "multinational nation."

The chapters that compose this volume use modern literature to reflect on the nature of national identity, together with the sorts of narrative processes on which that identity is partly predicated. We approach the taxonomical category of modern Chinese literature in broad terms, to include not only works from inland China but also works associated with border regions including Inner Mongolia, Macau, Manchuria, Hong Kong, Taiwan, and Sinophone Southeast

Asia. In addition to works composed in Mandarin Chinese, we examine ones written in regional dialects as well other languages including English, Japanese, and Korean. We consider works by conventionally "Chinese" authors, but also include some by authors belonging to other ethnicities and/or nationalities. In short, we approach both Chinese literature and Chinese national identity as flexible constructs that are not defined by any necessary and sufficient criteria but are instead the product of a disparate set of forces and tendencies.

In the introduction, Carlos Rojas examines the relationship between language and Chineseness by considering five contemporary works ranging from Beijing-based author Yan Lianke's 2004 novel *Lenin's Kisses* (*Shouhuo*), set in the author's home province of Henan, to Chinese émigré author Xiaolu Guo's debut English-language novel, *A Concise Chinese-English Dictionary for Lovers*, written in the voice of a young Chinese woman who has come to England from China. Starting with a work set in central China (the "Central Plains" region that is often regarded as the birthplace of Chinese civilization) and moving outward to China's border regions and beyond, this chapter examines different strategies that the authors use to address the heterogeneous linguistic environments within which they are each based.

The remainder of the volume adopts a similar structure, moving progressively outward from China's presumptive ideological center to the far reaches of the Chinese diaspora. In particular, the volume is divided into three sections, with Part I examining a set of authors associated with mainland China, Part II turning to literary phenomena associated with China's geographic margins, and Part III looking at works originating from the far reaches of the global Chinese diaspora. Through this comparative analysis, we examine the ways that even works that might be viewed as paradigmatically Chinese strategically incorporate a variety of "foreign" elements and influences, while works from the outer periphery of the Chinese global diaspora often remain deeply engaged with questions of how to understand concepts of China and Chineseness.

Part I opens with Mei-hwa Sung's discussion of Mo Yan, the first Chinese national to be awarded the Nobel Prize for literature. Sung focuses specifically on four novels published between 1987 and 2006, in which Mo Yan strategically interweaves historical and fantastical elements. In this way, Sung not only illustrates the ways Mo Yan draws on national conceits in his fiction but also shows how his approach underscores the fantastic underpinnings of the national imaginary. In the following chapter, XU Xi turns to Yu Hua, who similarly began his literary career in the 1980s. Xu looks specifically at Yu Hua's 1991 novel *Cries in the Drizzle*, arguing that it borrows some of the narrative conventions associated with the Western genre of the bildungsroman but strategically inverts them. Next, Lucas Klein considers two of contemporary China's most influential poets, Wang Ao and Xi Chuan, borrowing the tropes of Dracula and Frankenstein as metaphors for two distinct ways classic Romanticism has been reclaimed in contemporary Chinese poetry. The Dracula approach views Romanticism as a vampiric force closely allied with capitalism, while the Frankenstein approach emphasizes Romanticism's inherent "hybridity and adaptability." Finally, Wen Jin considers Shanghai author Jin Yucheng's 2012 novel *Fanhua* (Blooming blossoms). Although many discussions of the novel have tended to focus on its extensive use of local Shanghai dialect, Jin instead examines the ways the work challenges contemporary readers' expectations relating to narrative form and character development and draws on a narrative mode more commonly associated with Chinese literature from the late imperial period.

Part II turns to a set of works associated with the geographic border regions such as Inner Mongolia in the north, the region formerly known as Manchuria in the northeast, Macau in the southeast, and Sinophone territories in the Southeast Asia. First, Q. S. Tong considers the 2004 novel *Wolf Totem*, by Jiang Rong (the pen name of Lü Jiamin). Although Jiang Rong is ethnically Han, his quasi-autobiographical novel is set in Inner Mongolia and uses a celebration of Mongol culture to offer a broad critique of Han Chinese society and values. Next, Miya Qiong Xie examines a novel titled *The Myth of the Twentieth Century* (*20-segi ŭi sinhwa*) by ethnically Korean and China-based author Kim Hak-ch'ŏl. Kim wrote the novel in Korean between 1964 and 1965, then immediately began translating it into Japanese (the Korean version was not published until 1996, in Seoul, and Kim's Japanese translation of the work was never completed). Although Kim was still technically a North Korean citizen when he completed the novel in 1965, Xie argues that the work may be viewed as a Chinese novel on the grounds that Kim was living in the Korean Autonomous District in northeast China, and the novel itself deals with topics relating to modern Chinese history. In the third chapter, Rosa Vieira de Almeida turns to the Macau-born poet Yiling (pen name of Virginia Cheang Mio San), specifically, the way Yiling presents Macau during the "pre-postcolonial era" (the period between the 1987 Sino-Portuguese Joint Declaration that Macau would be returned to Chinese control and the eventual transfer of sovereignty in 1999) as a space of "insignificance." Rather than insisting on seeing literature as an affirmation of the significance of its subject matter, de Almeida sees something deeply productive in Yiling's emphasis on the structural "insignificance" of contemporary Macau. Finally, MEI Chia-ling looks at the work of the Mahua (Malaysian-Chinese) author Zhang Guixing. Taking inspiration from the title of China's earliest etymological dictionary, the second century CE *Shuowen jiezi* (說文解字) (which literally means "explaining graphs and analyzing characters"), Mei examines Zhang Guixing's use of and focus on Chinese characters in two of his novels, *Elephants* and *Monkey Cup*, arguing that the texts deviate from the locus of China/Chineseness that is their source text and the object of their pursuit.

Part III considers a set of contemporary works that are a product of Chinese literature's global dissemination. Written by authors currently based in Taiwan, the United States, Canada, and Great Britain, these could all be viewed as "Chinese" novels, though they were actually composed in English. First, Mary Goodwin considers several novels from Taiwan that feature romantic affairs between young female students and significantly older male teachers, all of whom happen to specialize in topics related to traditional Chinese culture, focusing in particular on two novels that were both composed in English. Next, Charles Lowe turns to the author Qiu Xiaolong and a series of crime novels that Qiu has written since he moved to the United States in 1988. Although the novels have subsequently been translated into a number of different languages, including Chinese, they were originally composed in English. Lowe, however, argues that they may be viewed as products of "virtual translation," written as though translated from Chinese originals, although in reality the English-language works have no prior source text. In the third chapter, Belinda Kong examines Chinese-Canadian author Larissa Lai's 2002 novel *Salt Fish Girl*. Drawing from Anna Tsing's anthropological study of the matsutake mushroom and the conceit of Lai's novel that its protagonist is a mortal reincarnation of the goddess Nu Wa (who is credited in Chinese mythology with having created humanity), Kong develops a conceptual model of what she calls the sinospore as a more flexible and productive alternative to the widely used concept of the Chinese diaspora. Finally, in the fourth chapter Carlos Rojas offers an analysis of Xiaolu Guo's 2014 novel *I Am China*. Following the novel's lead, Rojas looks at the relationship between linguistic copulas and processes of sexual copulation, and use an abstract understanding of translation (including nodes of untranslatability) to reflect on the significance of the novel's title.

In the end, this is a book about books, and specifically about how literature helps shape our vision of the nation and of the world. Our own book's cover image is of the spectacular wall of books in the Binhai Public Library in Tianjin, China. Designed by the Dutch architectural firm MVRDV, the library opened in 2017 and can hold more than 1.35 million volumes. When viewed from outside, the building resembles a giant eye staring into space; but when visitors enter the structure, they have a feeling of being immersed within an ocean of books. Although observers have noted the fact that a subset of the volumes visible in the building's main atrium are actually "fake" (consisting of embossed aluminum plates designed to resemble actual books), the library's use of these fake books could nevertheless be viewed as a reflection on the way in which our perception of reality is similarly mediated through simulacra – and more specifically, the way in which our view of social reality is itself mediated though an engagement with literature and other forms of cultural production. In other words, even as national and global communities are constituted through a set projective and imagined processes (i.e., they are "fake"), the resulting communities nevertheless have a very real existence within today's world.

INTRODUCTION

My language is not my own: translation, displacement, and contemporary Chinese literature

Carlos Rojas

Running like a mantra through Derrida's most acutely autobiographical book – his 1996 study *Monolingualism of the Other; or, The Prosthesis of Origin* – the assertion "I have only one language, but it is not mine" is both intimately personal and broadly universal.[1] That is to say, this claim not only speaks to the biographical specificities of Derrida's own relationship to language but also reflects more generally on humanity's relationship to language itself.

On one hand, although Derrida was fluent in several languages, he described how French was the only language in which he felt truly at home – despite the fact that, having grown up in Algeria, he spoke French with a distinctive southern accent and confesses that his entire life he looked down on accents like his own in favor of a more "standard" Parisian accent that he was never able to fully master. Moreover, as a French Jew growing up during World War II, Derrida was stripped of his French citizenship under the Vichy government and thereby legally separated from the nation-state with which he most directly identified. Accordingly, when Derrida states that he only has one language but it is not his own, he is referring to the fact that French is his first language and the only language he views as truly his, but it was never *truly* his, and he has continually felt alienated from it.

On the other hand, in *Monolingualism of the Other* Derrida is also making a broader claim about humanity's relationship to language itself. That is to say, we have only one language, in that we don't have access to any metalanguage or communicative space outside of language with which we can effectively discuss language itself. At the same time, natural language, in a very practical sense, can never be one's own; it is predicated on the existence of a set of communal (and, therefore, necessarily external) rules and conventions that make it intelligible to others. Accordingly, when Derrida states that he has only one language but it is not his own, he also means natural language is effectively the only language to which we have access, but it can never belong to any one individual and instead is generated through collective interactions. Language is never "one's own," precisely because, by its very nature, it is a product of interactions among individuals.

The paradoxical status of language that Derrida identifies in *Monolingualism of the Other* also has implications for corresponding ethnonational configurations, as well as taxonomical categories for various phenomena grounded on those configurations. Although it is often assumed that ethnonational and linguistic categories are closely linked, in reality no nation is truly monolingual, nor is there any language that is precisely coterminous with any single national configuration. By extension, while it may be true that in the modern world we can no more exist without ethnonational identity than we can exist without language, those ethnonational structures are always a product of interactions among people, and therefore are never one's own.

What is true of languages and ethnonational categories is also true of literary fields. Literature, understood in the general sense of storytelling, represents a fundamental aspect of how we engage with and make sense of the world, and in the modern world there has been a strong tendency to associate literary fields with national configurations. Literary associations, literary histories, academic departments, and literary prizes often categorize literary works based not only on the language in which they are written but also on their corresponding national configurations. As a result, the imagined coherence of the nation is used to naturalize inherently heterogenous groupings of literary texts. The resulting bodies of national literature, in turn, may play an important role in further consolidating the constructed nexus of national identity itself.

While modern Chinese literature has traditionally been viewed through the lens of the nation-state, many scholars have recently emphasized the need to consider other taxonomies that don't prioritize the nation. In particular, borrowing from notions of Anglophone or Francophone literature, which refer to literature written in English or French but originating from outside England or France, some scholars use the term *Sinophone* to refer to literature written in Chinese from outside China and to literature written by ethnic minority authors from within China. This use of language as a basis of classification, however, has its limits. Many diasporic Chinese authors do not write primarily or solely in Chinese, and even if they do, the fact that they use a common language does not guarantee that they share a common literary or cultural tradition. Furthermore, the emphasis on language as a determining criterion ignores the fact that Chinese is not a singular and self-contained category but a conglomerate of distinct dialects and languages.

In the following discussion, I use Derrida's aphorism from *Monolingualism of the Other* to examine the relationship between language and (national) identity in relation to Chinese literature, broadly understood. Although it is often assumed that Chinese literature is defined by the fact that it is written in Chinese, the relationship between the language and the literature is actually rather complex.

Chinese is not, of course, a unitary entity but an assortment of partly overlapping scripts and dialects. Furthermore, although the language often carries national and ethnic connotations, there is no coherent and unitary ethnonational identity to which it corresponds.

In particular, I will consider works by five authors who have very different relationships to both the Chinese language and corresponding ethnonational configurations. Although each of these works could be said to have been written in Chinese, broadly understood, they capture very different facets of the language while also foregrounding internal tensions within it. Fittingly, each work prominently features a dictionary-like text – though the dictionary functions as a symbol not of authority but rather of fragmentation and disjunction. In this respect, these dictionaries are reminiscent of Borges's figure of the Chinese encyclopedia, which suggests the possibility of a radical reconfiguration of existing taxonomical categories.

1. Yan Lianke

Born and raised in central China's Henan province, Yan Lianke 閻連科 frequently incorporates local Henan dialect into his fictional writings. This practice is most obvious in his 2004 novel *Shouhuo*, translated as *Lenin's Kisses*, which includes numerous notes (or *xuyan* 絮言) that explain terms and phrases with which a typical Chinese reader would not necessarily be familiar.[2] These are in both local dialect and language deriving from the specific (quasi-fictional) history of the remote region in which the novel is set. For instance, the novel's very first sentence includes the word *shouhuo* 受活, followed by a note explaining that this is a dialectal term used mostly in western Henan and in eastern Henan's Balou mountains, meaning "enjoyment, happiness, and passion, and also carries connotations of finding pleasure in discomfort, or making pleasure out of discomfort."[3]

Lenin's Kisses features a remote village known as Shouhuo, or "Liven," in which virtually all of the residents of the community are disabled – blind, deaf, paralyzed, missing a limb, and so forth. The villagers, however, are not overly troubled by their disabilities, and many have developed compensatory "special skills," which they use to accomplish daily tasks and sometimes to entertain each other. Legend has it that the village was founded as early as the Ming dynasty, but until the middle of the twentieth century it was so isolated that it wasn't even recognized by any of the surrounding counties. One day in the mid-1950s, however, the community's matriarch, Grandma Mao Zhi, ventures out of the village and discovers that nearby communities are actively pursuing collectivization efforts under the newly established PRC's Great Leap Forward campaign. Fearing that Liven risks being left out of an important sociopolitical development, Grandma Mao Zhi decides to help the village "enter society" and join the collectivization. To this end, she convinces the leaders of one of the three nearest counties to recognize her village as falling under their jurisdiction, but shortly afterward the initiatives pursued under the Great Leap Forward campaign backfire disastrously and result in a devastating famine, during which county officials repeatedly claim the village's precious grain reserves for themselves. Feeling deeply betrayed by this turn of events, Grandma Mao Zhi vows to help the village regain its original autonomy and spends the next several decades working to achieve this goal.

The novel's main plot line unfolds during the latter half of 1998 and involves a local bureaucrat named Liu Yingque who comes up with a harebrained scheme to purchase Lenin's embalmed corpse from Russia and bring it back to his county in China, where he plans to construct a Lenin Memorial Hall that could become a lucrative tourist site. To raise the money he needs, Liu Yingque recruits some of Liven's disabled villagers and arranges for them to form a performance troupe that will entertain audiences with displays of the "special skills" they have developed to compensate for their disabilities. Grandma Mao Zhi allows Liu Yingque to proceed with this plan, but on the condition that once he has raised the money, he will permit the village to withdraw from the county and finally regain its independence.

Grandma Mao Zhi's initial determination to help Liven "enter society" and her subsequent insistence on helping the village regain its autonomy parallels the novel's own use of language. To begin with, the narrative's incorporation of local Henan dialect functions as a reminder of the relative isolation that Liven enjoyed throughout much of its history, just as the novel's inclusion of dictionary-style explanations of that same terminology is symptomatic of the village's incorporation into the broader community in the 1950s, as well as the novel's own attempt to reach an audience far beyond a theoretical readership of residents of rural Henan. At the same time, many of the explanatory excurses contain not only definitions of local terminology but also important backstory detailing the village's history – meaning that the excurses function not merely as a supplement for readers who don't know local Henan dialect but rather as an integral component of the work itself.

The irony, however, is that the endnotes are able to function as intended precisely *because* the novel was theoretically written for a readership not expected to be familiar with local Henan dialect. That is to say, readers who are familiar with the local dialect would presumably not need to consult the notes for explanations and consequently they would miss not only the explanations of the words themselves but also the more open-ended historical background contained in the notes. The novel, in other words, is situated within the gap *between* standard Mandarin and Yan's local Henan dialect. Even in the original Chinese, it is designed to be read "in translation," such that it emphatically reminds readers of the linguistic fissures that run through Chinese itself.

2. Alai

An ethnically Tibetan author from an area of northern Sichuan that was traditionally considered part of "cultural Tibet," Alai 阿來 currently lives in Chengdu.

He is the editor of a major science fiction journal and also the author of fiction mostly set in the multilingual, multiethnic, and multicultural region of northern Sichuan where he was born and grew up. Alai writes exclusively in Mandarin but nevertheless describes how he found himself "destined to roam between two languages" – educated in Chinese but accustomed to using his "mother tongue" for casual conversations.[4] Although the implication is that Alai sees himself as moving back and forth between Mandarin and Tibetan, it is likely, based on his biographical information, that what he identifies as his mother tongue is not, in fact, Tibetan, but a different language altogether – specifically, the Maerkang subdialect of the language Jiarong.

Set in the ethnically Tibetan town of Jicun in western Sichuan, *Bald Mountain* consists of six overlapping novellas in three volumes (published in 2005, 2007, and 2008, respectively). I will focus here on the third novella, *Dase and Dage* (Dase yu Dage 達瑟與達戈). Set in the 1960s, it revolves around the two title characters: Dase, who left the village to study in the Chinese interior and subsequently returned in 1963 with a cartful of books, and Rejue Huaerdan (惹 覺 華爾丹) – also known as Dage, which is Tibetan for "idiot" – who was a hunter before joining the People's Liberation Army (PLA). Standing between them is Dage's lover, a local woman called Semei 色媒, who joins a Communist propaganda troop and dreams of becoming a professional singer. The novella is narrated by a young boy positioned throughout much of the work as a silent observer.

As he does throughout his fiction, in *Dase and Dage* Alai silently translates the "hometown speech" of the narrative into Chinese, while at the same time drawing attention to these underlying issues of language and translation. The first explicit reflection on issues of language in the novella occurs as Semei is discussing with Dage her plan to become a professional singer:

> "Dage, the world has changed. Can a good hunter help me become a singer?"
>
> Semei used the Chinese word *gechangjia* 歌唱家 (singer). After all, the dialect of Tibetan used in their village didn't really have this word yet. In this dialect, there were only words and phrases corresponding to "song," "to sing," "that person is singing a song," "that person singing a song," and similar expressions describing someone in the act of singing at a specific moment. Those formulations designate a condition that anyone could provisionally assume, rather than the glorious profession of singing itself.
>
> Now, however, this technical term referring to a kind of glorious profession tumbled out of Semei's beautiful throat in Chinese. The word had a spell-like allure, and as she uttered it her downcast face immediately lit up with an extraordinary glow.[5]

It is no coincidence that the first word in the novel spoken directly in Mandarin is *gechangjia* (singer). Not only is *singer* itself a metalinguistic term, referring to a practice wherein language itself is endowed with a "spell-like allure," but also it is being used here in a way that underscores an ontological distinction between singing as a discrete act and the concept of a singer as a fixed identity.

It is also no coincidence that Semei's comments come precisely in the context of a discussion of language itself. Semei's face lights up the instant she mentions the Chinese word for "singer," as she becomes infected with the enchanting power of the "glorious profession" of singing itself. Her use of a Chinese term is fitting, since it becomes clear that the songs she will be performing are actually Maoist propaganda pieces. For instance, she proceeds to sing a couple of lines from "The Brilliance of Chairman Mao" (*Mao Zhuxi de guanghui* 毛主席的光輝):

> The brilliance of Chairman Mao,
> *gelaya xi luoruo.*
> It shines on the snowy mountain tops,
> *yila qiang ba luoruo.*
> 毛主席的光輝
> 嘎拉呀兮咯若
> 照到了雪山上
> 一拉將把咯若 (28)

Notably, this song is not only one of the relatively few instances in the novella where a character is described as speaking Chinese rather than one of the region's local languages, but also one of the rare instances in Alai's work (with the exception of proper names like Dage) where Tibetan is transcribed and directly embedded within the fictional text. It is, therefore, significant that this inclusion of Tibetan occurs in one of the most explicitly Maoist passages in the novel.

The interweaving of Chinese and Tibetan phrases in this song has a specific history. The tune was originally adopted in 1951–1952 from a Tibetan folk song, and was given Chinese lyrics by Wang Ronghan 王蓉翰. The piece was modified again in 1964 when the Tibetan singer Tseten Dolma 才旦卓瑪 was invited to perform it at Zhou Enlai's multiethnic 1964 production of "The East Is Red" (*Dongfang hong* 東方紅), where she modified it by reinserting a Tibetan-language refrain into the Chinese lyrics. In his own citation of the song, meanwhile, Alai leaves Tseten Dolma's lines in the original Tibetan (though transliterated into Chinese) and emphasizes the fact that other characters in the novel perceive these lines as comparatively unintelligible "distant Tibetan (*yuanfang de Zangyu* 遠方的藏語), and not the local dialect of the village (*dangdi fangyan* 當地方言)" (28).

The song, accordingly, captures in miniature the translational nature of Alai's fiction, which takes inspiration from the local culture of the Greater Tibet region, is rendered mostly in standard Mandarin, and also occasionally includes Tibetan linguistic elements that help mark the text's non-Mandarin origins. The irony is that in this particular passage, Alai's fictional characters describe Tseten Dolma's reinserted Tibetan song lyrics as being a form of "distant Tibetan," which is perhaps even more alien to them than the song's original Mandarin lyrics.

3. Dung Kai-Cheung

Born in Hong Kong in 1967, Dung Kai-Cheung 董啟章 speaks Cantonese as his first language, but is also fluent in *putonghua* (Mandarin) and English. He received his BA and MA in literature from the University of Hong Kong and began publishing fiction in 1991. All of Dung's works are set either in Hong Kong or in a fictional space that clearly parallels that of Hong Kong, and many explore issues of Hong Kong's history and contemporary identity.

Like other Hong Kong authors, Dung writes fiction that uses a combination of different forms of Chinese – including a written form of Cantonese (which reflects Cantonese syntax and uses Cantonese-specific characters) for characters' dialogue, and what resembles standard Mandarin (but Dung himself prefers to call simply "written language" [*shumianyu* 書面語]) for the narrative portions. In some works he also includes phrases in English and other languages, depending on the context and the linguistic backgrounds of the corresponding fictional characters.

A good example of this heteroglossic practice can be found in Dung's Natural History trilogy (自然史三部曲), which began with his 2005 novel *Works and Creations* (*Tiangong kaiwu: Xuxu ruzhen* 天工開物. 栩栩如真), continued with his 2007 two-volume novel, *Histories of Time: The Luster of Mute Porcelain* (*Shijian fanshi: Yaci zhiguang* 時間繁史: 啞瓷之光), and concludes with *The Origin of the Species: The Educational Age of Beibei's Rebirth* (物種源始: 貝貝重生之學習年代) (of which the first volume was published in 2010, but the planned second volume was never completed). Though composed primarily in standard written Chinese (*shumianyu*), the trilogy includes significant amounts of English, and *Histories of Time* features so much Cantonese-language dialogue that a lengthy Chinese-Cantonese glossary is included at the end, for readers who don't speak Cantonese. In the following discussion, however, I will focus on volume one of the trilogy, *Works and Creations*, which not only includes considerable amounts of English but also culminates in a pivotal scene featuring a Chinese-English dictionary.

Works and Creations alternates between two interwoven storylines: the odd-numbered chapters consist of a series of excerpts from a fictional novel, and the even-numbered chapters consist of an epistolary exchange between the author of this fictional novel and a character, by the name of Xuxu, within that novel. Xuxu is initially presented as a cyborglike creature, with an alarm clock for a heart and pasta for hair, but as *Works and Creations* progresses she gradually acquires more human qualities, until roughly halfway through she finally crosses over into the "real world" inhabited by the narrator.

We are offered several different possible explanations for the significance of Xuxu and her relationship to the narrator. The most immediate explanation is that when the narrator was young, he had a friend named Ruzhen who subsequently disappeared from his life, and it is suggested that the fictional Xuxu was created as a symbolic substitute. Among several other explanations for Xuxu's origins and significance, the novel details different childhood experiences with trauma and loss, many of which revolve around dolls or doll-like figures. Perhaps the most intriguing of these childhood memories is in the final chapter and describes a copy of an *Illustrated English-Chinese Dictionary* that the narrator owned. The dictionary contained an illustration of a female body with the various body parts labeled in both English and Chinese, and the narrator notes that it was from this illustration that he first learned the English word *breast*. He recalls that the only part of the illustration that was *not* labeled was the figure's crotch – deliberately left blank so that young students would not learn inappropriate sexual terminology. Not only was this portion of the diagram left blank, it was explicitly labeled with the word *lack* (*wu* 無), and the narrator notes that "this was something that could not be named, and therefore it further stimulated my younger self's fascination with 'lack' (*wu*)."

The narrator then describes how he proceeded to rip out the page with the anatomical diagram:

> Why? Perhaps it was because I felt that it was inappropriate for children, or perhaps it was because it gave me an ineffable feeling of terror. In any event, I carefully, compulsively, and spontaneously ripped the page out. This certainly did not mean that when I was young my thoughts were utterly pure. Not at all. At that time, when I was still maturing and before I had taken any sex-ed classes, my mind was full of strange and fanciful notions. In my own personal material history, this had already been recorded in a manner that was detailed but difficult to read. However, I really did tear out that dictionary page with the female figure. Afterward, I felt an alternating sense of pride and regret, but in any event this is something I will never forget. That torn-out page was preserved as a form of "lack" (*wu*).[6]

Just as the narrator's attempt in an earlier rag doll scene to sew a doll's clothes back on functions as a site of traumatic investment in its own right, his act of tearing out the dictionary page further reaffirms the symbolic "lack" that had been the focus of the diagram itself.

While dictionaries typically function as sites of linguistic authority and bilingual dictionaries gesture to the possibility of complete translatability, the *Illustrated English-Chinese Dictionary* in Dung's novel functions instead as a symbol of linguistic aporia and the limits of translation. The novel as a whole revolves around anxieties about loss and attempts to find compensatory substitutes, and the dictionary scene at the end functions as a reminder of the degree to which a figure of lack is ultimately embedded within language itself.

4. Ng Kim Chew

Born in the Malaysian state of Johor, Ng Kim Chew 黃錦樹 grew up in a village in a rubber forest. In 1986 he went to Taiwan for college, where he received his

BA and PhD in Chinese literature. He is currently a professor of Chinese litera-ture at Taiwan's National Chi Nan University and also a prize-winning creative author in his own right, having published six volumes of fiction over the past two decades. Focusing on the interethnic and multicultural environment of Malaysia and Southeast Asia, Ng's fiction probes the distinctive peculiarities of the region he calls home, while helping interrogate some of the basic conceptual paradigms through which literary production itself is understood.

Ng Kim Chew's 1996 short story "Allah's Will" (阿拉的旨意) revolves around a Malaysian Chinese named Liu Cai, who is sentenced to death in 1957 on account of his affiliation with the Malayan Communist Party.[7] On the eve of his scheduled execution, however, a former childhood friend – who by this point has become a politically powerful Malay aristocrat – intervenes and arranges for Liu's life to be spared, but on the condition that Liu agree to relocate to a remote island and renounce all traces of his former identity. In particular, Liu's benefac-tor specifies that Liu must give up his name, family, community, and even his original language. Liu reluctantly agrees to these conditions, whereupon he is escorted to the island that has been selected as his new home.

The main body of the story focuses on the decades that Liu Cai spends in exile – having been assigned a new name, language, family, and religion. This process of radical reacculturation begins shortly after Liu arrives on the island. He is ritually circumcised and married to the daughter of the local village chief, with whom he proceeds to have over a dozen children. Each time a new child is born, Liu's benefactor sends him a gift, and as the children grow up the benefac-tor arranges for them to go to the Malaysian mainland to continue their stud-ies. Liu himself, however, is never permitted to leave the island to attend their graduations or their weddings, or even allowed to explain to his family *why* he is unable to leave – since another of the conditions his benefactor placed on their agreement was that he never tell anyone about it.

Near the end of the story, after Liu Cai has lived under his adopted identity for more than three decades, he becomes concerned about the name under which he will be buried, and specifically the possibility that he may be buried as a Malay. He therefore resolves to compose his own epitaph but, wary of the potential con-sequences of violating his agreement, decides to do so with invented ideographs inspired by ancient Chinese seal script:

> It would be too obvious if I were to carve actual Chinese characters, because they would immediately be recognized, leading to enormous problems.
>
> It occurred to me that ancient Chinese characters were all pictographs, but I hadn't learned ancient seal script and consequently could only imag-ine what it might have looked like. It would certainly not be a violation of our agreement if I were to carve some made-up designs or figures.
>
> First, I inscribed a lopsided pig – my zodiac birth sign.
>
> After writing a period, I then proceeded with my name. . . . I carved an ox together with several copper coins and the sort of cowrie shells that the

islanders occasionally collect along the seashore. My surname is *Liu*, which rhymes with *niu* [ox], and my given name is *Cai*, which is homophonous with the *cai* [wealth] that many parents dream their children will one day obtain. More specifically, my given name was inspired by the fact that just before I was born my father happened to find some coins in the courtyard.[8]

Using this invented script, Liu Cai is able to symbolically reclaim his Chinese name while technically continuing to honor his agreement with his benefactor. As a result, the epitaph comes to symbolize not only Liu Cai's attachment to his former identity but also the ways that identity is continually being transformed and reinvented.

Along these lines, Liu Cai's epitaph may be seen as operating on two distinct levels: the conventional meaning contained in the coded script (Liu's name, birth sign, and so forth) and the significance of his use of the coded script in the first place. While the former can be specified with some precision, the latter is necessarily indeterminate to outside observers: we know that Liu Cai's decision to write in code stems from his frustration at having been stripped of his language and his identity, but only *he* knows precisely how he feels. While on the level of conventional meaning the epitaph is a form of public language (albeit one that, at least within the story's diegesis, is intelligible to only this individual), on a deeper level it is an intensely private language that functions not so much to convey meaning itself but rather the protagonist's effort to grapple with the limits of language itself. The epitaph, in other words, functions as both a form of language proper and a nonlinguistic index of the subject's inner mental state.

These questions of language are also foregrounded in the story's narrative frame. The work opens with a Chinese translation of a short passage from the *Qur'an*, on "unbelievers," and is followed by the narrator's reflection, also in Chinese, on his decision to write the text in Chinese in the first place:

> I am very well aware of the fact that if the following story were to be revealed to the world, it would surely precipitate a grave crisis.
>
> It would have dire consequences not only for my wife, children, grandchildren, and many other descendants with whom I've already lost touch, but also for my "most cherished friend," the island where I live, my country, as well as my fellow countrymen.
>
> This is a very complicated matter, and I hardly even know where to begin. My thoughts are very confused – especially given that I haven't written in Chinese for over thirty years and there are therefore a lot of Chinese characters I've forgotten how to write (I often either add or leave out strokes, mistake one character for another, remember the character only vaguely, or only know its pronunciation . . .). But if I can't write a certain character, I refuse to transliterate it into Malay, and instead prefer to use another Chinese character with a similar pronunciation. Given that I've

already breached the contract that I signed on pain of death (and which I will describe below), I might as well go ahead and break it completely.

(85)

Embedded between the epigraph and the opening paragraph, however, is a parenthetical note that reads, in Chinese: *"Originally written in Malay."*

The precise significance of this paratextual remark is ambiguous. On one hand, the remark could be referring to the quote from the *Qur'an* that appears in the preceding epigraph – suggesting that the quote was translated into Chinese from Malay, rather than from Arabic (the story, though, mentions that at one point Liu Cai asked his benefactor for some Buddhist sutras in Chinese, but the latter instead sent him a copy of the *Qur'an* in Arabic). However, the font and positioning of the note suggest instead that it refers to the text immediately following – implying that the story itself was originally written in Malay. This stands in direct contradiction to the narrator's explicit claims, in the story's opening paragraphs, that he has made a point of composing the text in Chinese (and has even refused to use Malay transliterations for Chinese characters he has forgotten how to write). The opening parenthetical note, accordingly, doesn't identify the written language of the story at hand as much as it enacts a performative contradiction that illustrates some of the internal tensions (such as between "public" and "private" dimensions) that arguably characterize *all* language use.

The original language of "Allah's Will" (if we accept the fictional premise of the story itself) is similarly brought into question by the contradictory statements that appear at the beginning of the work. This indeterminacy, combined with the process of forcible reacculturation that Liu Cai undergoes while on the island, raises significant challenges with respect to whether Ng's story should be classified as Chinese, Malay, Mahua, or even something else entirely. This taxonomical indeterminacy, in turn, invites an approach to the story that doesn't prioritize the work's language of composition, its point of geographical origin, or the ethnic identity of its author but instead considers the way it explores issues of identity, displacement and loss, and yearning at the interstices of different languages and cultures.

5. Xiaolu Guo

Xiaolu Guo was born in a fishing village in Zhejiang province but relocated to London in 2002. Active as both a novelist and a filmmaker, Guo initially produced works in Chinese, but after relocating to London in 2002 she decided to write her third novel, *A Concise English-Chinese Dictionary for Lovers* (2007), in English, in order to reach more effectively a British and international readership.

Although most authors write in their dominant languages (which may or may not be their first), there is also ample precedent for authors who instead write in a second or adopted language. Some, like Vladimir Nabokov, are virtuosic in their mastery of their adopted language, while others, like the Boston-based

Chinese author Ha Jin, retain a distinct awkwardness in their adopted tongue but find ways to rationalize that awkwardness within the narrative logic of their fictional work. In her first English-language novel, Xiaolu Guo presents a combination of these two situations. The work is structured as a journal kept by a young Chinese woman after she comes to England from China. The protagonist – her name is Zhuang, but after arriving in England she asks people to simply call her Z – begins her journal on the day she lands at Heathrow, and she writes in English despite the fact that her command of the language is rudimentary at best. The early entries are written in a simple and error-riddled version of English, but as the novel progresses the protagonist's command of the language improves, such that by the end of the work – after she has been in Britain for a year – her written English is quite eloquent.

The novel opens with a chapter labeled "prologue," which begins with a definition of the word (in English), followed by the first diary entry:

> prologue ('prō-ˌlòg) *n.* 1. an introductory section or screen in a book, play or musical work; 2. an event or action leading to another.

Prologue
Now.

> Beijing time 12 clock midnight.
> Long time 5 clock afternoon.
> But I at neither time zone. I on airplane. Sitting on 25,000 km above to earth and trying remember all English I learning at school.
> I not met you yet. You in future.[9]

The emphasis on time and temporality in this first entry is prophetic, as time is a motif that runs through the novel as a whole. All of the diary entries are carefully dated and arranged in chronological order, and Z notes that that one of the key challenges in learning English is mastering the verb conjugations and tenses. Unlike English and other Indo-European languages, Chinese does not have tenses, and so has relatively few ways of syntactically designating temporality.

One of the novel's most explicit discussions of temporality can be found in the section titled "Timing":

Timing

Today I read about tense again. It is a sentence from Ibn Arabi, an old sage, a very wise man living in the early thirteen century. He said:

The Universe continues to be in the present tense.

> Does that mean English tense difference is just complicated for no reason? Does that mean tenses are not natural things at all? Does that mean love is a form of continues for ever and for ever, just like in my Chinese concept?

About *time*, what I really learned from studying English is: *time* is different from *timing*.

I understand the difference of these words so well. I understand falling in love with the right person in the wrong timing could be the greatest sadness in a person's life

(260)

In this poignant passage, Z struggles to use her not yet fully grammatical English to articulate complicated reflections on time and temporality, and specifically the difference between time as an abstract matrix and timing as the structure that is imposed on that matrix.

Near the end of the novel, after Z and her English boyfriend have broken up, she writes an entry in which she reminisces about the impact that her boyfriend had and continues to have on her, even now that they are separated:

People say nowadays there are no more boundaries between nations. Really? The boundary between you and me is so broad, so high.

When I first saw you. I felt I saw another me, a me against me, a me which I contradicted all the time. And now I cannot forget you and I cannot stop loving you because you are a part of me.

(279)

The remark that her boyfriend remains a part of her even after their separation reminds the reader of a curious remark in the novel's very first entry: "I not met you yet. You in future" (3).

Although the premise of the novel is that each entry is preserved as it was originally written (which explains why the poor English of the early entries has not been revised and corrected), the narrator's reference in her first entry to a "you" she has not yet met (presumably her future boyfriend) suggests that her lover is already part of her even before they actually meet, just as he remains a part of her after they have separated.

Z emphasizes that her lover, in addition to providing a source of emotional and physical comfort, is also an important conduit for her process of language acquisition. Her implication that he is always-already part of her and remains embedded within her after they have separated, accordingly, could also be seen as a commentary on her relationship to language – not only English, but even Chinese.

For Z, accordingly, her English lover functions not only as a useful entry point into a foreign language and a foreign culture but also as a symbol of the simultaneously intimate and alien quality of language. Just as Derrida suggests that we can never get outside language ("I have only one language") even as we remain fundamentally distanced from it ("but it is not mine"), Guo's novel suggests that, on some level, her lover (and the foreign language that he represents) was always a part of her, even as there was – and always will be – an irreducible gap between them.

Notes

1 Jacques Derrida, *Monolingualism of the Other; or, The Prosthesis of Origin*, trans. Patrick Mensah (Stanford: Stanford University Press, 1998).
2 Yan Lianke 閻連科, *Shouhuo* 受活 (Shenyang: Chunfeng wenyi chubanshe, 2004).
3 Yan Lianke, *Lenin's Kisses*, trans. Carlos Rojas (New York: Grove/Atlantic, 2012), 4.
4 Alai 阿來, "Zai Meiguo bijiao wenxue xuehui nianhui shang de yanjiang" 在美國比較文學學會年會上的演講 (A Lecture Delivered to the American Comparative Literature Association's Annual Conference], in Alai, *Aba Alai* 阿埧阿來 [Ngawa Alai] (Beijing: Zhongguo gongren chubanshe, 2004), 156–160, 157.
5 Alai, *Kongshan* 空山 (Bald Mountain), vol. II (Beijing: Renmin wenxue chubanshe, 2007), 28. Subsequent references to this novella will be noted parenthetically in the text.
6 Dung Kai-Cheung董啟章, *Tiangong kaiwu: Xuxu ruzhen* 天工開物: 栩栩如真 (Works and Creations: Vivid and Lifelike) (Taipei: Rye Field Publishing, 2005), 476.
7 Ng Kim Chew 黃錦樹, "Ala de zhiyi" 阿拉的旨意 ("Allah's Will"), in *Youdao zhidao* 由島至島 (From Island to Island] (Taipei: Rye Field Publishing, 2001), 85–109.
8 Ng Kim Chew, *Slow Boat to China and Other Stories*, trans. and ed. Carlos Rojas (New York: Columbia University Press, 2016), 103. Subsequent references to this novella will be noted parenthetically in the text.
9 Xiaolu Guo, *A Concise English-Chinese Dictionary for Lovers* (New York: Anchor, 2008), 3. Subsequent references to this novella will be noted parenthetically in the text.

Works cited

Alai 阿來. *Kongshan* 空山 (Bald Mountain). Vol. 2. Beijing: Renmin wenxue chubanshe, 2007.
———. "Zai Meiguo bijiao wenxue xuehui nianhui shang de yanjiang." 在美國比較文學學會年會上的演講 (A Lecture Delivered to the American Comparative Literature Association's Annual Conference). In *Aba Alai* 阿埧阿來 (Ngawa Alai), edited by Alai, 156–160. Beijing: Zhongguo gongren chubanshe, 2004.
Derrida, Jacques. *Monolingualism of the Other: Or, the Prosthesis of Origin*. Trans. Patrick Mensah. Stanford: Stanford University Press, 1998.
Dung Kai-Cheung 董啟章. *Shijian fanshi: Yaci zhiguang* 時間繁史: 啞瓷之光 (Histories of Time: The Lustre of Mute Porcelain). 2 Vols. Taipei: Rye Field Publishing, 2007.
———. *Tiangong kaiwu: Xuxu ruzhen* 天工開物: 栩栩如真 (Works and Creations: Vivid and Lifelike). Taipei: Rye Field Publishing, 2005.
———. *Wuzhong yuanshi: Beibei chongsheng zhi xuexi niandai* 物種源始. 貝貝重生之學習年代 (The Origin of Species: The Educational Age of Beibei's Rebirth). Taipei: Rye Field Publishing, 2010.
Guo, Xiaolu. *A Concise Chinese-English Dictionary for Lovers*. New York: Anchor, 2008.
Ng Kim Chew 黃錦樹. *Slow Boat to China and Other Stories*. Trans. and ed. Carlos Rojas. New York: Columbia University Press, 2016.
———. *Youdao zhidao* 由島至島 (From Island to Island). Taipei: Rye Field Publishing, 2001.
Yan Lianke 閻連科. *Lenin's Kisses*. Trans. Carlos Rojas. New York: Grove/Atlantic, 2012.
———. *Shouhuo* 受活. Shenyang: Chunfeng wenyi chubanshe, 2004.

PART I
Mainland China

1

ALLEGORIZING HISTORY

Realism and fantasy in Mo Yan's fictional China

Mei-hwa Sung

In awarding Mo Yan 莫言 the Nobel Prize in Literature in 2012, the Swedish Academy recognized his achievement in "merging hallucinatory realism with folk tales, history and the contemporary." All his works – including eleven full-length novels and thirty-odd novellas and short stories – are written in a quasi-autobiographical mode, deploying stories from his childhood memories or from his close observations of contemporary China. Among them, the novels *Red Sorghum* (紅高粱家族) (1987), *The Republic of Wine* (酒國) (1992), *Big Breasts and Wide Hips* (豐乳肥臀) (1996), and *Life and Death Are Wearing Me Out* (生死疲勞) (2006) collectively span a historical period from the Sino-Japanese War in the 1930s to the Reform Era in the 1980s and 1990s, and share an approach to history that blends realist and fantastic elements. Tending toward the episodic, the narratives draw inspiration from magical realism and from China's cultural, literary, and folkloric traditions, weaving religious belief, legend, and fantasy with historical subject matter. A forerunner in stylistic innovations new to China's literati of the mid-1980s, Mo Yan writes about China's contemporary history by allegorizing the here and now.

In a talk on Gao Xingjian 高行健 and Mo Yan, Liu Zaifu 劉再復 praised the avant-garde Chinese writers who emerged during the 1980s for their attempts to liberate literature from the political dictates of the ruling party, arguing that literature "freed the writers from political ideology, enabling life and talent to explode." Liu added that these writers were able to "break out of the blockade . . . [as a result of] opening and searching their souls."[1] A close look at how Mo Yan juggles history and imagination to represent contemporary China in his fiction may similarly shed light on his flair for presenting a satiric vision of China's national ethos during the first fifty years of the history of the People's Republic.

Historicity is a prominent feature in many of Mo Yan's works. Topical references to contemporary history pervade the narratives as they unfold the stories of individual characters, their families, and the actual events influencing human destiny. As Mo Yan explains in the postscript to *Big Breasts and Wide Hips*, the national history narrated through fiction needs to be derived from the common people. National history in fictional works, in other words, is not the history that one reads about in textbooks, but rather the common people's version told in the form of legend (*chuanqihua le de lishi* 傳奇話了的歷史). It is deinstitutionalized history. Remarking on *Red Sorghum*, Mo Yan observes, "The only history in my head is the legendary type,"[2] stressing the importance of a free-ranging imagination and the fact that the history he is writing is actually the version handed down from oral sources about historical figures acting under and upon real-life circumstances. In other words, style precedes content in what he conceives to be storytelling as history writing. This attempt to deinstitutionalize official national history carries a skeptical or even subversive overtone. Paradox may often serve as camouflage by which a confrontation of viewpoints becomes understated in equivocal language. Mo Yan is then capable of appealing to the proletarian values sanctified by national policy makers while debunking the grand narrative of national history.

Narrative authenticity, which ostensibly legitimizes official history, is deliberately problematized in Mo Yan's works. In this spirit, he allegorizes and comments upon the historical references made in his novels, employing a combination of symbolism, hyperbole, parody, satire, and fantasy to refract historical realities and discredit verisimilitude as a path to historical truth. The result is frequent shifting between fantasy and realism, to the point that the line between the two is emphatically blurred.

Reimagining the Sino-Japanese War

Like most of his fiction, Mo Yan's first full-length novel, *Red Sorghum*, is set in Northeast Gaomi township of Shandong province, and the main narrative unfolds against the historical backdrop of the 1930s, during which China was engaged in fierce resistance against the Japanese invaders while also caught up in a civil war involving the Nationalists, the Communists, and the collaborators (*hanjian* 漢奸) fighting for dominance. The narrator notes at the beginning that Northeastern Gaomi township is "easily the most beautiful and most repulsive, most unusual and most common, most sacred and most corrupt, most heroic and most bastardly, hardest-drinking and hardest-loving place in the world,"[3] and he has subsequently described how he hoped to make Northeast Gaomi township "a miniature of China and even the world."

The novel takes its title from a local variety of sorghum used for food and for brewing wine, which is identified with the spirit of the land – its shiny dark red color as the blood that flows through the veins of the heroic people who have lived there for centuries. Likewise, the Black Water River is described as being both fertile and toxic, a symbol of life and death: "a river as cumbersome as the great, clumsy Han culture" (102/88; translation revised). The geographic setting is also given a larger-than-life aura reflective of the paradox that Mo Yan sees in its people. In the same spirit, topicality and fabrication are interlaced to render the narrative a hybrid of realism and antirealism.

The narrator opens the story by matter-of-factly announcing the specific day (the ninth day of the eighth lunar month of the year 1939) on which an incident will dramatically change the fate of a family. The invading Japanese soldiers force the local conscripts to drag all vehicles and cattle to the riverbank to build a highway for moving troops and transporting military supplies. To establish the historical credibility of his narrative, the narrator cites from the county gazetteer, which records details of this historical incident: 400,000 shifts of hard labor, severe damage of the year's crop, and so forth. This military maneuver meets with fierce resistance, causing dire casualties among the locals, including the deaths of Grandma, Arhat Liu, and many other villagers. Amid the descriptions of killing and torturing and the intrigues and betrayals among the local factions, the reader is introduced to the lush waves of ripe red sorghum stalks.

The sorghum in the novel stands for the heroic ancestry of the Gaomi people, "lines of scarlet figures shuttled among the sorghum stalks to weave a vast human tapestry." Their "unfilial descendants who now occupy the land pale by comparison." The narrator laments that "surrounded by progress, I feel a nagging sense of our species' regression" (4). At the end of the novel, he mourns the vanished red sorghum, which "has been drowned in a raging flood of revolution and no longer exists," having been replaced by a hybrid green sorghum "bereft of tall, straight stalks . . . devoid of the dazzling sorghum color . . . they pollute the pure air of Northeast Gaomi Township with their dark, gloomy, ambiguous faces" (377). The red sorghum stands for the golden days of the land and its people that are extinct in modern-day Northeastern Gaomi township and, by extension, contemporary China.

There are, however, some modern-day heroes and heroines who challenge patriarchal constraints and foreign invaders. In flashbacks, the narrator relates the illicit romantic love between his grandparents, Commander Yu and Dai Fenglian. Commander Yu, a coolie turned bandit, is caught in a love triangle with two fearless, self-reliant women, Grandma and Lian'er. Commander Yu commits larceny and murder to snatch Dai, and shortly afterward falls in love with Dai's servant girl, Lian'er. Sex scenes are presented in an explicit and yet genteel language, highlighting sensuality and an urge to break out of social conventions. Grandma dies on the bank of the Black Water River in a gun fight against the Japanese soldiers, Commander Yu dies seeking to avenge her death, and Lian'er dies after offering herself to the Japanese soldiers in an attempt to save her daughter. The rape and murder scenes are described in graphic detail.

Up to the final chapter of the novel, the story line follows a more or less coherent structure despite the author's frequent use of flashbacks. The final chapter, however, features a number of unnatural deaths, including a weasel that is beaten to death by Lian'er in revenge for the chickens it has killed, the gruesome death of Lian'er's daughter at the hands of the Japanese soldiers, and Lian'er's own prolonged derangement and death when she is brought home by Commander Yu after having been raped by the Japanese soldiers. In his first attempt at the fantastic, Mo Yan turns to Pu Songling's 蒲松齡 *Liaozhai zhiyi* 聊齋誌異, a local literary legacy of the fantastic mode by which he often claims to be proudly inspired.[4] For instance, he describes how Lian'er was convinced that a weasel

> had absolute control over her in some deep, dark place. Whatever it ordered her to do, she did: cry, laugh, speak in tongues, perform strange acts. . . . Always, the image of the potent black-mouthed weasel swayed before her eyes, grinning hideously and whisking her skin vigorously with its tail.

After a long spell of whipping, shouting, and cursing, Lian'er "crumpled to the ground, spittle drooling from the corners of her mouth, her body lathered in sweat, her face the color of gold foil" (335). She dies only after a famed exorcist has finally been able to rid her of the sinister weasel.

Mo Yan repeatedly insists that he is not a writer of textbook history, but rather of fiction. Toward the end of the novel, in an episode dated to the early spring of 1940, Northeastern Gaomi township lies in ruins as rival local factions continue to fight the Japanese invaders and each other. The supernatural phenomena preceding Lian'er's death are interlaced with descriptions of gory battle scenes. Battlefield violence and rowdy exorcism are combined in a surreal manner, offering a satirical comment on this historical period.

In *The Republic of Wine*, Mo Yan further develops this sort of interplay between the realist and the fantastic mode of writing. Consisting of a series of overlapping narrative frames, *The Republic of Wine* includes fragments from a novel (also titled *The Republic of Wine*) being composed by a fictional character named Mo Yan, an epistolary correspondence between this fictional Mo Yan and a character named Li Yidou, together with a series of short stories that Li Yidou sends the fictional Mo Yan. Li Yidou is described as being an enthusiastic fan of (the fictional) Mo Yan's work, particularly his novel *Red Sorghum*, and the short stories that he sends – in the hope that the celebrated author can help him get published – are all ostensibly inspired by Mo Yan's own writings. When the fictional Mo Yan receives these manuscripts, however, he finds them utterly lacking in literary merit.

The novel that the fictional Mo Yan is attempting to write can also be viewed as an informal sequel to *Red Sorghum*. While the primary narrative plane of Mo Yan's first novel is set during the Sino-Japanese War and thematizes sorghum wine as a beverage for the common people, however, the embedded novel in *The Republic of Wine* is set in the post-Mao era and uses Maotai and other hyperexpensive versions of sorghum wine to critique the epidemic of collusion between businessmen and government officials that plagues contemporary China. However, a deeper irony lies in the sharp contrast between the two novels' subject matter and intent. While *Red Sorghum* reconstructs a historical period of war and individual sacrifice for the national cause, celebrating and lamenting sex and death in a grandiose manner, *The Republic of Wine* points to what Mo Yan identifies as "a unique problem in China," the pervasive corruption among government officials perpetrated over expensive food and wine.

The embedded novel in *The Republic of Wine* describes Special Investigator Ding Gou'er's attempts to investigate allegations that human cannibalism is being practiced in the city of Liquorland, and when he arrives at the city, he is treated to an extravagant banquet in which the pièce de résistance appears to be a roasted human boy. As Ding Gou'er is reacting with horror and revulsion, however, his hosts reassure him that this Meat Boy dish is actually a simulacrum – an elaborate facsimile of a human body constructed out of other edible items. Partly reassured, Ding Gou'er proceeds to consume the dish while getting progressively drunker and drunker, until he eventually passes out.

After partaking of the Meat Boy at the reception banquet, Ding Gou'er is invited to the Culinary Academy to learn the art of cooking babies and endangered species such as the platypus. The instructor's lecture offers a dark vision of contemporary China as a cannibalistic society, as she notes that

> a chef's heart is made of steel and . . . should never waste emotions. Rather than being human, the babies we are about to slaughter and cook are small animals in human form that are, based upon strict, mutual agreement, produced to meet the special needs of Liquorland's developing economy and prosperity. In essence, they are no different than the platypuses swimming in the tank waiting to be slaughtered.
>
> *(222)*

In this way, the work combines realism and fantasy, offering a vision of contemporary China as a land where fiction blends with reality. China as represented in the novel may be truer to life than China in reality, where things are often kept from public view.

A similar interweaving of realism and fantasy can be found in the epistolary exchanges between Li Yidou and the fictional Mo Yan. This dialogic device creates an open zone where realism and fiction meet and drift apart, a textual space constantly problematized by a subtext until authenticity is difficult to anchor. For example, in one of his letters, Li Yidou relays a detractor's diatribe against the fictional Mo Yan:

> Is that little rascal Mo Yan writing his *The Republic of Wine*? It's nothing but the ravings of a fool, someone who has no concept of his own limitations. How much liquor did he consume before he felt qualified to write *The Republic of Wine*?
>
> *(180)*

Mo Yan (the author) uses this fictional detractor to offer an ironic self-critique:

> There are four things you need to know about the little rascal: first, he likes women; second, he smokes and drinks; third, he's always strapped for

money; and fourth, he's a collector of tales of the supernatural and unexplained mysteries that he can incorporate into his own fiction.

(179)

In this way, the author satirizes himself in order to "sheathe the porcupine's quills" and deflect this acrimonious attack targeting the perpetrators of corruption in the public sphere.

Roughly halfway through *The Republic of Wine*, the fictional Mo Yan decides to abandon the novel he has been working on and instead visit Li Yidou in Liquorland – which is also presented as being the fictional space within which his own (incomplete) novel is set. In the concluding section of the original version of the novel (which was subsequently removed from later revised versions), there is a stream-of-consciousness passage alternating between two or more voices, which alludes to various episodes from the work itself as well as political campaigns of the 1950s and 1960s, a high-echelon Communist Party leader, and historical accounts of cannibalistic incidents. This section concludes with a speaker (presumably the fictional Mo Yan) reproaching Li Yidou for bringing him to Liquorland and holding Li responsible for his plight – dead drunk by the time the banquet thrown in his honor has ended. On this hallucinatory note, the novel ends.

Allegories of descent and reincarnation

While the primary narrative planes of both *Red Sorghum* and *The Republic of Wine* are narrowly bounded (focusing on the 1930s and the 1980s, respectively), the historical vision offered in *Big Breasts and Wide Hips* and *Life and Death Are Wearing Me Out* is more expansive – in each case spanning more than half a century. The two works use fantastic narratives centered around chains of reproduction and reincarnation in order to reflect on contemporary China's historical trajectory.

Big Breasts and Wide Hips uses a combination of realistic and fantastic narrative modes to trace the history of the Shangguang family from the 1920s to the 1990s. The dominant metaphor in the novel is the breast, which Mo Yan identifies as a symbol of the Chinese patriarchal culture that has long instituted social and sexual restraints. In the novel's postscript, the author pinpoints foot-binding as one such cultural inhibition, while in the novel itself sexual mores are clearly implied as the predominant constraint. The protagonist, Shangguang Lushi, survives war, famine, and political persecutions, and her breasts help nourish eight children – seven girls and one boy. By describing the protagonist's lifelong plight, Mo Yan criticizes China's patriarchy for privileging sons over daughters. Traditionally, girls' feet were bound when they were young, after which their primary expectation was to produce male heirs for their husband's clan. Having married an impotent husband, however, Shangguan Lushi finds her way out of her predicament by getting pregnant by other men. The last of her many extramarital relationships, with the Swedish pastor Malory, finally brings her a "Golden Boy," Jintong.

In the novel, Jintong narrates the Shangguan family history, including involvement in the war against the Japanese invaders, the civil war, and later the various political campaigns of the People's Republic. The daughters feud as a result of their marriages to men from opposing political camps: Eldest Sister Laidi (literally, "awaiting a brother") to Sha Yueliang, a collaborator with the invading Japanese troops; Second Sister Zhaodi (literally, "beckoning to a brother") to Sima Ku, commander of local anti-Japanese forces; Fifth Sister Pandi (literally, "expecting a brother") to Lu Liren, political commissar of the Communist Demolition Battalion; Sixth Sister Niandi (literally, "missing a brother") to American bomber pilot Babbitt; Seventh Sister Qiudi (literally, "wishing for a brother") is sold to a Russian woman as an orphan. With its multiple foreign relationships, the Shangguang family takes on an allegorical significance as China at war with itself and with foreign interests. As in *Red Sorghum*, historical incidents such as the Sino-Japanese War, the founding of the People's Republic, the Great Leap Forward, and the Cultural Revolution serve as backdrops while human suffering (including men and women, victims and villains) takes center stage. Again, historical authenticity is hardly the central concern. The novel instead tilts toward the fantastic, couching its moral in a language and events that defy societal and realist constraints. Realism is reserved for episodes such as the Famine Years, to foreground human misery.

Jintong's obsession with his mother's breasts until his mid-teens, and after that with other women's breasts, is offered as an allegory of the regression of the Han race. Mo Yan expresses ambivalence about this obsession in the postscript, where he acknowledges his gratitude to his own mother and identifies breasts as the spiritual root of the Chinese people. He admits that deep in his own heart there is a Jintong, not weaned from his Mother Culture, and blames himself for being an unworthy offspring of the heroic clan that once inhabited Northeastern Gaomi township. In the novel, Jintong is driven crazy when he sees or imagines his sisters' breasts falling prey to the gnawing teeth of their husbands, especially the American pilot. Jintong is in fact the antihero of the novel despite his angelic looks and his privileged status as the only son of the family. The climax of this "Golden Boy's" fate, as well as of the narrative fantasy, takes place at the Snow Fair (*xue ji*), where Mo Yan again demonstrates his flair for hallucinatory imagination.

At the Snow Fair of the first winter of the People's Republic, Jintong is chosen by some Taoist priests to be that year's Snow Prince. On the day of the first snow, Jintong is taken to the fair, dressed in a white robe and cap made of glossy satin, and given a white horsetail whisk to hold. He is placed in a litter and taken on a parade. His final, most important duty comes when he is to give blessings to women and girls by touching their breasts with his snow-chilled hands to bring them good luck. On that day, Jintong assesses countless breasts of women from Northeastern Gaomi township by cupping them in his hands. The ecstatic state of his mind goes on for some time until he finally encounters "a lonely mountain peak" spread across the right side of a woman's breast. This episode ends in a catastrophe, with a woman called Old Jin screaming with joy and breaking the snow fair's rule of absolute silence. The Taoist organizers are subsequently condemned as spies and executed. In this way, reality intrudes to overturn the carnivalesque aura of this sexual escapade.

In the latter half of the novel, the narrative dwells on the hardships endured by the Shangguan clan in the early decades of the People's Republic. Due to the family's diverse associations with the opposing factions during the Sino-Japanese War and the ensuing civil war, Shangguan Lushi loses her daughters and grandchildren to enemies from different factions, and her other offspring perish during the famine that follows the Great Leap Forward. Shangguang Lushi works for meager wages at a soybean mill and, unable to feed her family, she steals beans by swallowing them at her workplace and regurgitating them at home. After being washed and strained, these beans are then fed to the children raw – for fear that smoke produced from cooking them would attract the attention of local officials. In her old age, Shangguang Lushi becomes a fearless matriarch who is nevertheless disillusioned about Jintong's future. Although readers might have expected the family's hybrid son to be capable of transmitting the family's "essence," he turns out to be merely a foil for his mother. This irony unsettles patriarchal values and, by extension, linear progression in the family and national history.

In *Big Breasts and Wide Hips*, the decline of the Shangguan clan functions as an allegory for the regression of the Han race, beginning with the failure of the Westernization movement that started in the late Qing. In this way, Mo Yan uses fantasy to reflect on the nation's awkward process of modernization and historical development.

In *Life and Death Are Wearing Me Out*, Mo Yan revisits the traditional Chinese fantastic narrative. The Buddhist motif of transmigration gives structure to the Ximen family saga, with an allegorical intent to polarize good and evil and query the lack of justice in the several lives of the protagonist, Ximen Nao. The novel spans the entire latter half of the twentieth century, with the narrative voice following the multiple reincarnations of Ximen Nao as a donkey, ox, pig, dog, monkey, and finally a human again. Ximen Nao's transmigrations parallel many of the political movements taking place in the first five decades of the People's Republic, including the Great Leap Forward, the Commune period, the Cultural Revolution, and the Reform era. In the novel, the interplay between fantasy and realism is exemplified in the episodes describing Ximen Nao's five resurrections, four of which involve a relationship with a character known simply as Blue Face (Lan Lian).

In a recurrent master–slave dialectic, Blue Face and Ximen Nao (in his various incarnations) sustain unusual feelings for each other throughout the half-century span of the narrative. Mo Yan affirmed that Blue Face is modeled upon a real person from Northeastern Gaomi county who refused to join the local commune despite tremendous pressure from both the authorities and the townspeople. During the Cultural Revolution, this peasant continued to insist on farming on his own, independent of the commune's authority. He was bullied and beaten to death by a mob of villagers. In an interview in which he reminisces about this tragedy he learned of as a child, Mo Yan reaffirms the essence of China's rural history as being rooted in "peasants' rebellions" (*nongmin qiyi* 農民起義).[5] In this remark, he suggests a critique of the misguided political campaigns that had disastrous consequences throughout the entire country and for particular individuals such as Blue Face – whom Mo Yan lauded as "a living fossil of China's classic farmer" (539) who devoted himself heart and soul to the land. The commune was doomed to fail because it attempted to sever this primordial bond.

In the novel, Blue Face is picked up from the street by Ximen Nao and works as his farmhand for a few years. After Ximen Nao is executed for being a landlord, Blue Face becomes an independent farmer and marries Ximen Nao's first concubine. From this point onward, Ximen Nao's fate – as donkey, ox, pig, dog, and "Big Head" Lan Qiansui – continues to be interwoven with that of Blue Face. The animals are born successively to the family of Blue Face, his wife, and his children and grandchildren. Thus, transmigration affords Mo Yan a narrative framework to deploy episodes set during a span of fifty years and involving three generations. The narrative voices shift between "Big Head" Lan Qiansui (Ximen Nao's last transmigration), Lan Jiefang, and the fictional Mo Yan. This postmodernist narrative device reflects the author's attempt to satirize history by presenting poignant criticism as hilarious fantasy. Mo Yan has already prescribed a playful tone for the subject matter of the novel: for instance, by naming his protagonist "Nao" (鬧, which literally means "rowdiness"), Mo Yan strikes an ironic note that helps refract the story's stark realism.

However, a theme that runs through the narrative is "grievance" (*yuanwang* 冤枉). At the beginning of his transmigration journey, Ximen Nao repeatedly screams "I am innocent" at the court of Lord Yama. He protests to the emperor of the Underworld his wrongful execution for alleged bullying and exploitation of his tenant peasants. Near the end of the novel, Big Head relates a scene in his previous life as a dog where the moribund Blue Face comments on wretched landlords like Ximen Nao living in China in those days. Blue Face, coming to realize who the dog is, says, "Old Master, you shouldn't have died the way you did, but then again the world has seen more people like you who shouldn't have died the way they did over the past decades" (500; my translation). While Blue Face dies an outcast on the strip of land to which he has clung, the historical individual on whom Mo Yan based the character actually died a violent death at the hands of the mob during the Cultural Revolution.

Fantasy and realism come head to head, creating a scene where a realistic coda abruptly disperses the phantasmagoric aura. By a pond where the villagers have traditionally dumped dead infants, man and ox engage in dancelike plowing movements under the eerie moonlight with a myriad of infant spirits looking on and cheering them:

> Dad and the ox were performing drills out on the threshing floor as more
> red children than I could count appeared on the top of the wall. . . . He had
> painted the right side of his face with red grease paint, creating a stunning

contrast with the blue birthmark on the left side. . . . At the same time, our family ox, sporting red satin cloth on his horns and a big red satin flower on his forehead, which made him look like a jubilant bridegroom, was running around the outer edge of the threshing floor. His body glistened, his eyes were bright as crystal, his hooves like lit lanterns. . . . In all, he circled the floor ten times or more before joining Dad in the center.

(144)

The dreamy narrative snaps when the narrator Lan Jiefang finds Big Head puzzled, not recalling this episode from one of his previous lives. He quickly admits to Big Head that "maybe what I saw that night was just a fanciful dream. But dream or no dream, you played a role" (145). Here, Mo Yan juggles fantasy and realism, attempting to use fantasy to comment on the actual history behind the fictional story. Making use of a dual-layered narrative, referring to history by way of fantasy, he succeeds in depicting the grievances caused by erroneous state policies and, ultimately, foregrounding the beauty of humanity under distress.

Despite the fantastic framework that allows the supernatural to coexist and interact with the mundane, the moral intent of this family saga is evident. For example, when Ximen Nao complains about the brutality of the land reform movement, he remarks that "the big estates had been piecemealed out to landless peasants; naturally mine was no exception. Parceling out land has its historical precedents, I thought, so why did they have to shoot me before dividing up mine?" (7). Later, Ximen Nao, in the form of a pig, is overjoyed by his luxurious new abode paved with new earth, fresh parasol wood, and fresh sorghum stalks, and, above all, equipped with electricity. Seemingly immersed in naïve ecstasy, he eulogizes the commune's campaign to raise pigs:

> I have a premonition that I was born into an unprecedented time of pigs who are enjoying a dignified status that has never been accorded to us before. . . . There will be hundreds of millions of people flocking to pay homage to us, answering to the call of our great leader. . . . Many will crave being reincarnated as a pig, and even more will opine that humans are lesser than pigs.
>
> *(202: my translation)*

In the voice of a pig, Mo Yan ridicules the folly of the state policy and its implementation regarding food production. The campaign ends in a catastrophic failure when all the pigs raised in the commune perish from an epidemic.

In the novel, satire and sarcasm are directed against failed state maneuvers, as the author comments critically on political campaigns that wreaked havoc on the lives of millions of Chinese people. With subdued "righteous indignation" couched in humor, Mo Yan revisits some gloomy moments in China's contemporary history to mete out poetic justice to those victimized, and the result stands in stark contrast with the free-ranging fantasy of *The Republic of Wine* and *Big Breasts and Wide Hips*.

What is Mo Yan's vision of China as represented in these works? In the four novels considered here, he writes about women with stamina and strong willpower, including Dai Fenglian and Lian'er in *Red Sorghum*, the truck driver who thwarts Ding Gou'er's task in *The Republic of Wine*, and Jintong's mother in *Big Breasts and Wide Hips*. The author's heroes and heroines often show a mixture of lawless bravado and unconventional sexuality. For example, in *Big Breasts and Wide Hips*, Sima Ku is a patriot leaning toward the Nationalists during the Sino-Japanese War who decides to give himself up to the Communists in exchange for the release of the Shangguang clan from captivity. Mo Yan praises him as a hero and laments that such types are nowhere to be found in his native land today.

In the four novels, there are episodes of illicit love and sex, such as the love triangle involving Commander Yu, Dai Fenglian, and Lian'er in *Red Sorghum*; the affairs between Third Sister and Birdman Han and between Mother and Pastor Malory in *Big Breasts and Wide Hips*; and between Lan Kaifang and Pang Fenghuang in *Life and Death Are Wearing Me Out*. Mo Yan questions traditional patriarchy while also relishing the memory of his own mother's bound feet, appreciating her resilience all the more because of this handicap. He sees heroism among lowly and unsanctified humans and animals. For example, in *The Republic of Wine*, the characters Black Mule and Scaly Boy, who ambush corrupt Party officials, are represented as harbingers of justice. Scaly Boy "has become the embodiment of justice, the enforcer of the people's will, the pressure valve of law and order. . . . He may not be able to stop the officials' corrupt behavior, but he can reduce the people's anger" (158). Among these representations of the dark side of human nature and Chinese culture, Mo Yan entrusts hope in larger-than-life individuals of common stock. For him, fiction can be closer to life's higher reality; in fantasy, the creative psyche is emancipated to utter unsaid words by way of allegorical writing.

The national identity of contemporary China represented in these four quasi-historical novels may well be seen as a Jintong figure, effeminate due to his addiction to maternal nourishment, identified by Mo Yan as China's patriarchal culture (*lijiao* 礼教). The mixed blood circulating in Jintong has done him no good, to the point that he may be viewed as a symbol of China's inchoate modernization. The Han people's character has regressed to an infantile state and, worse, appears to be arrested in a Freudian oral stage. Mo Yan's vision is satirical, gloomy, and antiprogressive, summed up in a nostalgic reminiscence about the red sorghum of the old days. Hybrid sorghum has prevailed. An exclamation at the end of *Red Sorghum*, "How I loathe hybrid sorghum," sums up the allegorical message of Mo Yan's dramatization of war, suffering, love, death, and human destiny in these novels. Writing under sociopolitical constraints, the author resorts to indirect modes of storytelling, even as he refuses to suppress the moral under fantasy or drown it in seeming hilarity. These four novels feature a combination of fantasy and realism wherein fantasy serves as an artistic means to an etiological end that is achieved only in finally saying unsaid or prohibited messages – a self-styled mission signaled by his pen name, Mo Yan, which literally means "don't speak."

Notes

1 Liu Zaifu 劉再復, "Gao Xingjian Mo Yan fengge bijiao lun" 高行健莫言風格比較論'(A Comparative Study of Gao Xingjian and Mo Yan), *Huawen wenxue* 華文文學(Literatures in Chinese) 1 (2013): 13–18.
2 Arthur Sze, ed., *Chinese Writers on Writing* (San Antonio, TX: Trinity University Press, 2010).
3 Mo Yan, *Red Sorghum*, trans. Howard Goldblatt (New York: Arrow Books 2003), 4. Subsequent citations from this novel will be referenced parenthetically in the text.
4 The supernatural forces that are shown to cause Lian'er's derangement and uncanny death are familiar to readers of Pu Songling, whom Mo Yan often refers to as coming from a neighboring township and as his own role model.
5 See Appendix, *Shengsi pilao* 生死疲勞 (Beijing: Zuojia chubanshe, 2013), 538.

Works cited

Chen Sihe 陳思和. "Lishi – jiazu: minjian xushi moshi de chuangxin changshi." "歷史-家族"民間敘事模式的創新嘗試 (History: Family: Folk Narrative Mode and Innovative Narrative Devices). *Dangdai zuojia pinglun* 當代作家評論 (Contemporary Writers Review) 6 (2008): 90–101.
———. "Wo dui Mo Yan san ge gushi de jiedu." 我對莫言三個故事的解讀 (My Interpretation of Three Stories by Mo Yan). *Shanghai caifeng* 上海采風 (Shanghai Style) 2 (2013): 94–95.
Liu Zaifu 劉再復. "Gao Xingjian Mo Yan fengge bijiao lun" 高行健莫言風格比較論' (A Comparative Study of Gao Xingjian and Mo Yan). *Huawen wenxue* 華文文學 (Literatures in Chinese) 1 (2013): 13–18.
Mo Yan 莫言. *Big Breasts and Wide Hips*. Trans. Howard Goldblatt. New York: Arcade Publishing, 2012.
———. *Fengru feitun* 豐乳肥臀 (Big Breasts and Wide Hips). Beijing: Zuojia chubanshe, 2013.
———. *Honggaoliang jiazu* 红高粱家族 (Red Sorghum Family Saga). Beijing: Zuojia chubanshe, 2013.
———. *Jiuguo* 酒國 (The Republic of Wine). Beijing: Zuojia chubanshe, 2013.
———. *Life and Death Are Wearing Me Out*. Trans. Howard Goldblatt. New York: Arcade Publishing, 2012.
———. *Red Sorghum*. Trans. Howard Goldblatt. New York: Arrow Books, 2003.
———. *The Republic of Wine*. Trans. Howard Goldblatt. New York: Arcade Publishing, 2012.
———. *Shengsi pilao* 生死疲勞 (Life and Death Are Wearing Me Out). Beijing: Zuojia chubanshe, 2013.
Sze, Arthur, ed. *Chinese Writers on Writing*. San Antonio, TX: Trinity University Press, 2010.

Wang, David Der-wei 王德威. "Kuangyan liuyan, wuyan moyan." 狂言流言，巫言莫言 (Rhapsody, Rumor, Silence, and Words of a Shamaness.) *Jiangsu daxue xuebao* 江蘇大 學學報 (Journal of Jiangsu University) 11, no. 3 (2009): 1–10.
———. "The Literary World of Mo Yan." Trans. Michael Berry. *World Literature Today* 74, no. 3 (Summer 2000): 487–494.

2

UNATTAINABLE MATURITY

Yu Hua's *Cries in the Drizzle* as an anti-bildungsroman

XU Xi

At the end of Yu Hua's 余華 1991 novel *Cries in the Drizzle* (在細雨中呼喊), twelve-year-old Sun Guanglin, the work's protagonist and narrator, embarks on a journey back to the village of Southgate, where he was born. Upon reaching a crossroads, he encounters an old man who begins to follow him. Guanglin initially urges him to go away, but it turns out that the man is actually his grandfather, Sun Youyuan, who suffers from dementia and has forgotten his way home. When Guanglin and his grandfather finally arrive at Southgate, they discover that their former home is in flames, and consequently what should have been a happy reunion mutates into a family tragedy. This moment marks both the end and the beginning of this story of Sun Guanglin's maturation: it is positioned at the end of the novel, though chronologically it antedates the events described in the main narrative.

During the five years preceding this scene, Sun Guanglin had been living in a town called Sundang (rendered as "Littlemarsh" in Alan Barr's translation) with a childless couple who had adopted him, but after the suicide of his foster father and the sudden departure of his foster mother, he had little choice but to try to return to his natal family. When Guanglin arrives and discovers that his parents' house is in the process of burning down, his father suspects that it is Guanglin and his grandfather's return that has brought him bad luck. In the days that follow, Guanglin becomes alienated from his natal family and comes to view his foster parents as his real parents. This sense of alienation haunts Guanglin, and distinguishes him from typical protagonists of the traditional coming-of-age novel, or bildungsroman.

In the following discussion, I begin with a brief overview of the bildungsroman genre, including its relationship with the historical and political discursive constructions of youth in modern China. I then offer an analysis of Yu Hua's *Cries in the Drizzle*, highlighting the ways it diverges from the generic conventions of the bildungsroman. The sense of abandonment and betrayal that Guanglin experiences prevents him from identifying with any ideals that might have helped guide him to maturity, but also makes it impossible for him to reconcile himself with existing social norms. In this work, Yu Hua creates a peculiar protagonist who is neither a fully developed individual realizing his personal ideals nor an institutionalized subject governed by dominant ideologies, and instead appears trapped in a state of arrested development. In this sense, the novel can be read as an *anti*-bildungsroman, because it challenges the stylistic conventions and the ideological tendencies of the traditional bildungsroman by foregrounding the protagonist's inability to attain maturity.

Although *Cries in the Drizzle* is, in many respects, a rather unusual work, it nevertheless reflects the sociopolitical circumstances of the period in which it was composed. Accordingly, I position the novel within the context of early 1990s China and argue that the protagonist's sense of disorientation and inability to attain maturity reflect the anxiety and despair that Chinese youth experienced during the historical watershed moment in which the work was composed – a period in which past values were being discredited and future hopes were being shattered. Like the protagonist, whose life is presented as a closed circle, many Chinese youth during this period were denied the possibility of maturing fully, and Yu Hua's novel reflects this plight.

Novels of education

The German term *Bildungsroman*, meaning "novel of education," refers to a genre that typically features a young person in the process of reaching maturity. Goethe's *Wilhelm Meister's Apprenticeship* (1795–1796) is frequently viewed as a seminal example, and after being translated into English by Thomas Carlyle in 1824 it helped inspire many British novels, including Charlotte Brontë's *Jane Eyre* (1847), George Eliot's *The Mill on the Floss* (1860), and Charles Dickens's *Great Expectations* (1861). The primary concern of the typical European bildungsroman is the process by which the protagonist successfully establishes a stable identity through a series of trials. M. H. Abrams, for instance, argues that the subject of the typical bildungsroman

> is the development of the protagonist's mind and character, in the passage from childhood through varied experiences – and often through a spiritual crisis – into *maturity*, which usually involves *recognition of one's identity* and role in a world.[1]

Chris Baldick similarly defines the bildungsroman as "a kind of novel that follows the development of the hero or heroine from childhood or adolescence into adulthood, through a troubled *quest for identity*."[2] In contrast, Richard Salmon argues that "at its most prescriptive, the Bildungsroman has been defined as a form of autobiographical narrative which should end in a compromise between the desires of the individual and the normative values of existing society."[3] Maturity, in this sense, means being a socialized, institutionalized individual rather than a fully fledged self, and the process of growing up involves ridding oneself of personal desires in order to meet society's expectations.

Although in the Western context the bildungsroman has been viewed as inherently conservative, reaffirming the importance of traditional institutions and social values, the genre was introduced into China as a fundamentally progressive one. In fact, as Leo Ou-fan Lee argues, Western fiction in general carried radical connotations when it was promoted by Chinese reformers in the late imperial and early Republican period.[4] For instance, Yan Fu 嚴復 believed that a new kind of fiction from the West and Japan could function as a powerful instrument to re-educate the Chinese people, and Liang Qichao 梁啓超 argued that in order to reform the nation's people it was necessary to first reform the nation's fictional literature.[5] Rather than advocating an idealized notion of "art for art's sake," accordingly, intellectuals like Yan Fu and Liang Qichao instead tried to appropriate fiction in service of the modernization and nation building of China.

This celebration of Western literature also was particularly true of fictional depictions of youth, which were invested with national and political connotations. Liang Qichao also played a major role in the construction of the radical discourse of youth in modern China, and in his famous essay "Ode to Young China" (*Shaonian Zhongguo shuo* 少年中國說, 1900) he claimed that the future of old China lay in its youth. Throughout the twentieth century, youth-centered discourses remained central to political and cultural efforts to modernize the nation. In the May Fourth era, the most influential cultural magazine was titled *New Youth* (*Xin qingnian* 新青年), and the celebration of youth continued after the founding of new China. When Mao Zedong visited the Soviet Union in 1957, he delivered a speech to Chinese students studying in Moscow, in which he famously proclaimed:

> The world is yours, as well as ours, but in the last analysis, it is yours. You young people, full of vigor and vitality, are in the bloom of life, like the sun at eight or nine in the morning. Our hope is placed on you. The world belongs to you. China's future belongs to you.[6]

During the Rustication Movement from the 1960s to the 1970s, millions of urban educated youth (*zhishi qingnian* 知識青年, or *zhiqing* 知青 for short) were dispatched to rural areas so that they might live with and learn from the workers and peasants. This *zhiqing* generation was nurtured to value revolutionary heroism and idealism, and at that time the highest ideal for Chinese young people was to be a revolutionary youth (*geming qingnian* 革命青年) – to fully integrate oneself with the masses and devote oneself to the pursuit of a wealthy and powerful nation. In this sense, youth could be considered mature only when they actively engaged with the ideals of revolution. From the late Qing to the Cultural Revolution, accordingly, Chinese youth were interpellated by various political ideologies, such that self making and nation building constituted an influential reciprocal allegory that subsumed individual desires under the grand narrative of building up national identity.

Given that the Western-style novel was promoted as a powerful tool to rejuvenate the Chinese nation, just as youth were given the task of realizing this national rejuvenation, it is no surprise that the genre of the bildungsroman attracted particular attention from Chinese translators and novelists throughout this century-long period. Beginning in the late Qing, many classic European bildungsroman novels were translated into Chinese, including Charles Dickens's *David Copperfield* and *Oliver Twist* (trans. Lin Shu 林紓, 1908), Goethe's *Sorrows of Young Werther* (trans. Guo Moruo 郭沫若, 1922), Charlotte Brontë's *Jane Eyre* (trans. Li Jiye 李霽野, 1935), Romain Rolland's *Jean-Christophe* (trans. Fu Lei 傅雷, 1941), and Goethe's *Wilhelm Meister's Apprenticeship* (trans. Feng Zhi 馮至, 1943), all of which were enthusiastically read and discussed by Chinese readers.[7]

During the Cultural Revolution, however, many of these works were attacked for being poisonous weeds and were either treated as politically taboo or read in accordance with the dictates of communist ideology. Nevertheless, many of these titles, both reprints of earlier works and new translations, reentered the Chinese market during the early 1980s Reform Era. For instance, Fu Lei's translation of *Jean Christophe* was republished by People's Publishing House in 1980 with a print run of 350,000 copies,[8] and by 2011 there were no fewer than 167 Brontë books on the market in China, including 94 different editions of *Jane Eyre* alone.[9]

Although prior to the twentieth century there had not been an indigenous tradition of the bildungsroman in China, the genre was enthusiastically adopted by Chinese authors in the May Fourth period. Mingwei Song observes that in May Fourth works such as Ye Shengtao's 葉聖陶 *Ni Huanzhi* (倪煥之; 1928) and Ba Jin's 巴金 *Family* (家; 1931), youth are closely associated with a sense of "newness and progress, the future and hope, and the development of transpersonal entities like nations."[10] The protagonists of these works are assigned the role of renovating the nation by challenging conventional social constraints, which became the central trope of youth discourse in modern China. In the 1950s, socialist bildungsromans like Yang Mo's 楊沫 *The Song of Youth* (青春之歌; 1958) celebrated new youth ready to set aside their personal desires and devote themselves to the grand cause of building a socialist society. The Chinese version of *How the Steel Was Tempered* (鋼鐵是怎樣練成的), translated from a Russian work by Nikolai Ostrovsky, became one of the most popular foreign novels in the early years of the new China. Its protagonist, Pavel Korchagin, provides a perfect role model of a socialist youth who sacrifices his personal love and even his own health to realize the communist ideal.

Although, like the translated works discussed above, many of these indigenous bildungsromans were censored during the Cultural Revolution, they returned with a vengeance in the 1980s. Despite the substantial differences between the protagonists of European bildungsromans and the youth portrayed in these modern Chinese novels, the two sets of works share several important characteristics. First, in both cases self-identity is typically achieved by successfully integrating oneself with normative social values, whether these be bourgeois or socialist; second, both sets of youth express confidence in their ability to mature into an ideal self, whether this be an enlightened individual or a socialist new man.

Cries in the Drizzle

Born in 1960, Yu Hua grew up during the Cultural Revolution and began writing fiction in the 1980s. Many of his early short stories feature extreme violence and revolve around characters who appear lost and disillusioned. In the short story "1986," for instance, the protagonist is a former history teacher who is taken away during the Cultural Revolution. When he returns to his hometown ten years later and finds that no one remembers him, he proceeds to inflict on them (in his imagination) a series of violent punishments, including branding them with a hot iron, slicing off their noses, and chopping off their legs. When these imagined acts of violence elicit no response from the townspeople, the man turns around and performs a similar series of punishments on his own body, but he is still ignored. As a history teacher victimized during the Cultural Revolution, the protagonist appears to represent the traumatic legacy of that event, and his experience reflects the inability of Reform Era society to fully process its significance. *Cries in the Drizzle*, published in 1991, was Yu Hua's first full-length novel, and although from a narrative perspective it is somewhat more conventional than the author's earlier short stories, it continues to explore many of the same themes of loss, confusion, and disillusionment. *Cries in the Drizzle* shares several important commonalities with European bildungsroman works – it has a quasi-autobiographical component, is narrated from the first-person perspective of an adult, and focuses on the development of selfhood – but departs from the European model in one crucial respect: the protagonist's expectations of maturity are never realized.

In many societies, family is important in a youth's development, and paternal figures function as important role models for their sons. In traditional bildungsroman works one often finds a benevolent paternal figure who not only provides support at critical moments but also is a role model for the young hero. In *Cries in the Drizzle*, by contrast, fathers are depicted as negative figures with deep moral flaws. Most obviously, the protagonist's biological father, Sun Guangcai (rendered as Sun Kwangtsai in Barr's translation), fails to embrace any of his traditional social roles. Not only is he unable to serve as a model for his sons, he even rejects his filial obligations to his own father, Sun Youyuan. Sun Guangcai's father is a stonemason who has lost the ability to work due to illness, and Sun Guangcai even rejoices when he learns that his father is about to die. In order to hasten his father's death, Sun Guangcai assures him that a carpenter had been hired to build a coffin, while in reality he has merely instructed his sons to beat some wooden blocks to imitate the sound of a carpenter working. Forced to trick his own dying grandfather, thirteen-year old Guanglin is disconsolate, and this memory of having hastened his grandfather's death continues to haunt the grown-up narrator – who recalls how, at the time, he was "like a convict on death row who is forced to carry out the execution of another hapless inmate."[11] Meanwhile, Guanglin's foster father, Wang Liqiang, has an affair with a young widow for two years, until finally one day they are caught by the wife of one of his co-workers. Wang Liqiang subsequently takes revenge on the informer, and after accidentally killing her two sons, he commits suicide using a hand grenade. The elder brother of another friend, Liu Xiaoqing, is an educated youth sent down to work in the countryside; he dies from hepatitis after his father urges him to hurry back to the village – and although his father was unaware of the illness, the narrative suggests that the son's death was accelerated by his father's actions.

If fathers in the novel are unfaithful and irresponsible, mothers tend to be powerless figures who simply resign themselves to adversity. For instance, Guanglin's mother endures her husband's callousness and betrayal for many years, but her only act of resistance is enacted on his mistress, not her husband himself. Similarly, Guanglin's foster mother remains locked in her house for the entire five years Guanglin lives with his foster family, only to depart mysteriously shortly after her husband dies. The mother of another character is arrested for prostitution and imprisoned when her son is but a child, leaving him effectively orphaned. All three mothers are presented as being relatively powerless, and they all ultimately disappear from their children's lives.

If families and parents in the novel are unreliable, what about schools and teachers? In the Confucian tradition, teachers were traditionally highly respected, but during the Cultural Revolution their authority was seriously undermined. In Yu Hua's novel, teachers occupy an ambiguous role: they are nominally in positions of authority, but they either are disrespected by their students or abuse their power. For instance, Guanglin admires his high school music instructor, who is cultivated, easygoing, and the only teacher who speaks to the class in standard Chinese, but the teacher is subsequently humiliated by a student who disrespects him by putting his bare feet on his desk and throwing the teacher's songbook out the window. Conversely, one afternoon, two of Guanglin's friends tell him that someone has made a big-character poster calling for the ouster of one of their teachers, and they praise Guanglin for having written the slogan. He replies that he was not the one who wrote it, but adds, "If you'd asked me to do it, I would have written it too."[12] This remark is relayed to Guanglin's teachers, who punish him not for what he has actually done, but rather for what he *could have* done.

In short, Sun Guanglin stands in sharp contrast to both the protagonists in European bildungsroman and the vigorous youth who are associated with modern China. Guanglin is abandoned by his parents, unjustly accused by his teachers, and betrayed by his friends. He craves acceptance but remains isolated and disoriented. For him, achieving maturity is impossible because he cannot reconcile himself with the chaotic and miserable society in which he lives.

In a recent study, Li Hua notes that Yu Hua and fellow novelist Su Tong "turn their narratives from mass movement (the Cultural Revolution) to individual heroism, from the collectivist mentality to private identity, and from political enlightenment to personal spiritual exploration,"[13] and contends that Su Tong's and Yu Hua's presentation of their young protagonists as distanced from revolutionary activity may be read as a gesture of bidding farewell to revolution. Li Hua's argument accords with the critique of radical revolution by Li Zehou and Liu Zaifu, who attribute the tragedy of twentieth-century China to the violent revolutions that produced life-or-death political struggles and conclude that a thorough reassessment of twentieth-century China must include a profound rethinking of revolution. They argue that China should give up radical revolution and instead adopt peaceful evolutionary reform.[14] This critique echoes Li Zehou's earlier claim that a nascent enlightenment movement in China was overwhelmed by discourses of national salvation in the post–May Fourth period. In this context, Li Hua's reading of the novel suggests that Yu Hua shares Li Zehou and Liu Zaifu's liberal enlightenment stance, but reading Yu Hua's work as an act of bidding farewell to revolution oversimplifies his contemplation of the spiritual trauma caused by the Cultural Revolution and ignores his concern with the destructive power that continues to haunt Chinese youth.

I agree that these protagonists' failure to attain maturity may be seen as a parody of a traditional political discourse of serving the nation or party at the expense of the youth's own autonomy, but do not think that Yu Hua presents his protagonist as independent of the revolutionary movement. Instead, Guanglin's inability to reach maturity may be directly attributed to the legacy of the destructive power of the Cultural Revolution. In particular, I would argue that Yu Hua's critique of the Cultural Revolution is unmistakable, but it does not simply call for a clear break with history. Peng Mingwei observes that Yu Hua "does not view himself as an intellectual and advanced enlightenment torchbearer," and that he "avoids general political judgment and secular moral standards, and is opposed to the rigid and stereotyped understanding of characters and history."[15] In contrast to an enlightenment view of history, Yu Hua's literary representation is much more pessimistic, suggesting that revolution is not simply something to which one may bid farewell but rather is a force that inevitably continues to haunt the present.

The 1980s are often regarded as a peak of liberal enlightenment in China, during which individuals were able to free themselves from narratives of national salvation and revolutionary ideals. At the time, the nation seemed to be moving toward a liberal democracy in which the rights of the individual would be respected and people's potential could be fully developed. In other words, the conflict between self-realization and nation building seemed to dissolve, as the two processes reached a mutually beneficial relationship. This was derailed by the crackdown on the democracy movement protesters in the summer of 1989, after which the future of China's modernization and reform appeared unclear and young people's pursuit of self-realization was stymied. It was no longer possible for these young people to identify with prior social norms such as Confucian values of filiality or Marxist revolutionary ideals, which had been undermined during the Cultural Revolution. However, new models of self-realization embodied in individual economic success and material fulfillment in the market had not yet been fully established. Yu Hua's *Cries in the Drizzle*, accordingly, reflects the anxiety and despair felt by many of China's youth during this key transitional period. The novel raises important questions about how an individual might grow up, achieve self-realization, and become a complete human being – but the only answers offered are at best highly pessimistic. The novel suggests that the mature self cannot be realized because the individual cannot reconcile him- or herself with this historical legacy, and consequently remains disoriented within society.

Apart from Guanglin's conflict with his father and betrayal by his friends, there are other instances of disorientation in the work. Guanglin's elder brother, Guangping, changes quickly after going into town for high school. He distances himself from the village boys and attempts to ingratiate himself with his classmates from the town. His parents are flattered by the regular visits of his new friends, and some villagers even predict Guangping "would have the brightest future of any of the village children."[16] Despite his efforts to maintain the friendships, however, Guangping is abandoned after graduation, and when the other boys are assigned jobs, he has to return to the village.

Guangping is not the only student in his school who is abjectly abandoned. For instance, one morning his classmate Su Yu suffers an aneurism, and as he is fighting for his life his mother arrives but virtually ignores him. Su Yu's father also has a chance to help, but instead merely yells at Su Yu for not getting up. Su Yu's death is described as "an unstoppable fall that accelerated and turned into a tailspin."[17] Rather than growing up, the town's youth spiral toward death and despair, as their parents and siblings – who should have been able to provide support in their process of development and maturation – instead are cold-hearted and negligent.

A state of dull captivity

From the preceding examples, we can see that even as the Cultural Revolution overturned existing norms and regulations, it did help some youth to achieve emancipation. The youthful characters in *Cries in the Drizzle*, however, are unable to reach maturity and find themselves lost and ignored. Living in a society full of violence, cruelty, and betrayal, some even follow the evil examples that they find in the adult world. Rather than characterizing an enlightened young hero, this work describes a group of lost children whose growth was seriously hindered by the revolution.

Although Yu Hua's novel adopts the general narrative framework of the bildungsroman, it differs from this enlightenment model in several important respects. First, while Franco Moretti argues that the classic bildungsroman relies on a teleological logic whereby "events acquire meaning when they lead to one ending, and one only,"[18] Yu Hua's novel instead has a cyclical structure, with the narrative concluding where it began. Second, while protagonists in traditional bildungsromans are oriented toward certain ideals, in Yu Hua's novel all possible role models – including parents and teachers – are overthrown either by excessive personal desires or by distorted ideological discipline. Furthermore, the toppling of these role models does not necessarily result in a process of healthy maturation and self-cultivation. Instead, the younger generation finds itself in a state of confusion and despair.

This younger generation's quest for identity cannot rely on external institutions, such as family, school, or community; these youth are left like the six-year-old boy at the beginning of the novel, who is haunted by a "nameless dread."[19] In particular, one rainy night he hears a woman's anguished wails and expects to hear another voice respond, but it never materializes. The latter absent voice subsequently haunts the protagonist, because he cannot figure out a meaning in the nothingness. Chinese youth in the early 1990s were caught in what Georg Lukács describes as a state of "dull captivity within a merely present reality – a reality that is heterogeneous in itself and meaningless to the individual."[20] These youth had to face the nothingness of history and attempt to find self-realization within it. In this sense, Yu Hua is more of an existentialist writer than an enlightenment one.

Notes

1 M. H. Abrams, *A Glossary of Literary Terms*, 7th ed. (Beijing: Foreign Language Teaching and Research Press, 2004), 193, italics added.

2 Chris Baldick, *The Concise Oxford Dictionary of Literary Terms* (Oxford: Oxford University Press, 2001), 27, italics added.

3 Richard Salmon, "The English *Bildungsroman*," in *The Oxford History of the Novel in English*, vol. 3: *The Nineteenth-Century Novel 1820–1880*, ed. John Kucich and Jenny Bourne Taylor (Oxford: Oxford University Press, 2012), 91.

4 See Merle Goldman and Leo Ou-fan Lee, eds., *An Intellectual History of Modern China* (Cambridge: Cambridge University Press, 2002), 146–147.

5 For Yan Fu, see Goldman and Lee, eds., *An Intellectual History of Modern China*, 146–147. See Liang Qichao, "On the Relationship Between Fiction and the Government of the People," in *Modern Chinese Literary Thought: Writings on Literature, 1893–1945*, ed. Kirk Denton (Stanford: Stanford University Press, 1996), 74–81.

6 Mao Zedong, "Talk at a Meeting with Chinese Students and Trainees in Moscow" (17 November 1957), in *English Quotations from Chairman Mao Tse-tung* (Beijing: Foreign Language Press, 1966), 288.

7 Guo Moruo's translation of Goethe, for instance, went through more than fifty printings between 1922 to 1932. Liu Xiang 劉香, "Zhongguo 'Weite re' yu 20 niandai wenhua shichang" 中國 "維特熱" 與20年代文化市場 ("Craze for Werther" and the Cultural Market in 1920s China), *Guo Moruo xuekan* 郭沫若學刊 (Guo. Moruo Journal) 3 (2001): 44.

8 Tu Hui 涂慧, "*Luoman Luolan zai Zhongguo de jieshou fenxi — yi <Yuehan Kelisiduofu> wei zhongxin*" 羅曼・羅蘭在中國的接受分析 – 以〈約翰克裏斯朵夫〉為中心 (An Analysis of Romain Rolland's Reception in China: Centering on *Jean Christophe*) MA thesis, Beijing Normal University, 2008, 12.

9 Shouhua Qi, "' . . . [A]s Much Soul . . . and Full as Much Heart': Translation and Reception of the Brontë Sisters in China," British Library, www.britishlibrary.cn/en/articles/much-soul-full-much-heart%e2%80%a8-translation-reception-bronte-sisters-china/ (accessed February 1, 2018).

10 Mingwei Song, *Young China: National Rejuvenation and the Bildungsroman, 1900–1959* (Cambridge: Harvard University Asia Center, 2015), 42.

11 Yu Hua, *Cries in the Drizzle,* trans. Allan H. Barr (New York: Anchor Books, 2007), 196.

12 Yu Hua, *Cries in the Drizzle,* 268.

13 Li Hua, *Contemporary Chinese Fiction by Su Tong and Yu Hua: Coming of Age in Troubled Times* (Leiden: Brill, 2011), 191.

14 Li Zehou 李澤厚 and Liu Zaifu 劉再復, *Gaobie geming: Huiwang ershi shiji Zhongguo* 告別革命：回望二十世紀中國 (Bidding Farewell to Revolution: Looking Back to Twentieth-Century China). (Hong Kong: Tiandi tushu. 2004), 60, 69.

15 Peng Mingwei 彭明偉, *"Ziwo lingchi de yishu: Lüelun Yu Hua <Zai xiyu huhan>"* 自我凌遲的藝術：略論余華〈在細雨呼喊〉 (The Art of Self-Dismembering: On Yu Hua's *Cries in the Drizzle*). March 11, 2016. http://yuhua.zjnu.cn/ArticleOne.aspx?id=2055.

16 Yu Hua, *Cries in the Drizzle,* 16.

17 Yu Hua, *Cries in the Drizzle,* 120.

18 Franco Moretti, *The Way of the World: The Bildungsroman in European Culture* (London: Verso, 1987), 7.

19 Yu Hua, *Cries in the Drizzle,* 3.

20 Georg Lukács, *The Theory of the Novel,* trans. Anna Bostock (Cambridge: MIT Press, 1971), 80.

Works cited

Abrams, M. H. *A Glossary of Literary Terms.* 7th ed. Beijing: Foreign Language Teaching and Research Press, 2004.

Baldick, Chris. *The Concise Oxford Dictionary of Literary Terms.* Oxford: Oxford University Press, 2001.

Goldman, Merle, and Leo Ou-fan Lee, eds. *An Intellectual History of Modern China.* Cambridge: Cambridge University Press, 2002.

Li, Hua. *Contemporary Chinese Fiction by Su Tong and Yu Hua: Coming of Age in Troubled Times.* Leiden: Brill, 2011.

Liang Qichao. "On the Relationship between Fiction and the Government of the People." In *Modern Chinese Literary Thought: Writings on Literature, 1893–1945,* edited by Kirk Denton, 74–81. Stanford: Stanford University Press, 1996.

Liu Xiang 劉香. "Zhongguo 'Weite re' yu 20 niandai wenhua shichang" 中國"維特熱"與20年代文化市場 ("Craze for Werther" and the Cultural Market in 1920s China). *Guo Moruo xuekan* 郭沫若學刊 (Guo. Moruo Journal) 3 (2001): 44.

Li Zehou 李澤厚 and Liu Zaifu 劉再復. *Gaobie geming: Huiwang ershi shiji Zhongguo* 告別革命: 回望二十世紀中國 (Bidding Farewell to Revolution: Looking Back to Twentieth-Century China). 5th ed. Hong Kong: Tiandi tushu, 2004.

Lukács, Georg. *The Theory of the Novel.* Trans. Anna Bostock. Cambridge: MIT Press, 1971.

Mao Zedong. "Talk at a Meeting with Chinese Students and Trainees in Moscow." (November 17, 1957). In *English Quotations from Chairman Mao Tse-tung,* 288. Beijing: Foreign Language Press, 1966.

Moretti, Franco. *The Way of the World: The Bildungsroman in European Culture.* London: Verso, 1987.

Peng Mingwei 彭明偉. *""Ziwo lingchi de yishu: Lüelun Yu Hua <Zai xiyu huhan"* 自我凌遲的藝術: 略論余華<在細雨中呼喊 (The Art of Self-Dismembering: On Yu Hua's *Cries in the Drizzle*). March 11, 2016. http://yuhua.zjnu.cn/ArticleOne.aspx?id=2055.

Qi, Shouhua. "' . . . [A]s Much Soul . . . and Full as Much Heart': Translation and Reception of the Brontë Sisters in China." *British Library*. www.britishlibrary.cn/en/articles/much-soul-full-much-heart%e2%80%a8-translation-reception-bronte-sisters-china/. Accessed February 1, 2018.

Salmon, Richard. "The English Bildungsroman." In *The Oxford History of the Novel in English, Vol. 3: The Nineteenth-Century Novel 1820–1880*, edited by John Kucich and Jenny Bourne Taylor, 90–105. Oxford: Oxford University Press, 2012.

Song, Mingwei. *Young China: National Rejuvenation and the Bildungsroman, 1900–1959*. Cambridge: Harvard University Asia Center, 2015.

Tu Hui 塗慧. "*Luoman Luolan zai Zhongguo de jieshou fenxi — yi <Yuehan Kelisiduofu> wei zhongxin*" 羅曼·羅蘭在中國的接受分析 – 以<約翰克裏斯-夫>為中心 (An Analysis of Romain Rolland's Reception in China: Centering on *Jean Christophe*). MA thesis, Beijing Normal University, 2008.

Yu Hua. *Cries in the Drizzle*. Trans. Allan H. Barr. New York: Anchor Books, 2007.

3

FRANKENSTEIN VS. DRACULA

Romanticisms and the ideologies of poetry in contemporary China

Lucas Klein

> *The hemophagous mosquito, the female of the species, is in the same category as the leech and the vampire, to which could be added the bloodsucking bureaucrat, the landlord, the capitalist.*
>
> – Xi Chuan, *"Notes on the Mosquito"*

一只吸血的蚊子，母蚊子，與水蛭、吸血鬼同歸一類，還可加上吸血的官僚、地主、資本家。[1]

> – 西川, "蚊子志"

In Al Adamson's 1971 movie *Dracula vs. Frankenstein*, Dr. Durea, a descendent of Dr. Victor Frankenstein, announces that his guests "do not realize that reality itself is the grandest illusion of all, that human blood is the essence from which future illusions may be created."[2] Moments later, Count Dracula appears and orders the doctor to re-reanimate his ancestor's monster – "Your mind and certain skill were meant to fulfill the Frankenstein dream, and to infuse life into that artificially created man, the likes of which civilization will never forget" – whose remains the count happens to possess. Dracula and Frankenstein's monster team up to take vengeance on Dr. Durea's enemies, but at the climax of the movie Frankenstein's monster, moved by the beauty of one of their victims, turns against the vampire. Dracula manages to kill the monster by decapitating him and pulling off his arms – "I'll destroy you piece by piece," he threatens, "as Dr. Frankenstein created you!" – but he is himself turned to ash in the light of the rising sun.

We have never stopped resurrecting and reanimating the monsters of Romanticism. Both Mary Shelley's *Frankenstein* and John Polidori's "The Vampyre" – a predecessor of Bram Stoker's *Dracula* – were products of the Year Without a Summer (1816) jaunt to Lord Byron's Lake Geneva Villa Diodati, a grouping that Elma Dangerfield has described as "the most brilliant and romantic circle of poets, writers and personalities which Switzerland – and Europe – has ever seen."[3] While Dracula's and Frankenstein's continued reimaginings in cinema owe more to tropes set in F. W. Murnau's *Nosferatu* (1922) and James Whale's *Frankenstein* (1931) and *Bride of Frankenstein* (1935) than to the literature they adapt, the remakes nevertheless demonstrate the hold the gothic has on our imagination and the Romantic has on our epistemology.[4] Here, I use the terms *Frankenstein* and *Dracula* to refer not to characters of a monolithic Romanticism but rather to two distinct ways of configuring Romanticism in contemporary literature, the hybrid and the ideological. I will argue for the ethics of the former against those of the latter in contemporary Chinese poetry.

Since Leo Lee's *Romantic Generation of Modern Chinese Writers* we have had no problem admitting that "the impact of Western romanticism . . . provided the prevalent ethos and dominated at least a decade of literary development in China," and we should have no problem acknowledging Romanticism's revivification in Chinese poetry today.[5] We have not yet, however, focused sufficiently on the internal differences within Chinese poetry's revivals or re-uses of Romanticism. Using the symbolism of vampires and Frankenstein's monster, my analysis is partly inspired by Karl Marx's remark that "capital is dead labour, that, vampire-like, only lives by sucking living labour, and lives the more, the more labour it sucks."[6] Franco Moretti builds on this observation to argue that Dracula represents capital, "impelled towards a continuous growth, an unlimited expansion of his domain: accumulation is inherent in his nature"; by contrast, Frankenstein's monster represents the proletariat, in that "denied a name and an individuality . . . he belongs wholly to his creator (just as one can speak of a 'Ford worker')."[7] But while I like Moretti's close reading of what he calls the Dialectic of Fear, my emphasis is on how these two *"totalizing* monsters" represent not social or psychological forces, but rather alternate options for how to handle Romanticism.[8]

What was – or is – Romanticism? Marx's notion of capitalism as the idea of the blood-sucking ruling class provides for what Jerome McGann has called the Romantic Ideology, "a synthetic program whose center has been shifted from rational inquiry to imaginative pursuit," under the illusion that "only a poet and his works can transcend a corrupting appropriation by 'the world' of politics and money."[9] In this reading, Romanticism represents poetry's inward turn in opposition to an industrialism it cannot successfully combat. But because it accepts its own social irrelevance in the face of paper mills and printing presses (and novels and newspapers), Romantic poetry assents to the underlying logic of capitalism.[10] The vampiric, accordingly, represents the ideological force of capitalism that has proven very hard to kill, while the Frankensteinian offers an alternative that emphasizes Romanticism's hybridity and adaptability. For poetry to be Frankensteinian, as I use it here, it must be open to the translingual and translational, availing itself of and updating some of the attributes of Romanticism without succumbing to it entirely.[11] I will elaborate on these notions via recounting a debate on Romanticism between Xi Chuan 西川 (b. 1963) and Wang Ao 王 敖 (b. 1976), in which one argues for what I call the Frankensteinian and the other for the vampiric – to be contextualized in terms of claims of Chineseness, modernity, and translation. At stake is not only how we read and write Chinese culture's relationship to the rest of the world and its own cultural history but also how we understand the notion of modernity, especially as it applies to China.

The best words in the best order?

Footnoting the first paragraph of his multivolume history of modern Europe and the world, Eric Hobsbawm writes that the words coined early on in modernity that are definitive of that era – such as *industry, factory, strike, capitalism, socialism,* and *nationality* – "either have international currency, or were fairly literally translated into various languages. Thus . . . the combination 'iron road' is the basis of the name of the railway everywhere except in its country of origin."[12] Moreover, the international currency of modernity changed the definitions of certain words and concepts. For instance, along with the conscious adoption of a Western-centered modernity in the twentieth century, the translation of *poetry* into Chinese involved a redefinition of *shi* (詩) from one genre among several (*ci* 詞, *fu* 賦, *qu* 曲, etc.) into an umbrella concept renamed *shige* (詩歌). This translational redefinition, creating what Lydia Liu would call a "supersign," has built into it ideological implications of both irrelevance and aesthetic beauty, or subjective definition – so that while we are not able to say *poetry* in classical Chinese, neither are we able to define poetry very easily in modern Chinese.[13] Rather than the stiff yet clear prescriptions of *shi* or *ci* before the twentieth century, we have a Chinese approximation of Samuel Taylor Coleridge's adage, "the *best* words in the best order," with all the subjectivity that that entails.[14] This definition is wholly unsatisfying (is a bad poem, with inferior words in an inferior order, not a poem?), yet this kind of definition, whose pose of objectivity masks an assertion of subjective taste, is the product of modernity and Romanticism.[15]

Romanticism also gives us the idea of poetry as marginal – or rather, capitalism gives us the idea of poetry as marginal, and Romanticism revels in it. This allows Romantic poets to think of themselves, in the words of *Frankenstein*'s author's husband, as "the unacknowledged legislators of the world."[16] Michelle Yeh uses a similar metaphor in her 1992 edited *Anthology of Modern Chinese Poetry*, the introduction to which is titled "From the Margin."[17] But with any claim of marginality, it is always necessary to ask, as Maghiel van Crevel does, "Whose margins? . . . Whose center?"[18] In this instance, it is not so much that Chinese poetry today is marginal to industrialized Chinese society, but rather that contemporary Chinese poetry appears marginal only against a fantasy of a premodern China in which poetry could be central to everyone: "What," van Crevel continues, "makes the classical poetry paradigm, socio-economic development or power relations the center?"[19] Since opposition to a thing so often only reifies the power that thing has, my underlying standpoint is *against* the radical epistemological break between premodern and modern Chinese poetry (as Stephen Owen has written, "an embalmed version of the past was constructed by May Fourth scholars" as "a pure act of ideological will").[20] Rather, the distinction appears to us as a result of translation and our framework for understanding translation.

Creating the appearance of an epistemological split through the simultaneous use and denial of translation is in fact a common trait of Romanticism. Romanticism often casts translation as a kind of transcendence, but the truly transcendent is the national as an expression of the individual. At the end of "Song of Myself," Walt Whitman writes, "I too am not a bit tamed – I too am untranslatable."[21] Similarly, Guo Moruo 郭沫若 (1892–1978) wrote that "translated poetry must be like poetry" (譯詩得像詩) – as if, only a matter of years after the advent of vernacular verse, what "poetry" was like were a clear proposition.[22] Yet by a few decades into the People's Republic of China, the dominance of such poetry-translational norms ended up constructing a certain sense of Chineseness in Chinese poetry. Guo's "Praise Song for the Sun" (太陽禮贊), for instance, includes the lines

> Oh Sun! Please shine the whole of my life into a stream of flowing red blood!
> Oh Sun! Please shine the whole of my poetry into golden froth!

> 太陽喲! 你請把我全部的生命照成道鮮紅的血流!
> 太陽喲! 你請把我全部的詩歌照成些金色的浮漚!

This poem rhapsodizes in a manner drawn from Whitman, even as it prefigures the Communist iconography of literalized metaphor and revolutionary red flowing through one's veins.[23] But if the author of these lines can have adhered to normative, nativizing translational ethics (a modern definition of poetry, but not the modernity of an amorphous "best words in the best order"), then behind the national as an expression of the individual we have evidence of the ossification of poetry and the denial of translation's importance.

We cannot, therefore, look at modern Chinese poetry only in terms of what, in a modern context, it has been translated *into*, but must also consider what, in a premodern context, it was translated *from*. In short, poetry in China today is not solely a translation of a Western notion implanted onto a colonized locale; it is simultaneously a translation of a premodern tradition resuscitated in the contemporary moment, attempting to reconcile these competing notions into a cohesive text – which is, of course, what translation so often is and does, anywhere.

Awareness of contemporary Chinese poetry's translational status is on full display in Xi Chuan's essay, "The Notion of the Poet and the Notion of Poetry – A Historical Abyss" (詩人觀念與詩歌觀念的歷史性落差). Arguing, as the title implies, that a gap exists in China today between poetry as poets write it and poets as society imagines them, Xi Chuan proposes that "the poet's self-construction . . . is accepted by the reader, misread and recreated, with this misread and recreated self-image of the poet then reincorporated by later poets into the work of self-construction." In public discourse, then, "we have a hard time distinguishing between the image of poets' own self-creation and the image of poets re-created by readers in the process of acceptance. In many ways, the two kinds of images fuse together."[24] The result is what Xi Chuan calls the Chinese poet's "nineteenth-centurification" (十九世紀化), and as he traces this history, he notes that a "superstition of the era took shape: only the Romantic poet could be the true poet."[25]

Xi Chuan describes Zhu Naizheng's 朱乃正 (b. 1935) 1984 oil portrait of Bronze Age poet Qu Yuan 屈原 (c. 339–278 BCE), *The Nation's Spirit – for Qu Yuan* (國魂 – 屈原頌), wherein Qu Yuan, feet in the Miluo River, stands adamantly against the wind, hair and beard blown back. Xi Chuan contrasts this image with those by late imperial artists Chen Hongshou 陳洪綬 (1598–1652) and Xiao Yuncong 蕭雲從 (1596–1673), both of whom paint Qu Yuan with billowing robes and a sword, hair tucked under a coronet, and beard drooping – a morose-looking official.[26] "The image of the poet as a poet-official or poet-scholar eventually simplified into that of the poet himself," Xi Chuan writes, "and the poet who lost the image of the official or scholar took on the image of the poet as Western Romanticism knew it."[27] Xi Chuan notes that Zhu's Qu Yuan looks to have been informed and inspired by the 1977 film *Chu Yuan* (屈原), directed by Fong Pau 鮑方 (1922–2006) – the first Hong Kong movie to be released in the People's Republic of China, and an adaptation of a 1942 play script by Guo Moruo. As Xi Chuan points out, Guo's play at key moments sucks its lifeblood from other famous works of literature: Guo has Qu Yuan scream into a storm, "Wind! Roar, roar! Roar with all your might!" (風, 你咆哮吧! 咆哮吧! 盡力地咆哮吧!) – echoing King Lear's "Blow, winds, and crack your cheeks! rage! blow!"[28] Of course, Shakespeare was canonized and turned into the exemplar of genius by the Romantics.[29] So the Chinese image of the paradigmatic poet comes to us through being reimagined in terms set by a poet from another culture, made paradigmatic through the auspices of Romanticism.

For my purposes here, it is important to highlight that Romanticism or the changing definitions of poetry under modernity constituted not an epistemic rift but rather merely a shift in Chinese understandings of the poet and poetry. As Xi Chuan observes,

> The image of Qu Yuan as a poet, including his spirit, personality, cultivation, taste, dress, hairstyle, and manner of speech, is the collective construction of Qu Yuan, Wang Yi, Liu Xie, Chen Hongshou, Xiao Yuncong, Guo Moruo, Zhu Naizheng, and others.[30]

Of course, to talk about the image of a poet as a construct that has undergone change over time is to argue against an essential spirit of poetry and therefore against one of the pillars of the Romantic ideology, and Xi Chuan's implicit critique of Romanticism has indeed engendered a vociferous reaction.

Published later the same year, Wang Ao's "How to Synchronize the Watches of Running Poets" (怎樣給奔跑中的詩人們對錶) takes issue with a number of

Xi Chuan's secondary points and implications. Where Xi Chuan worried about the "nineteenth-centurification" of Chinese poetic selves, Wang Ao notes that "'Century,' of course, is a Western invention."[31] The aim of Wang's criticism is not to show Xi Chuan as an epistemological running dog to Western cultural hegemony. Rather, it is to promote Romanticism as "providing hope for transcendence beyond religious orthodoxies and official philosophies, as well as helping poets expand their fields of fantasy to actively pursue more revelatory dialogues for the transcendence of the limits of space and time, as John Ashbery demonstrated for us in 'Self-Portrait in a Convex Mirror.'"[32] To do this, Wang Ao partakes in a long discursus of Harold Bloom – inspireds readings of Romantic and post-Romantic poets such as Ashbery, Hart Crane, W. H. Auden, and Wallace Stevens, primarily to displace the Modernist interest in Ezra Pound and Gary Snyder that Wang sees as dominant in China.[33] For Wang Ao, Xi Chuan buys into a Modernist myth of progress, at the cost of believing in the universal value of creativity.

As Eric Hayot has observed, Modernism and Romanticism share "the unusual characteristic of denoting both an attitude and a period."[34] The debate between Xi Chuan and Wang Ao, then, is at base about this dual feature of Romanticism as written upon the world with the pen of global power. At a certain level this is only a matter of taste, leading to the moral quandaries in differences of worldview we often think underlie our likes and dislikes. But for all that it is common to fault fascist Pound for his representation of other cultures, and he may indeed lead to no end of ethical troubles, Wang Ao finds himself making some discomfiting statements as well – at least if you want to be critical of capitalism, empire, cultural plunder, and vampires. On "the other side of the Möbius strip" from "ready-made theoretical discourse" such as "*This is the consequence of cultural colonialism,*" Wang Ao says, "people will believe that we Chinese just got started early in grand-scale cultural plundering of the West, taking these poems of intermingled nativeness and foreignness as proof."[35] Later, he refers to Marx's comparison of capitalism to vampires as if it were praise:

> As [Marx] said, capitalism has become a vampire, still standing even after having been cut down countless times. . . . Thus, despite having been hacked at by Modernism, overturned by New Criticism, and deconstructed from every theoretical angle, Romanticism can not only come back to life, it is even able to consume the Modernism that murdered it.[36]

Defending grand-scale cultural plunder and promoting the undying spirit of capitalism? If Romanticism is an attitude, what is the attitude that it has about the rest of the world?

While Wang Ao offers a valuable rereading of Romanticism, his article neither solves nor refutes the problem raised by Xi Chuan. Wang Ao defends his defense of Romanticism by explaining that if we say that the Romanticist transcendence of history is a myth, we must also acknowledge that the automatic explanation of everything with history (or historical determinism) is also a myth – and between these two myths, both of which require reflection, many poets will lean to the former.[37]

In other words, he ignores the gap between the craft of poetry as poets have pursued it and the Romantic image of poetry within which Chinese society confines poets, simply because he prefers to stay caught (up) in that Romantic image.[38] Wang Ao writes about Auden's reversal of his own earlier Romantic aesthetics and politics "as stuck in the same rut as Hitler's and Mussolini's making themselves into the spiritual leaders of their nations," but here he falls into a similar, related ditch.[39] Even as he presents his argument as merely one among many – "my version is not the only one," he says, "but I hope it can . . . help clarify some long-standing confusions that have entangled the minds of readers of Chinese poetry" – his advocacy of Romanticism belies his pluralism because it cannot get past the problems inherent in Coleridge's definition of poetry as "the *best* words in the best order."[40] Ultimately, what seems so individual and empowering about Romanticism leads to a reliance on authority that will, just like capitalism's vampire sucking the blood out of other cultural imaginations of and attempts at freedom, prove very hard to kill.

I propose that, while Wang Ao's vampiric approach effectively leads to a defense of capitalist plunder and revels in its own marginality, Xi Chuan's Frankensteinian approach can instead, by helping reshape notions of intercultural interaction in poetry, offer a way for poetry to gain cultural relevance. To pursue this argument is to look to Xi Chuan's "Historical Abyss" article not for a defense of Modernism against Romanticism, but rather for a different way to approach Romantic poetry, from within or without – or even an attempt at both simultaneously. Despite Wang Ao's framing of him, Xi Chuan is not in fact an anti-Romanticist; his essay is not in fact a critique of Romanticism. Though he states that "As a literary tendency, Romanticism has its problems, such as when it makes itself into a *cliché*," he also notes that he is only

> inadvertently mocking the great spirit of Romanticism . . . today, after Western civil society has been basically finalized, Romanticism's advocacy of the spontaneous overflow of powerful feelings, as well as the relationship between man and nature, gain a new necessity even among the bourgeoisie.[41]

Against such criticisms, Wang Ao wants to reestablish the Romantic ideology as fitting, proper, and inevitable for poetry: "Not only has Romanticism not left the stage, it has continued to demonstrate its vivacity and adaptability; not only is it not to be pronounced obsolete, it has turned into a power strong enough to cross international and ethnic boundaries."[42] But is there a way to demonstrate and embrace some of Romanticism's adaptability without copping to the queasy triumphalism of "strong enough to cross international and ethnic boundaries"? As Xi Chuan himself writes, "either Romanticism must be twentieth or twenty-first-centurified . . . or else we must be vigilant against Romanticism's incursion into modern poetry."[43] How, then, do we update Romanticism in Chinese poetry for the twenty-first century?

To ask this question is to focus on how to write Chinese poetry – a question that, for understandable reasons, literary scholarship on modern China has not often asked. Instead, the stakes of talking about modernity in China and Chinese literature – our *Search for Modern China* – often have to do with our own comfort or discomfort with Chinese literature's alleged Westernization, whether we can allow China to take on and develop aspects that remind us of things we know from the West, like skyscrapers and traffic jams and free verse poetry.[44] One critic asks, "Is this Chinese literature?"[45] Others respond that such a question denies China its "historically specific modernity" and ability to formulate "an historically specific cultural response," as "the modern intellectual tradition in China began" not with wholesale acquiescence but rather "translation, adaptation, appropriate, and other interlingual practices related to the West."[46] There are treatments of Chinese modernity that more or less bracket the West, describing instead a "dialectics of the heroic and the quotidian," or else basing modernity in the specifics of urban culture, but most seem to talk about the instability of the ground "upon which the dialectic between 'Chinese' and 'Western' is played."[47] But isn't all this just a specific response to modernity as brought by the West? Doesn't it just acknowledge "the lure of global modernity," "oriented toward the West's imposition of itself on the Rest," and that at "the periphery of the literary system . . . the modern novel first arises not as an autonomous development but as a compromise between a western formal influence (usually French or English) and local materials"?[48] What if there's something wrong with our understanding of modernity vis-à-vis China itself? The standard narrative is that modern China began in the twentieth century, but was there not a "Chinese contribution to global modernity" in the late Qing that was "subsequently denied and repressed"?[49] The Western formal influence/local materials compromise theory, for instance, relies on the post-1500 historiography of world-systems theory.[50] Andre Gunder Frank, in contrast, asks whether there may have been an earlier "Sinocentric international order" in which "Ming China was the driving force behind global trade in the early-modern period."[51] Other scholars, from Naitō Konan 内藤湖南 to David Porter to Wang Hui 汪暉, have similarly proposed that the origins of Chinese modernity may be found as early as the Song dynasty (960–1279).[52] My own suspicion is that modernity has a multiplicity of sources, but the implications of this have not been fully developed, given that modernity is only spoken of in the abstract, in place of more emotionally pressing questions like whether or not we can tolerate a China with traffic jams and free verse poetry.

My question, then, is how contemporary Chinese poets should approach questions of modernity and sharper awareness of multiple modernities, taking the West not as a force to be resisted or acquiesced to but rather as a fact of modernity that requires negotiation, to be handled tactically and strategically. In the debate between Wang Ao and Xi Chuan I see opposing ideas of how to engage in such negotiations, which I have named vampiric and Frankensteinian, but they have in common an understanding that the force of Romanticism demands questions of *how* rather than of *whether*. They both have a sense of the stakes of writing Chinese poetry in the face of the West.

Late trains or learning languages

In *Dracula*, Jonathan Harker writes in his diary, "It seems to me that the further east you go the more unpunctual are the trains. What ought they to be in China?"[53] In contrast, Dr. Victor Frankenstein tells of a mentor interested in "making himself complete master of the oriental languages . . . Persian, Arabic, and Sanscrit [*sic*]," which "easily induced" Victor himself "to enter on the same studies."[54] As trains were the height of modern transportation circa 1897, when *Dracula* was published, to imagine Chinese trains as perennially unpunctual was to think of China's modernity as belated – and believe that the "History of the World," per Hegel, "travels from East to West."[55] As for mastery of oriental languages in *Frankenstein*, since Edward Said we have not been able to pretend that such knowledge would be innocent (in the same breath, Victor writes that in "oriental" literature "life appears to consist in a warm sun and a garden of roses, – in the smiles and frowns of a fair enemy, and the fire that consumes your own heart. How different from the manly and heroical poetry of Greece and Rome!").[56] While we may balk at the binary oppositions and the assertion of mastery over the oriental, aware that knowledge production imbues ideological and material power, I still think this limited and impure knowledge is better than ignorance. And that is what the Frankensteinian in Chinese poetry can achieve.

Statements such as these suggest the stakes of the struggle between the vampiric and the Frankensteinian. As modernity configures poetry as marginal, the vampiric view sees China as being on the margins of the world's project of modernity. The Frankensteinian, on the other hand, believes that both China and the rest of the world can be known, and though such knowledge is not without problems, the way through those problems should be founded on the integration of such knowledge. To write vampiric poetry, then, is not only to kowtow to the Romantic ideology but also to jettison belief in China's ability to have anything to say about or to that Romanticism. To write Frankensteinian poetry, though, is to believe that Romanticism does not have to come from the Roman, and that a hybrid is available between the Asiatic garden of roses and the manly heroic poetry of the European classics (and that these descriptions do not exhaust the categories they purport to describe). The Frankensteinian is the mode more likely to bring China's present – as well as China's past and the hybrids it has created in its interactions with foreign pasts – into the poetry of the world. It is also, as has been my argument, a better politics for building the worlds in and of poetry.

In this I have a reason for using the terms *vampiric* and *Frankensteinian* rather than trying to retrofit the square pegs of Modernism and Romanticism into a new framework. Modernism and Romanticism have both had their political problems: Xi Chuan is astonished that Wang Ao lauds "the 'Romantic' poems of Guo Xiaochuan 郭小川 (1919–1976) for 'resurrecting' the 'imperial imagination,'" as this representative poet of the "political lyric" was a Mao-era employee of the Publicity Department of the Communist Party of China (Xi Chuan quotes Alain Badiou: "The only maxim of contemporary art is: do not be imperial").[57] Wang Ao retorts, "Do not forget, as far as twentieth-century poetry goes, the greatest enthusiasts for the 'imperial imagination' were Pound and Eliot."[58] But although Pound and Eliot were racists, this doesn't mean that their writing necessarily embodied their racism. Moreover, literary movements are not necessarily reducible to the politics of their most famous figures. As Raymond Williams pointed out, the antibourgeois politics of Modernism divide

> not just between specific movements but *within* them. . . . [I]ts representatives either choose the formerly aristocratic valuation of art as a sacred realm above money and commerce, or the revolutionary doctrines, promulgated since 1848, of art as the liberating vanguard of popular consciousness.[59]

But if the movements cannot determine the politics of the writing, and if the authors themselves are either dead or merely serving ideological functions that mark our fear of "proliferation of meaning," can there be a politics or ethics in the writing *itself* – under labels such as *vampiric* and *Frankensteinian*?[60]

My use here of *itself*, as if either such politics or its language could ever be decontextualized or anything but contingent, suggests not. At the same time, in writing's engagement with its various contexts, there can be no escape from questions of politics. Too much of our analysis has focused on whether or when or on what terms modernity came to China, rather than on the more political question of what China should do with that modernity. Such questions cannot be explored without at least implicit proposals for the when and what of modernity, but when poets get together they debate the *how* of Chinese modernity, and how their writing should respond to it and bend it in the directions they'd like it to go. That is the politics, at any rate, in which this essay has been participating.

So although many have run in fear from Frankenstein's monster, I believe the case can be made for an ethics and positive politics behind its hybridity. I've elsewhere argued for a "translational reading," which can see ideology and discourse at work when paying attention to the role of the translator in shaping a text amid the various needs and interests of a range of powers in both source and target cultural contexts, even as the translational reading derives its main legitimacy from detailed attention to the text. The Frankensteinian hybrid, as I see it operating in contemporary Chinese poetry, can offer a corollary in writing to such imperatives for a critical reading that is "constantly shifting its own point of view" to "remain fluid, seeing and at times reconciling but not speaking from the perspective of any stable global position."[61] Seeing the ideological vampire of Romanticism – but as one further iteration not only of the transnational modernity that created both Romanticism and modern Chinese poetry but also of the hybrid and translingual practices that have propelled Chinese poetry for centuries, and thus resisting its ideological overdetermination – the Frankensteinian takes what it needs from Romanticism and combines it with Modernism, to avoid either succumbing to Romanticism's ideological power or otherwise reifying it through outright opposition. In this way, the Frankensteinian synthesis can re-create – and validate – a Romanticism for the twenty-first century.

Notes

1　Xi Chuan 西川, *Notes on the Mosquito: Selected Poems*, trans. Lucas Klein (New York: New Directions, 2012), 101. Reproduced with permission.
2　Al Adamson, *Dracula vs. Frankenstein* (1971).
3　Elma Dangerfield, *Byron and the Romantics in Switzerland, 1816* (London: Ascent Books, 1978), 91. See John William Polidori, *The Vampyre: A Tale* (London: Sherwood, Neely, and Jones, 1819); Mary Wollstonecraft Shelley, *Frankenstein, Or, The Modern Prometheus* (London: H. Colburn and R. Bentley, 1831); and Bram Stoker, *Dracula* (New York: Grosset & Dunlap, 1897).
4　F. W. Murnau, *Nosferatu, Eine Symphonie Des Grauens* (Germany: Prana Film, 1922); James Whale, *Frankenstein* (United States: Universal Pictures, 1931); and James Whale, *The Bride of Frankenstein* (United States: Universal Pictures, 1935).
5　Leo Ou-fan Lee, *The Romantic Generation of Modern Chinese Writers*, Harvard East Asian Series 71 (Cambridge: Harvard University Press, 1973), 279. Lee notes that both Romanticism and realism "held sway in China" (276), but argues that even realism was understood in a romantic light, and that "the leftist tendency on the literary scene was due to the impact more of romanticism than of theoretical Marxism" (289). My analysis of an opposition within how Chinese poetry handles romanticism differs from Lee's, which sees a "Wertherian (passive-sentimental) and Promethean (dynamic-heroic)" binary (280).
6　Karl Marx, *Capital, Volume One*, in *The Marx-Engels Reader*, ed. Robert C. Tucker, trans. Samuel Moore and Edward Aveling, 2nd ed. (New York: Norton, 1978), 250. Cf. Slavoj Žižek, *For They Know Not What They Do: Enjoyment as a Political Factor* (London: Verso, 2002), 197–198, 221; and *Tarrying with the Negative: Kant, Hegel, and the Critique of Ideology* (Durham: Duke University Press, 1993), 222, 12.
7　Franco Moretti, *Signs Taken for Wonders: Essays in the Sociology of Literary Forms*, trans. Susan Fischer, David Forgacs, and David Miller (London: NLB, 1983), 91, 85. The quoted chapter is translated by Forgacs.
8　Franco Moretti, *Signs Taken for Wonders*, 84, 83.
9　Jerome J. McGann, *The Romantic Ideology: A Critical Investigation* (Chicago: University of Chicago Press, 1983), 10, 13.
10　On the novel and the newspaper, see Benedict Anderson, *Imagined Communities: Reflections on the Origin and Spread of Nationalism* (London: Verso, 2006), 24–25, where he says the "two forms of imagining which first flowered in Europe in the eighteenth century . . . provided the technical means for 're-presenting' the *kind* of imagined community that is the nation."
11　For "translingual," see Lydia Liu, *Translingual Practice: Literature, National Culture, and Translated Modernity–China, 1900–1937* (Stanford: Stanford University Press, 1995).
12　Eric Hobsbawm, *The Age of Revolution: 1789–1848* (New York: Vintage, 1996), 1.
13　See Lydia He Liu, *The Clash of Empires: The Invention of China in Modern World Making* (Cambridge: Harvard University Press, 2004).
14　Samuel Taylor Coleridge, *Specimens of the Table Talk of the Late Samuel Taylor Coleridge* (New York: Harper & Brothers, 1835), 76.

15 Samuel Taylor Coleridge, *Poetical Works*, ed. J. C. C. Mays, The Collected Works of Samuel Taylor Coleridge 16 (Princeton: Princeton University Press, 2001), 1:511.

16 Percy Bysshe Shelley, "A Defence of Poetry," in *Essays, Letters from Abroad, Translations and Fragments*, ed. Mary Wollstonecraft Shelley, vol. 1 (London: Edward Moxon, 1840), 57.

17 Michelle Yeh, ed., *Anthology of Modern Chinese Poetry*, xxiii–l. For more Yeh on marginality, see "Light a Lamp in a Rock: Experimental Poetry in Contemporary China," *Modern China* 18, no. 4 (October 1, 1992): 379–409; and "'There Are No Camels in the Koran': What Is Modern about Modern Chinese Poetry?," in *New Perspectives on Contemporary Chinese Poetry*, ed. Christopher Lupke (New York: Palgrave Macmillan, 2008), 9–26.

18 Maghiel van Crevel, *Chinese Poetry in Times of Mind, Mayhem and Money*, Sinica Leidensia, v. 86 (Leiden: Brill, 2008), 49.

19 Van Crevel, *Chinese Poetry in Times of Mind, Mayhem and Money*, 89. See Yeh, "There Are No Camels in the Koran": "Although quantitatively speaking, Classical Poetry was primarily written by and for members of the literati, it occupied a central position in culture and society" (13).

20 Stephen Owen, "The End of the Past: Rewriting Chinese Literary History in the Early Republic," in *The Appropriation of Cultural Capital: China's May Fourth Project*, ed. Milena Doleželová-Velingerová, Oldřich Král, and Graham Martin Sanders, Harvard East Asian Monographs 207 (Cambridge: Harvard University Asia Center, 2001), 168, 188. For an example of such reification, see Yeh, "There Are No Camels in the Koran": "Why do I enjoy reading Modern Poetry? A simple answer would be: because it is not Classical Poetry" (25).

21 Walt Whitman, *Leaves of Grass* (Brooklyn, 1855), 55.

22 Guo Moruo 郭沫若, "Tan wenxue fanyi gongzuo" 談文學翻譯工作 (On the work of literary translation], in *Fanyi lunji* 翻譯論集 (A collection of translation theories), ed. Luo Xinzhang 羅新璋 (Beijing: Shangwu chubanshe, 1984), 498. Bian Zhilin 卞之琳 (1910–2000) critiqued Guo's statement on turning translation "into Chinese traditional poetry," as once "like poetry" (像詩) "becomes the most disseminated model, it also becomes the tool most conducive to generalization and vulgarization" ("Fanyi duiyu Zhongguo xiandaishi de gongguo" 翻譯對於中國現代詩的功過 [An assessment of the effects of translation on modern Chinese poetry], in *Bian Zhilin wenji* 卞之琳文集 [The collected writings of Bian Zhilin], vol. 2 [Hefei: Anhui jiaoyu chubanshe, 2002], 537).

23 Guo Moruo, *Xin Shi* 新詩 (New-Style Poems) (Beijing: Beijing dianzi chubanwu chuban zhongxin, 2001), 67–68. This poem was first published in 1921, but its afterlife in the Mao era, when the Chairman was unfailingly compared to the sun, is not hard to imagine.

24 Xi Chuan, "Shiren guannian yu shige guannian de lishixing luocha" 詩人觀念與詩歌觀念的歷史性落差 (The Notion of the Poet and the Notion of Poetry–A Historical Abyss), *Jintian* 今天 (Today) 80 (Spring 2008): 121.

25 Xi Chuan, "Shiren guannian," 128.

26 Xi Chuan, "Shiren guannian," 122–124.

27 Xi Chuan, "Shiren guannian," 128.

28 Guo Moruo 郭沫若 [as Kuo Mo-jo], *Chu Yuan: A Play in Five Acts*, trans. Gladys Yang and Yang Hsien-yi (Beijing: Foreign Languages Press, 1953), 109; Guo, Qu Yuan: *Wu mu lishi huaju* 屈原：五幕曆史話劇 (Qu Yuan: A Historical Drama in Five Acts) (Beijing: Renmin wenxue chubanshe, 1980), 125; cited in Xi Chuan, "Shiren guannian."

29 Samuel Taylor Coleridge, "Shakspeare [*sic*] Appears . . . to Have Possessed all the Conditions of the True Poet," in *Coleridge's Essays & Lectures on Shakespeare: & Some Other Old Poets & Dramatists* (London: J. M. Dent, 1907), 42.

30 Xi Chuan, "Shiren guannian," 124.

31 Wang Ao 王敖, "Zenyang gei benpaozhong de shirenmen duibiao: Guanyu shigeshi de wenti yu zhuyi" 怎樣給奔跑中的詩人們對錶：關於詩歌史的問題與主義 (How to Synchronize the Watches of Running Poets: On Some Questions and -Isms in the History of Poetry), *Xinshi pinglun* 新詩評論 (New Poetry Critique) 8, no. 2 (2008): 5. For a continuation of the debate, see Xi Chuan, "Zhongguo xiandai shiren yu Nuositi, Kabala, Langmanzhuyi, Bulumu–du Patelika Laolunsi zhu 'Lili Buruisike de Zhongguo

Yanjing,' bing huiying Wang Ao 'Zenyang gei benpaozhong de shirenmen duibiao: Guanyu shigeshi de wenti yu zhuyi' yiwen" 中國現代詩人與諾斯替、喀巴拉、浪漫主義、布魯姆 – 讀帕特麗卡·勞倫斯著《麗莉·布瑞斯珂的中國眼睛》，並回應王敖《怎樣給奔跑中的詩人們對錶：關於詩歌史的問題與上義》一文 (Modern Chinese poets and Gnosticism, Kabbalah, Romanticism, and Bloom – Reading Patricia Laurence's *Lily Briscoe's Chinese Eyes*, and a reply to Wang Ao's essay "How to Synchronize the Watches of Running Poets: On Some Questions and -Isms in the History of Poetry'), *Xinshi pinglun* 新詩評論 [New Poetry Critique] 10, no. 2 (2009): 3–23; then Wang Ao, "Guanyu 'Duibiao' yiwen de chengqing" 關於《對錶》一文的澄清 (Some Clarifications Concerning 'How to Synchronize the Watches of Running Poets'), *Xinshi pinglun* 新詩評論 (New Poetry Critique) 11, no. 1 (2010): 63–69. Both Xi Chuan's essays have been reprinted in his collection *Dahe guai dawan: Yi zhong tanqiu kenengxing de shige sixiang* 大河拐大彎: 一種探求可能性的詩歌思想 (A Bend in the Great River: Thoughts in Search of Poetic Possibility) (Beijing: Beijing daxue chubanshe, 2012).

32 Wang Ao, "Zenyang gei Benpaozhong de shirenmen," 8.

33 Wang Ao, "Zenyang gei Benpaozhong de shirenmen," 25, cites the attention Marjorie Perloff draws to Harold Bloom's statement that "Modernism in literature has not passed; rather, it has been exposed as never having been there," and his suggestion that "the Stevens Era" replace what Hugh Kenner called *The Pound Era* (Berkeley: University of California Press, 1971) (e.g., Harold Bloom, *A Map of Misreading: With a New Preface*, 2nd ed. [New York: Oxford University Press, 2003], 28; and *Wallace Stevens: The Poems of Our Climate* [Ithaca: Cornell University Press, 1980], 152). See Marjorie Perloff, "Pound/Stevens: Whose Era?," *New Literary History* 13, no. 3 (April 1, 1982): 486.

34 Eric Hayot, "Chinese Modernism, Mimetic Desire, and European Time," in *The Oxford Handbook of Global Modernisms*, ed. Mark A. Wollaeger and Matt Eatough (New York: Oxford University Press, 2012), 150.

35 Wang Ao, "Zenyang gei benpaozhong de shirenmen," 3–4.

36 Wang Ao, "Zenyang gei benpaozhong de shirenmen," 7.

37 Wang Ao, "Zenyang gei benpaozhong de shirenmen," 8.

38 In his follow-up essay, Wang continues ignoring the matter of the gap between the craft of poetry as poets have pursued it and the Romantic image of poetry within Chinese society. Wang's criticism is that, "According to Xi Chuan, for Chinese poets in the twentieth century to construct Romanticist images of poets is, in fact, to nineteenth-centurify themselves. According to this logic, poets from around the world who have been influenced by the image of Hamlet must be stuck in the era of Queen Elizabeth. Poets in the West who emulated Hanshan collectively returned to the eighth century. Pound's deference to the image of Confucius proves he never let himself be twentieth-centurified" ("Guanyu 'duibiao' yiwen de chengqing," 63–64). But Xi Chuan's point is not, in fact, that poets are turning themselves into nineteenth-century versions of themselves, but rather that broader society has a nineteenth-century notion of poets, which keeps it from appreciating the work of contemporary poetry.

39 Wang Ao, "Zenyang gei benpaozhong de shirenmen," 28.

40 Wang Ao, "Zenyang gei benpaozhong de shirenmen," 8–9.

41 Xi Chuan, "Lishixing luocha," 129.

42 Wang Ao, "Zenyang gei benpaozhong de shirenmen," 7. He even adds a footnote at this point citing McGann's *The Romantic Ideology*. He continues: "The other side of this is, after deep understanding of Romanticism, we find it to be all the more pervasive, penetrating the depths of our modern consciousness, and, after being proclaimed dead numerous times, follows the expansion of capitalism into the era of globalization."

43 Xi Chuan, "Lishixing luocha," 130.

44 Jonathan D. Spence, *The Search for Modern China* (New York: Norton, 1991).

45 Stephen Owen, "What Is World Poetry? The Anxiety of Global Influence," *New Republic* 203, no. 21 (November 19, 1990): 31. Owen was reviewing Bei Dao, *The August Sleepwalker*, trans. Bonnie S. McDougall (New York: New Directions, 1990).

46 Gregory B. Lee, *Troubadours, Trumpeters, Troubled Makers: Lyricism, Nationalism and Hybridity in China and Its Others* (Durham: Duke University Press, 1996), 127; Liu, *Translingual Practice*, 25.

47 Xiaobing Tang, *Chinese Modern: The Heroic and Quotidian* (Durham: Duke University Press, 2000), 1; Rey Chow, *Woman and Chinese Modernity: The Politics of Reading between West and East*, Theory and History of Literature, v. 75 (Minneapolis: University of Minnesota Press, 1991), xi–xii. See Leo Ou-fan Lee, *Shanghai Modern: The Flowering of a New Urban Culture in China, 1930–1945* (Cambridge: Harvard University Press, 1999).

48 Shu-mei Shih, *The Lure of the Modern: Writing Modernism in Semicolonial China, 1917–1937* (Berkeley: University of California Press, 2001), 14; Rey Chow, *The Protestant Ethnic and the Spirit of Capitalism* (New York: Columbia University Press, 2002), 83; Franco Moretti, "Conjectures on World Literature," in *Debating World Literature*, ed. Christopher Prendergast (London: Verso, 2004), 152.

49 David Wang, *Fin-de-Siècle Splendor: Repressed Modernities of Late Qing Fiction, 1849–1911* (Stanford: Stanford University Press, 1997), 1.

50 Alexander Beecroft, "World Literature Without a Hyphen: Towards a Typology of Literary Systems," *New Left Review* 54 (December 2008): 87–100. See Immanuel Wallerstein, *World-Systems Analysis: An Introduction* (Durham: Duke University Press, 2004).

51 Andre Gunder Frank, *ReOrient: Global Economy in the Asian Age* (Berkeley: University of California Press, 1998), 116; Dennis O. Flynn and Arturo Giráldez, "China and the Spanish Empire," *Revista de Historia Economica–Journal of Iberian and Latin American Economic History* 14, no. 2 (September 1996): 311.

52 See Hisayuki Miyakawa, "An Outline of the Naitō Hypothesis and Its Effects on Japanese Studies of China," *The Far Eastern Quarterly* 14, no. 4 (August 1, 1955): 533–552; David Porter, ed., *Comparative Early Modernities, 1100–1800* (New York: Palgrave Macmillan, 2012); and Wang Hui, *China from Empire to Nation-State*, trans. Michael Gibbs Hill (Cambridge: Harvard University Press, 2014). For further analysis, see Sheldon Lu, "Re-Visioning Global Modernity through the Prism of China," *European Review* 23, no. 2 (May 2015): 210–226.

53 Bram Stoker, *Dracula* (New York: Grosset & Dunlap, 1897), 2, http://archive.org/details/draculabr00stokuoft.

54 Shelley, *Frankenstein*, 54.

55 Georg Wilhelm Friedrich Hegel, *The Philosophy of History*, trans. J. Sibree (New York: Dover, 1956), 103. See Wang, *Fin-de-Siècle Splendor*, on the problems of China's "belated modernity."

56 See Edward W. Said, *Orientalism* (New York: Pantheon, 1978). Shelley, *Frankenstein*, 54. Later the novel mentions a young Arab woman taught "to aspire to higher powers of intellect, and an independence of spirit, forbidden to the female followers of Mahomet . . . The prospect of marrying a Christian, and remaining in a country where women were allowed to take a rank in society, was enchanting to her" (106).

57 Xi Chuan, "Xiandai Shiren Yu Nuositi, Kabala, Langmanzhuyi, Bulumu," 23; Alain Badiou, "Fifteen Theses on Contemporary Art" (*Thèses sur l'art contemporain*), trans. uncredited, *Performance Research* 9, no. 4 (January 1, 2004): 86 (in the book publication of his essay, Xi Chuan cites Alain Badiou, "Dangdai yishu de shiwu ge mingti–zenyang bu zuo yige Langmanzhuyizhe?" 當代藝術的十五個命題 – 怎樣不做一個浪漫主義者? (Fifteen Theses on Contemporary Art–How Not to be a Romantic), trans. Sun Yi 孫怡, *Xinshi pinglun* 新詩評論 [New Poetry Critique] 11, no. 1 [2011]).

58 Wang Ao, "Guanyu 'Duibiao' yiwen de chengqing."

59 Raymond Williams, *The Politics of Modernism: Against the New Conformists* (London: Verso, 1989), 34. For every "D'Annunzio, Marinetti, Wyndham Lewis, Ezra Pound . . . who moved towards Fascism," he writes, there is a "Mayakovsky, Picasso, Silone, Brecht . . . who moved into direct support of Communism." Not that Communism represents the pinnacle of moral political belief, as we who study Chinese culture know well.

60 Michel Foucault, "What Is an Author?," in *The Foucault Reader*, ed. Paul Rabinow, trans. Josué V. Harari (New York: Pantheon, 1984), 119. See also Roland Barthes, "The

Death of the Author," in *Image-Music-Text*, trans. Stephen Heath, Fontana Communications Series (London: Fotana/Collins, 1977), 142–148.
61 Lucas Klein, "A Dissonance of Discourses: Literary Theory, Ideology, and Translation in Mo Yan and Chinese Literary Studies," *Comparative Literature Studies* 53, no. 1 (2016): 191.

Works cited

Adamson, Al. *Dracula vs. Frankenstein*. United States: Independent-International Pictures, 1971.

Anderson, Benedict. *Imagined Communities: Reflections on the Origin and Spread of Nationalism*. London: Verso, 2006.

Badiou, Alain. "Dangdai yishu de shiwu ge mingti – zenyang bu zuo yige Langmanzhuyizhe?" 當代藝術的十五個命題 – 怎樣不做一個浪漫主義者? (Fifteen Theses on Contemporary Art: How Not to Be a Romantic). Trans. Sun Yi 孙怡. *Xinshi pinglun* 新詩評論 (New Poetry Critique) 11, no. 1 (2011).

———. "Fifteen Theses on Contemporary Art" (Thèses sur l'art contemporain). Trans. uncredited. *Performance Research* 9, no. 4 (January 1, 2004): 86.

Barthes, Roland. "The Death of the Author." In *Image-Music-Text*, translated by Stephen Heath, 142–148. London: Fotana/Collins, 1977.

Beecroft, Alexander. "World Literature without a Hyphen: Towards a Typology of Literary Systems." *New Left Review* 54 (December 2008): 87–100.

Bei Dao 北島. *The August Sleepwalker*. Trans. Bonnie S. McDougall. New York: New Directions, 1990.

Bian Zhilin 卞之琳. "Fanyi duiyu Zhongguo xiandaishi de gongguo." 翻譯對於中國現代詩的功過 (An Assessment of the Effects of Translation on Modern Chinese Poetry). In *Bian Zhilin Wenji* 卞之琳文集 (The Collected Writings of Bian Zhilin). Vol. 2, 534–552. Hefei: Anhui jiaoyu chubanshe, 2002.

Bloom, Harold. *A Map of Misreading: With a New Preface*. 2nd ed. New York: Oxford University Press, 2003.

———. *Wallace Stevens: The Poems of Our Climate*. Ithaca: Cornell University Press, 1980.

Chow, Rey. *The Protestant Ethnic and the Spirit of Capitalism*. New York: Columbia University Press, 2002.

———. *Woman and Chinese Modernity: The Politics of Reading between West and East*. Theory and History of Literature, Vol. 75. Minneapolis, MN: University of Minnesota Press, 1991.

Coleridge, Samuel Taylor. *Coleridge's Essays & Lectures on Shakespeare: & Some Other Old Poets & Dramatists*. London: J. M. Dent, 1907.

———. *Poetical Works*. Ed. J. C. C. Mays. 2 Vols. The Collected Works of Samuel Taylor Coleridge 16. Princeton: Princeton University Press, 2001.

———. *Specimens of the Table Talk of the Late Samuel Taylor Coleridge*. New York: Harper & Brothers, 1835.

Crevel, Maghiel van. *Chinese Poetry in Times of Mind, Mayhem and Money*. Sinica Leidensia 86. Leiden: Brill, 2008.

Dangerfield, Elma. *Byron and the Romantics in Switzerland, 1816*. London: Ascent Books, 1978.

Flynn, Dennis O., and Arturo Giráldez. "China and the Spanish Empire." *Revista de Historia Economica – Journal of Iberian and Latin American Economic History* 14, no. 2 (September 1996): 309–338.

Foucault, Michel. "What Is an Author?" In *The Foucault Reader*, edited by Paul Rabinow, translated by Josué V. Harari, 101–120. New York: Pantheon, 1984.

Frank, Andre Gunder. *ReOrient: Global Economy in the Asian Age*. Berkeley: University of California Press, 1998.

Guo Moruo 郭沫若. *Chu Yuan: A Play in Five Acts*. Trans. Gladys Yang and Yang Xianyi. Beijing: Foreign Languages Press, 1953.

———. *Qu Yuan: Wu mu lishi huaju* 屈原: 五幕歷史話劇 (Qu Yuan: A Historical Drama in Five Acts). Beijing: Renmin wenxue chubanshe, 1980.

———. "Tan wenxue fanyi gongzuo." 談文學翻譯工作 (On the Work of Literary Translation). In *Fanyi lunji* 翻譯論集 (A Collection of Translation Theories), edited by Luo Xinzhang 羅新璋, 498–499. Beijing: Shangwu chubanshe, 1984.

———. *Xin shi* 新詩 (New-Style Poems). Beijing: Beijing dianzi chubanwu chuban zhongxin, 2001.

Hayot, Eric. "Chinese Modernism, Mimetic Desire, and European Time." In *The Oxford Handbook of Global Modernisms*, edited by Mark A. Wollaeger and Matt Eatough, 149–170. New York: Oxford University Press, 2012.

Hegel, Georg Wilhelm Friedrich. *The Philosophy of History*. Trans. J. Sibree. New York: Dover Publications, 1956.

Hobsbawm, Eric. *The Age of Revolution: 1789–1848*. New York: Vintage Books, 1996.

Kenner, Hugh. *The Pound Era*. Berkeley: University of California Press, 1971.

Klein, Lucas. "A Dissonance of Discourses: Literary Theory, Ideology, and Translation in Mo Yan and Chinese Literary Studies." *Comparative Literature Studies* 53, no. 1 (2016): 170–197.

Lee, Gregory B. *Troubadours, Trumpeters, Troubled Makers: Lyricism, Nationalism and Hybridity in China and Its Others*. Durham: Duke University Press, 1996.

Lee, Leo Ou-fan. *The Romantic Generation of Modern Chinese Writers*. Harvard East Asian Series 71. Cambridge: Harvard University Press, 1973.

———. *Shanghai Modern: The Flowering of a New Urban Culture in China, 1930–1945*. Cambridge: Harvard University Press, 1999.

Liu, Lydia He. *The Clash of Empires: The Invention of China in Modern World Making*. Cambridge: Harvard University Press, 2004.

———. *Translingual Practice: Literature, National Culture, and Translated Modernity: China, 1900–1937*. Stanford: Stanford University Press, 1995.

Lu, Sheldon. "Re-Visioning Global Modernity through the Prism of China." *European Review* 23, no. 2 (May 2015): 210–226.

Marx, Karl. *Capital, Volume One*. In *The Marx-Engels Reader*, edited by Robert C. Tucker, translated by Samuel Moore and Edward Aveling, 2nd ed., 294–438. New York: Norton, 1978.

McGann, Jerome J. *The Romantic Ideology: A Critical Investigation*. Chicago: University of Chicago Press, 1983.

Miyakawa, Hisayuki. "An Outline of the Naitō Hypothesis and Its Effects on Japanese Studies of China." *The Far Eastern Quarterly* 14, no. 4 (August 1, 1955): 533–552.

Moretti, Franco. "Conjectures on World Literature." In *Debating World Literature*, edited by Christopher Prendergast, 148–162. London: Verso, 2004.

———. *Signs Taken for Wonders: Essays in the Sociology of Literary Forms*. Trans. Susan Fischer, David Forgacs, and David Miller. London: NLB, 1983.

Murnau, F. W. *Nosferatu, Eine Symphonie Des Grauens*. Berlin, Germany: Prana Film, 1922.

Owen, Stephen. "The End of the Past: Rewriting Chinese Literary History in the Early Republic." In *The Appropriation of Cultural Capital: China's May Fourth Project*, edited by Milena Doleželová-Velingerová, Oldřich Král, and Graham Martin Sanders, 167–192. Harvard East Asian Monographs 207. Cambridge: Harvard University Asia Center, 2001.

———. "What Is World Poetry? The Anxiety of Global Influence." *New Republic* 203, no. 21 (November 19, 1990): 28–32.

Perloff, Marjorie. "Pound/Stevens: Whose Era?" *New Literary History* 13, no. 3 (April 1, 1982): 485–514.

Polidori, John William. *The Vampyre: A Tale*. London: Sherwood, Neely, and Jones, 1819.

Porter, David, ed. *Comparative Early Modernities, 1100–1800*. New York: Palgrave Macmillan, 2012.

Said, Edward W. *Orientalism*. New York: Pantheon, 1978.

Shelley, Mary Wollstonecraft. *Frankenstein, or, the Modern Prometheus*. London: H. Colburn and R. Bentley, 1831.

Shelley, Percy Bysshe. "A Defence of Poetry." In *Essays, Letters from Abroad, Translations and Fragments*, edited by Mary Wollstonecraft Shelley, Vol. 1, 1–57. London: Edward Moxon, 1840.

Shih, Shu-mei. *The Lure of the Modern: Writing Modernism in Semicolonial China, 1917–1937*. Berkeley: University of California Press, 2001.

Spence, Jonathan D. *The Search for Modern China*. New York: Norton, 1991.

Stoker, Bram. *Dracula*. New York: Grosset & Dunlap, 1897.

Tang, Xiaobing. *Chinese Modern: The Heroic and Quotidian*. Post-Contemporary Interventions. Durham: Duke University Press, 2000.

Wallerstein, Immanuel. *World-Systems Analysis: An Introduction*. Durham: Duke University Press, 2004.

Wang, Ao 王敖. "Guanyu 'duibiao' yiwen de chengqing." 關於《對錶》一文的澄清 (Some Clarifications Concerning 'How to Synchronize the Watches of Running Poets'). *Xinshi pinglun* 新詩評論 (New Poetry Critique) 11, no. 1 (2010): 63–69.

———. "Zenyang gei benpaozhong de shirenmen duibiao: guanyu shigeshi de wenti yu zhuyi." 怎樣給奔跑中的詩人們對錶：關於詩歌史的問題與主義 (How to Synchronize the Watches of Running Poets: On Some Questions and -isms in the History of Poetry). *Xinshi pinglun* 新詩評論 (New Poetry Critique) 8, no. 2 (2008): 3–48.

Wang, David Der-wei. *Fin-de-Siècle Splendor: Repressed Modernities of Late Qing Fiction, 1849–1911*. Stanford: Stanford University Press, 1997.

Wang Hui 汪暉. *China from Empire to Nation-State*. Trans. Michael Gibbs Hill. Cambridge: Harvard University Press, 2014.

Whale, James. *The Bride of Frankenstein*. Universal City, CA: Universal Pictures, 1935.

———. *Frankenstein*. United States: Universal Pictures, 1931.

Whitman, Walt. *Leaves of Grass*. Brooklyn, 1855.

Williams, Raymond. *The Politics of Modernism: Against the New Conformists*. London: Verso, 1989.

Xi Chuan 西川. *Dahe guai dawan: Yi zhong tanqiu kenengxing de shige sixiang* 大河拐大彎：一種探求可能性的詩歌思想 (A Bend in the Great River: Thoughts in Search of Poetic Possibility). Beijing: Beijing daxue chubanshe, 2012.

———. *Notes on the Mosquito: Selected Poems*. Trans. Lucas Klein. New York: New Directions, 2012.

———. "Shiren guannian yu shige guannian de lishixing luocha" 詩人觀念與詩歌觀念的歷史性落差 (The Notion of the Poet and the Notion of Poetry: A Historical Abyss). *Jintian* 今天 (Today) 80 (Spring 2008): 118–132.

———. "Zhongguo xiandai shiren yu Nuositi, Kabala, langmanzhuyi, Bulumu – du Patelika Laolunsi zhu 'Lili Buruisike de Zhongguo yanjing,' bing huiying Wang Ao 'Zenyang gei benpaozhong de shirenmen duibiao: guanyu shigeshi de wenti yu zhuyi' yiwen." 中國現代詩人與諾斯替、喀巴拉、浪漫主義、布魯姆 – 讀帕特麗卡·勞倫斯著《麗莉·布瑞斯珂的中國眼睛》，並回應王敖《怎樣給奔跑中的詩人們對錶：關於詩歌史的問題與上義》一文 (Modern Chinese Poets and Gnosticism, Kabbalah, Romanticism, and Bloom: Reading Patricia Laurence's Lily Briscoe's Chinese Eyes, and a Reply to Wang Ao's Essay 'How to Synchronize the Watches of Running Poets:

On Some Questions and -isms in the History of Poetry'). *Xinshi pinglun* 新詩評論 (New Poetry Critique) 10, no. 2 (2009): 3–23.

Yeh, Michelle, ed. *Anthology of Modern Chinese Poetry.* New Haven: Yale University Press, 1992.

———. "Light a Lamp in a Rock: Experimental Poetry in Contemporary China." *Modern China* 18, no. 4 (October 1, 1992): 379–409.

———. "'There Are No Camels in the Koran': What Is Modern about Modern Chinese Poetry?" In *New Perspectives on Contemporary Chinese Poetry*, edited by Christopher Lupke, 9–26. New York, NY: Palgrave Macmillan, 2008.

Žižek, Slavoj. *For They Know Not What They Do: Enjoyment as a Political Factor.* London: Verso, 2002.

———. *Tarrying with the Negative: Kant, Hegel, and the Critique of Ideology.* Durham: Duke University Press, 1993.

4

FANHUA, GLOBAL MODERNISM, AND THE ART OF DETACHMENT

Wen Jin

Jin Yucheng's 金宇澄 2012 novel *Fanhua* 繁花 – which won several major literary awards in China, including the 2015 Mao Dun Literature Prize – is perhaps the most formally sophisticated, stylistically conscious novel to come out of China in recent decades, and many critics have commented on its use of Shanghai dialect syntax and vocabulary. Unlike earlier novels, such as the late Qing dynasty *Haishanghua liezhuan* 海上花列傳 (Singsong girls of Shanghai), which uses Wu (Suzhou) dialect, *Fanhua* captures the rhythm of Shanghai dialect while remaining legible to Chinese readers from other regions. More striking, however, are the multiple temporalities of the work's mixed style. The novel makes use of the arsenal of narrative techniques associated with modernist novels, such as splicing together two time frames separated by about a decade and incorporating a number of "magic realist" plot twists. At the same time, however, *Fanhua* is hard to position within the context of world novels. It rejects the convention, common in modernist fiction, wherein the narrative voice delves into the psyche of individual characters; instead, in the epilogue Jin cites Walter Benjamin's 1936 essay "The Storyteller": "As I moved away from 'psychological shadings,' I started to narrate in a spoken dialect, settling into an unperturbed mood."[1]

Fanhua also features other structural oddities. It has a decentered network of characters, almost doing away with the notion of a singular protagonist. Also, it describes things and urban architectural structures and elevates them to the same level as the human characters, in ways reminiscent of a number of modern literary movements. So to come to terms with the way the work straddles different literary genealogies, we would do well to examine the novel as a species of its own, mindful of its inbuilt fluidity and elusive position in the scheme of world literatures.

The form of contemporary Chinese novels has long been a vexed issue. The end of Maoist China in the early 1980s ushered in a decade of trepidatious formal experimentation under the influence of European and Latin American modernism (understood broadly as including everything from symbolism to magic realism), with an attendant anxiety about mimicry and belatedness. The late 1980s witnessed a heated debate around what was called China's "faux modernism,"[2] but also the emergence of a host of Chinese novelists who displayed a certain flexible sensibility in mixing outside influences and local inspirations. The celebration of Mo Yan 莫言 after he won the Nobel Prize in 2012 reminds us of just such a productive blend of modernist influences and local innovations, including an instinct for a good story and a gift for narrating floods of sensory experiences. This history underscores the futility of attempts to date literary movements, like modernism, across national boundaries. Even though modernism (like postmodernism) is relevant to a host of writings from contemporary China, its usage is by no means straightforward. As Eric Hayot and Rebecca Walkowitz observe, "there is no modernism without the 'global' in it," and modernism generates itself from "the interaction between the local and the regional, the local and the foreign, the local and the global."[3] It is, therefore, not inappropriate to characterize the style of *Fanhua* as modernist, though this is a modernism characterized by hybrid formal tactics, including borrowing, revision, and innovation. In this chapter, accordingly, I propose to investigate this strange species of Chinese fiction as just that – strange, multilayered, and yet part of global modernism as a fluid, loosely structured global movement.

Before writing *Fanhua*, Jin Yucheng was known primarily as an accomplished literary editor, even though in 1992 he published an early collection of short stories titled *Mystified Night* 迷夜. Building on Jin's command of Shanghai history and culture, *Fanhua* germinated as a series of online postings on the website Longtang wang (The alleyway) 弄堂網 that drew an increasingly large following. The innovative, decentered form of the resulting novel reflects the digital environment in which it first appeared, but this is more than happenstance. Evident in the text is a rich accumulation of formal features associated with different times and spaces, and the result is fascinating and enigmatic – a small archive of seemingly incompatible narrative forms. Having maintained a low profile during the first few decades of the post-Mao period, when a variety of different literary movements emerged in rapid succession and contended with one another, Jin Yucheng was not tethered to any of the labels familiar to students of contemporary Chinese literature, and instead was free to mix and innovate.

Fanhua is also an archive of the emotional lives taking place in twentieth-century Shanghai. Whereas Eileen Chang 張愛玲 and Wang Anyi 王安憶, two famous female predecessors in writing fiction about Shanghai, were distinguished by their love tragedies featuring women of different social classes, Jin instead portrays a city of male underdogs and upstarts – including victims of the Cultural Revolution and those who flourished or floundered in the commercialized era of the 1990s – and the women they never seem to get, all with a formal flair that resists simple characterization.

Return to tradition

Fanhua exhibits the kind of sizable, scattered network of characters and the *guanxi*-centered narratives that Franco Moretti argues are endemic to Chinese imaginings of the human world.[4] This is but a small facet of the homage the novel pays to the tradition of Chinese vernacular fiction. It is unconcerned about disrupting its own narrative flow with anecdotes, digressions, lengthy descriptions, and poetic insertions. Even as it sets up two parallel story lines, the novel cares little about a continuous plot. Instead it strings together scenes from real life, almost unadorned and unedited, giving the novel a documentary-like and essayistic style. How do we understand its complex, deconstructive approach to narrative?

It is significant that Jin has been working with a publisher to prepare an annotated version of *Fanhua* and has expressed a desire to model the annotations upon literati commentaries in traditional Chinese vernacular novels.[5] This gives us a clue as to where to find possible sources of the antinarrative elements of the novel. For much of Chinese history, there was not a single category of writings that was purely narrative, in the sense of presenting a connected sequence of events. What we today refer to as "narrative" was instead grouped under the "talk" category 說部 in the Chinese taxonomy – a notoriously fluid and catch-all category that became largely associated with narrative writings during the Ming dynasty. Even at the height of vernacular Chinese novels in the late Ming, however, narrative writings of different lengths customarily incorporated significant numbers of original poems or verse set pieces, a convention going back at least to the Tang dynasty.

To elaborate a bit, even though the contemporary term for long Chinese narrative works that resemble nineteenth-century English novels is *xiaoshuo* 小說, this word actually carries a variety of different meanings. Literally meaning "small talk," the term traditionally encompassed, at least until the Ming dynasty, everything that did not fall under the categories of the classics and official history. The category included arguments, narrative representations of history, and other writings that combine history and argument, as well as *chuanqi*, or vernacular tales of fictional events, and the collections of witty, ironic remarks and jokes that were popular among the literati.[6] In its various guises, *xiaoshuo* appears in either classical or vernacular Chinese (both of which include a range of styles). Examples can be as short as a few lines or as long as many chapters, and either based on historical events or completely fictional. Not until the late Qing did the term *xiaoshuo* come to be used as roughly equivalent to the Western "novel." If we limit ourselves to narrative writings, we can move from *chuanqi* 傳奇 through *huaben* 話本 (scripts for extended oral storytelling in vernacular Chinese), to *nihuaben* 擬話本 (prose narratives modeled on scripts for oral performances), and to long prose narratives based on fictional events rather than preexisting stories. *Xiaoshuo* became associated exclusively with long fictive narratives in the late Qing for complicated reasons. The translation of Western-language novels into

Chinese is one factor, and so is the association of narrative works with the Western novel on the part of missionaries and their Chinese collaborators. And the development of indigenous long prose narratives (the four masterworks of the Ming novel and their Qing successors) almost certainly factors into this process as well. That is why the famous late Qing translator Wang Tao 王韜 uses the term "odd book" (*yishu* 異書) to describe the early nineteenth-century *Jinghua yuan* 鏡花緣 (Flowers in the mirror), an encyclopedic novel that devotes elaborate sections to displays of learning. Wang's verdict on *Jinghua yuan's* oddity may well signal a certain dominance that the Western-style novel had achieved in China by the turn of the twentieth century, though this dominance does not need to be exaggerated.

A productive way to sort through the meaning of *Fanhua's* narrator is to reconsider the tradition of Chinese fiction. It is customary for Chinese vernacular novels to attribute the story to sources other than the narrator, sometimes several steps removed from the narrator, or to present the narrative as a dream that descends on the narrator out of the blue. These conventions create the peculiar effect of distancing the narrative from the narrator, absolving him or her of any responsibility to interpret what's inside or underneath the surface. It is difficult to find in the masterworks of the Chinese novel either summary distillations of personalities (as one finds in eighteenth-century prose comedies or character sketches) or minute self-reflections.

Many Chinese critics have pointed out this phenomenon, though they have not yet fully spelled out its implications. Zhao Yiheng 趙毅衡 famously notes that narrators of Chinese novels are often modeled upon the oral storyteller, "disembodied, nameless, and half hidden."[7] The narrative perspective often switches between omniscient and limited third person, sporadically focalized through a specific character. Zhao speculates that the enduring dominance of the oral storyteller turned narrator masks the written nature of the vernacular novels (most of which borrowed plots from earlier sources), thus abrogating the need to consider the problem of copyrights.[8] Zhang Yong 張勇, meanwhile, observes that the narrator styled upon the oral storyteller adheres to the protocol of *ruhua* 入話 (preface) and *zhenghua* 正話 (main story). In most cases, the *ruhua* explains how the story originates. By citing a dream or other sources (as shown in the eighteenth-century *The Dream of the Red Chamber* 紅樓夢, which has an innovative Russian doll structure that influenced later novels), the narrator refrains from claiming ownership over the story.[9] Both Zhao and Zhang gesture toward the question of ownership, but they do not fully explain how the self-disowning narrator affects the imagining of characters in vernacular Chinese novels or relates to their quality of otherness.

Fanhua features a detached narrator who stands apart from the characters, without getting inside their heads or showing comprehension of their psyches. Chinese critic Huang Ping 黃平 suggests that *Fanhua* counters Japanese scholar Karatani Kojin's argument about the rise of the "inner man" as a sign of modern literature.[10] It can equally be argued that the work runs counter to a strain of modernist writings that Erich Kahler has famously described as exhibiting an "inward turn."[11] But the detached tone of the novel – inducing both opaque characters and a disavowal of anything that seems contrived – is also a conscious effort to harken back to a tradition of fiction still alive today.

This is the kind of antimodernism that we see in a range of contemporary Chinese novels. The influx of Western modernist writings by authors such as Faulkner, Kafka, and others in 1980s China inspired considerable soul-searching among Chinese literary critics, some of whom believed that Chinese mimicry of modernist techniques lacked authenticity. Many Chinese writers and critics started to reflect on the possibility of rejuvenating formal elements in vernacular Chinese fiction to engender a different type of modern writing. For instance, Wang Zengqi 汪曾祺 looked back to Song-dynasty *biji xiaoshuo* 筆記小說 (notebook-style fiction) to identify a type of fiction that does not aim to construct artificial interest but rather seems unadorned and almost essayistic.[12] Jin Yucheng's novel begins with a narrative hook (in which a crab merchant tells a lurid story of neighbor in love) to lure the reader, but then proceeds with considerably less interest in narrative continuity and intensity.

The technique of external focalization that we see in *Fanhua*, likewise, is an index to how contemporary Chinese novelists have weathered the shock of imported modernism and coped by drawing on local history and indigenous narrative styles. It would be more productive to relate Jin's novel not just to previous Shanghai-based novels but also to other works that draw on local history – such as Jia Pingwa's 賈平凹 Shangzhou-centered works, which attempt to replicate the local speech style (often a mixture of period expressions, peasant slang, and encyclopedic references to local history, landscape, and traditions). Jia Pingwa adheres much more closely than Mo Yan to the task of a storyteller and the effects of an opaque psyche. *Fanhua* is a relative newcomer to this tradition, and distills this particular brand of antimodernism more intensely than its predecessors.

Affective implications of detachment

Antimodernism, however, may not be entirely accurate as a genre label for Jin Yucheng's novel. The work shows a kind of countermodernism, in the sense of echoing many urban novels from the twentieth century. Even as it pays homage to Chinese literary predecessors, it also suggests intriguing parallels with fictional representations of modern cities in other parts of the world. Whether or not the author is aware of these parallels, his work manages to stage the muted drama of a particular metropolis while registering the melancholy permeating global writings of the modern city.

As pointed out earlier, distance figures in *Fanhua* as both a central trope and a key structural principle. The novel is set in a dual time frame, chronicling events in Shanghai from the 1960s and 1970s as well as the 1990s, when the urban space is torn apart by either political strife or increased uncertainty in a commercialized society. The narrator stands apart from the characters, seeing everything yet offering no insights or epiphanies, just as the characters remain disconnected from one another. Distance is also integral to the novel's chronotope. The different sections in the same time frame are only loosely connected, and are repeatedly interrupted by sections set in a period twenty years apart. Ironically, distance becomes a unifying formal and thematic feature of the novel, which exhibits a certain ease with its own disjunction.

This situation can be described as an ethos of detachment. Detachment is, of course, a key concept in theories of aesthetic judgment and literary studies of emotion. On one hand, it is associated with the absence of meaning and the disconcerting experience of being thrown or projected out of sites of meaning. And that is perhaps why modern urban fiction is often filled with a wistful awareness of brittle, transitory social relationships. On the other hand, detachment obtains an affirmative meaning as a condition for valid aesthetic judgment in Kantian philosophy or respect for otherness in aesthetic activities from an Adornian perspective. It has thus been associated also with cosmopolitanism – which is to say, an ability to imagine and embrace impersonal relations that allows us to go beyond our narrow set of allegiances.[13] *Fanhua* is closely related to all these meanings of detachment, in that it approaches the question of otherness, both within and without, with a shifting stance that is only consistent in its elusiveness and slipperiness. It projects moodiness without a specific mood, plumbs the depths of urban life without insisting on depth.

The novel's structural omission of the 1980s is part and parcel of what can be described as a distancing mechanism that permeates the work. The narrator seems unwilling to probe into the "whys" of interior transformation. Elaborate attention is devoted to things and urban places, to manners, everyday speech, and hearsay (gossip, confessional narratives), but very little is revealed of motivations and inner thoughts. The novel employs an omniscient perspective that avoids, or refuses to claim, certain knowledge, a refusal stemming from what has been described in narratology as "external focalization," where the narrator stands outside the characters and knows less than they do.

The permeating trope of distance in *Fanhua* conveys a mood of alienation and angst, but it is not to be conflated with just any other modern urban novel. The angst permeating *Fanhua* is symptomatic of specific historical moments – and specifically, the Cultural Revolution and the early 1990s. If the commercialized era of the 1990s seems like a reversal of the earlier episode, it is shown in the novel to evacuate the human soul just as the Cultural Revolution once did. The muted pain that colors the novel's tone results from a double affliction: those who go on a downturn in the Cultural Revolution find themselves once more cast adrift in the unscrupulous go-getter decade of the 1990s.

The narrator accentuates this double affliction by presenting many characters whose fluctuating fortunes do not cohere into meaningful, empowering personal trajectories. One of the most enigmatic may be Hu Sheng. Literally meaning "born in Shanghai," the name Hu Sheng suggests that the corresponding fictional character may be rather generic, though in fact he is by no means ordinary. In the opening episodes of the novel, set in the 1990s, he is revealed to have both a fiancée and a girlfriend, though he loses the latter after she becomes attracted to his friend Ah Bao, the work's other male protagonist. Hu Sheng then marries his fiancée, only to see his wife relocate abroad indefinitely. He does not initiate a divorce, however, even after he feels quite certain that she is now with someone else.

Meanwhile, we learn about Hu Sheng's upbringing in the interspersed chapters about the 1960s and 1970s, during which Hu Sheng comes of age and has an early love affair, which dissipates along with his privileged social position (as the son of an army cadre) at the onset of the Cultural Revolution. The illuminating episodes from his earlier life may or may not perform an explanatory function in relation to the ambiguous, self-distancing attitudes he exhibits toward the important people in his life. The narrative's braidlike structure is at odds with the linear bildungsroman form and the sort of character development found in many modern novels. Instead, the work reverts to narrative conventions found in late imperial Chinese fiction, which typically reflects little interest in the explanatory drive of depth psychology. Indeed, as the narrator puts it in the work's final chapter, "If you want to learn about male psychology, just go to the bookstore and pick up a few artsy books."

The most poignant moments in Hu Sheng's life occur during his ambiguous relationship with Shu Hua, a high-strung young woman who has a deeply empathetic, sensitive, and vulnerable mind and, judging from the books she collects, an interest in sophisticated matters like desire and anatomy.[14] Ironically, he reminisces about how Shu Hua liked to speak of life as a "desolate journey" and wanting to pull her out of this mood.[15] Hu Sheng, however, is inevitably engulfed in the same mood. His desperation to get to know Shu Hua is suggested by the shenanigans in which he is engaged while working as a postman. He and his co-workers pick out envelopes with "delicate" handwriting and open and read them, before throwing them out the window.[16] Here we see an act of penetration followed quickly by an act of projection. And this is but a minor variation on the pattern into which all of Hu Sheng's relationships fall. Hu Sheng poses as an inadequate emotional detective, spying on Shu Hua without being able to reach beneath the surface. On their outing to Zhongshan Park, they barge into an abandoned lab on the campus of East China Normal University but are scared off by the broken specimens and an unidentified, sticky, unnamable substance; they "run away and dare not stop until they're far off."[17] After Shu Hua leaves Shanghai for a distant province, as was common for Chinese youth during the Cultural Revolution, Hu Sheng receives only one letter from her. As the narrator transcribes the letter, Hu Sheng senses that "she would not write again."[18] This judgment is a correct reflection less of Shu Hua's intent than of Hu Sheng's own pessimism about the extenuating effects of distance and the possibility of accessing female interiority.

Hu Sheng's inability to cement his social position and gain access to other people places him in the ranks of besieged males in fictional writings, but he does not react to this condition with deep frenzy or palpable anxiety, suggesting instead an inscrutable, pervasive aloofness to suffering. Furthermore, the unperturbed narrative tone merges with Hu Sheng's apparent lack of concern. Nihilism is too dark, and insouciance seems too light. The double affliction that Hu Sheng suffers in the novel is subtly disguised, yet loudly accentuated through the very disguise.

The syndrome of detachment might well be read as a sign of the kind of psychological trauma that Dominick LaCapra described as absence and Sianne Ngai more recently categorizes as anxiety.[19] Hu Sheng's voyeurism and emotional escapism may authorize the label of anxiety, though trauma in the sense of a historical loss is, of course, also present. The other protagonist, Ah Bao, is first introduced as a heartless dandy; then the second chapter opens with him sitting on rooftop with a neighborhood girl named Betty. The narrator tells us, in a significant aside, that "this is a memory he forever holds,"[20] suggesting an idyllic time before the "primal scene" that is to come. The primal scene, of course, is more aptly described as a series of primal scenes that come in scattered places, revolving around the disappearance of Betty. One could argue that the episode changes Betty into a fetish, highlighting the prior losses that can never be precisely pinpointed. The novel blurs the two types of trauma in generating a tone of muted pain that keeps clawing at the reader.

This feature in *Fanhua* has clear resonance with a range of twentieth-century urban novels outside of China. Ann Beattie comes in particular to mind. Beattie is great at creating characters who, like Karen in "A Vintage Thunderbird," feel deeply disaffected with life in New York and are unable to figure out how to remedy the lack. They form shallow bonds out of a habit of alienation, in the same way that Hu Sheng drifts through life in perpetual angst. Ultimately, we may trace characters like Hu Sheng and Ah Bao to the disintegration of individuality in postmodern Western fiction, a medium that Jin Yucheng utilizes to portray a locally grounded angst.

A penchant for description

Not only does *Fanhua* flout modern literary expectations of coherent plot and character development; it also shows a peculiar penchant for detailed description. Indeed, *Fanhua* is full of details that display an extreme literalism that resists symbolic interpretation. Moreover, the novel marshals the Shanghai dialect in its full richness: the lingo and idiom of different trades; stories and urban legends; dinner table gossip; fashion and food; films, novels, and poetry; even hand-drawn graphs of neighborhoods and period objects flesh out its conception of Shanghai. The author proudly states his ultrarealist aesthetic by saying that many of the dialogues and anecdotes are lifted whole from his real-life experiences.

How material environment and inanimate things are cast into complex interplay with interiority would be a separate topic in its own right, but what I focus on here is the way the author assumes the responsibility of a docudrama writer. One could argue that Jin Yucheng is attempting a certain form of documentary fiction, or perhaps even what Edward Mendelson calls encyclopedic fiction.[21] This term has come to refer to exhaustive, maximalist writings, such as Babette Factory's 2005 novel *2005 Dopo Cristo* and Roberto Bolaño's 2006 novel *2666*.[22] Contemporary China has produced its own share of such works, including novels like Wang Anyi's *Documentation and Fiction* 紀實與虛構 (1993), Han Shaogong's 韓少功 *A Dictionary of Maqiao* 馬橋詞典 (1996), and Jia Pingwa's *Qin Opera* 秦腔 (2003). *Fanhua*'s desultory details, meanwhile, betray a similar impulse toward giving historical gravitas to his fiction. He is preserving the dense texture of a period of urban history, with a particular focus on the life of the lower social classes in Shanghai in the 1960s and 1970s. A large segment of the objects described in the novel are work tools and cheap trinkets, which gives the Shanghai workers a sensuality that explicitly contradicts the logic of class narratives underlying the Cultural Revolution. The narrator says at one point that individuals relate to one another more "based on smell"[23] than on social identification, using smell as a synecdoche for the senses. In an interview, Jin Yucheng further elaborates the intent behind sensualizing the experiences and craft of the workers: he had researched this period and found that working-class people lacked a clear identity that a class narrative would accord to them.[24]

In one episode set in the late 1960s, the narrator starts to catalogue a line of stainless steel bottle openers that were "in vogue in Shanghai."[25] The novel goes to great lengths to describe how one experienced worker uses various machines – a stamping press, pincer pliers, and so forth – to give these openers an incredible amount of detail, including "eagle feathers, horseshoes, beautiful women's hair and shins, as well as high heels – which come in different sizes, all skinny, with the right curvature and marvelous delicacy."[26] The relish with which these trinkets are described cannot be reduced to a process of commodity fetishism, and in fact the 1990s chapters consistently challenge a logic of commercialization that turns men and women into lifeless commodities. This scene, instead, suggests an unalienated form of labor and a detached, nonpossessive mode of psychic investment. The nostalgic depiction of the work ethic of the 1960s is presented as a counterpoint to the logic of the commodity and to the homogenizing class-based politics during the Cultural Revolution.

Collectible items also appear in the novel, as cascades of nouns. A similar episode occurs earlier, when the narrator veers away from the story line as if drawn by the magnetic power of things. One would never imagine that collectible stamps from 1960s Shanghai displayed such an array of different flowers, or that these flowers had so many names:

> daffodils, also known as "*yao* girls" and "female literati"; chrysanthemums, also known as "emperor girls"; cherry apple flowers with layered petals, also known as "return of life"; magnolias, also known as "maidens"; jade hairpin flowers, also known as "seasonal girls"; day lilies, also known as "remedy for sorrows"; balsamine blossoms, also known as "inverted reflections"; cassia blossoms, also known as "a look at Jiangnan"; and hydrangea, also known as "snow blossom flowers."[27]

The proliferation of obscure nouns violates every rule that Lukács institutes for descriptive passages in narrative fiction in his 1934 essay "Describe or Narrate,"[28] apparently contributing very little to the social critique the novel performs. But that is precisely the point the novel makes: the critical implications of a narrative do not solely hinge upon the elements that make it a narrative. What gets excluded from the narrow idea of narrative is foregrounded, in a reversal formally correlated with the novel's critical contestations of conventional attachments driven by utility. The workers in *Fanhua* embody a set of subversive attitudes toward labor and commodity that extend the novel's configuration of detachment. Detachment now goes over and beyond muted pain to become equated with a nonpossessive, sensually driven relation to the inanimate things of the urban environment.

Jin's use of the documentary and encyclopedic style does more than accentuate the sensual quality of scenes, objects, and sights in Shanghai. Like his predecessor Eileen Chang, Jin endows his native city with a mixture of sensual glory often associated with the decadent old Shanghai. But he broadens the producers and consumers of this sensuality to the social underclass, who unexpectedly become the center of a world of hidden objects and luxury. The novel's most riveting male character is Xiao Mao, who, along with Hu Sheng and Ah Bao, connects the various episodes of the novel. The son of a migrant family from the impoverished area north of the Yangtze, Xiao Mao is a watch and clock maker who is laid off in the early 1990s, yet he is the character in the novel with the richest sensuality: he not only throws himself into a heated, though innocent affair with a neighbor's wife but also has a habit of culling soulful lines from poetic collections.

We can take a close look at the opening of the novel, which contains a virtuoso descriptive passage about the end of Wong Kai-wai's 王家衛 1990 film *Days of Being Wild* (阿飛正傳), which combines a fascination with materiality with an attention to social underdogs:

> The best time to ascend to a high place alone is at night. At the end of *Days of Being Wild*, Tony Leung Chiu-wai steals a quiet moment from a life of wild treachery, haggard but not broken. Bathed in electric light, he picks up a stack of bank notes, counts them, and puts them into a jacket pocket; then he grabs a pack of playing cards, which he spreads apart between pressed fingers, and repeats the process with another. After that, he takes a comb to his hair, parts it on the side, near the three-seven line, and combs it smooth before a mirror, his body straight as a pole, dripping with an easy callousness. Finally, the light goes off, signaling the hero's confidence in surviving the seedy underworld. Half of a minute for all this, and that is the Shanghai flavor distilled.[29]

> 獨上高樓，最好是夜裏。《阿飛正傳》結尾，梁朝偉騎馬覓馬，英雄暗老，電燈下面數鈔票，數清一沓，放進西裝內袋，再數一沓，拿出一副撲克牌，捻開先看，再摸出一副。接下來梳頭，三七分頭，對鏡子梳齊，全身筆挺，骨子裏疏慢，最後，關燈。否極泰來，這半分鐘，是上海味道。

The passage describes nothing more than a hooligan who makes his fortune by cheating at card games. What is impressive about Tony Leung's role is his suaveness – his appearance of having everything down pat. His personal style and the novel's narrative style become indistinguishable. It is a style that places everything in order, though of nobody's design, pointing to no hidden or more complicated meaning. There is confidence and fulfillment in this smoothness, but also a profound lack of higher meaning. The mood of the paragraph is poised precariously on the edge between a wistful realization of lack and a sensual insouciance. What I have referred to as the aesthetic of detachment enables this mode of intermingling precisely by precluding the desire for incorporation, appropriation, or domination.

Ultimately, the novel projects notions of narrative, narrative tone or mood, and subjectivity in ways that question their conventional meanings. It speaks to certain strains of modernist fiction in the West (urban fiction like the works of Hemingway and Beattie and anti-interiority modernist fiction like Robbe-Grillet's "nouveau novel") and, equally important, taps into formal resources of conventional Chinese novels. It creates an image of Shanghai, as well as a Shanghai style of narrative, that differs from though partly parallels the angst of modernist and contemporary English fiction, turning it into a methodological lens for studying a distinctly non-Western urban culture and narrative form.

Conclusion: a look into the past

Fanhua is both conventional and innovative, bringing vernacular Chinese fiction into an age of internet-generated literature, gesturing toward a certain capaciousness, the appropriation of narrative inclinations from both East and West. The "Shanghai flavor" marking the novel revolves around a distinct brand of detachment, with layered meanings extending from muted pain to impersonal sensuality.

It is no surprise that *Fanhua* has been compared to earlier fictional writings on Shanghai, especially those by Eileen Chang, and the novel is no less successful in turning Shanghai into a discursive method and aesthetic. It is also fitting that Wong Kar-wai has acquired the rights to adapt this novel for the big screen. After all, *Fanhua* starts with a scene from Wong's *Days of Being Wild* and is poised to be recognized as just the type of masterpiece exemplified by that film.

Notes

1 Jin Yucheng 金宇澄, *Fanhua* 繁花 (Blooming Blossoms) (Shanghai: Shanghai wenyi chubanshe, 2015), 443.
2 Li Tuo 李陀, "Ye tan 'wei xiandaipai' jiqi piping" 也談"偽現代派"及其批評 [On "Faux Modernism" and Its Criticisms], *Beijing Literature* 4 (1988): 4–10. See also Huang Ziping 黃子平, "Guanyu 'wei xiandaipai' jiqi piping 關於"偽現代派"及其批評 [On "Faux Modernism" and Its Criticisms], *Beijing Literature* 2 (1988): 11–16.
3 Eric Hayot and Rebecca L. Walkowitz, eds., *A New Vocabulary for Global Modernism* (New York: Columbia University Press, 2016), 7.

4 Franco Moretti, "Network Theory and Plot Analysis," *Literary Lab Pamphlet* 2 (2011): 9, https://litlab.stanford.edu/LiteraryLabPamphlet2.pdf (accessed August 24, 2017).

5 Conversation with the author, August 27, 2016. The annotated edition is not yet published as of spring 2020, but is said to be undergoing final edits.

6 See Li Junjun 李軍均, "Mingqian 'xiaoshuo' yuyi yuanliu kaolun" 明前"小說"語義源流考論 (A Study of the Semantics of "*Xiaoshuo*" Before the Ming), *Zhongguo wenxue yanjiu* 中國文學研究 (Chinese Literature Studies) 2 (2013): 41–50. In this article, Li analyzes these three primary meanings of *xiaoshuo*.

7 Zhao Yiheng 趙毅衡, *Kunao de xushizhe* 苦惱的敘事者 (Troubled Narrator) (Chengdu: Sichuan wenyi chubanshe, 2013), 28.

8 Zhao, *Kunao de xushizhe*, 28.

9 Zhang Yong 張勇, "Ruhe kaikou" 如何開口 (How to Start Narrating), in *Zhongguo wenxue gujin yanbian yanjiu lunji sibian* 中國文學古今演變研究論集四編 (Essays on the Historical Evolution of Ancient Chinese Literature, vol. 4) (Shanghai: Shanghai Ancient Books Press, 2015), 1078–1092.

10 Huang Ping 黃平, "Cong chuanqi dao gushi: *Fanhua* yu shanghai xushu" 從"傳奇"到"故事"：《繁花》與上海敘事 (From Romance to Fiction: *Fanhua* and Shanghai Narratives). *Dangdai zuojia pinglun* 當代作家評論 (Reviews of Contemporary Chinese Writers) 4 (2013): 58.

11 Erich Kahler, *The Inward Turn of Narrative*, trans. from the German by Richard & Clara Winston (Princeton: Princeton University Press, 1973).

12 Wang Zenqi 汪曾祺, *Zhongguo dangdai zuojia xuanji congshu·Wang Zenqi* 中國當代作家選集叢書·汪曾祺 (Selected Works by Contemporary Chinese Writers: Wang Zenqi) (Beijing: Remin wenxue chubanshe, 1992), 5.

13 See Amanda Anderson, *The Powers of Distance: Cosmopolitanism and the Cultivation of Detachment* (Princeton: Princeton University Press, 2001), 63–90. Whereas Anderson associates the omniscience of nineteenth-century Victorian novels with the ethos of detachment, this essay suggests that *Fanhua* projects a unique conception of detachment by resisting omniscience.

14 Jin Yucheng, *Fanhua*, 76.

15 Jin Yucheng, *Fanhua*, 197.

16 Jin Yucheng, *Fanhua*, 195.

17 Jin Yucheng, *Fanhua*, 201.

18 Jin Yucheng, *Fanhua*, 197.

19 See Sianne Ngai, *Ugly Feelings* (Cambridge: Harvard University Press, 2007), 209–247; Dominick LaCapra, "Trauma, Absence, Loss," *Critical Inquiry* 25, no. 4 (Summer 1999): 696–727.

20 Jin Yucheng, *Fanhua*, 13.

21 Edward Mendelson, "Encyclopedic Narrative: From Dante to Pynchon," *MLN* 91 (1976): 1267–1275.

22 See Stefano Ercolino, "The Maximalist Novel," *Comparative Literature* 64, no. 3 (2012): 241–256.

23 Jin Yucheng, *Fanhua*, 171.

24 Interview with the author, September 16, 2016.

25 Jin Yucheng, *Fanhua*, 193.

26 Jin Yucheng, *Fanhua*.

27 Jin Yucheng, *Fanhua*, 65.

28 Georg Lukács, "Narrate or Describe?" in *Writer and Critic and Other Essays*, trans. Arthur Kahn (London: Merlin Press, 2005), 110–148.

29 Jin Yucheng, *Fanhua*, preface.

Works cited

Anderson, Amanda. *The Powers of Distance: Cosmopolitanism and the Cultivation of Detachment*. Princeton: Princeton University Press, 2001.

Ercolino, Stefano. "The Maximalist Novel." *Comparative Literature* 64, no. 3 (2012): 241–256.

Hayot, Eric, and Rebecca L. Walkowitz, eds. *A New Vocabulary for Global Modernism.* New York: Columbia University Press, 2016.

Huang Ping 黃平. "Cong chuanqi dao gushi: *Fanhua* yu shanghai xushu" 從"傳奇"到 "故事":《繁花》與上海敘事 (From Romance to Fiction: *Fanhua* and Shanghai Narratives). *Dangdai zuojia pinglun* 當代作家評論 (Reviews of Contemporary Chinese Writers) 4 (2013): 54–62.

Huang Ziping 黃子平. "Guanyu 'wei xiandaipai' jiqi piping" 關於"偽現代派"及其批評 (On "Faux Modernism" and Its Criticisms). *Beijing wenxue*北京文學 (Beijing Literature) 2 (1988): 11–16.

Jin Yucheng 金宇澄. *Fanhua* 繁花 (Blooming Blossoms). Shanghai: Shanghai wenyi chubanshe, 2015.

Kahler, Erich. *The Inward Turn of Narrative.* Trans. German by Richard and Clara Winston. Princeton: Princeton University Press, 1973.

LaCapra, Dominick. "Trauma, Absence, Loss." *Critical Inquiry* 25, no. 4 (Summer 1999): 696–727.

Li Junjun 李軍均. "Mingqian 'xiaoshuo' yuyi yuanliu kaolun" 明前"小說"語義源流考論 (A Study of the Semantics of "*Xiaoshuo*" before the Ming). *Zhongguo wenxue yanjiu* 中國文學研究 (Chinese Literature Studies) 2 (2013): 41–50.

Li Tuo 李陀. "Ye tan 'wei xiandaipai' jiqi piping" 也談"偽現代派"及其批評 (On "Faux Modernism" and Its Criticisms). *Beijing wenxue*北京文學 (Beijing Literature) 4 (1988): 4–10.

Lukács, Georg. "Narrate or Describe?" In *Writer and Critic and Other Essays*, translated by Arthur Kahn, 110–148. London: Merlin Press, 2005.

Mendelson, Edward. "Encyclopedic Narrative: From Dante to Pynchon." *MLN* 91 (1976): 1267–1275.

Moretti, Franco. "Network Theory and Plot Analysis." *Literary Lab Pamphlet* 2 (2011): 9. https://litlab.stanford.edu/LiteraryLabPamphlet2.pdf. Accessed August 24, 2017.

Ngai, Sianne. *Ugly Feelings*, 209–247. Cambridge: Harvard University Press, 2007.

Wang Zenqi 汪曾祺. *Zhongguo dangdai zuojia xuanji congshu·Wang Zenqi* 中國當代作家選集叢書·汪曾祺 (Selected Works by Contemporary Chinese Writers: Wang Zenqi). Beijing: Remin wenxue chubanshe, 1992.

Zhang Yong 張勇. "Ruhe kaikou." 如何開口 (How to Start Narrating). In *Zhongguo wenxue gujin yanbian yanjiu lunji sibian*中國文學古今演變研究論集四編 (Essays on the Historical Evolution of Ancient Chinese Literature), Vol. 4, 1078–1092. Shanghai: Shanghai Ancient Books Press, 2015.

Zhao Yiheng 趙毅衡. *Kunao de xushizhe* 苦惱的敘事者 (Troubled Narrator). Sichuan wenyi chubanshe, 2013.

PART II
Border regions

5

WOLF TOTEM

An allegory of the future

Q. S. Tong

The 2004 novel *Wolf Totem* (*Lang tuteng* 狼圖騰), by Jiang Rong 姜戎 (the pen name of Lü Jiamin 呂嘉民), is a story of contradictions. It is at once a celebration of Mongolian wolves and an elegy for them as an anachronism in modern times, a critique of the innate defects of the Han race and an expression of desire for its improvement, a tale of haunting nostalgia for a lost past and an allegory of our bleak future. The novel presents a simple linear narrative, but the author's insertion of discursive comments disrupts, redirects, and reorganizes its temporal linearity, as if recommending it to be read as a text different from a traditional realist novel. Its reflections on the mythical origins of Mongol warriors, their worship of wolves, and their heroism on one hand, and the defects of the Han Chinese and the irremediable lethargy of agrarian culture on the other, dramatically spatialize the plot and foreground its central thematic concerns.

Critics have noted several controversial motifs in the novel, including its critique of the Han Chinese and their historical failures, its admiration for masculine power, and its unconcealed aestheticization of violence. And yet, it is a moving story of the relationships – or rather, the breakdown of the relationships – between men, wolves, and the grassland. Should the militaristic tradition be revived in order to strengthen the Chinese nation? Should one accept that lupine heroism is not constitutive of Chinese national character, and therefore it is important to cultivate it in order to be globally successful? Questions of this kind are often put forward by critics to demonstrate how politically and ethically limited the novel is. However, though potentially of heuristic value, these questions are mostly informed by historical hypotheses.[1] History cannot be repeated, let alone revived. Celebration of a lost past does not have to be advocacy of its return. Instead, it could be yet another attempt to understand what historical and ethical responsibilities we should bear for that lost past and what we could realistically do to avert future failures and disasters.

Primitive heroism and Chinese national character

The narrator, Chen Zhen, a Beijing student in his early twenties, is dispatched to Inner Mongolia for reeducation in the early days of the Cultural Revolution (1966–1976). Indeed, he is reeducated, not through physical labor or ideological indoctrination, but by the wolves. The Mongolian wolves – especially the cub that Chen takes and attempts to raise – are at the center of the novel's drama. The use of the wolves as narrative focus is simultaneously realistic and allegorical. In its description of the vicissitudes of the wolves' life on the grassland, the novel critically reflects on issues of national character by way of comparison between Mongolian nomads and Han Chinese, and between what the author calls the "freedom and independence" of lupine life on the vast, masculine, and sublime steppes and the squalor and boredom of the routinized Han Chinese life in their enclosed and isolated spaces.

As Silvia Sebastiani notes, notions like nation and national character were "central topics in the new science of man taking shape in the eighteenth century" in Europe.[2] The novel's narrator is apparently committed to the Enlightenment classification of peoples in accordance with their perceived collective or national character, which is typically understood as being biologically defined or conditioned.[3] Starting from the fatalistic pronouncement "character is destiny," which George Eliot attributes to the German author known as Novalis,[4] the narrator enters upon a discussion of the causes for ethno-physical and civilizational/cultural divergences among peoples and nations: "Character determines the fate not only of individuals but also of the entire race. Farming people are domesticated, and faintheartedness has sealed their fate."[5] By this logic, just as the wolf is superior to sheep, the Mongolians are (or at least were) superior to the Han Chinese. Of all the world's great agrarian societies, only China has survived – not because it possesses exceptional national qualities or a better governmental system, but rather because it is fortunate enough to be protected by its vast territory, by the Yellow and the Yangtze Rivers, and by its large population, which have helped to prevent its total collapse at various historical junctures (*WT* 174).

In the early twenty-first century, when China has gone through radical historical transformation and regained much of its confidence, it is rather unsettling that the May Fourth enlightenment language is invoked to mount this radical critique of China and Chinese national character. Even more unsettling, however, is the narrator's fatalistic verdict on the irremediable genetic formation of the Han Chinese – not only do they possess a set of objectionable qualities, but also these qualities are inherited and thereby unalterable and reproducible:

> People say you can tell what a person will grow up to be at the age of three and what he'll look like in old age at seven. The same holds true for a race of people. In the West, primitive nomadic life was their childhood, and if we look at primitive nomads now, we are given access to Westerners at three and at seven, their childhood, and if we take this further, we get a

clear understanding of why they occupy a high position. Learning their progressive skills isn't hard. China launched its own satellite, didn't it? What's hard to learn are the militancy and aggressiveness, the courage and willingness to take risks that flow in nomadic veins.

(WT 303)

This is perhaps not the place to discuss in detail whether "militancy and aggressiveness, the courage and willingness to take risks," should be considered the biohistorical conditions of Western nations' achievement. The narrator clearly enjoys the exhibition of what he considers to be Chinese "national defects": complacency and selfishness; lack of courage, bravery, and commitment. Earlier in the book, for example, the narrator elaborates on the historical incompetence of Han Chinese thus:

> In ancient times . . . the impact of Mongols on the world was far greater than that of the Han, who outnumbered them a hundred to one. . . . I tell you, I feel sorry for the Han Chinese. We built the Great Wall and crowed about what an achievement it was, considering ourselves to be the center of the world, the central kingdom. But in the eyes of early Western people, China was only a "silk country," a "ceramic country," a "tea country."
>
> *(WT 34)*

Again, in the context of China's ascendance on the global stage, the novel's rejection of the ethnographical development of the Han Chinese could alienate many of its Chinese readers. Into this critical language is woven a thread of linguistic *chinoiserie* in such decorative and consumerist commodities as silk, ceramics, and tea, which are not just products greatly desired in eighteenth-century Europe but also figures representing the infirmity and fragility of Han Chinese.

The narrator seems obsessed with the issue of Chinese national character, but the comparison between Han people and Mongols is strategically developed to foreground the flaws and defects of Han Chinese and their historical failures. At one point the narrator mentions to his friend Yang Ke: "Lu Xun had noted the major problems in the national character of the Hua-Xia race."[6] Here, the early twentieth-century reformer Lu Xun is singled out as the intellectual inspiration for the kind of critique of Chinese national character the author attempts to mount in the novel. Later in the book, again invoking Lu Xun to support his view on the hierarchical differences among the nations in the world, the narrator states: "Westerners are brutish, while we Chinese are domesticated" (*WT* 173). Situating the novel's thematic concern within the discourse of the May Fourth critique of Chinese tradition, the narrator urges readers to note the discursive continuity between Lu Xun's and his own reflections on Chinese national character and to recognize the urgent need to renew the May Fourth discussion of Chinese modernity.

Perhaps nowhere is the narrative more manifestly allegorical than when the narrator draws an analogy between sheep and Han Chinese. Describing a scene where the wolves were slaughtering sheep, Chen feels repulsed more by the sheep's imperviousness to the killing of other sheep – being torn, destroyed, and devoured by the wolves – than by their physical meekness and weakness. He is instantly reminded of Lu Xun's description of the unfeeling Chinese onlookers watching a fellow countryman being executed by a Japanese soldier:[7]

> Sheep are truly stupid animals. When the wolf knocked the unfortunate sheep to the ground, the other sheep scattered in fright. But the entire flock soon calmed down, and there were even a few animals that timidly drew closer to watch the wolf eat a number of their flock. As they looked on, more joined them, until at last a hundred sheep had virtually penned the wolf and its bloody victim in; they pushed and shoved and craned their necks to get a better look.
>
> (WT 319)

The narrator asks rhetorically: What is the difference between Lu Xun's description of Chinese and sheep? A wolf eating a sheep may be abhorrent, but "far more loathsome," he concludes, "were cowardly people who acted like sheep" (WT 319). As is well known, Lu Xun, who had decided to abandon his medical studies in Japan, reinvented himself as a writer in order to address what he perceived to be his compatriots' lethargy and numbness; the publication of his short story "Diary of a Madman" (1918) was the first major assault on Confucianism in the May Fourth New Cultural Movement. Wolf Totem's preoccupation with the allegorical similarity between sheep and Han Chinese serves as a timely reminder that the May Fourth enlightenment project remains incomplete. The narrator suggests a straightforward, though perhaps less nuanced, way to renew the May Fourth project, by abandoning Confucianism and adopting the wolf totem:

> The wolf totem has a much longer history than Han Confucianism with greater natural continuity and vitality. In the Confucian thought system, the main ideas, such as the three cardinal guides and the five constant virtues, are outdated and decayed, but the central spirit of the wolf totem remains vibrant and young, since it's been passed down by the most advanced races in the world. It should be considered one of the truly valuable spiritual heritages of all humanity. There'd be hope for China if our national character could be rebuilt by cutting away the decaying parts of Confucianism and grafting a wolf totem sapling onto it.
>
> (WT 377)

Dismissing Confucianism as "outdated" and "decayed" and proposing a familial relationship between the two cultures, the narrator interrogates the long-held value system and Han national character. In the lengthy afterword, "Rational Exploration: Lectures and Dialogues on the Wolf Totem," the author attempts to clarify and rectify Chinese history, which, he says, has been willfully distorted by the Confucians. The Han Chinese, if willing, could also take the wolf, rather than the dragon, as their primal totem, origin of thought, and source of inspiration. Against the nationalistic grain in contemporary China, therefore, the novel urges a more self-reflexive understanding of Han Chinese along the lines of the May Fourth rejection of Confucianism.

In the epilogue, the narrator and his friend Yang Ke return to the grassland after a hiatus of three decades. It is an emotional journey home, and the question of Chinese national character that the narrator identified shortly after his arrival on the Mongolian grassland continues to bother him: "It's been twenty years since the launching of the reforms, and we've made quite a bit of progress, but we're still on shaky legs" (*WT* 513). Wealth and technological advances are insufficient for building a strong nation, and human progress does not depend on economic and technological development. More often than not, the narrator suggests, the opposite is true. It is the practice of social developmentalism that has brought about a whole series of disasters, including the destruction of the Mongolian grassland.

The novel's comparative, historical, and anthropological reflections on the Chinese national character are reminiscent of the Darwinian notion of civilizational development. Its explicit endorsement of the principle of the survival of the fittest, its unconcealed admiration for the wolves' techniques of war, and its unqualified celebration of the victor as hero are the most controversial aspects of the novel. The conception of lupine heroism and its human expression of courage, bravery, and military superiority is nowhere more manifest than the author's unconcealed admiration for the military successes of Genghis Khan and his children in conquering China and the world. The destruction of the Song dynasty is repeatedly cited as evidence of the radical difference between the Mongols and Han Chinese. René Grousset's *The Empire of the Steppes*, on which the narrator draws for historical information about the Mongols, records the tragic fall of the Song dynasty thus:

> The last of the Chinese "patriots," under the leadership of the heroic Chang Shih-kie, took refuge aboard their fleet with a new little Sung prince, Ti-ping, aged nine. On April 3, 1279, this fleet, attacked by the Mongol squadron near the islet of Yaishan southwest of Canton, was destroyed, taken, or scattered, and the child Ti-ping was drowned.
>
> This was the first time that the whole of China, including the south had fallen into the hands of a Turko-Mongol conqueror. . . . With [Kublai] the roving herdsmen of the steppe, "all the sons of the Gray Wolf and the Hind," became at last the lords of China – that is, of the densest community of sedentary farmers in all Asia.[8]

Confucian historians might consider the last "patriots" or "loyalists" of the Song dynasty to be heroes, but insofar as the narrator is concerned, the victor was the only hero the world would recognize and remember. In toppling the Song dynasty, the Mongol soldiers under Kublai Khan, the grandson of Genghis Khan (1162–1227), asserted their dominance over the territory corresponding to the Central Kingdom – though it may be argued that Han Chinese civilization remained intact, unified, and strong despite such disruptions. As they moved from periphery to center, the Mongol conquerors adopted a Han Chinese way of life and were thereby assimilated into Chinese culture. If so, the Mongol empire testifies to the very impossibility of speaking of a unitary and continuous Chinese national identity.

One of the novel's subplots involves the Mongol empire led by Genghis Khan, whose name, reports historian Urgunge Onon, means "greyish white wolf."[9] The empire's legendary military successes and achievements are recorded in the rich archive of literary memories. In world literature, the expansion of this largest geographically contiguous empire in history was a monumental event that inspired not only a range of imaginative works but also early Western knowledge of China. Prominent examples of literary works that reference the Mongol empire include Marco Polo's *Travels*, Voltaire's play *The Orphan of China*, Arthur Murphy's drama by the same title, and Samuel Taylor Coleridge's poem "Kubla Khan."

Wolf Totem taps into this rich archive of historical memories. In its celebration of the Mongol conquest, the novel does not conceal its enthusiasm for a revival of Mongol militarism. The military success of the empire was achieved through a process of violence and destruction – such that its imperialism served as a powerful instrument for dissemination of its legend and its myth. Jiang Rong's novel, meanwhile, has been criticized for its advocacy of militarism, imperialism, and fascism, as evidenced by its celebration of the Mongol empire's primitive force and animalistic vitality, vividly figured in the wolf. Wolfgang Kubin, for example, argues that the novel is an allegory of fascism and has brought shame on China.[10] Some of the narrator's comments on Chinese national character and his celebration of lupine violence and militarism, taken in isolation, could be easily viewed as racist or even fascist. However, to the extent that the novel could be described as racist, it is actually an *internal* racism – in that the author's critique is nearly entirely directed at his own race. In response to his critics, Jiang Rong in an interview insists that he is only interested in critically interrogating his own race and country, and categorically denies that there are any commonalities between his rejection of Han national character and Nazi anti-Semitism.[11] If the novel were intended, as Kubin understands it, to "disgrace" the Chinese, then to reduce its critique of Chinese national character to the fascist ideology would constitute a total rejection of the tradition of serious critical reflection on Chinese culture and Chinese people that Lu Xun championed. And it would have been a fascist novel if the author had celebrated his own race's superiority and justified his country's invasion and colonization of others.

Wolf, dog, and man

The story of the wolf is intended not only to set off and foreground the lack of spirit, vision, energy, and bravery of the Han Chinese but also to show that the Han's merciless campaigns against animals and nature have eroded not just their environment but also their very humanity. The story is at its most powerful in its description of the Mongolian grassland replete with wolves, dogs, horses, birds, sheep, and so forth, and most poignant in its elegiac conclusion that the shrinking of the grassland and the disappearance of wildlife foreshadow a future the narrator does not look forward to. In his cruelty against animals, man embarks on a journey to his self-destruction.

Central to the novel's narrative is the narrator's memorable portrayal of the wolf cub, a symbol of lupine animality, identity, and heroism. The cub's bravery and courage, unwavering commitment to his species, native wisdom for survival, readiness to fight, and discipline are some of the exceptional qualities the author foregrounds and eulogizes, and are also imagined to be the qualities of the Mongol warriors. The allegorical significance of the cub is brought to the fore in his refusal to live together with human beings; his final tragic death seems to mark the death of the organic relationship among people, wild animals, and grassland.

Out of curiosity, Chen Zhen takes the cub from a burrow and tries to raise and domesticate him. In return, Chen hopes that the cub will accept him as a friend, who, though of a different species, genuinely loves it.

> Every day at mealtime he called out to the cub, hoping that would spark a bit of gratitude. He often found himself thinking that when the day came that he married and started a family, he'd probably not be as fond of his own children as he was of the young wolf. Since he had taken it upon himself to raise the cub, his mind was often tormented by mythlike dreams and fantasies.
>
> *(WT 329)*

The narrator is fascinated by the cub, and by the mysterious affinity between wolf and man. On the steppes, a female wolf would breastfeed an abandoned human child, and the whole pack of wolves would take care of the child and raise it as their own. There would not be such myths had there not been any connection between man and wolf, and the narrator's love for the cub is manifest in his admiration for the cub's beauty:

> His eyes were the most fearsome and yet the most fascinating part of his face. They were round, but slanted upward and outward, and were more striking than the eyes painted on the face of a Beijing Opera performer. The inner corners of his eyes slanted downward to form a dark tear-duct line, giving them an especially eerie appearance. . . . The cub's eyes differed fundamentally from those of humans or other animals. The "whites"

were more an amber yellow, which, Chen felt, had a penetrating power over human and animal psychology. The cub had small irises, dark and forbidding, like the tiny opening in the blowpipe used by the black man in one of Sherlock Holmes's stories. When the cub was angry, Chen dared not look him in the eye.

(WT 399)

The narrator never fails to direct attention to the details of everyday care of the cub: how the cub responds to captivity, attempts to understand himself in relation to other wolves and to the human world, and attempts to develop an understanding of the self and a sense of identity. Making constant efforts to humanize and domesticate the cub, the narrator hopes that one day the young wolf might become like a dog and live confidently in the human world. In captivity, the cub is naturally confused about his identity, and one of the novel's most moving episodes involves his efforts to acquire a "language" by learning from dogs:

> The cub could not yet make wolf sounds, so he'd tried to imitate the barking of a dog, but that was simply too hard. . . . Yet even as the cub fretted over his inability to bark like a dog, he refused to stop trying. . . . Erlang came running over, stood beside the cub, and began to bark, slowly, like a patient teacher. A moment later, Chen heard the cub cry out in the cadence of a dog's bark, but without the sound a dog makes – *orf orf.* The cub was so excited he leaped into the air and began licking Erlang's mouth. . . . The strange sound brought the three puppies running, while the other dogs made deriding sounds as if mocking the cub. . . . The cub may well have been aware that the man and the dogs were making fun of him. . . . The puppies were so happily caught up in the atmosphere that they were rolling on the ground.
>
> (WT 357–358)

This loving picture of the cub, dogs, and narrator helping one another shows a remarkable community that does not recognize the deep-seated Han prejudice against animals, and particularly dogs. The cub wants to learn to articulate, but has no one to teach him how to make wolf sounds and is unable to produce a dog's barking. After all, "[he] was a wolf, not a dog" (*WT* 360), though the narrator notes that they are genetically related (*WT* 111). When the cub begins to howl, however, Chen Zhen and the dogs are thrilled:

> With the aid of his flashlight, Chen spotted the cub, crouching next to the wooden post, his snout pointing into the sky as he howled. So that's where the sound was coming from! It was the first time Chen had heard the cub actually bay like a wolf, something he thought the cub wouldn't do until he was fully grown. But here he was, only four months old, and

already sounding and acting like a mature wild animal. Chen was thrilled as a father hearing his son say "Daddy" for the first time. He bent down and stroked the cub's back; the cub turned and licked the back of his hand, then went back to baying.

(WT *360*)

Only when he is able to howl and bay does the cub express his presence and identity before humans and dogs. Unlike dogs that bark at people or other animals, he instead bays with his snout pointing into the air. This is, according to the narrator, how the cub communicates with faraway kin – as if saying: I'm here, in captivity. The cub's howling and scent draw packs of wolves that are willing to risk their lives to liberate him from captivity. As the wolves close in, the human world becomes enveloped by "the walls of sound" they create. Unfolding in the grand theater of the grassland is the drama of collisions between wolves and humans. Though chained, the cub gets excited and attempts to escape when he hears the other wolves' howling. Just four months old, he has not yet lived with other wolves, but his instinct is to leave the human world. Something in his bones and blood leads him to seek a life elsewhere:

> [The cub] was jumping up and down outside the hole, snarling and baring his claws, wildly excited by the sound-and-light war between humans, wolves, and dogs. . . . His fighting instincts had been stimulated by the pre-battle tension and palpable sense of fear in the air, and he seemed incapable of distinguishing between friend and foe, so long as he could enter the fray on any side. It seemed as if killing a puppy or killing another cub would have made him equally happy.
>
> (WT *356*)

The prolonged and deep baying of the wolves trigged a profound sense of self in the cub. He is a natural fighter, though he does not even know that he has an enemy.

In theorizing the wolf's cultural significance, the narrator explains that "the wolf is the ancestor of the dog" (*WT* 111). The dog is the wolf's other and vice versa, and they require each other. One of the important things the narrator has learned on the grassland, something he would never have known in Beijing, is this vital organic unity of men, dogs, and wolves: "Heaven, earth, and man are a unity; it's impossible to categorically separate men, dogs, and wolves" (*WT* 94). But compared with wolves, dogs have an advantage in that they understand both men and wolves. Erlang and Huang Huang, the two dogs who play a major role in assisting people in their fight against the wolves, are instrumental in the formation of the community of men, dogs, and wolves. The novel suggests that those who respect wolves would love dogs; those who have no respect for wolves would similarly dislike dogs. By this logic, Han Chinese hate dogs, and the novel suggests that Mongols cannot understand why Han Chinese eat dogs if they hate them, curse them, and even kill them (*WT* 196). On the grassland, by contrast, men consider dogs their comrades-in-arms, their best friends, and their brothers, while women treat dogs almost as though they were their own children (*WT* 195). For Mongols, "eating dog meat, skinning a dog, or sleeping under a dog skin" are "acts of unforgivable betrayal" (*WT* 196). The narrator's love for dogs, like his love for wolves, should not be read as just personal inclination or private sentiment; in his conception of the organic community of people, dogs, and wolves, his love of the dogs constitutes a major ideological and ethical challenge to Han people's inveterate cruelty toward and cultural stereotyping of them.

Admittedly, the issue of animal rights is not on the narrator's agenda in *Wolf Totem*. As far as the narrator is concerned, in the animal world there is a hierarchical structure in which the wolf is *the* natural ruler, lord, and god. If the book is an elegy, it is an elegy for the wolf and its ecological space, the grassland, rather than for animals in general. But Chen Zhen's raising of the cub offers a perfect opportunity for the narrator to reflect on the human causes of natural disasters and the ethical implications of human cruelty to animals. Overexploitation of Mongolian grassland only exhibits human stupidity and selfishness. Organized slaughter of wolves during the Cultural Revolution was stimulated by misunderstanding of and ignorance about the human need for animals. In denouncing the human-centered view of social development and its consequences, the narrator argues for the urgent need to recognize that protection of animals is also protection of our humanity. What is human must be considered in terms of what is not; one's understanding of humanity depends on one's understanding of animality. In the story of the wolves, therefore, readers are urged to think about the future of humanity in conjunction with the future of nature, and of human rights with animal rights.[12]

Immanuel Kant argues in the *Lectures on Ethics* that even though animals are not rational or self-conscious and humans may not have direct duties to them, humans can nevertheless protect and promote their own humanity by being kind and dutiful to animals. Significantly, Kant invokes the dog as an example of the importance of animals to human self-understanding:

> Since animals are an analogue of humanity, we observe duties to mankind when we observe them as analogues to this, and thus cultivate our duties to humanity. If a dog, for example, has served his master long and faithfully, that is an analogue of merit; hence I must reward it, and once the dog can serve no longer, must look after him to the end, for I thereby cultivate my duty to humanity, as I am called upon to do. . . . So if a man has his dog shot, because it can no longer earn a living for him, he is by no means in breach of any duty to the dog, since the latter is incapable of judgement, but he thereby damages the kindly and humane qualities in himself, which he ought to exercise in virtue of his duties to mankind. Lest he extinguish such qualities, he must already practise a similar kindliness towards animals; for a person who already displays such cruelty to animals is also no

less hardened towards men. We can already know the human heart, even in regard to animals.[13]

Human respect for animals, or lack thereof, is analogous to the way we see each other socially. We can only be good and kind to each other by not being cruel to animals. Jeremy Bentham believed that abuse of animals is not very different from racism, and called for the organized protection of animal rights:

> The day may come, when the rest of the animal creation may acquire those rights which never could have been withholden from them but by the hand of tyranny. The French have already discovered that the blackness of skin is no reason why a human being should be abandoned without redress to the caprice of a tormentor. It may come one day to be recognized, that the number of legs, the villosity of the skin, or the termination of the *os sacrum*, are reasons equally insufficient for abandoning a sensitive being to the same fate. What else is it that should trace the insuperable line? Is it the faculty of reason, or perhaps, the faculty for discourse? . . . The question is not, Can they reason? nor, Can they talk? but, Can they suffer? Why should the law refuse its protection to any sensitive being? . . . The time will come when humanity will extend its mantle over everything which breathes.[14]

Do animals have rights? Should we begin to develop and establish an animal ethics? Why should we consider the moral implications of our relationship with animals? Many defenders of Guangxi's infamous Yuling "dog-meat festival" argue that dogs are not rational and cannot speak, and we must be more concerned with human suffering than with dog rights. Animals merely exist in the form of bare life, and can thus be eliminated when they are perceived as invasive or useless. But the point is that we should not consider the rights of animals in human terms. And, as Bentham noted, we must not ask whether dogs can reason or talk, but should instead ask: Can they suffer? Should they suffer? Would their suffering alleviate or decrease human suffering brought about by human beings themselves? To make a distinction between animal life and human life in terms of human properties such as reason and language, which give human life its political forms, and thereby to justify the killing of animals is the most negative politicization of bare life. However, such a distinction, as Foucault shows, did not exist before the eighteenth century: "All that existed was living beings, which were viewed through a grid of knowledge constituted by *natural history*."[15] Giorgio Agamben similarly argues that the dichotomy between animal life or bare life (*zoē*), on one hand, and political or social life (*bios*), on the other, is a modern invention that has led to catastrophic consequences, such as the implementation of genocidal policies during World War II.[16] Slaughtering wolves with the help of modern military technology, as described in Jiang Rong's novel, is not dramatically different from the practice of such biopolitics.

For pastoral Mongols, there is only bare life on the grassland. Although the author of *Wolf Totem* is not exactly an environmentalist, he nevertheless suggests that humans would be dehumanized without proper love and respect for nature. Human cruelty as revealed in the slaughtering of wolves with machine guns is presented as not only a crime against nature but also a crime against humanity. After years of being hunted, the wolves are not to be seen anywhere on the grassland. The narrator makes clear that it is a tragic political and ideological blunder to hunt down wolves and to reclaim Mongolian grassland for farming. What would the postwolf grassland be like? Would it still be the grassland as we know it? Would we have a future without wolves? Human beings must take responsibility for their own actions. The story concludes with the cub's death. As if making an effort to redeem his foolishness in attempting to domesticate the cub, the narrator performs a ritualistic burial in the traditional Mongolian style. In his imagination, the narrator watches the cub "[ride] the clouds and mist, travelling on snow and wind, soaring happily toward Tengger, to the star Sirius, to the free universe in space, to the place where all the souls of Mongolian wolves that died in battles over the millennia congregated" (*WT* 503).

Coda

Just as it is nostalgic, focusing on a lost past, *Wolf Totem* is an allegory of our potential future. In contrast with Han Chinese – and the novel underscores the Han's cruelty toward animals, conservatism and shortsightedness, and lack of courage and bravery, as figured in the image of sheep – Mongols are presented as being like wolves, as warriors who could not survive in the modern world. Only sheepish people seem able to thrive on modernization and urbanization. The novel originated, Jiang Rong explains, from his "love for the grassland." He saw with his own eyes the destruction of the fecund and beautiful grassland and of what it has represented:

> I'm so distressed to see such radical change. Over the past several decades since I left the grassland, I have seen more destruction and sensed the coming of even greater disasters. This is precisely why I feel that I'm emotionally closer to the beautiful grassland in my memory and why I have developed an even greater emotional attachment to it.[17]

Wolf Totem is a memoir of the author's emotions about the grassland and its wolves.
   The novel is probably the first sustained modern effort since Lu Xun to develop an informed critique of China's civilization, national character, and history, as well as the Han mode of being. It requires moral courage to take such a stand on the self with its historical baggage when Chinese nationalism is on the rise. In the epilogue, the author articulates his wish for the establishment of the wolf as the symbol of the nation. But how would this be possible? Earlier in the book, the narrator commented on the civilizational telos of the Han race in the following terms:

We're a farming race, and a fear and hatred of wolves is in our bones. How could we venerate a wolf totem? We Han worship the Dragon King, the one in charge of our agrarian lifeline – our dragon totem, the one we pay homage to, the one to whom we meekly submit. How can you expect people like that to learn from wolves, to protect them, to worship and yet kill them, like the Mongols?

(WT 33–34)

The author knows, of course, that there is no hope for the wolves to return to the grassland, and no possibility to revive the legacy of the Mongolian wolves – their glory and their heroism. *Wolf Totem* is a book of radical pessimism. "Now that the wolves are gone, the dogs will disappear, and when they are gone, there'll be no more battles. Without battles, only sloth and inertia remain" (*WT* 512). Chen Zhen confesses emotionally, "I truly miss Erlang," the brave giant dog who had faithfully fought alongside him.[18] By killing wolves and dogs, Han Chinese have denied themselves a future that is worth living.

Notes

1. Critical responses to *Wolf Totem* include Li Xiaojiang 李小江, "Lun *Lang tuteng* de hexin yuyi: guominxing, minzuxing yu minzuzhuyi wenti" 論"狼圖騰"的核心寓意 – 國民性、民族性與民族主義問題 (*Wolf Totem's* Allegorical Meanings: National Character, Ethnicity and Nationalism), *Wenyi yanjiu* 文藝研究 4 (2009); Wu Xiuming 吳秀明and Chen Lijun 陳力君, "Cong *Lang tuteng* kan dangdai shengtai wenxue de fazhan" 從《狼圖騰》看當代生態文學的發展 (*Wolf Totem* and the Development of Contemporary Environmental Literature), *Wenyi yanjiu* 4 (2009); Zhou Yan 周晏, "Shengtai wenxue shiyu xia *Lang tuteng* de xianshi yiyi" 生態文學視閾下《狼圖騰》的現實意義 (The Meaning of *Wolf Totem* from the Perspective of Environmental Literature), *Wenyi zhengming* 文藝爭鳴 (November 2013); Chen Guo'en 陳國恩, "*Lang tuteng* yu 'zhongguo' xingxiang wenti" 《狼圖騰》與"中國"形象問題 (*Wolf Totem* and the Image of "China"), *Tianjin shehuikexue* 天津社會科學 2 (2012); Song Ru 宋茹, "Cong *Menggu mishi* kan caoyuan minzu de lang tuteng yu yingxiong chongbai" 從《蒙古祕史》看草原民族的狼圖騰與英雄崇拜 (Wolf totem and Hero Worship in *The Secret History of the Mongols*), *Shanxi Shifandaxue xuebao* 山西師範大學學報 (September 2014); Jiang Rong (姜戎), "Peitong A Nuo zhuixun lang tuteng wenhua" 陪同阿諾追尋狼圖騰文化 (In Search of the Culture of Wolf Totem with Jean-Jacques Annaud), *Xibu Menggu luntan* 西部蒙古論壇 3 (2010).

2. See Silvia Sebastiani, "Nations, Nationalism and National Characters," in *The Routledge Companion to Eighteenth-Century Philosophy*, ed. Aaron Garrett (London: Routledge, 2014), 593–617.

3. For example, Carolus Linnaeus, in *Systema natura*, divides *Homo sapiens* into four main varieties – Americans, Europeans, Asiatics, and Africans – each of which has a distinctive physiognomy and character: the American appears choleric and governed by customs, the sanguine European is ruled by laws, the melancholic Asiatic by opinions, and the phlegmatic African by caprice. See Linnaeus, *Systema naturae*, trans. A. Drace-Francis, 10th ed., 2 vols. (Stockholm, 1758), 1: 22–23. In Britain, David Hume was one of the earliest to reflect on the causes of the formation of national character. In "Of National Characters," he discusses two types of causes: moral and physical. The physical causes include "those qualities of the air and climate which are supposed to work insensibly on the temper, by altering the tone and habit of the body and giving a particular

complexion." David Hume, "Of National Characters," in *Essays: Moral, Political, and Literary* (Indianapolis: Liberty Fund, 1985), 198.

4 See George Eliot, *The Mill on the Floss*, ed. A. S. Byatt (London: Penguin, 1985), 514.

5 Jiang Rong, *Wolf Totem*, trans. Howard Goldblatt (New York: Penguin, 2008), 174 (translation revised). Hereafter quotes from this text will be cited parenthetically.

6 Jiang Rong, *Lang tuteng* (Wolf Totem) (Wuhan: Changjiang wenyi chubanshe, 2004), 195.

7 See Lu Xun, "Tengye xiansheng" 藤野先生 (Mr. Fujino), in *Lu Xun quanji* 魯迅全集 (Complete Works of Lu Xun) (Beijing: Renmin wenxue chubanshe, 1992), 2: 302–309.

8 René Grousset, *The Empire of the Steppes: A History of Central Asia*, trans. Naomi Walford (New York: Barnes & Noble, 1970), 287–288.

9 Urgunge Onon, *The Secret History of the Mongols: The Life and Times of Chinggis Khan* (Surrey: Curzon, 2001), 39.

10 Wolfgang Kubin, "*Lang tuteng* rang women xiangqi Xitele shidai" 《狼圖騰》讓我們想起希特勒時代 (*Wolf Totem* Reminds One of the Hitler Era), *International Sinological Studies*, www.sinologystudy.com/news.Asp?id=282&fenlei=7 (accessed February 16, 2016).

11 Jiang Rong, "Huan 'langxing' yige gongdao: Jiang Rong fangtan" 還"狼性"一個公道 – 姜戎訪談 (Rehabilitate the Wolf: An Interview with Jiang Rong), *Nanfang zhoumo* 南方週末(Southern Weekend), May 1, 2008.

12 In an attempt to deconstruct the human-centered view that man is radically opposed to animals, Jacques Derrida urges the transcendence of "the confines of man" and "the crossing of borders" between man and animal: "Crossing borders or the ends of man I come or surrender to the animal – to the animal in itself, to the animal in me and the animal at unease with itself, to the man about which Nietzsche said . . . something to the effect that it was an as yet undetermined animal, an animal lacking in itself." Jacques Derrida, "The Animal That Therefore I Am," *Critical Inquiry* 28, no. 2 (Winter 2002): 372.

13 Immanuel Kant, *Lectures on Ethics*, ed. Peter Heath and J. B. Schneewind, trans. Peter Heath (Cambridge: Cambridge University Press, 1997), 212.

14 Jeremy Bentham, *An Introduction to the Principles of Morals and Legislation* (London: Printed for W. Pickering, 1823), 2: 235–236n.

15 Michel Foucault, *The Order of Things* (London: Routledge, 1989), 139.

16 Giorgio Agamben, *Homo Sacer: Sovereign Power and Bare Life*, trans. Daniel Heller-Roazen (Stanford: Stanford University Press, 1998), 9.

17 Jiang Rong, "Rehabilitating the Wolf, an Interview with Jiang Rong," *Nanfang zhoumo* (Southern weekend), May 1, 2008.

18 Jiang Rong, *Lang tuteng*, 358.

Works cited

Agamben, Giorgio. *Homo Sacer: Sovereign Power and Bare Life.* Trans. Daniel Heller-Roazen. Stanford: Stanford University Press, 1998.

Bentham, Jeremy. *An Introduction to the Principles of Morals and Legislation.* London: Printed for W. Pickering, 1823.

Derrida, Jacques. "The Animal That Therefore I Am." *Critical Inquiry* 28, no. 2 (Winter 2002): 369–418.

Eliot, George. *The Mill on the Floss.* Ed. A. S. Byatt. London: Penguin, 1985.

Foucault, Michel. *The Order of Things.* London: Routledge, 1989.

Grousset, René. *The Empire of the Steppes: A History of Central Asia.* Trans. Naomi Walford. New York: Barnes & Noble, 1970.

Hume, David. "Of National Characters." In *Essays: Moral, Political, and Literary.* Indianapolis: Liberty Fund, 1985.

Jiang Rong. "Huan 'langxing' yige gongdao: Jiang Rong fangtan." 還"狼性"一個公道 – 姜戎訪談 (Rehabilitate the Wolf: An Interview with Jiang Rong). *Nanfang zhoumo* 南方周末 (Southern Weekend), May 1, 2008.

———. *Lang tuteng* 狼圖騰 (Wolf Totem). Wuhan: Changjiang wenyi chubanshe, 2004.

———. *Wolf Totem*. Trans. Howard Goldblatt. New York: Penguin, 2008.

Kant, Immanuel. *Lectures on Ethics*. Ed. Peter Heath and J. B. Schneewind, Trans. Peter Heath. Cambridge: Cambridge University Press, 1997.

Kubin, Wolfgang. *Lang Tuteng* rang women xiangqi Xitele shidai《狼圖騰》讓我們想起希特勒時代 (*Wolf Totem* Reminds Us of the Hitler Era). *International Sinological Studies*. www.sinologystudy.com/news.Asp?id=282&fenlei=7. Accessed February 16, 2016.

Linnaeus, Carolus. *Systema naturae*. Trans. A. Drace-Francis, 10th ed., 2 Vols. Stockholm, 1758.

Lu Xun. "Tengye xiansheng" 藤野先生 (Mr. Fujino). In Volume 2 of *Lu Xun quanji* 魯迅全集 (Complete Works of Lu Xun). Beijing: Renmin wenxue chubanshe, 1992.

Onon, Urgunge. *The Secret History of the Mongols: The Life and Times of Chinggis Khan*. Surrey: Curzon, 2001.

Sebastiani, Silvia. "Nations, Nationalism and National Characters." In *The Routledge Companion to Eighteenth-Century Philosophy*, edited by Aaron Garrett. London: Routledge, 2014.

6

WRITING THE MOTHERLAND(S) ON THEIR BORDERS

Kim Hak-ch'ŏl and his cultural criticism of Maoist China

Miya Qiong Xie

In *Modernity with a Cold War Face: Reimagining the Nation in Chinese Literature across the 1949 Divide*, Xiaojue Wang cites contemporary Chinese writer Ye Zhaoyan's 葉兆言 lament over the absence of intellectual heroes or martyrs under the totalitarian regime in socialist China. According to Wang, Ye and his fellow authors admire the Russian poets and writers who openly defied Stalinist totalitarianism, including Boris Pasternak and Alexander Solzhenitsyn. In China, by contrast, all they find is stifling silence.[1] This chapter is about a striking exception. Positioned outside the Chinese-speaking community but within the territory of the People's Republic of China, the ethnic Korean writer Kim Hak-ch'ŏl wrote an intriguing novel in Korean titled *The Myth of the Twentieth Century* (*20-segi ŭi sinhwa*) in the mid-1960s, criticizing the Anti-Rightist Campaign, the Great Leap Forward, the People's Commune, and Mao Zedong's cult of personality. Kim began the work in 1964, completed it in 1965, and then started to translate it into Japanese himself – probably in the hope of publishing both the Korean and the Japanese versions outside of mainland China. When he was only halfway through, however, the Cultural Revolution started, and the Red Guards broke into his home and happened upon the manuscript. What followed was a seven-year imprisonment for the author and a thirty-year publication delay for the novel. The Korean version of the work was published in 1996 in Seoul, and the Japanese translation remains incomplete to this day.[2]

Rather than treating Kim as a "Chinese Solzhenitsyn" – an intellectual hero and martyr – my chapter approaches his work as an example of borderland writing. I investigate how socialist China was imagined and criticized from the periphery and how the borderland conditions both enabled and circumscribed Kim's writing. The French thinker Edgar Morin conceptualizes the frontier as a liminal space that is at once closed and open, both forbidding and authorizing, and argues that "we need . . . to go beyond the simple idea of closing which excludes opening, beyond the simple idea of opening which excludes closing."[3] This observation applies to geographical borderlands as well, for borderlands are where boundaries form and dissolve simultaneously and where identities and allegiances are constantly shifting. In the case of Kim's novel, I argue that the borderland conditions – manifested as much in Kim's personal experience as in that of the broader ethnic Korean community – provided him with the intellectual resources to construct his subversive political critique. His comparative perspective on contemporary Soviet, Chinese, and North Korean society allowed him to observe China as both an insider and an outsider. It lent support to his intrasocialist dissent against Maoist totalitarianism from a transnational point of view. His trilingual skills in Korean, Chinese, and Japanese made it possible for him to envision spreading his works about China outside the iron curtain. However, it was precisely the same set of conditions that prevented him from engaging with the totality of each political entity and led him, paradoxically, to embrace an abstracted, idealized, essentialized, and thus unrealistic illusion of socialist China. He then used this illusion as the yardstick to gauge the complex Chinese reality.

Postcolonial scholars often celebrate ethnic minority borderlands as sites of literary diversity and political resistance. Within the field of China studies, Shumei Shih's notion of Sinophone literature highlights the frontier ethnic regions of mainland China as the places where minority writers write to challenge the "internal colonialism" emanating from the center.[4] In the global context, the Chicana writer Gloria Anzaldúa, in *Borderlands/La Frontera: The New Mestiza*, conceptualizes the Chicano/a borderland between the United States and Mexico as "*una herida abierta* [an open wound] where the Third World grates against the First and bleeds."[5] In particular, Anzaldúa proposes a border-crossing consciousness that allows her to move freely across different types of geographical and imaginary boundaries, including the US-Mexico border, which was firmly but rather arbitrarily drawn by the United States, and those of sex, language, and race. Apparently, she conceived this border-crossing consciousness as a political critique of and solution to social demarcation. At first glance, Kim's novel seems a perfect case of cultural and political resistance to the hegemony of the center from the margins and the marginalized, a show of the workings of border-crossing consciousness. And yet, just as borders are challenged and crossed in his writing, they are also re-enforced and reproduced; the territories demarcated by various borders are opened and traversed, but are in the meantime stratified and essentialized, all within the same process of borderland writing. This critical stance allows us to fully appreciate the insights and pitfalls of Kim's extraordinary text, the image of China it re-creates, and the broader challenges that others writing from the borderlands may also have faced.

The multinational confluence

In the early 1950s, when Chinese Communist Party (CCP) cadres were preparing for the establishment of the Korean Autonomous District in the northeast of the new China, they were confronted with what the ethnic Koreans called "the theory of multiple motherlands" (Kor. *tajogungnon*; Chin. *duozuguolun*). Simply put, ethnic Koreans wondered whether they could claim the Soviet Union as their proletarian motherland (Kor. *musankyegŭp ŭi choguk*; Chin. *wuchanjieji de zuguo*), North Korea as their ethnic motherland (Kor. *minjok ŭi choguk*; Chin. *minzu de zuguo*), and China as their realistic motherland (Kor. *hyŏnsil ŭi choguk*; Chin. *xianshi de zuguo*). Although the theory was never sanctioned by the Chinese Communist Party, it found a sympathetic ear among some ethnic Koreans throughout the 1950s and illustrated the structure of multinational identification in the ethnic Korean community.[6] Kim never endorsed this theory himself, but we can nevertheless use it to help explore the different layers of the transnational perspective Kim entertained in the novel *The Myth of the Twentieth Century*.

The Chinese Korean community developed along the border between China and the Korean Peninsula, in a region that took on the name "In-Between Island" (Kor. *Kando*; Chin. *Jiandao*) in the late nineteenth century. In the early 1930s, part of the region became one of the most important Communist bases in northeast China, known then as Manchuria. Koreans in the base areas operated under the leadership of the Chinese Communist Party, but also received heavy Soviet influence. The much larger Korean population outside the Communist base areas had to bear the blunt force of Japanese colonial rule under the Manchukuo regime (1932–1945). Between the end of World War II in 1945 and the establishment of the Korean Autonomous District in 1953,[7] Chinese Koreans had a certain degree of freedom to choose between returning to South or North Korea or staying in the Chinese northeast. The majority of those who chose to stay in China acquired Chinese nationality but were allowed to keep Korean as their primary language and continue their Korean lifestyle within the district.[8]

Although Kim Hak-ch'ŏl did not share in the struggles of the Korean community in northeast China until he moved into the region in 1952, his personal experience exhibits a similar structure of multinational confluence. Born in 1916 in Korea, Kim received a Japanese colonial education and was involved in the resistance movement during his school years. In 1935, he moved to China to join other Korean exiles in fighting for the independence of their nation outside its colonized territory. In China, he took part in several anarchist assassinations and was then sent to study at the Republic of China Military Academy, the successor of Sun Yat-sen's Whampoa Academy. After the outbreak of the Sino-Japanese War (1937–1945), Kim joined the Korean Volunteer Unit (Kor. *Chosŏn Ŭiyongdae*; Chin. *Chaoxian yiyongdui*) of the Chinese army, believing that the liberation of Korea could be realized only after China had defeated Japan. In the process, he gradually metamorphosed from a Korean nationalist to a communist and joined the Chinese Communist Party in 1940. In 1942, he was captured by the Japanese and sent to prison in Japan, where he lost a leg due to injury.[9]

After his release in 1945, Kim settled in South Korea, North Korea, and subsequently Beijing, but ultimately none of these environments proved safe and productive for him. As a communist, he had little chance of surviving the increasingly repressive anticommunist campaigns in South Korea, but North Korea proved just as inhospitable when the Korean War (1950–1953) broke out and a domestic political purge followed. In Beijing, Kim enjoyed the patronage of Ding Ling and managed to publish a few pieces in Chinese, but he felt like a "potted plant" without his Korean compatriots.[10] Consequently, soon after he learned about and visited the Korean Autonomous District, newly created in the former "in-between island" area in 1952, he decided to move there. After that, he lived, wrote, and published in the district, later renamed the prefecture, although he maintained North Korean citizenship until 1983.

In 1964, Kim started to write the novel *The Myth of the Twentieth Century.* The novel is divided into two parts: Part I focuses on the protagonists Im Il-pyong, a former literary journal editor; Shim cho-kwang, former chair of the Writers Association of the Korean Autonomous Prefecture; and their friends' experiences in an Anti-Rightist labor camp; Part II depicts their life after being released from the camp. The narrator attributes most of the social and political disorder in contemporary Chinese society to the personality cult of Mao Zedong. The targets of his criticism range from the lofty to the mundane. He blasts the deprivation of the freedom of speech among writers and intellectuals, but also jokes about the poorly manufactured toothbrushes whose bristles "fall out elegantly" whenever they are used (100). Moreover, the novel explicitly labels the Maoist party-state a Nazi regime, and it periodically draws parallels between Maoist China and both Nazi Germany and Imperial Japan. This starts with the novel's title, which mirrors the title of Alfred Rosenberg's foundational book of German Nazism.

Critiquing Maoist socialism, Kim drew his ideological inspiration from the Soviet Union. He took seriously Khrushchev's denunciation of Stalinism in his speech titled "On the Cult of Personality and Its Consequences" at the Twentieth Party Congress (1956), referencing the event multiple times in the novel. This crucial event leads to the protagonist Shim's political awakening – albeit a belated one, since it takes Shim a long time to associate the cult of personality with Mao and Maoist China. Kim's criticism of Mao's domestic and international policies was also in tune with Khrushchev's relatively moderate socialist position as outlined in his speech and elsewhere. This includes the protagonists' lament over the economic catastrophe that occurred during the Great Leap Forward, regret about Mao's prioritization of the nuclear arms race over people's livelihood, mockery of the unstable intrasocialist anti-Soviet bloc consisting of China, North Korea, and Albania, and so on. Contemporary Soviet dissident literature was another source for ideological emulation. For instance, after a description of a hard day at the labor camp, the narrator cites the protagonist of Solzhenitsyn's *One Day in the Life of Ivan Denisovich* when he remarks that "were Ivan Denisovich here for a week, he would feel homesick for his Siberian camp" (104). Published in 1962 with Khrushchev's permission, Solzhenitsyn's novella depicts the harsh conditions in a Soviet socialist labor camp and was one of the earliest pieces of dissident literature in the Soviet Union. Although Kim may not have read the full novella by 1965,[11] he clearly knew Solzhenitsyn's writing and situated his own work in the same literary lineage.

What Kim's Koreanness offers him, I argue, is a critical stance toward China's Han chauvinism and a perspective that compares Maoist China and contemporary North Korea. Many of his accusations concerning the deprivation of freedom of speech have to do with censorship of Korean publications that highlight the community's Korean origin in the prefecture. For example, a character who writes a poem about missing his old hometown across the Tumen River is considered by the authorities to be "announcing that the People's Republic of China is not his motherland" (33). Another character complains that "it's not fun that there's no bar here selling raw rice wine," and is immediately labeled a "bourgeois rightist" on the grounds that he "demonizes socialist China as being inferior to the living hell of South Korea" (33). Similarly, the protagonist, Im, is discontented because not a single Korean literary work has been allowed to appear in the prefecture's Korean textbooks; instead the texts are all Korean translations of Chinese literary works (285). Being ethnically Korean, Kim strongly identifies with a Korean language and culture that are not necessarily tied to any political regime, and this makes him sensitive to Party policies – often sanctioned by the authorities in Beijing – that erase the community's Korean roots and replace them with a Chinese identity with chauvinistic Han undertones.

Moreover, Kim's connection to North Korea provided him with a contemporary reference point for his China critique. In his eyes, China under Mao mirrored North Korea under Kim Il-sung, in that both endured a cult of personality, social poverty, and endless political purges. Most important, Kim's writing on the situation in China was likely inspired by the North Koreans' political struggle against Kim Il-sung in 1956, commonly known as the August Incident (P'arwŏl sakŏn). This began with Yi Sang-cho, the North Korean ambassador to the Soviet Union, dispatching a secret letter to Soviet leaders accusing Kim Il-sung of encouraging a cult of personality and recommending his impeachment, and it ended with Kim Il-sung executing most of the dissidents, including Kim Hak-ch'ŏl's own sister-in-law. Yi Sang-cho lived in the Soviet Union under asylum until 1989.[12] In Kim's novel, a key motif that runs through Part I involves a set of "unsent letters" that the protagonist Shim writes to "his friend currently seeking refuge in the Soviet Union" (18). Often at the close of an episode the narrator quotes passages from these letters as a commentary on the preceding events, thereby offering a critique of various aspects of contemporary Chinese society. In reality, Kim knew Yi Sang-cho personally, and in 1953 when Kim considered returning to North Korea from China after the Korean War, it was Yi Sang-cho who persuaded him to give up the idea.[13] I read this motif of the unsent letters as an allusion to, a repercussion of, and a tribute to the August Incident in North Korea, just as the reference to a "friend currently seeking refuge in the Soviet Union" is reminiscent of Yi Sang-cho's subsequent exile.

If the Soviet presence in the novel is ideological and the Korean connection is historical, then the Chinese background tends to be realistic, or even pragmatic.

In the theory of multiple motherlands, ethnic Koreans call China the "realistic motherland" (Kor. *hyŏnsil ŭi choguk*; Chin. *xianshi de zuguo*). The Korean word *hyŏnsil*, like the Chinese word *xianshi* 現實, can be translated as both "realistic" and "pragmatic." In Kim's novel, this realistic motherland represents an environment where basic human needs such as those for food, home, and safety can be met, and where writers and intellectuals like Kim himself can write and publish freely and safely as long as they do not challenge the laws of socialist China. I will elaborate on his imagination of China as a realistic motherland in the following section to investigate its literary and ideological implications.

As should now be clear, the conditions of the borderland – on the periphery of the Chinese nation yet at the top of a multinational cultural network – enabled the author's transnational interrogation of the social malaise in Maoist China. This interrogation consists of not a simple, random juxtaposition of different national perspectives but rather a structure of stratified multinational identification. Each national perspective has its own significance within a certain stratum of the author's epistemological complex, pointing to a different kind of political engagement and sentimental attachment. This pattern captures the lived conditions of the borderland inhabitants more generally, for no matter how multifarious and precarious their identifications are, each represents to them a unique institutional history, emotional investment, and set of temporal and spatial associations. While the notion of fluidity is commonly applied to intellectuals from the borderland regions, it may be more difficult than we think for them to fully blend into and freely move between the different layers of affiliation and allegiance that are the sediment of decades and generations of individual and collective experience.

In addition to a multinational identification, the borderland conditions also include the author's non-Chinese linguistic skills, which made the novel possible in the first place. Writing secretly in Korean and then translating his work into Japanese, Kim confessed that he worked under the fear that he would be executed as soon as the work was published.[14] According to Kim's son, Kim had considered having the two versions of the novel published in the Korean Peninsula or in Japan.[15] By comparison, Chinese-speaking intellectuals and writers in the core regions of China had fewer options. They were not unfamiliar with anti-Stalinist trends in the socialist bloc,[16] but it was much harder to find an alternative. The prospect of redemption in an external national/political space was dim and, for many, a pure fantasy.

China as the realistic motherland

A closer examination of Kim's imagination of China as a realistic motherland will demonstrate its literary and ideological implications. Central to this configuration of socialist China, I argue, is Kim's belief in the possibility of a reciprocal relationship between the nation and the people. For him, while the people are responsible for working and fighting for the nation, the nation is most valuable when it offers them a livable environment. This view was certainly not Kim's own invention, but it is closely related to his transnational outlook and ethnic background. First, the reason the realistic dimension of China is foregrounded and other dimensions are downplayed is that these other dimensions are displaced onto other polities in Kim's transnational intellectual world. Moreover, Kim's identity as a member of China's ethnic Korean community – a community with an immigrant history and a language and culture distinct from those of the Han Chinese – allows him to treat Han-dominated China as a land of settlement instead of a land of origin, and as part of an exchange economy instead of an overarching totality.

In the novel, the main Han Chinese character, nicknamed "Dope Peng" for his below-average intelligence, is characterized as a pathetic creature perpetually wracked by hunger. The only other Han Chinese character in the work, Wang, is an intellectual who has been assimilated into the Korean community and speaks perfect Korean. Peng, in contrast, barely speaks any. Aside from Peng and Wang, all of the other main characters are ethnic Korean intellectuals. Dope Peng ended up in the labor camp because he felt his living conditions had not improved much after the liberation and complained at a meeting: "I was starving before liberation, and am still starving now. So, to be honest, I don't know how the socialist society that everyone praises is actually good." He believed that once the Party cadres knew his problems, they would help solve them, but instead they simply labeled him an antirevolutionary and threw him into the labor camp. The scarcity of food there only makes his poor physical condition worse:

> As the Communist Farm [the formal name of the labor camp] has literally turned into a living hell of hunger after the Great Leap Forward, he [Dope Peng] has become even weaker and more aged. Maybe because wrinkles all go to his face, within months his dry gourd-like face has been completely covered by small lines. He said several of his teeth had been loose, and within months more than ten upper and lower teeth had fallen out. His hair has turned half-white and his eyes are always watery. Moreover, his hearing has gone bad and he can't make out what other people are saying. Even his back is bent. Now this thirty-five- or thirty-six-year-old man has become like an old man over sixty. He can't stay calm during meals and instead always ducks his head and looks around. He peeks anxiously at other people's bowls and doesn't put down his own empty bowl even after he has finished. Instead, he holds on to it for a while, examining the table to see if someone happens to have spilled something. Once he finds even a grain of sorghum rice, he immediately reaches out his hand, seizes it, and puts it in his mouth. He acts at lightning speed for fear there might be competitors.
>
> *(155–156)*

One day in the labor camp, the administrator Park accidentally spills Peng's portion of porridge. Because the administrator's father has been helping Peng tremendously all his life, Peng has been looking after Park ever since he was a child. The moment Peng loses his food, however, he cannot help but grab Park's arm and demand to know what he plans to do about it. Park dismisses Peng's question and instead simply demands, in Chinese, that Peng release his arm. Following the episode, the narrator notes that

> what grabbed Park's arm was not Peng himself but his blind appetite that broke out by instinct. If he had had a clear head, he would not have grabbed Park's arm, nor would he have asked Park to give him another bowl of porridge.
>
> *(156)*

Fortunately, Im witnesses the whole scene and leaves a portion of his own food for the desperate Peng.

This image of Peng functions as both a synecdoche and a metaphor of Maoist China as a failed realistic motherland. Peng is agonized by the fanatical socialist revolutions that have worsened rather than improved his living conditions. Extreme hunger leaves him desperate and crazed and deprives him of basic human affection and morality. He is not an intellectual like the other characters in the work, so his misfortune involves no political ideals or intellectual activities. Furthermore, given that he is Han Chinese, his suffering is unrelated to the interethnic relationship between the Han and the Koreans that proves problematic for other characters. Peng simply but powerfully represents the most ordinary but also most typical man in China who needs to be fed before fulfilling any political responsibilities. He emblematizes what Kim perceives to be the biggest failure of socialist China, which is that it starves its people, regardless of their ethnicity, age, or other factors. For Kim, this failure nullifies both the ideological superiority and the ethnic bond that the nation claims to possess and serves as the point of departure of his China criticism in the novel.

Although Kim's expectations for the nation are not ethnically specific but rather apply to all Chinese citizens, I argue that what makes him approach socialist China as first and foremost a realistic motherland has to do with his own ethnic background. That is to say, his conceptual schema is deeply connected to an immigrant mentality that did not necessarily apply to his own life but was common among ethnic Koreans. These ethnic Koreans were not born Chinese, but rather voluntarily stayed in China amid the postwar chaos. For them, China became their motherland of choice, and like any other choice, theirs involved pragmatic calculations and expectations of reward. Accordingly, central to Kim's configuration of China as a realistic motherland is his belief in a relationship of exchange and reciprocity between the country and the people. This view of the nation-state, as well as its clashes with the view sanctioned by the propaganda organ of the government, is illustrated in a story embedded within the novel.

In Part I, the narrator quotes in full a short story by an ethnic Korean titled "A Place to Take Root" (*Ppuri pagŭn t'ŏ*). The main body of the work adopts an epistolary form, written in the voice of a young man proudly introducing the immigration history of his family and their current village home to his friend. This story was in fact originally published by the author himself as the opening work in the first literary collection from the district, the 1953 collection *A Place to Take Root*,[17] and was subsequently included in the district's middle school textbook.[18] In the novel too, the narrator recalls that the short story was so popular that it was included in the textbook in local schools. Both in real life and in the novel, the work was picked up by the authorities as "poisonous grass" that represented rightist values during the Anti-Rightist Campaign. In the novel, after its denunciation, "all schools received notifications and were obliged to tear the pages containing the story out of their textbooks" (89). The inclusion of the story in Kim's later novel can be seen as both the author's and the narrator's protest of its undeserved removal from the textbooks, and their reaffirmation of the values represented in the short story.

The title of the story, "A Place to Take Root," suggests an immigrant view of hometown. For the characters, their hometown is not where they or their ancestors were born but the soil in which they may put down new roots. This title metaphorically depicts an encounter between the people and the land, emphasizing the process through which people who are initially outsiders may establish a new life in a new land. The story concludes with the narrator's observation that "I don't know very well, but I think socialism and communism are something that will be realized naturally when each person loves and respects the place where he puts down roots, and works and struggles for its infinite prosperity" (97). The identification of the ideological ideal – the realization of socialism and communism – with local material prosperity prioritizes the realistic dimension of the nation. In this context, it is the narrator's immigrant mentality that necessarily leads to his awakening. In the literary collection published in 1953 with the same Korean title, however, the title is translated into Chinese as "Love My Hometown" (*re'ai wode jiaxiang*).[19] In this translation, the indication of an immigrant history is removed and replaced with a neutral concept of hometown.

Throughout the story, the author also implies an economy of exchange between the nation and the people. The epistolary part of the story reviews how the narrator's grandfather moved from Korea to this land some thirty-seven years before, and how the three generations of the family have worked hard and are finally able to live a happy life in the new China. In the version Kim first finished, the narrator comments, "the sight of the grandfather – already in his seventies – taking his grandson to the park is very heartwarming." However, when Kim submitted the story for publication, the reviewer from the propaganda organ objected,

> How can you let this grandfather play around and not work, just because he is in his seventies? . . . You should say "the sight of the grandfather – already in his seventies – working in the rice paddies every day is very heartwarming."[20]

Kim followed this suggestion, but not without discontentment, as can be seen from the final published version of the passage:

Last winter, as soon as I returned from the front, I wanted to separate my grandfather from work, Grandfather's dearest company that has shared his joys, griefs, sorrows, and pleasures for half a century. This is because I believe that for old people in their seventies, in this time when we have become the owners of the country, their proper life is not to work but to always wear new clothes and visit restaurants, parks, or theaters with their grandsons and granddaughters. Wouldn't you think the same? But Grandfather is still working every day now.

(96)

The narrator evidently is not convinced that the grandfather should continue to work and instead believes that the country, owned by the working people, should provide old people with the necessary conditions for them to fully enjoy their life of leisure – which is what they deserve after half a century of hard work. While the narrator insists that the country owes a reward to the people who have worked hard for it, the reviewer demands that the people be represented in literature not as the country's mere beneficiaries but rather as its creators and the symbolic embodiment of its essence.

Upon closer examination, we find that some aspects of the unique history of the ethnic Korean community underlie Kim's conception of the economy of exchange. In the opening sentence of the story, the protagonist explains why he writes the letter: "Several days ago, I received a letter from the comrade who was demobilized from the Korean front and returned to my hometown with me on the same day." In the original Korean version, the sentence, as well as the entire story, opens with the phrase "from the Korean front." This phrase highlights the unique contribution that the ethnic Korean community made to the newly established People's Republic of China: serving as a major force in the Chinese Volunteer Army during the Korean War and sacrificing for China, the new motherland. Furthermore, as the above quote illustrates, the moment that the narrator wants his grandfather to stop working and enjoy life happens when the narrator has just returned from the front. In other words, behind the narrator's judgment that the grandfather now deserves a reward from the country is the implication that the narrator has just fought for his country. I therefore argue that for Kim, the relation of exchange exists not merely between the grandfather and the nation, but more importantly, between the entire ethnic Korean community and the nation.

The immigrant background of the community also makes the idea of exchange and reward tangible to its people, including Kim. When recalling the difficulties the protagonist's family encountered after immigrating to China, the story's narrator recalls that his grandfather, having no money to buy an ox, pulled the soil rake himself, as a result of which he was given the nickname "ox without a tail" (94). In the novel, however, the fictional author of the story is accused by the district's leadership of literature and art of having "scorned the modest peasant as an ox without a tail," and so the author himself is consequently nicknamed by other camp members "an ox without a tail" (89). The short story does not glorify the new immigrants' struggle for survival in the unclaimed land but rather recognizes that such struggle can be abject and demeaning, to the point of transforming humans into animals. However, it all seems worth it now that they are able to live a happy life in their new country. This suggests that for an immigrant community, the idea of exchange and justification between working like an animal and living like a human is inherent in its history. In this sense, we may consider the notion of a realistic motherland to be an upgraded version of the immigrants' economy of exchange, aspiring to improved living conditions in the future as a reward for all that they have suffered in the past. The attackers, in contrast, would not tolerate an animalized image of the peasant conditioned by future compensation. Instead, they consider the peasants to be the nominal ruling class and therefore the sacred symbol of the nation, and they under no circumstances allow their glory to be impaired.

Outside the embedded short story, Kim's criticism of China – the realistic motherland – based on this economy of exchange is crystallized in his description of a children's word game involving a (mis)translation of Mao Zedong's name. One day, from the window of his home, Im sees a young woman beating her child while mimicking what the child has done and said to merit the beating to a neighborhood old woman:

> Her first move was to stretch out her neck, tap her nape with her fingers, and utter the word, "*Mok* [meaning "neck")."
> She then raised her chin, lifted it with her fingers, and said, "*Taek* ["chin"]."
> Finally, she bent her back, pushed out her butt, and hit it. "*Dong* [shit]!"
>
> (190)

When the old woman asks what this means, one of the children answers, "This is how we say Mo-T'aek-tong [the Korean pronunciation of Mao Zedong]!"

Echoing the concept of the realistic motherland and the immigrant mentality, a relation of exchange is implied in this game in which the secret political icon of the nation, Mao's name, is translated into three biological features of the human body, starting where one eats and ending with what one excretes. Kim invokes this pun to smash the idol, as if announcing, through the children's innocent voices, that there is no such thing as the cult of personality. Instead, there are only real people whose real life consists of food and shit. The implication is that all political capital must be translated into productive and reproductive material before it can acquire meaning for the people. Moreover, with an exclamation mark following the word "shit," the description arouses a sense of catharsis and revenge, as if what has been ingested and then expelled is precisely the political icon of Mao himself, conscripted to fill the people's stomachs that are empty because of him, then consumed and discharged by his own people. In the context of the many examples of supply shortage and fatal poverty that Kim enumerates in his novel, this episode is one of the rare moments in which the power relationship between the national elites and the common people is inverted.

Furthermore, in the description of this game, as in earlier examples, the embedded criticism is possible thanks to Kim's ethnic background and perspective. The ingenious wordplay is enabled by the linguistic difference between Chinese and Korean, when the three awe-inspiring Chinese characters are mistranslated into Korean in a sarcastic, playful, and blasphemous way. In other words, the linguistic difference creates a space of interethnic mediation from which a critical distance and a language of criticism can be generated. More broadly, Kim's general criticism of China as a realistic motherland that develops throughout the book is enabled within a similar space of interethnic mediation based on cultural translation. For example, when he depicts all the ridiculous scenes of daily life during supposedly serious political movements, such as the toothbrushes whose bristles fall out that were manufactured during the Great Leap Forward, he is doing exactly what the children were doing in their game: translating, reductively but subversively, sacred political symbols into something material, mundane, inferior, but nevertheless tangible. In this sense, the pun in the game may be read as a linguistic metaphor for Kim's overall critique of China: he translated China as a totality into China as a realistic motherland while embedding his criticism in the process of an interethnic cultural translation.

To some extent, Kim's imagination of China as first and foremost a realistic motherland and his stratified multinational identification synergistically empower his criticism. This criticism strips off the nation's glorious veil sustained by the claim of a transcendental or indisputable ideological superiority and a long and harmonious ethnic history, thereby revealing the barren conditions within which contemporary Chinese people actually live. His ethnic background, furthermore, conditions his view of China and provides critical distance. In reality, it was a difficult task for any writer to represent Maoist China in a way that deviated from the totality that identified the nation, the Party, the Party leader Mao, the political ideals of socialism and communism, and the nation's various ethnicities as one and the same thing – or at least as elements inseparable from one another. But in Kim's literary world, these elements are subjected to independent scrutiny. For instance, Kim differentiates between Mao and the Chinese Communist Party, asking, "Who can say the sun does not shine because there are sunspots?" and adding that Mao is the "dirt floating on the clear river" (87). This is a different collective identification from the nationalist-socialist type that China and many other socialist countries at the time forced on their people, and I argue that it arose from the multinational borderland milieu surrounding Kim and his work.

Meanwhile, the same identification and imagination may have prevented Kim from engaging the full totality of socialist China and instead encouraged him to idealize other spaces, creating unrealistic expectations for China. Most prominently, he derived his theoretical resources from the latest developments in the contemporary Soviet Union, though the real domestic conditions in the Soviet Union not only were far from ideal but also shared many similarities with China. The Khrushchev regime successfully abolished the cult of Stalin, but not the political system associated with him. With respect to the rural economy, Khrushchev's reform also suffered from radicalism and subjectivism.[21] When looking to the Soviet Union, a country he had never visited, Kim abstracted the layer of political theory and ideology from the total reality of the country, in the hope that it could be grafted onto the realistic roots he was witnessing in China. This is precisely the logic by which Kim first assumed a stratified multinational identification and then sought to synthesize all the strata within the one body of China. In an essay published in 1998, Kim admitted the political limits of his novel, including "firmly believing that socialism could be realized in this century" and "firmly believing that as long as the cult of personality was eliminated, the socialist paradise would be realized."[22] To some degree, this blindness can be attributed to his identification with the Soviet Union as a prior and superior source of political ideology, as well as to his flattened understanding of the thorny reality of Maoist China.

The polemics of borderland writing

Kim's realistic critique of socialism from the borderland reveals much more than his stratified structure of cultural identification. It exposes the potential and pitfalls of border crossing, in literature and beyond. Having lived in all four countries of Northeast Asia, Kim was the border crosser par excellence. His rather subversive fiction writing derives its critical power precisely from the perspective attained through his distinctive lived experience. However, his case also vividly illustrates that a border crossed is never a border erased. In this final section, departing from Kim's case, I want to discuss the three intertwined and circulating processes that are often at work when the act of border crossing takes place: hybridization, demarcation, and essentialization.

Hybridization occurs when the boundaries of cultural demarcation are blurred or crossed, a process that is often suppressed by political authorities, such as colonial regimes, whose dominance is secured through the maintenance of certain social or ethnic divisions. In postcolonial studies, therefore, borderland literature emerging from transcultural encounters is often celebrated as embodying a creative and critical synergy that may problematize or subvert geographical and conceptual borders that entail suppression. For example, Gloria Anzaldúa argues for a border-crossing consciousness – a radically inclusive synthesis of different social and cultural investments – that aims to transcend various geographical and imaginary borders demarcating the US-Mexico frontier. Some recent scholars in Chicano/a cultural studies, such as Carl Gutiérrez-Jones and Kavita Panjabi, however, contend that this consciousness may in fact work to reinforce borders: repeated crossing over between binary conceptual poles – two sides of a border, two ends of the gender spectrum, or two categories in the racial mix – may end up reinforcing "repetition scenarios" and reproducing the very boundaries that have been traversed.[23] The sociologist Pablo Vila, in his research of narratives of identities by members of different ethno-racial communities living along the US-Mexico border, also notices that as hybridization occurs and identities become more fluid, there are also efforts to "reinforce the bold limits – the strict categorical distinctions, . . . the logic of either/or – that are the antipodes of a 'hybrid' or 'mestiza' way of thinking."[24]

Inspired by these discussions, in Kim's work I observe a similar triple dialectic in the borderland complex composed of the actions of crossing, drawing, and essentializing the border. First, a degree of productive cultural mixing, or so-called hybridity, exists in virtually all borderland spaces, including where Kim lived and wrote. However, hybridity is not a magic word that bridges differences. Rather, the fluidity of boundaries that hybridity implies sometimes leads to a heightened sense that boundaries are being violated: boundaries need to be redrawn as soon as the elements of supposedly separated things blend. This is true in colonial states that are sustained by a hierarchical boundary between the colonizer and the colonized, and also in places where the smaller ethnic group feels insecure, as was the case in the Korean Autonomous Prefecture at certain historical moments. The revolving operations of hybridization and boundary redrawing lead to – and are accompanied by – the overarching process of essentialization. I use this term to describe the paradoxical effect of border crossing reinforcing what was putatively bridged. In crossing between different realms, one often essentializes and rationalizes the differences encountered at the border itself, and what lies on each side of it. These perceived and often imaginary differences justify the crossing, just as they create ingrained ideas about the essence of each of these spaces. The processes of hybridization, demarcation, and essentialization don't occur independently from one another; instead, one often triggers another. As a result, the borders grow stronger with each crossing.

This triple dialectic is manifested in Kim's borderland writing in many aspects, but certain linguistic issues concerning the ethnic Korean community that he features in the novel most clearly illustrate the case. The modern Korean language uses a phonetic alphabet, but there is still one-to-one correspondence between most of its vocabulary and Chinese characters. In the prefecture, where bilingualism was the norm, this allowed Han Chinese words to easily enter the daily language of the ethnic Korean Chinese – in their original form but pronounced in Korean. Most of the new words created through this special translingual hybridization process circulated widely among the ethnic Koreans. In the Korean version of Kim's novel that was published in South Korea, there are many cases where the author chose to keep such new words distinctive to the prefecture and then match them with the corresponding words used in South Korea in parentheses. For example, the author used the word 소개신 (sogae sin, lit. "letter of introduction"), the transliteration of the Chinese characters 紹介信 (shaojie xin), to refer to the letter of introduction, an important document in socialist China (55). This is a typical new hybrid word among the ethnic Korean

Chinese, who combined the first two characters of the original Korean word referring to the document (소개장 *sogaechang*, lit. "paper of introduction") with the third character of the Chinese word for the same concept (介紹信 *jieshaoxin*, lit. "introductory letter") and then pronounced the whole word in Korean. South Korean readers would have found this awkward, for they would not have known the meaning of the new word that the ethnic Korean Chinese coined. So Kim appended the common South Korean word (소개장 *sogaechang*) in parentheses, acknowledging the hybridity while bridging the difference. Like most other local intellectuals, Kim did not find the use of these new words problematic.

However, after both Chinese and Korean were declared the official languages of the prefecture in the 1950s, ethnic Korean Chinese witnessed a rapid inflow of new Chinese words that often confused or even offended them. Some were simply arbitrary transliterations of Chinese characters for concepts that could have been expressed more naturally with original Korean words, while others conflicted with existing words. This was when hybridization became enmeshed with the counterprocess of boundary redrawing. Around 1957, a group of concerned ethnic Korean intellectuals launched a movement called the campaign for "linguistic purification" (Kor. *ŏnŏ sun'gyŏlhwa*; Chin. *yuyan chunjiehua*), seeking to rid the prefecture of awkward Chinese words and to restore the elegance of the Korean language. The Party organization denounced the movement as a manifestation of harmful local nationalism (*difang minzu zhuyi* 地方民族主義) – referring to the tendency of minority nationalities to secede from the country – and quickly suppressed it in 1958 and 1959.[25] Kim did not participate in the campaign directly, but he was targeted. One article published in 1959 picked up several cases of Kim's translation of Chinese words into Korean in his literary translations. One example is "Women's Association" (*funühui* 婦女會), for which Kim used the Korean word *nyŏmaeng* rather than *punyŏhoe*, a Korean transliteration of the Chinese. The author criticizes this choice of translation for demonstrating that "Kim is not happy with the numerous new words generated from the new political, economic, and cultural environment in our big motherland family, or that he objects to the communion of language and intends to create divergence."[26] This criticism replicates the main point of the authorities' denunciation of the "linguistic purification" campaign.

In the novel, however, Kim subtly but firmly demonstrates his support for the campaign. Among the characters ensnared in the labor camp, one is nicknamed "flexible savings" (활기존관 *hwalgi chongwan*). This was a new word in the prefecture to refer to current deposits, and was a direct transliteration of the Chinese word 活期存款 (*huoqi cunkuan*). The character in question got his nickname because at an academic conference he argued that "it is improper to use transliterated Chinese words arbitrarily, such as 'flexible savings.'" Instead, he advocated using the original Korean term, 당좌예금 (*tangchwa yegŭm*), as a result of which he and his supporters were accused of "attempting to undermine the linguistic unification of the socialist big family" and labeled antirevolutionaries (33). This character reappears several times in the novel and repeatedly appeals to the Chinese authorities to defend his linguistic view, but every time he does so, he slips further down the slope. Kim's own experience in the campaign and the "flexible savings" episode in the novel both suggest that at the time, Kim felt the necessity of linguistic purification, or of the reinforcement or redrawing of the line between the language of the ethnic Korean Chinese and that of the Han Chinese.

What is implied in the Korean intellectuals' advocacy of linguistic purification, though, is not merely boundary drawing but also a tendency to essentialize a Korean linguistic identity that is intrinsically differentiated from a Chinese one. The term *purification* implies that deep in the minds of the ethnic Korean intellectuals, there was a linguistic state that was pure, original, authentic, and uncontaminated – a belief that they held dear even as they themselves used hybrid new words on a daily basis. Kim had a lifelong obsession with the idea of an authentic Korean language. He adored the authentic Seoul dialect, which he acquired during his school years when he was first enlightened about literature, naming it the most beautiful dialect of the Korean language. His literary model was the Korean writer Hong Myŏng-hŭi's multivolume novel *Im Kkŏk-chŏng*, a work known for its use of a rich Seoul vocabulary. During the turbulent years in China, Kim preserved his Seoul dialect and took a copy of *Im Kkŏk-chŏng* with him wherever he went. The ethnic Korean dialect, on the contrary, did not please him; it simply "made the whole world boring."[27] Kim's support for the campaign of linguistic purification can therefore be understood in light of his own linguistic obsession. His personal identification with a particular dialect of the Korean language as a diaspora writer and his concern with the proper use of Korean in the diaspora community at large were both motivated by a belief that a hierarchy existed among different forms of the Korean language, depending on their proximity to the language used in the ethnic homeland or the language used by the diaspora subjects when they lived there. Accordingly, as Kim joined other ethnic Korean intellectuals in redrawing the boundaries between the Korean and the Chinese languages in a condition of linguistic hybridity, he was simultaneously essentializing a Korean linguistic identity as a nostalgic and authentic expression of proper Koreanness.

This is what I call the trilateral dialectic of the borderland in the linguistic realm, as manifested in the novel and beyond. It is never a purely linguistic issue but has political and cultural implications. Linguistic hybridity has long existed in the ethnic Korean community, especially in vocabulary. However, in the minds of ethnic Korean intellectuals, including Kim, there was a clear line up to which such hybridity could be tolerated. While most supporters of linguistic purification justified this line on pragmatic grounds, such as the need to preserve semantic clarity, the convenience of use, or the elegance of the language, they likely did so because this was the safest way to advocate a Korean linguistic identity. Manfred Henningsen's observation of movements for linguistic purity in multiple locations across the world shows that the politics of purity and exclusion often "originates in the quest for the identity and authenticity of a cultural

Self that feels threatened by the hegemonic presence of another culture."[28] Lara Maconi, in his study of the language debate among minority Tibetan intellectuals, also notes that "the negotiation of linguistic idiom is never a neutral matter," but "expresses concrete concerns with tangible implications for every aspect of Tibetan literary life."[29] Similarly, for the ethnic Korean Chinese, the question whether or not to cross a linguistic boundary was not merely an academic discussion but rather signified the extent to which they could accept Han influence without endangering their own culture. For the authorities, this linguistic choice was an indicator of whether this ethnic minority community was displaying a tendency toward national secessionism. Essentially, the linguistic choices among ethnic Koreans were a question of when to cross, when to draw, and when to essentialize the inter-ethnic and inter-national borders in their social and cultural lives.

The linguistic pattern therefore epitomizes the mechanisms of Kim's borderland writing in general. The three processes concerning the border happen simultaneously in his literary-political world. Crossing into China by choice, Kim worked hard to maintain an imaginary "inclusive synthesis" that was an ideal socialist Chinese space. This ideal space would accept and respect the language and culture of the ethnic Koreans while integrating them into a welfare system modeled on that of the Soviet Union, again in his imagination. It was the synthesis of all the layers in his stratified identification complex: a rich, humane, and diverse socialist paradise. However, his critique of the actually existing China from this idealistic, synthetic point of view worked to erect and reinforce the many boundaries of the borderland: between China and the Soviet Union and between ethnic Koreans and Han Chinese. While China and the Soviet Union had their own difficulties and shared many systematic problems, Kim essentialized one as the superior, absolute antithesis of the other. This, along with his worship of an authentic Korean language, hints at cross-border essentialization in his multinational identification system. In other words, each layer of his identity was a storage site for a different, yet equally essentialized image of a national/ethnic/political space. As he moved between these spaces in physicality and imagination, he reinforced these images, ingraining them into his texts.

Conversely, we could also say that the act of border crossing did not necessarily predate these essentialized images; rather, it was the essentialized images of an ideal motherland that drove Kim to cross the geographic borders. To put it differently, we could consider the idealist, essentialist part of Kim not as the result of his border-crossing consciousness but as precisely what drove him across the borders again and again. Refusing to compromise with the colonial reality in the Peninsula, he left his hometown to fight the Japanese in China. Firmly believing in the Chinese Communist cause, he joined the Chinese Communist Party and stayed in the Korean Autonomous Prefecture in the postwar years. Moreover, in 1961, disillusioned with Maoist China and identifying Soviet ideology as ideal and authentic, he went to Beijing and attempted to break into the Soviet embassy to apply for asylum in the Soviet Union. He was always pursuing something better, purer, and more authentic. Precisely because he could not compromise these spiritual boundaries in his heart, he constantly had to cross geographic borders and was perpetually disappointed – not so much by the failure of these societies to fulfill their promises as because of the mismatch between a border crosser's idealistic image of an inclusive synthesis and the bare reality.

Conclusion

Kim Hak-ch'ŏl is an influential writer in Korean-speaking communities in East Asia. In China, he is often celebrated as an ethnic Korean Lu Xun for his uncompromising spirit and his fierce criticism of the darkness of society, although his novel *The Myth of the Twentieth Century* remains unpublished today.[30] In Korea, Kim's series of autobiographical novels about his experience in anti-Japanese struggle and in socialist China, including *The Myth of the Twentieth Century*, distinguishes him from the large number of Korean writers writing in the Peninsula under colonial and postcolonial conditions. As the renowned Korean critic Kim Yoon-sik observes, the "straightforwardness and optimism" found in Kim's work form a sharp contrast with the inwardness and melancholy that many colonial Korean writers could not escape even during the postcolonial period.[31] This encourages Korean readers to revere Kim as a heroic diasporic Korean writer whose sole existence redeemed the Peninsula colonial literature that they often associate with shame and guilt. It also makes Kim's work an exceptional case that fits only uneasily into the landscape of Korean national literature. Between mystification and forgetfulness, Kim's work deserves a more nuanced and contextualized treatment than what it has received so far in either China or Korea.

This chapter has investigated Kim's political novel *The Myth of the Twentieth Century* as part of Chinese minority literature – ethnic Korean literature – and examined the author's China criticism in the novel. Approaching it from the perspective of borderland writing, I argue that the borderland writer's stratified identification with the three nations of China, North Korea, and the Soviet Union offered him a creatively critical perspective on the reality of China at the zenith of the socialist revolution. Kim's perspective is influenced by and epitomizes the "theory of multiple motherlands" that many ethnic Korean intellectuals embraced in the 1950s. But the same multinational identification prevented the author from fully engaging with the complex totality of socialist China and led him to consider China as first and foremost a realistic motherland whose priority was to reward her hardworking people with adequate living conditions and reasonable freedom of speech. Moreover, he measured the living reality of this realistic motherland against his idealized conception of the Soviet Union, his ideological motherland, thus coming to the conclusion that Maoist China had betrayed the socialist and communist cause and was fascist in nature. Finally, in the broader context of borderland literature, and departing from existing studies of its pattern and character, I propose a trilateral dialectic consisting of the three processes of hybridization, demarcation, and essentialization that I find essential to Kim's borderland writing.

Kim is no doubt both a hero and a martyr under the totalitarian regime in socialist China. In this sense, he fills the embarrassing absence that Ye Zhaoyan lamented. What I consider to be the limitations of his borderland writing in no way obscure all the acclaim he has received from both Chinese and Korean readers. They show how far a borderland writer can go under a totalitarian regime in navigating a polarized world divided by the Cold War, and how difficult his journey is doomed to be.

Notes

1 Xiaojue Wang, *Modernity with a Cold War Face: Reimagining the Nation in Chinese Literature across the 1949 Divide* (Cambridge: Harvard University Asia Center, 2013), 10–12.
2 Kim Hak-ch'ŏl, *20-segi ŭi sinhwa* [The Myth of the Twentieth Century] (Seoul: Ch'angjak kwa Pip'yŏngsa, 1996).
3 Edgar Morin and J. L. Roland Bélanger, *Method: Towards a Study of Humankind*, vol. 1 (New York: Peter Lang, 1992), 133.
4 Shu-mei Shih, "Against Diaspora: The Sinophone as Places of Cultural Production," in *Sinophone Studies: A Critical Reader*, ed. Shu-mei Shih, Chien-hsin Tsai, and Brian Bernards (New York: Columbia University Press: 2013), 35–36.
5 Gloria Anzaldúa, *Borderlands/La Frontera: The New Mestiza* (San Francisco: Spinster/ Aunt Lute, 1987), 3.
6 There are multiple versions of the theory of multiple motherlands. For example, one claims "the Soviet Union as the first motherland, Korea as the second, and China as the third." In other versions, China is called "the motherland of liberation" instead of "the realistic motherland." For more about the theory of multiple motherlands throughout the 1950s, see Haiying Li, "Chungguk Chosŏnjok ŭi sŏnt'aek kwa Chosŏnin kanbudŭl ŭi yŏkhal: Chosŏnjok ŭi Changp'yŏn sosŏl kwa Chosŏnin kanbudŭl ŭi hoegorok kwa ŭi taebi rŭl t'onghayŏ" (Chinese Ethnic Koreans' Choices and the Role of the Ethnic Korean Cadres: A Comparison of Ethnic Korean Novels and Memoirs by Ethnic Korean Cadres), *Han'guk hyŏndae munhak yŏn'gu* (Journal of Modern Korean Literature) 45 (2015): 298. See also Pak Chong-ch'ŏl, "Chungguk ŭi minjok chŏng p'ung undong kwa Chosŏnjok ŭi Pukhanŭro ŭi iju" (The Ethnic Reformation Movement in China and the Migration of Chinese Ethnic Koreans to North Korea), *Pundan 70-yŏn, Pukhan ch'eje ŭi pyŏnhwa p'yŏngka wa chŏnmang* (Seventy Years of Division: The Change, Evaluation and Prospect of the North Korean System), Conference Proceedings, Pukhan Yŏn'gu Hakhoe, June 26, 2015, 130. For discussions in English, see Adam Cathcart, "Nationalism and Ethnic Identity in the Sino-Korean Border Region of Yanbian, 1945–1950," *Korean Studies* 34 (2010): 34; Hyun Ok Park, *The Capitalist Unconscious: From Korean Unification to Transnational Korea* (New York: Columbia University Press, 2015), 154–155.
7 The district was later upgraded to be the Korean Autonomous Prefecture in 1955, so in this chapter, I use both *district* and *prefecture* to refer to the region, depending on the time concerned.
8 For more about the history of the Chinese Korean community and China's policies concerning its population, see Shen Zhihua 沈志華, "Dongbei chaoxianzu jumin kuajing liudong: Xinzhongguo zhengfu de duice jiqi jieguo 1950–1962" 東北朝鮮族居民跨境流動: 新中國政府的對策及其結果1950–1962 (Movements across the Border among Ethnic Korean Residents in the Northeast: The Response from the New Chinese Government and Its Result '950–1962), *Shixue yuekan* 十月學刊 (October Academia) 11 (2011).

9   Kim Hak-ch'ŏl, "Na ŭi kil" (My way) in Kim Hak-ch'ŏl, *Na ŭi kil* (My way) (Yanbian: Yanbian renmin chubanshe, 1999), 1–4.
10 Kim Ho-ung and Kim Hae-yang, *Kim Hak-ch'ŏl p'yŏngjŏn* (A Biography of Kim Hak-ch'ŏl with Commentary) (Seoul: Silch'ŏn Munhaksa, 2007), 246.
11 Kim Ho-ung and Kim Hae-yang, *Kim Hak-ch'ŏl p'yŏngjŏn*, 301.
12 Kim Ho-ung and Kim Hae-yang, *Kim Hak-ch'ŏl p'yŏngjŏn*, 286.
13 Yu Lei 于雷, *Tieguai xia de zuhen* 鐵枴下的足痕 (Footsteps under the Iron Crutch) (Beijing: Zuojia chubanshe, 2013), 890–891.
14 Kim Hak-ch'ŏl, *Ch'oehu ŭi pundaejang: Kim Hak-ch'ŏl chasŏjŏn* (The Last Squad Leader: An Autobiography of Kim Hak-ch'ŏl) (Seoul: Munhak kwa Chisŏngsa, 1995), 376–377.
15 Interview with Kim Hak-ch'ŏl's son Kim Haeyong.
16 Following the Twentieth Congress in the Soviet Union, *China Daily*, the authoritative organ of the Chinese Communist Party, published an article titled "The Historical Experience of the Proletarian Dictatorship" on April 5, 1956, to introduce the key elements of Khrushchev's speech. Wu Lengxi, the chief editor of the newspaper, recalls how Mao and other Party leaders carefully positioned the article so that readers would not associate the cult of personality with China. Nevertheless, entries in the Chinese Anti-Rightist Campaign Database show that some Chinese intellectuals claimed that Mao was the object of a cult of personality in China. Wu Lengxi 吳冷西, *Shinian lunzhan: 1956–1966 Zhong Su guanxi huiyilu* 十年論戰：1956–1966中蘇關系回憶錄 (Ten Years of Disputation: A Memoir of the Sino-Soviet Relations from 1956 to 1966) (Beijing: Zhongyang wenxian chubanshe, 1999), 20–33. Song Yongyi, ed., *Chinese Anti-Rightist Campaign Database* (2nd ed.), 2013, http://ccrd.usc.cuhk.edu.hk/Default. aspx (accessed December 1, 2017).
17 Kim Hak-ch'ŏl, et al., *Ppuri pagŭn t'ŏ* (A Place to Take Root) (Yanbian: Yanbian jiaoyu chubanshe, 1953).
18 Kim Chong-guk, "'Ppuri pagŭn t'ŏ' e taehayŏ" (On "A Place to Take Root"), *Arirang* (Arirang) 2 (1958): 61.
19 Kim Hak-ch'ŏl, et al., *Ppuri pagŭn t'ŏ*, copyright page.
20 Kim Hak-ch'ŏl, *Ch'oehu ŭi pundaejang: Kim Hak-ch'ŏl chasŏjŏn*, 358.
21 William Taubman, *Khrushchev: The Man and His Era* (New York: Norton, 2003), 371–378.
22 Kim Ho-ung and Kim Hae-yang, *Kim Hak-ch'ŏl p'yŏngjŏn*, 292.
23 Carl Gutiérrez-Jones, "Desiring B/orders," *Diacritics* 25, no. 1 (1995): 100–101.
24 Pablo Vila, *Crossing Borders, Reinforcing Borders: Social Categories, Metaphors, and Narrative Identities on the US-Mexico Frontier* (Austin: University of Texas Press, 2000), 9.
25 For more on the debate about "linguistic purity," see Wu Yanghao 吳養鎬, *Yanbian ribao wushinianshi* 延邊日報五十年 (Fifty Years of *Yanbian Daily*) (Yanbian: Yanbian renmin chubanshe, 1998), 182–195. The PRC's campaign against local nationalism was not confined to the ethnic Korean community but was a nationwide policy regarding minority nationalities in the 1950s and 1960s. See Colin Mackerra, *China's Minorities: Integration and Modernization in the Twentieth Century* (Hong Kong: Oxford University Press, 1994), 145–153.
26 Hyŏn Nam-gŭk, "Pŏnyŏk munhak ŭl hoesang hayŏ" (A Review of Translation Literature), *Yŏnbyŏn munhak* (Yanbian Literature) 10 (1959): 54.
27 Li Haiying, *Ch'ŏngnyŏn Kim Hak-ch'ŏl kwa kŭ ŭi sidae* (The Youth Kim Hak-ch'ŏl and His Time) (Seoul: Yŏngnak, 2006), 221–224.
28 Manfred Henningsen, "The Politics of Purity and Exclusion: Literary and Linguistic Movements of Political Empowerment in America, Africa, the South Pacific, and Europe," in *The Politics of Language Purism*, ed. Björn H. Jernudd and Michale J. Shapiro (Berlin: Mouton de Gruyter, 1989), 31–32.
29 Lara Maconi, "One Nation, Two Discourses: Tibetan New Era Literature and the Language Debate," in *Modern Tibetan Literature and Social Change*, ed. Lauran R. Hartley and Patricia Schiaffini-Vendani (Durham: Duke University Press, 2008), 173.

30 For example, see the essays included in "Part II: Lu Xun and Kim Hak-ch'ŏl" (Ro Sin kwa Kim Hak-ch'ŏl) in *Ro Sin kwa Kim Hak-ch'ŏl* (Lu Xun and Kim Hak-ch'ŏl), ed. Kim Hak-ch'ŏl Munhak Yŏn'guhoe (Yanbian: Yŏnbyŏn Inmin Ch'ulp'ansa, 2011), 167–566.

31 Kim Yoon-sik, "Hangil ppaltchisan munhak ŭi kiwŏn" (The Origin of Anti-Japanese Guerilla Literature) in *Chosŏn Ŭiyonggun ch'oehu ŭi pundaejang Kim Hak-ch'ŏl Book II* [The Last Squad Leader of the Korean Volunteer Army Kim Hak-ch'ŏl Book II], ed. Kim Hak-ch'ŏl Munhak Yŏn'guhoe (Yanbian: Yŏnbyŏn Inmin Ch'ulp'ansa, 2007), 143–186 and 160 in particular.

Works cited

Anzaldúa, Gloria. *Borderlands/La Frontera: The New Mestiza*. San Francisco: Spinster/Aunt Lute, 1987.

Cathcart, Adam. "Nationalism and Ethnic Identity in the Sino-Korean Border Region of Yanbian, 1945–1950." *Korean Studies* 34 (2010): 25–53.

Gutiérrez-Jones, Carl. "Desiring B/orders." *Diacritics* 25, no. 1 (1995): 100–101.

Henningsen, Manfred. "The Politics of Purity and Exclusion: Literary and Linguistic Movements of Political Empowerment in America, Africa, the South Pacific, and Europe." In *The Politics of Language Purism*, edited by Björn H. Jernudd and Michael J. Shapiro, 31–52. Berlin: Mouton de Gruyter, 1989.

Hyŏn, Nam-gŭk. "Pŏnyŏk munhak ŭl hoesang hayŏ." (A Review of Translation Literature). *Yŏnbyŏn munhak* (Yanbian Literature) 10 (1959): 53–55.

Kim, Chong-guk. "'Ppuri pagŭn t'ŏ' e taehayŏ." (On "A Place to Take Root"). *Arirang* (Arirang) 2 (1958): 61.

Kim, Hak-ch'ŏl. *20-segi ŭi sinhwa* (The Myth of the Twentieth Century). Seoul: Ch'angjak kwa Pip'yŏngsa, 1996.

———. *Ch'oehu ŭi pundaejang: Kim Hak-ch'ŏl chasŏjŏn* (The Last Squad Leader: An Autobiography of Kim Hak-ch'ŏl). Seoul: Munhak kwa Chisŏngsa, 1995.

———. "Na ŭi kil" (My Way). In *Na ŭi kil* (My Way), edited by Kim Hak-ch'ŏl, 1–6. Yanbian: Yanbian renmin chubanshe, 1999.

Kim, Hak-ch'ŏl, and Munhak Yŏn'guhoe, eds. *Ro Sin kwa Kim Hak-ch'ŏl* (Lu Xun and Kim Hak-ch'ŏl). Yanbian: Yŏnbyŏn Inmin Ch'ulp'ansa, 2011.

Kim, Hak-ch'ŏl, et al. *Ppuri pagŭn t'ŏ* (A Place to Take Root). Yanbian: Yanbian jiaoyu chubanshe, 1953.

Kim, Ho-ung, and Kim Hae-yang. *Kim Hak-ch'ŏl p'yŏngjŏn* (A Biography of Kim Hak-ch'ŏl with Commentary). Seoul: Silch'ŏn Munhaksa, 2007.

Kim, Yoon-sik. "Hangil ppaltchisan munhak ŭi kiwŏn." (The Origin of Anti-Japanese Guerrilla Literature). In *Chosŏn Ŭiyonggun ch'oehu ŭi pundaejang Kim Hak-ch'ŏl Book II* (The Last Squad Leader of the Korean Volunteer Army Kim Hak-ch'ŏl Book II), edited by Kim Hak-ch'ŏl Munhak Yŏn'guhoe, 143–186. Yanbian: Yŏnbyŏn Inmin Ch'ulp'ansa, 2007.

Li, Haiying. *Ch'ŏngnyŏn Kim Hak-ch'ŏl kwa kŭ ŭi sidae* (The Youth Kim Hak-ch'ŏl and His Time). Seoul: Yŏngnak, 2006.

———. "Chungguk Chosŏnjok ŭi sŏnt'aek kwa Chosŏnin kanbudŭl ŭi yŏkhal: Chosŏnjok ŭi Changp'yŏn sosŏl kwa Chosŏnin kanbudŭl ŭI hoegorok kwa ŭi taebi rŭl t'onghayŏ." (Chinese Ethnic Koreans' Choices and the Role of the Ethnic Korean Cadres: A Comparison of Ethnic Korean Novels and Memoirs by Ethnic Korean Cadres). *Han'guk hyŏndae munhak yŏn'gu* (Journal of Modern Korean Literature) 45 (2015): 285–312.

Mackerra, Colin. *China's Minorities: Integration and Modernization in the Twentieth Century*. Hong Kong: Oxford University Press, 1994.

Maconi, Lara. "One Nation, Two Discourses: Tibetan New Era Literature and the Language Debate." In *Modern Tibetan Literature and Social Change*, edited by Lauran R. Hartley and Patricia Schiaffini-Vendani, 173–201. Durham: Duke University Press, 2008.

Morin, Edgar J. L., and Roland Bélanger. *Method: Towards a Study of Humankind*. Vol. 1. New York: Peter Lang, 1992.

Pak, Chong-ch'ŏl. "Chungguk ŭi minjok chŏng p'ung undong kwa Chosŏnjok ŭi Pukhanŭro ŭi iju." (The Ethnic Reformation Movement in China and the Migration of Chinese Ethnic Koreans to North Korea). In *Pundan 70-yŏn, Pukhan ch'eje ŭi pyŏnhwa p'yŏngka wa chŏnmang* (Seventy Years of Division: The Change, Evaluation and Prospect of the North Korean system), 125–143. Conference Proceedings, Pukhan Yŏn'gu Hakhoe, June 26, 2015.

Park, Hyun Ok. *The Capitalist Unconscious: From Korean Unification to Transnational Korea*. New York: Columbia University Press, 2015.

Shen Zhihua 沈志華. "Dongbei chaoxianzu jumin kuajing liudong: Xinzhongguo zhengfu de duice jiqi jieguo 1950–1962." 東北朝鮮族居民跨境流動: 新中國政府的對策及其結果1950–1962 (Movements Across the Border among Ethnic Korean Residents in the Northeast: The Response from the New Chinese Government and Its Result '950–1962). *Shixue yuekan* 十月學刊 (October Academia) 11 (2011): 69–84.

Shih, Shu-mei. "Against Diaspora: The Sinophone as Places of Cultural Production." In *Sinophone Studies: A Critical Reader*, edited by Shu-mei Shih, Chien-hsin Tsai, and Brian Bernards. New York: Columbia University Press, 2013.

Song Yongyi, ed. *Chinese Anti-Rightist Campaign Database*. 2nd ed., 2013. http://ccrd.usc.cuhk.edu.hk/Default.aspx. Accessed December 1, 2017.

Taubman, William. *Khrushchev: The Man and His Era*. New York: Norton, 2003.

Vila, Pablo. *Crossing Borders, Reinforcing Borders: Social Categories, Metaphors, and Narrative Identities on the US-Mexico Frontier*. Austin: University of Texas Press, 2000.

Wang, Xiaojue. *Modernity with a Cold War Face: Reimagining the Nation in Chinese Literature across the 1949 Divide*. Cambridge: Harvard University Asia Center, 2013.

Wu Lengxi 吳冷西. *Shinian lunzhan: 1956–1966 Zhong Su guanxi huiyilu*. 十年論戰: 1956–1966 中蘇關係回憶錄 (Ten Years of Disputation: A Memoir of the Sino-Soviet Relations from 1956 to 1966). Beijing: Zhongyang wenxian chubanshe, 1999.

Wu Yanghao 吳養鎬. *Yanbian ribao wushinianshi*. 延邊日報五十年 (Fifty Years of *Yanbian Daily*). Yanbian: Yanbian renmin chubanshe, 1998.

Yu Lei 于雷. *Tieguai xia de zuhen*. 鐵枴下的足痕 (Footsteps under the Iron Crutch). Beijing: Zuojia chubanshe, 2013.

7

KEEPING TO THE MARGINS

Macau literature and a pre-postcolonial "poetics of insignificance"

Rosa Vieira de Almeida

This chapter proposes that the position of marginality, often read as one of weakness, can be wielded as a resource for the benefit of a marginal literary project. Considering Macau, one of the lesser-studied Sinitic literary spaces, the chapter examines Sinophone literature during the pre-postcolonial era of 1987–1999.[1] In the work of the Macau-born poet Yiling 懿靈 (pen name of Virginia Cheang Mio San 鄭妙姍) (b. 1964), I identify what I am calling a poetics of insignificance, in which the poet attempts to use Macau's historical peripherality to situate the city outside a Manichaean struggle for centrality. Proposing that minor sites of literary construction can harbor little interest in displacing Sinocentrism, I argue that Yiling's work is an example of how transition-era Macau Sinophone literature can be read as opting to wield marginality as a niche in its own right.

While many authors who have written on Macau call attention to the city's minute size and negligible import in matters political and economic, few can be said to have made "insignificance" into a constituent component of their literary project, as Yiling has done. Fewer still can be read as having taken insignificance from the superficial level of a localized lament to a viable category of Macau literature and culture. Following Yiling, this chapter takes insignificance not as a plaint but as a productive element in the negotiation of the city's pre-postcolonial and postcolonial relations in the region. Reading Yiling's poetics of insignificance as a rhetorical intervention in Sinitic center-periphery dynamics, I argue that insignificance allows Macau to make use of the asymmetry in the relationship. A position of insignificance is not about challenging or even subverting asymmetry (through, for instance, structured anticolonialist or localist literary discourses) but rather offers the possibility that reinforcement of asymmetrical relations may in fact serve the interests of the Sinitic periphery. In placing the burden of inconsequentiality on Macau, a poetics of insignificance situates the city as the most peripheral of peripheries, a "margin outside the margins" (邊緣

外的邊緣), as one Macau author has put it.[2] I contend that such a position permits Macau the leeway to participate in the center-periphery relationship, but also to extricate itself from the system without having to challenge it. Yiling's poetics of insignificance, in proposing value in a position of liminal peripherality, enables us to consider how the periphery can also be a place where Chinacentrism is strategically articulated and marginality is bent at will.

My use of "insignificance" echoes Shu-mei Shih's lament on the insignificance of Taiwan. "Studying Taiwan," Shih claims, "is an *impossible* task . . . because Taiwan is always already written out of mainstream Western discourse due to its *in-significance*."[3] This diagnosis of Taiwanese inconsequentiality can be equally – if not further – applied to Macau: "too small, too marginal, too ambiguous, and thus too insignificant."[4] Shih's approach relies not only on the adoption of a Western critical idiom (in this case, globalization) but also on a concurrent departure from China. Putting Taiwan "on the map" (making it "legible"), she argues, requires "displac[ing] Sinocentric influence and invent[ing] new forms of trans-culture."[5] By contrast, Macau barely registers. According to Macau author Agnes Lam 林玉鳳, "Macau is like dipping a strand of hair into ink and using it to dot a world map, it is only *so* big."[6] While signification in the form of an urgent scaling upward and outward may prove a worthwhile strategy for the comparatively more significant Taiwan, the example of Macau shows how for the most marginal of margins, there may be value in a commitment to insignificance that allows for greater flexibility of scale. Building on Jing Tsu's recent work on "weak links," this chapter proposes that the predicament of insignificance can also be articulated as a resource for an otherwise under-resourced margin. Writing on the weak links of Taiwan, Hong Kong, and Macau, Tsu claims that "a common sense of under-endowment and lack of prestige in the literary world in and beyond the Sinophone system drives them to develop their own scales of literary capital with whatever available means."[7] Thus, the question is not one of simply finding strength in weakness, but of finding the means by which the realization of one's weakness, or insignificance, propels the underendowed margin to forge novel (and what may at times appear to be counterintuitive) responses. Insignificance, rather than condemning Macau to impossibility and illegibility, appears instead as an approach that makes possible the consideration of Macau as a "margin outside the margins" – its reliance on Sinocentrism and its reluctance to take an antihegemonic stance that would compromise the Sinitic center-periphery dynamic.

However, insignificance is not a strategy devoid of risks. At minimum, employing insignificance as a form of self-discursive description risks undermining the validity of one's voice and, at the extreme, a strategy of insignificance places in jeopardy the possibility of having a voice at all: if Macau is so insignificant, why bother hearing what its authors have to say? My reading of Yiling's poetics of insignificance holds that the poet is aware of the potential pitfalls of such a position. With the "precarity of literary and linguistic resources," as Tsu argues, "the particular challenge faced by the weaker links in a given literary system,"[8] the shift from insignificance as predicament to insignificance as solution is a gamble. It follows, then, that any potential gains through insignificance should be greater than the possible loss of the viability of voice. As I will show, though a poetics of insignificance may articulate only a faint murmur at the periphery, its being excused from the demands of centrality permits signification through the development of related resources that the periphery can grasp, thereby increasing the stability and discernibility of even the faintest peripheral voices. A poetics of insignificance is thus to be read not as a lament, but as a means of imagining the necessary – or at least the *possible* – resources to deal with the difficult condition of insignificance. More crucially, such resources permit Yiling to accede to Sinocentrality as a condition of her literary project while also allowing for the development of an antihegemonic discourse that does not challenge China-centrism. It is in this sense that I argue that a poetics of insignificance enables a modulated Sinocentrality in which the periphery has room to maneuver in dictating not *whether* but *how* it is peripheral.

Insignificance and indifference

Three years following the signing of the 1987 Sino-Portuguese Joint Declaration that promulgated Macau's transfer of sovereignty from Portuguese administration to Chinese rule in 1999, Yiling launched her first book of poetry, titled *The Drifting Isle* (流動島, 1990). At a time when local authorities celebrated the city's unique cultural syncretism (a move that reclaimed Macau's colonial history as one of benign cultural encounters between two equals, not as an instance of violent domination of one people over another[9]), Yiling's first work assumed a contrarian stance: that Portuguese colonialism – and hence the violence of the colonial experience – existed, and yet was irrelevant.

If the juxtaposition of the two preceding statements appears striking, it is because we hardly expect an anticolonial discourse to align itself with an understanding of colonialism as an irrelevant historical experience. Anticolonial stances tend to rely, instead, on the *significance* of the colonial power – of colonization as a violent appropriation and reorganization of land and labor – as just cause for their existence and as rallying cry for resistance.[10] And while Yiling has been described as "one of the bravest voices" among Macau poets,[11] she is certainly not alone in critiquing coloniality, having for company other outspoken and prolific authors such as Wong Mun-fai 黃文輝 and Agnes Lam. Yiling is, however, singular in her detachment of significance from the colonial experience, turning the expectation of the importance of coloniality on its head. In proclaiming coloniality as fact, not as a euphemistic "encounter" of cultures, and simultaneously underscoring that coloniality has had few lasting effects on Macau, Yiling makes the case for a radical anticolonial stance based on the fundamental insignificance of the Portuguese colonial project in the territory.

Together with Yiling's later publications, *Collective Games* (集體遊戲, 2005) and *Collective Death* (集體死亡, 2005), *The Drifting Isle* appears to touch upon a question related to that posed by Rey Chow in her seminal article "Between Colonizers: Hong Kong's Postcolonial Self-writing in the 1990s." In this text on Hong Kong's imminent handover, Chow asks: "How do we talk about a postcoloniality that is a forced return to a 'mother country,' itself as imperialistic as the previous colonizer?"[12] As Chow asserts, because Hong Kong breaks with the teleological narrative of decolonization being followed by independent statehood, one cannot address the issue of decolonization without also addressing the issue of the transfer of sovereignty. In other words, the development of a discourse on Western colonization and decolonization of these Sinophone spaces cannot be conceived without a concomitant engagement with the hegemonizing Chinese nation-state that will incorporate these territories following their "handovers."[13]

Within this framework, I argue that in Yiling's poetry the anticolonial stance should not be read exclusively as an engagement with and an indictment of the colonizer, but instead as a means of mediating dialogue with Macau's primary partner in defining its fraught cultural and political position in the world – mainland China. Rather than reading Yiling's Macau as simply caught "between colonizers,"[14] in Rey Chow's terms, and attempting to shake off the yoke of both, I propose that Yiling devises a poetic strategy that plays off the peripherality of one against the centrality of the other. That is to say, the accusation of ineffectual coloniality is not a red herring serving to distract the reader's attention from the postcolonial tensions at hand; rather, an anticolonial stance based on the insignificance of the colonial experience is employed as a possible resource for an otherwise under-resourced margin operating within a postcolonial Sinocentric dynamic. In this way, Yiling's poetics of insignificance develops an anticolonial stance that seeks to dislodge the colonial center-periphery relationship while also borrowing the language of anticoloniality to disrupt the national center-periphery relationship.

My argument proceeds in two parts. First, drawing on the poetry of Yiling that directly engages with the colonial experience, I tease out the poet's complaints about the lack of a colonial consciousness in the Macau colonized subject. That colonial insignificance has come to define postcolonial indifference is a charge that Yiling, a committed democrat and activist, cannot ignore. In my reading, the poet weaves a lack of colonial consciousness into an integral aspect of a possible anticolonial stance, where indifference is both a regrettable consequence of and a provocative response to insignificance. Second, I depart from the colonial moment to suggest that a poetics of insignificance will serve as a resource to assess Macau's postcolonial relationship with mainland China. Turning to the poetry of Yiling that focuses on the transition period, I contend that a poetics of insignificance can be read as a form of further buttressing Sinocentrality.

Yiling's anticolonial stance does not develop as a politics of mass appeal. Instead, the critique of coloniality is construed as a personal experience engaging only the poetic subject herself. The primary task for the recognition of the violence of coloniality occurs as a personal unearthing of hidden histories – a task made all the more difficult as it runs counter to both official Portuguese and Chinese narratives on Macau. In "The Spies on the Ruins of St. Paul" (牌坊上的窺探, 1985), Yiling's attention turns to the archaeological, and she revisits that most famous of Macau historical sites and celebrated symbol of the architectural syncretism of religio-colonial construction in Asia. In the first two stanzas, a calm coastal scene at dawn is quickly overshadowed by the imposing figure of colonial history:

> The seagulls fly off with
> The last of the water-reflected starlight,
> A morning breeze raises
> The hairs of Jinghai[15] fisherwomen;
> A half-perched broken imperial crown,
> Hangs despondently atop sixty-eight steps,[16]
> For the creatures living on the hillock,
> It towers over as proof of history.
>
> Stones are mute;
> the confession of a mute is blank.
> Only attentive people
> are able to, between the cracks,
> find residues of blood –
> the proof of crimes of sailors and soldiers.

> 海鷗叼去
> 水面最後一片星輝,
> 晨風撩起
> 鏡海漁女的鬢髮;
> 半頂殘缺的皇冠,
> 垂著六十八層抑鬱,
> 為小丘上聚居的螻蟻,
> 矗立著歷史的佐證。
>
> 石頭是啞巴,
> 啞巴的供詞是空白。
> 只有細心的人
> 才能在裂縫裏,
> 覓到點點殘存的血漬 –
> 水手和武士的罪證。[17]

The decision to set this scene at the façade of the Ruins of St. Paul (牌坊) is particularly relevant considering how, during the transition years, this monument was restored from a largely abandoned ruin surrounded by overgrown vegetation into the city's ex libris, representing Macau's "unique cultural identity."[18] The recognition of colonial violence is a delicate forensic task constituted by a careful gathering of incriminating evidence. Colonial violence is not merely stumbled upon; finding it requires an attentiveness to fissures, to the interstitial spaces within the elements of the built environment. The metonymic use of colonial architecture to denote the brutality of the colonial experience might appear anything but extraordinary, yet in turning to "stones" (石頭), Yiling does not claim that Macau's landscape of colonial architecture yields a readily legible narrative of imperialist brutality. On the contrary, the recognition of such violence is achieved not by cursory glance but through the sustained effort of sifting through fleeting fragments – as is also evident in this extract from the title poem of the collection, "The Drifting Isle" (流動島) (1987):

> The lifeless harbor   and
> The muddy yellow seawater
> In [my] mind a unique manuscript
> On the clear watershed
> Before vanishing
> Seeks poetry on the rocky beach
> Before decaying
> Picks up the fragments left behind by brothers
> Unfortunately
> So small
> So quick

> 蒼白的港灣   和
> 泥黃色的海水
> 腦海中以上獨特的原稿
> 在明顯的分水線
> 消失以前
> 尋找亂石灘上的詩篇
> 在腐化以前
> 拾起弟兄遺下的片斷
> 可惜是
> 那樣的小
> 那樣的短速[19]

Of all the violent acts committed by Portuguese colonialism in Macau, the poet singles out this colonialism's ability to conceal itself, making the recognition of its crimes a particularly laborious task. Hiding behind the veneer of cultural exchange and unable to own up to its own brutal history, coloniality offers its subjects something wholly insignificant, as Yiling states in the first verses of a poem critiquing the monument mania of the transition years, "Reportage Literature: Macau Legislative Council Engages in Aesthetic Quibbling" (報告文學: 澳門立法會內有關藝術之詭辯, 1997):

> The beautiful Portuguese arts
> the singular Western aestheticism

this doglike East-West cultural exchange
entrusts us with chicken-ribbed food for thought

美麗的葡國藝術
獨特的西方審美
這狗樣的東西文化交流
賦予我們雞肋一樣的精神食糧[20]

Refusing to make itself known, coloniality remains conveniently hidden in Macau. By whitewashing the colonial project down to harmless banalities and persistently denying the antagonism of the colonial relationship, the poet states, the city's Portuguese administration has made it difficult for local residents to recognize the colonial strictures under which they live. In a later poem titled "Memorial Tablet of a Colonial Government" (殖民政府的墓誌銘, 1999), Yiling fantasizes about what a "nearly dead colonial government would write" on its gravestone, attributing to it all manner of brazen declarations of pillage and plunder.[21]

In contrast to the individual anticolonial stance discussed above, Yiling perceives also a collective apathy toward coloniality. Her claim of a lack of colonial consciousness and political awareness among the local population is in line with similar opinions by scholars of Macau,[22] but Yiling is singular in articulating popular indifference as a result of an insignificant coloniality that seeks to conceal itself. Left only with "chicken-ribbed food for thought," she suggests, it is no surprise that Macau's residents remain largely unable to articulate their own colonial experiences, let alone to structure them as an anticolonial discourse. Turning directly to the question of the muted colonial subject, in "Happiness Is by No Means Necessary" (幸福並不是必然的, 1989), Yiling establishes a direct link between the silence of Macau residents and that of their representatives in the colonial Legislative Council (LegCo),

> The children at home are very quiet
> Because at home the children's parents are even more quiet
> The children in front of LegCo are very quiet
> Because the people in front of LegCo never discuss anything
> The children of Macau are very quiet
> Because the children of Macau have an apparently quiet home
> The children at home are very noisy
> Because at home the parents of children are even noisier
>
> The children in front of the Kwangju graves are very noisy
> Because the children inside the Kwangju graves are still making noise
> The children of South Korea are very noisy
> Because the children of South Korea have a chaotic home
>
> Noisy homes
> Will probably not have peaceful children, but

Silent children, tomorrow, will have ever more
Difficulty in having long-lasting peace at home
When they leave their "guardians"
Or rather
When our "guardians" depart from us

孩子在家很静
因為孩子的父母在家更静
議事亭前的孩子很静
因為議事亭前的人們從不議事
澳門的孩子很静
因為澳門的孩子有個看似平静的家
孩子在家很吵
因為孩子的父母在家更吵
光州墳前的孩子很吵
因為光州墳裏的孩子仍然在吵
南韓的孩子很吵
因為南韓的孩子有個紛亂的家
嘈吵的家
難以有個偷安的孩子但
沉默的孩子明天更
難以有個長久安寧的家
當離開「家長」以後
又或者
當「家長」背離我們以後23

The poem's patronizing and even condemnatory tone, identifying a cross-generational pedagogy of indifference, shifts only in the final verse when the children are identified in the first-person plural, as "we." The implication is that the children can only repeat parental patterns; unable to grow up and leave home, they have to endure parental abandonment (note also the change from the intimate "parents" [父母] in the first verses to the more official-sounding "guardians" [家長] in the final). Such an approach to indifference functions as a face-saving gesture – it is not that the people of Macau are uninterested in their situation, but that having been subject to a coloniality of little effect, they cannot but respond indifferently. It is in this sense that the removal of a ground of significance from coloniality can be seen as a form of colonial violence that ultimately robs the subject of the possibility of a sustained anticolonial discourse.

This charge of political indifference at once furthers the claim of colonial insignificance and aids a shift in focus from a colonial past to a pre-postcolonial and postcolonial political reality that has China as its core concern. The poet's insertion of herself into the text – as one among the muted masses of Macau people – attests to the poem's strategic use of indifference. For if, on one hand, the poetic subject's frustration with the perpetuation of a generalized sense of political apathy is readily apparent, equally visible is the shift in the last verse, which, though ostensibly maintaining a passive tone, introduces the possibility that in a post-1999 era, silence is no longer a guarantor of peace. Though the greatest violence of the Portuguese colonial experiment in Macau may have been, through Macau's persistent refusal to admit to its own coloniality, a denial of the possibility of a sustained anticolonial discourse, the 1999 transfer of sovereignty does not necessarily imply a similar acquiescence. Insignificance can be seen as a source of violence, but it can also be read as a rallying point for pushback. Although Yiling is unable to transform her fellow colonial subjects into like-minded attentive investigators examining fissures in the colonial architecture and identifying mistruths in the historical record, she can instead claim that the inability of Macau people to pronounce themselves on political matters is itself a consequence of an insignificant colonialism. Although she is unable to rally the masses around an anticolonial project, she can fashion a retroactive anticolonial stance based on indifference, imagining an anticolonial community into existence by claiming that apathy too is a political act.

Insignificance and the transfer of sovereignty

At the same time, the suggestion that an indifferent colonized subject is the inevitable consequence of an insignificant coloniality, while disturbing the supposed primacy of the relationship between colony and metropole, also allows for a reevaluation of the relationship between Macau and China. Indeed indifference, as a corollary of insignificance, betrays the larger truth that despite five hundred years of colonial history, Macau's primary relationship is not with a faraway metropole but with the neighboring power to which it is tied geographically and with which it maintains its main commercial, political, and cultural links. In view of the transfer of sovereignty that would soon take place, Yiling's anticolonial stance is thus a commitment less to a destruction of the colonial status quo – for this was assured by 1999 – and more to the establishment of (an insignificant) coloniality as a fundamental element in Macau history, and one that marks Macau as not-China. This is not to say that Yiling is a reluctant anticolonialist, but that she is a peculiarly strategic anticolonialist who steers that stance to more pressing concerns.

While much of her work directly relates to the colonial experience, Yiling's poetry also gives a cursory impression of coloniality where what appear to be the concerns of a pre-postcolonial period are, in fact, more aptly understood as the preoccupations of the impending postcoloniality. In such poems, coloniality is engaged with more out of duty to historical accuracy than from any current concerns about the strictures of the colonial and postcolonial moments. One poem in which this is particularly evident is "The Third Identity" (第三重身份, 1989), where Yiling directly addresses the impending handover of sovereignty and what this means for the colonial enclave. Here, both Macau's and Hong Kong's colonialities appear in the form of mundane bureaucratic detail, manifested in the fungibility of colonial travel documents:

From a Hong Kong C.I. to a Portuguese PASSPORT (Switching from a green booklet called 'The Hong Kong Certificate of Identity' to a previously-seen-but-largely-unfamiliar blueish booklet in order to choose between what others have decided about my life-and-death) And so what

從香港 C.I. 到葡國 PASSPORT (從一個綠色的叫做 [香港身份証明書] 的本子轉到一個曾經見過面但印象豪不深刻的大概是藍色的本子裡來選擇別人所說的生死存亡) 又如何[24]

Like many of Macau's permanent residents, through both collective (colonialism) and individual (familial migration) historical accident, the poet has gathered a small array of travel documents issued by different authorities.[25] While symbolic of a loss of self-determination – the "choice" (選擇) to use one document or the other is limited to what unelected authorities have dictated regarding one's "life-and-death" (生死存亡) – the reduction of the documents to their colors attests to their merely functional role and ultimate interchangeability as the tools of border crossing. And though colonial travel documents may well constitute the first verses of this poem, the focus quickly shifts from the green and blue booklets to documents of a different hue:

Anyhow, being unwilling to enter the common market   and obtaining the red book   simply being unable to imagine what importance it has   At worst, rather getting a version of a very red travel permit   And calling oneself a resident of such and such a Special Administrative Region   And when in profitable or uncommon situations Or   when after a certain number of years on another uncommon day forgetting of which Special Administrative Region one is a citizen   When regional (neither racial nor national) discrimination occurs   Then   As long as you have money   As long as   you are a patriot   As long as you have good connections   No-one will dare "bug you"

反正不願入共市   取紅薄   就想象不到那有多重要   大不了就改拿一本紅色不過的通行證   然後稱自己為某某特區的居民   當有利可圖或與別不同的時候   又或者在若干年後另一個與別不同的日子裡忘掉自己是什麼特區的人   當區族 (非種族、非民族) 歧視發生的時候   總之   只要有錢   只要愛國   只要關係良好   無人敢 「詐你形」[26]

The transfer of sovereignty occasions yet another unsatisfying choice of official papers, this time forcing the decision between the "red book" (紅簿) that is metonymic of Chinese nationality or the "very red travel permit" (紅色不過的通行證) that grants Macau and Hong Kong residents the right to enter mainland China while holding a non-Chinese passport. The dispassionate nature of paperwork reduces any possible postcolonial identification with the nation-state to its bureaucratic actuality and transactional value. Therefore, the poet's initial peremptory refusal to "enter the common market" is either hopelessly naïve or, as I read it, uttered with tongue firmly in cheek. Such choices are ineffectual not because of coloniality or the charge of its insignificance but, according to Yiling, because by the time Macau is due to become a full-fledged participant in the Chinese nation-state, national belonging has been eroded by the demands of the socialist market economy:

> Moreover, no type of IDENTITY has ever existed here   And in the process of separating colors and analyzing   The embryonic form of a game has begun to develop   A game with the strictest of rules that can calculate the value of the people of a region which like a currency that has undergone national regulation can still appreciate and depreciate only that it can no longer be laissez-faire like a laissez-faire economy Just as there are people who are devalued by a parenthesis   Others appreciate in a concept   But these are mere symbols and ABC[27]   And the question of the psychological needs of the markets   Probably also include the question of the quota and proportion of people to place

> 何況這裡從不存在任何一種IDENTITY   而在分色與分析間   一種遊戲的雛形已經開始成為定局   一種最規條不過的遊戲大概可以計算一個地區的人的價值像貨幣一樣經過國家調節後同樣有升值與貶值的可能只是不再自由放任如自由放任的經濟   正如有人貶值於一個括弧裡   有人升值在一個概念中   但這些都不過是符號與ABC及其市場之間的心理需求問題   也許還包括人與地的配額及其比例的問題[28]

Despite the prehandover official pronouncements on Macau's strategic importance (due to its role as a crucial link between China and Lusophone Africa and Brazil), ultimately the territory is at risk of being no different from any other Chinese city, subject to both the fluctuations of global capital and the constraints of an autocratic national state. Here, Yiling makes reference to the Reform and Opening Up campaign, a series of economic measures introduced under Deng Xiaoping 鄧小平 (1904–1997) in the late 1970s and 1980s that established the so-called Special Economic Zones (經濟特區), urban areas that the central government had made particularly attractive to foreign investment through a combination of tax and business incentives. Witnessing the rapid growth of these new centers of capital just across the border, and despite its impending gain of the official designation of Special Administrative Region (特別行政區), Macau suffers the loss of the status it shares with Hong Kong as the bridge between China and the West, becoming just one among the many free-market cities along the coast of South China. According to the poet, in a nation filled with special regions, it becomes increasingly difficult to detect the specialness of one region versus another, whether their ostensible difference is based on economic or administrative factors. Whatever historical or contemporary importance Macau may have possessed is diluted by such interchangeability, its "value" (價值) being decided merely by how it can contribute to the continued growth of the socialist market economy. In this way, post-1999 Macau joins a collection of interchangeable Chinese cities that, like the travel documents mentioned earlier in the poem, possess no intrinsic value. Read in these terms, the poetic lament regarding a lack of identity "here" refers not to Macau alone, but also to any other Chinese city that has been swept up in contemporaneous market reforms.

The notion of insignificance thus emerges anew, this time as a consequence not of coloniality but of capital. Subsequently, insignificance also becomes an integral consequence of Sinocentrism, here seen as the combination of the homogenizing power of capital and the hegemonizing weight of the state, as is particularly evident in a subsequent poem, "Socks-on Policy" (不脫襪政策, 1989):

> Lu Ping said
> Macau is tranquil suitable for living
> Hong Kong is still a gold mine
> suitable for making money   So
> Macau's value resides in tranquility
> Hong Kong's value resides in making money
> So Macau needs to be tranquil
> Hong Kong needs to make money   If
> Macau is no longer tranquil   Hong Kong
> no longer makes money Then
> Macau and Hong Kong are but
> two bunions on China's feet
> To remove them or not is actually irrelevant
> Just keep socks on so outsiders can't see
> That's all   And when it is time
> remove them   And no one will know

> 魯平說
> 澳門安靜適宜居住
> 香港仍然是一塊寶地
> 適宜搵銀   這樣看來
> 澳門的價值在於安靜
> 香港的價值在於搵銀
> 所以   澳門要安靜
> 香港要賺錢   如果
> 澳門再不安靜   香港
> 再不賺錢那麼
> 澳門和香港只不過是
> 中國腳下的兩粒雞眼
> 拔不拔反正也不礙事
> 不脫襪不讓外人看到
> 就是了   適當的時候
> 拔掉   還沒有人知道[29]

Constructed as a series of incremental, logical steps following a pronounce-ment by Lu Ping 魯平 (1927–2015), the Chinese representative for the Macau and Hong Kong handover negotiations, the poem concludes with a damning declaration of Macau's and Hong Kong's insignificance: whether they exist or not is irrelevant. Lying somewhere between a government diktat and the quoted words of sage-philosophers, the formulation "Lu Ping says" establishes what fol-lows as the assertion of the territory's insignificance by the Chinese state. In fact, the message is in line with Deng Xiaoping's well-known 1984 pronouncement that "the Macau question can be solved only when it does not affect Hong Kong's prosperity and stability."[30] Macau is only significant for the PRC in its ability to remain "quiet" (安靜) so that Hong Kong can remain profitable. Beyond the conspicuous difference between the active and passive "value" attributed to Hong Kong and Macau – where the latter is again associated with tranquility – in placing the discourse of Macau insignificance in the hands of Beijing, the poem abruptly raises the stakes of insignificance to the existential. The incorrect per-formance of one's prescribed value – or of one's prescribed insignificance – leads to annihilation and substitution by another of interchangeable value. By shifting from a poetic voice that claims insignificance to a voice that is the recipient of such a claim – or insignificance rendered from attribute of subject to attribute of object – Yiling in fact maneuvers insignificance into the realm of the significant.

Insignificance again hinges on Sinocentrism, both as its localized counter-discourse and as, consequently, that which cannot but reify the centrality of the Chinese state, upon which insignificance-as-peripherality is dependent. Having ceased to be that which defines Macau through ineffectual coloniality, insignifi-cance comes to be what draws the city back into the fold of a post-1999 capital-ist China. In crossing geographical and conceptual scales from the local to the national, the particular to the universal, insignificance shifts from being what differentiates Macau as not-China to that which solidifies Macau *as* China. Thus pivoted, insignificance as an equalizing force between Sinitic spaces conveys two different, though by no means contradictory, possible attitudes for pre-postcolonial and postcolonial Macau: the ability to develop a discourse between Macau and other Sinitic spaces that is contingent upon their common definition against Chi-nese state hegemony; and the fear of admission into a fully flattened Chinese world where localisms have been quashed and Macau is unable to claim its own place. The potentially unresolvable tension between these two drives will be a recurring theme in the literary production of pre-postcolonial and postcolonial Macau, where the expansion of the periphery through insignificance may well provide a network of coperipherals that act as a balm for the city's own irrelevance, yet ultimately provide little solace for the disquiet of one's own disappearance.

Concluding remarks

What then, to borrow from Roland Barthes, is "the significance of this insig-nificance"? Writing on those discursive details ("insignificant notation") that can be omitted without detriment to the plot (the color and size of extraneous objects, for instance), Barthes considered them to be the "irreducible residues" of the realist novel, or that which creates the *effect* of the real.[31] Like the Barthesian model, Yiling's poetics of insignificance becomes significant not through a shedding of its inconsequentiality, but through an understanding of the discursive function of such insignificance. Unburdened by the impossible task of battling for centrality in a Sinophone literary system, a poetics of insignificance permits Yiling's literary work the development of related resources that will serve to relocate it in the China-centric world, on which it also depends. As Tsu reminds us, literary life in a resource-poor margin demands creative workarounds and pliable responses.[32] The forms of a poetics of insignificance I have analyzed endow Yiling's work with the ability to engage with Sinocentrality in the context of an overwhelming disparity of resources within the Sinitic world. Through the development of locational awareness, Yiling's poetics of insignificance proposes the resources needed for Macau literature to exceed its local scale, allowing it to move up and down regional and national scales – possibly even participating in alternate and overlapping scales of its own co-creation.

Notes

This text is an edited excerpt from my dissertation, *Writing the Margins: Sinophone Macau Literature in the Pre-postcolonial era, 1987–1999*, Yale University, March 2018.

1 This period is more commonly referred to as the "transition era" (過渡時期), corresponding to the years between the 1987 Sino-Portuguese Joint Declaration and the 1999 transfer of sovereignty from Portugal to China. Christina Miu Bing Cheng, *Macau: A Cultural Janus* (Hong Kong: Hong Kong University Press, 1999).

2 Lei Chin Pang 李展鵬, *Zai shijie bianyuan yujian Aomen* 在世界邊緣遇見澳門 (Encountering Macau at the Margins of the World) (Macau: Macao Daily News, 2013), 84.

3 Italics in original. Shu-mei Shih, "Globalisation and the (In)significance of Taiwan," *Postcolonial Studies* 6, no. 2 (2003): 144.

4 Shu-mei Shih, "Globalisation and the (In)significance of Taiwan," 144.

5 Shu-mei Shih, "Globalisation and the (In)significance of Taiwan," 145 and 146.

6 Agnes Lam 林玉鳳, "Wu ziwo shiyi de chengshi," 無自我意識的城市 (A City with No Self-Consciousness), *Aomen ribao* 澳門日報 (Macau Daily), August 12, 2010. Emphasis added.

7 Jing Tsu, "Weak Links, Literary Spaces, and Comparative Taiwan," in *Comparatizing Taiwan*, ed. Shu-mei Shih and Ping-hui Liao (New York: Routledge, 2014), 134.

8 Jing Tsu, "Weak Links," 128.

9 For a brief overview of this period, see the introductory chapter in Cathryn H. Clayton, *Sovereignty at the Edge: Macau and the Question of Chineseness* (Cambridge: Harvard University Asia Center, 2009).

10 For instance, bell hooks's anticolonialist stance is purposely "marginal," seeking to strategically center coloniality. She explains, "I was not speaking of a marginality one wishes to lose – to give up or surrender as part of moving into the center – but rather of a site one stays in, clings to even, because it nourishes one's capacity to resist. It offers to one the possibility of radical perspective from which to see and create, to imagine alternatives, new worlds." bell hooks, "Choosing the Margin as a Space of Radical Openness," in *The Feminist Standpoint Theory Reader: Intellectual and Political Controversies*, ed. Sandra Harding (New York: Routledge, 2004), 157.

11 Scholar, translator, and fellow poet Yao Feng 姚風 (pen name of Yao Jingming 姚京明) claims that Yiling is among the few who "molds her poetic discourse with a profound socially interventionist conscience." According to Yao, this is not common for local literature because despite Macau's larger degree of freedom of expression when compared to mainland China, it is still a city unaccustomed to "the critical voice." This is why, he claims, many authors prefer silence to an interventionist stance. Yao Feng, "Antologia de Poesia Contemporânea de Macau" [Anthology of Contemporary Macau Poetry], *Sibila: Revista de Poesia e Crítica Literária* (April 2009).

12 The question of whether the People's Republic of China constitutes a power as imperialist as Great Britain or Portugal vis-à-vis Hong Kong or Macau does not particularly interest me. If the statement can perhaps be understood as an expression of the heat of the prehandover years, it is now less acceptable to lump together the colonial projects of Great Britain (and Portugal) and the hegemonizing and homogenizing centripetal force exerted by the Chinese state in pursuit of territorial "integrity." In fact, in the same text, Chow offers what could be an apt retort to such a statement in her take on "the postmodern hybridite." Such a character, Chow argues, would, rather than condemn British colonialism in Hong Kong (seeing it as "international openness"), instead critique "Chinese nationalism (read: 'native conservatism'), thus obliterating or blurring the complex history of the rise of modern Chinese nationalism as an overdetermined response to Western imperialism of the past few centuries." Rey Chow, "Between Colonizers: Hong Kong's Postcolonial Self-writing in the 1990s," *Diaspora: A Journal of Transnational Studies* 2, no. 2 (1992): 151–170.

13 Rey Chow puts the question another way when she aligns her own work in relation to Hong Kong to Dipesh Chakrabarty's project of "provincializing" Europe: "Similarly," she writes, "in the context of Hong Kong one cannot but problematize 'China' at the same time as one dismantles 'Britain'" ("Between Colonizers," 156).

14 Rey Chow, "Between Colonizers," 156.

15 Jinghai 鏡海 (Sea of mirrors) is a common poetic epithet for Macau.

16 The façade of the Ruins of St. Paul sits on top of a small hill and may be reached by climbing sixty-eight stone steps.

17 Yiling 懿靈, *Liudong dao* 流動島 (The Drifting Isle) (Hong Kong: Shifang, 1990), 52.

18 Clayton, *Sovereignty at the Edge*, 2.

19 Yiling, *The Drifting Isle*, 34.

20 Yiling 懿靈, *Jiti siwang* 集體死亡 (Collective Death) (Macau: Pin-to Books, 2005), 37.

21 Instead of concealed histories that are revealed only to the most attentive, Yiling offers four ways a colonial government might want to be remembered after its demise, two of which are quoted below. In the first option, she writes: "December 20, 1999 / I steal a plot of land and a gravestone here / to bury / myself / and / the pirate ships from when I got here / if you want compensation / you can always come down and find me" (一九九九年十二月二十日／ 我在這兒偷去了一把泥土和一塊石牌／ 用來埋葬／ 我／ 和／ 我來時那艘海盜船／ 如果你需要償還／ 大可下來找我). In the fourth, she writes: "When I came / I was bare-bodied / when I left / I was covered in jewels / my loyal followers, / remember that here you still have riches" ("來的時候／ 赤身露體／ 去的時候／ 珠光寶氣／ 我的遺民／ 記得這兒尚有你的財富"). On Yiling's imagined gravestones, the colonial government speaks out defiantly of its territorial occupation and its pillaging, even reminding the Portuguese of post-1999 Macau (Yiling uses the term *yimin* [遺民], which may be translated as "loyal followers" but also carries connotations of adherents of a lost dynasty) that there is still much money to be extracted from the ex-colony. In this alternate version of a colonial government, there is no burial of criminal evidence; the only interment happening is that of a colonial government that has reached the end of its days. *Jiti siwang*, 40–41.

22 Local sociologist Hao Zhidong states that "political apathy continues to be a problem," and cites a 2009 survey in which 54.3% of Macau respondents claimed to not be interested in politics, slightly down from a 2005 survey in which the figure stood at 60% (with 27.5% claiming to be "not very interested" and 32.1% choosing "not interested at

all"). Hao cites another study, a comparative survey of Hong Kong and Macau views on free speech in which 71% of Hong Kong respondents believed that people with "different, even radical, opinions like people who believe in Falun Gong" should be permitted to voice their views publicly, compared to only 48.95% of Macau respondents. Hao Zhidong, *Macau History and Society* (Hong Kong: Hong Kong University Press, 2011), 50 and 184.

23 Yiling, *The Drifting Isle*, 51.
24 Yiling, *The Drifting Isle*, 8.
25 Clayton places the number of ethnic Chinese with Portuguese passports at approximately 30% of the Macau population. Clayton, *Sovereignty at the Edge*, 21. For further reading on the complexities of multiple passports in colonial and postcolonial Macau, see 291–297.
26 An author's footnote explains that the phrase "詐你形" is a colloquial Hong Kong and Macau expression meaning to "cause you trouble" (找你麻煩) or "to censure or rebuke you" (向你作出非議). Yiling, *The Drifting Isle*, 9.
27 An author's footnote clarifies that ABC refers to "American-Born-Chinese" (美國土生華人). Yiling, *The Drifting Isle*, 9.
28 Yiling, *The Drifting Isle*, 8.
29 Yiling, *The Drifting Isle*, 16.
30 In addition, Deng clarified that "there is no urgent need to solve the Macau question. . . . Now it is more important to maintain the stability and prosperity in the Hong Kong/Macau region." The pronouncements were made during a meeting with Macau business leader and local leader Ma Man-kei (馬萬祺) (1919–2014) shortly after similar meetings had begun with Hong Kong authorities. Cited in Herbert S. Yee, *Macau in Transition: From Colony to Autonomous Region* (London: Palgrave, 2001), xv.
31 Roland Barthes, "The Reality Effect," in *The Rustle of Language*, trans. Richard Howard (Berkeley: University of California Press, 1989), 142, 143 and 146.
32 Jing Tsu, "Weak Links, Literary Spaces, and Comparative Taiwan," 134.

Works cited

Barthes, Roland. *The Rustle of Language*. Trans. Richard Howard. Berkeley: University of California Press, 1989.
Chow, Rey. "Between Colonizers: Hong Kong's Postcolonial Self-Writing in the 1990s." *Diaspora: A Journal of Transnational Studies* 2, no. 2 (1992): 151–170.
Clayton, Cathryn H. *Sovereignty at the Edge: Macau and the Question of Chineseness*. Cambridge: Harvard University Asia Center, 2009.
Hao Zhidong. *Macau History and Society*. Hong Kong: Hong Kong University Press, 2011.
Lam, Agnes 林玉鳳. "Wu ziwo shiyi de chengshi." 無自我意識的城市 (A City with No Self-Consciousness). *Aomen ribao* 澳門日報 (Macau Daily), August 12, 2010.
Lei Chin Pang 李展鵬. *Zai shijie bianyuan yujian Aomen* 在世界邊緣遇見澳門 (Encountering Macau at the Margins of the World). Macau: Macao Daily News, 2013.
Shih, Shu-mei. "Globalisation and the (In)significance of Taiwan." *Postcolonial Studies* 6, no. 2 (2003): 143–153.
Tsu, Jing. "Weak Links, Literary Spaces, and Comparative Taiwan." In *Comparatizing Taiwan*, edited by Shu-mei Shih and Ping-hui Liao, 123–144. New York: Routledge, 2014.
Yee, Herbert S. *Macau in Transition: From Colony to Autonomous Region*. London: Palgrave, 2001.
Yiling 懿靈. *Liudong dao* 流動島 (The Drifting Isle). Hong Kong: Shifang, 1990.
Yiling 懿靈. *Jiti siwang* 集體死亡 (Collective Death). Macau: Pin-to Books, 2005.

8

EXPLAINING "GRAPHS" AND ANALYZING "CHARACTERS"

Zhang Guixing's novels and Sinophone literature's cultural imaginings and representational strategies

MEI Chia-ling

In recent years, thanks to efforts by scholars such as Shu-mei Shih, David Der-wei Wang, and Jing Tsu, Sinophone literature has emerged as an important topic within international Sinological discussions. Whether it be Shih's notion of "antidiaspora," Wang's discussion of "the politics of 'roots' and poetics of 'propensity,'" or Tsu's concept of "literary governance," these scholars have opened up a variety of new perspectives with respect to the study of contemporary Chinese-language literature. These approaches include attempts to question and challenge an essentialized notion of Chineseness, using a dialectical method to examine the spatiotemporal boundary within Sinophone theory, and considering the new linguistic formations that may develop through a process of circulation through time and space.[1] At its core, the Sinophone obviously takes sound as a key element, but as soon as it adopts the form of literature it must instead rely on the graphic and semantic function of written characters. Many commentators have pointed out that although humans created writing, when they use written language it inevitably shapes their perceptual and cognitive activity, producing a dialectical relationship. This is particularly true when it comes to literature. Therefore, regardless of whether one uses a Sinophone literary framework, it can still be viewed in terms of concepts of postcolonialism or "postloyalism," and regardless of whether at a linguistic level Sinophone literature has characteristics of a "minor literature" or is able to manifest a function of literary governance, the more fundamental question is, what kind of perceptual or cognitive change can help challenge the Chinese writing system's essential Chineseness? What kind of representational strategies can trace the meandering history of Sinophone literature's process of self-creation (and self-deconstruction)? It is precisely on this point that Zhang Guixing's 張貴興 novels offer a useful perspective.

Zhang Guixing was born in Sarawak, on the eastern Malaysian island of Borneo. In the 1970s, however, he came to study in Taiwan, where he has lived ever since. He began writing fiction in the 1980s, using a combination of intricate plot lines and dense language to compose numerous works about Southeast Asian migration, including *Siren Song* (賽蓮之歌), *Rogue Clan* (頑皮家族), *Elephant Tropes* (群象), *Monkey Cup* (猴杯), and *My South Seas Sleeping Beauty* (我思念的長眠中的南國公主). From the beginning, Borneo's mysterious rain forests have been an important setting for Zhang's novels, with their countless monkeys and elephants, lizards and crocodiles, together with the tempestuous relationship between Chinese and Malays. Given Zhang's background as a Malaysian Chinese (i.e., an ethnic Chinese from Malaysia), critics have tended to focus on issues of hometown consciousness and national identity in his works.[2] His novels are composed in very exquisite language, and they certainly can be viewed as oriented toward a classical Chinese civilization, though his characters also have a strong "savage" inclination that inevitably weakens the works' homeland consciousness.[3] The critic Tee Kim Tong 張錦忠 has discussed Zhang Guixing's entry into a "fortress of language,"[4] Li Youcheng 李有成 has observed that *Elephant Tropes* is "a cultural history that is critically collecting collective memories,"[5] and Ng Kim Chew 黃錦樹 has employed a concept of linguistic exile to analyze his works, using the mutual germination of "characters" (*zi* 字) and "forms" (*xiang* 象) to reflect on the works' fluctuating relationship to a notion of Chineseness.[6] While all of these critics emphasize the significance of "writing/culture" (*wenzi/wenhua* 文字／文化) in Zhang Guixing's novels, I instead will use a strategy of explaining "graphs" (*wen* 文) and analyzing "characters" (*zi* 字) as my own entry point into an analysis of the novels *Elephant Tropes* and *Monkey Cup*. More specifically, I will ask what is the impetus behind Zhang's characters' "savage" inclination? What kind of cultural imagination is contained therein? After the nation collapses and the homeland ceases to exist, will *wen* 文 (which is to say, the broad category that includes both "human culture" [*renwen* 人文] and "civilization" [*wenming* 文明]) also collapse? Conversely, how does the mutual germination of "characters" (*zi* 字) and "forms" (*xiang* 象) come to be implemented as a representational strategy, to the point that it can continuously increase Sinophone literature's self-dialectical power?

"Characters" (*zi* 字) and "graphs" (*wen* 文): in the land of elephants and monkeys

Malaysia has a complex ethnic and cultural background. Due to a variety of political factors, the plight of the country's ethnic Chinese has long been extremely difficult. Positioned at the interstices of Malaysian literature, Malaysian Indonesian literature, and Malaysian British literature, and composed by Chinese authors who occupy a subordinate position within Malaysia, "Mahua" (Malaysian Chinese) literature, from nearly the very beginning, has had to shoulder a heavy political and cultural burden. Meanwhile, the very act of writing in Chinese – combined with attendant cultural rituals that have a performative dimension in everyday life – has come to function as a way of distinguishing between Chinese and Malays, and is among the most important markers of cultural identity in the region.[7] Therefore, beginning with Li Yongping 李永平, many Mahua authors have made a focus on Chinese writing a central element of their literary practice. Zhang Guixing's novels use brilliant and complicated language, and at first glance, they would not appear to be exceptions to this rule. However, even as he eloquently narrates on a grand scale many different stories and legends relating to tropical rain forests, he simultaneously uses a variety of plot lines, narrative structures, and rhetorical strategies to observe and reflect on questions relating to the formation, transmission, and divergence of language, writing, and civilization. This characteristic can already be observed in his early works such as "Entry into a Besieged City" (圍城進出) and *Rogue Clan*, and is more fully developed in his more recent novels *Elephant Tropes* and *Monkey Cup*.

"Entry into a Besieged City" uses a chess metaphor to retell the history of Japan's invasion of China, while underscoring the entangled and mutually contested relationship between the two nations. In this work, the phrase "Wu Dalang creates Japanese *kanji*" is used to mock the way *kanji*, or the Japanese versions of Chinese written characters, rely on a sense of national distinctiveness. Meanwhile, *Rogue Clan* describes an ethnically Chinese family surnamed Kui who have immigrated to the South Seas region. Without getting into the work's characters and plot, we may note that every chapter opens with a passage from a family chronicle written by the family's son, Wanbao, and every Chinese character included in these excerpts is accompanied by phonetic notation. Although Wanbao writes in childlike language, he is fond of using unusual characters and likes to use a dictionary to look up each character's form and meaning. For instance, at the beginning of the novel, Wanbao participates in an essay contest organized by a church and uses "several ambiguous and unusual characters" to describe his father:

> *Long hair, a thoughtful expression, a crazed temperament, a tired expression, and sunken features.* Because [Wanbao] was unable to write the character for *bie* 瘪 ("sunken"), he suddenly had a strange thought as he was looking up the character in the dictionary. He studied several other characters with an "illness" (疒) radical, then selected more than ten of them to describe his father. Given that when characters with the "illness" radical are used as adjectives they mean "the appearance of someone sick who is leaning to one side," and given that the Kui family, who lived in a tilted house, shared this basic characteristic, all of the "illness" radical characters in the dictionary could be used to describe the Kui family. Wan Bao himself was "obsessed" (癖) with writing, and was a "bookworm" (書癡) who was "crazed" (瘋) about reading.[8]

Zhang's obsession with the form and meaning of Chinese characters, together with his multifold reflection on their significance, is developed even further in *Elephant Tropes*. The first chapter opens with a lengthy passage describing

Teacher Shao giving a lecture on Chinese cultural history, which is undoubtedly a major point in the novel:

> Teacher Shao shook his head as he used a very precise pronunciation to read Han Yu's essay "An Offering to a Crocodile," adding an explanation of every character:
>
> " . . . in appearance, the crocodile has the head of a dragon, the claws of a tiger, the eyes of a crab, and the scales of a lizard. Its teeth are as large as saw blades; its tail is several *zhang* long, with hook-shaped thorns, and is covered in sticky slime. When it is submerged near the riverbank, people or animals who approach may be struck by its tail and eaten."
>
> Behind Teacher Shao, there was the blackboard that students had wiped with their hands, on which was written, like a strange new flower, the following passages:
>
> "Crocodile: a large type of animal with a dragon head, horse tail, and tiger claws. It can reach a length of up to four *zhang*, crawls well, and eats humans."
>
> *Records on Impressions of Animals*
>
> "Crocodiles are more than two *zhang* long, have four legs, and resemble alligators. Their snout is three *chi* in length, with very sharp teeth. When tigers and deer try to ford the river, crocodiles may attack."
>
> *Records of Extraordinary Things*
>
> "In the South Seas there are crocodiles, which resemble alligators."
>
> *Records on Diverse Matters*[9]

Given that this is a lecture on Chinese cultural history, the "character-by-character" explanations do not focus solely on the form and meaning of each individual character, but rather attempt to approach the characters' cultural source and trace their subsequent development. Therefore, the various quotes about crocodiles taken from classical texts and their commentaries cannot be ignored. More important, however, Teacher Shao wants to explain crocodiles' environment and living habits while also addressing the relationship between crocodiles and "dragons." He notes that, based on archaeological research, there is abundant evidence that "in the past, there were countless crocodiles in the Yangtze, Huai, and Yellow Rivers, all the way to where the rivers emptied into China's South Sea, East Sea, and Bohai Sea, respectively." In ancient China, many jade vessels, bronze vessels, stone chimes, and bell drums were inscribed with enormous images of crocodiles, while "on one Shang dynasty stone chime, the inscribed image of a dragon is actually a crocodile. Crocodiles frequently appeared on ritual vessels and musical instruments in the form of dragons." Nevertheless, "in the central plains region, dragons were indeed frightful. They were enormous man-eating crocodiles" (20–21).

The relationship between crocodiles and dragons, together with their symbolic significance in the novel, is further elaborated on in the work's afterword. What I'd like to emphasize here, however, is how in this carefully presented classroom scene every Chinese character, in addition to specifying its referent, also carries rich cultural connotations as a result of its position within multilayered historical resonances, together with complex sensory structure and emotional sedimentation. Therefore, in the process of "analyzing characters (zi 字)," it is also necessary to "explain graphs (wen 文)." That is to say, it is necessary to view the characters within the context of a broader course of cultural development. The processes of analyzing characters and explaining graphs, accordingly, are actually two sides of the same coin. At the same time, however, unlike alphabetic writing systems, Chinese characters are replete with pictorial significance; not only do the characters' forms carry semantic connotations, but the act of writing them is also a kind of art. Therefore, with respect to the characters written on the blackboard, "even if students don't consider their meaning and only focus on their form, that is still enough to energize them, to the point that they pick up their pens and sigh with regret."

Elephant Tropes also touches on the cultural perspective contained within Chinese characters, together with the interrelationship between the various different pronunciations of certain characters. This point is suggestively illustrated in the scene where the novel's protagonist, Shi Shicai, has just taught an aboriginal girl named Fadiya how to read:

> "Female (女). The first character in 'woman' (女人). Three strokes. Most Chinese characters are pictographic, and this one represents a woman bowing and kneeling. Here are her knees, and here are her hands. Female. You. Woman. I. Man. Male (男). Seven strokes. Man labors, plowing the fields. The character for male has 'field' (田) on top, and 'force' (力) on the bottom. I'll teach you how to write your Chinese name. Fa. Di. Ya." – "'Di' (蒂) is difficult to write," Fadiya remarked, as she furrowed her thick brows. – "You can also leave off the grass radical (艹) on top. Or else you can use the character 'di' (娣), which is a homophone. Which do you prefer?"
>
> (99)

Throughout this passage, it is evident that the relationship among the form, sound, and meaning of Chinese characters (zi) and their corresponding graphs (wen) is extraordinary and very deliberate. Furthermore, the character xiang (象) in the Chinese title of *Elephant Tropes*, Qun xiang 群象, refers not only to real life "elephants" (大象) but also to "pictographic" (象形) characters, the "real appearance" (真象) of things, and to a literary "imagination" (想像), and can be linked to the rhetorical techniques of "imagery" (意象) and "symbolism" (象徵).

Accordingly, the work's referent is not limited to a legend that unfolds in the rain forest; its circuitous twists also deserve attention.

As for *Monkey Cup*, in addition to the relationship between "characters" (*zi* 字) and "forms" (*xiang* 象), the novel also attends to the relationship between "graphs" (*wen* 文) and "marks" (*wen* 紋), between characters and mimicry, as well as between sound and language. At the beginning of the work, for instance, the protagonist, Zhi – who is about to leave his teaching position in Taiwan and return to Borneo – is in the process of straightening up his office. The inscription on the side of the bamboo pen holder on his desk reveals the relationship among "graphs/marks" (文/紋), "characters" (*zi* 字), and "things of the world":

> The pen holder resembled a three-legged *ding*. . . . The outer housing resembled snake tracks that Zhi would draw when he was bored, using knives he had confiscated from students. Zhi knew this image so well that he could trace it with his eyes closed. . . . Although his drafting technique was poor, after considerable effort he was nevertheless able to produce something of beauty. Of several overly complex patterns, he only inscribed one or two, as though he were taking a cumbersome human body and simplifying it down to an embryo with only a head and tail. He felt that these patterns resembled the world's myriad things; insects, fish, birds, and animals; grass and trees; the sun, moon, stars, clouds, water, and fire; and even hair, eyebrows, ears, and noses; toes and claws. But he couldn't find a single clear attribution. Sometimes these inscriptions were so abstract that they resembled characters.[10]

Actually, Zhi's drafting skills are influenced by the rain forests in his homeland, where "in the living room of the stilt house, the inscriptions on a number of plastic artifacts had influenced him over the years." Borneo's inscribed artifacts and decorative arts are mostly related to the Dayak art master Ah Banban. Apart from inscribing weapons, building materials, jewelry, and assorted tools with images of various sorts of insects, fish, and plants, what interested Ah Banban most were tattoos. Not only did he tattoo his own body, such that

> his torso was covered in countless animals running around, as though it were a forest; his four limbs were covered in flowers, leaves, birds, and insects, as though they were tree branches; his back was covered in wind, fire, and lightning, as though it were the vast sky; his hands and feet were covered in reptiles; his buttocks were covered in skulls; his entire face was covered in fairies; and even his phallus was covered in marks,

he also took pleasure in marking up the bodies of his wife and relatives. The patterns he created were wide-ranging, and he never repeated the same pattern twice.

It was said that Ah Banban, from the time he was young, was fascinated by the art of inscription:

> In order to penetrate the intricacies of Borneo's decorative arts, in the middle of the night he would go out alone into the rain forest, pursuing animals and chasing the moon. During the day he would climb trees and scale cliffs, observing bushes and trees; insects, fish, and birds; feet, talons, and fangs. He would wander all over the island, serving his apprenticeship, and like a chameleon he would prey mimetically on the mysterious mottling of the tattoos of various different ethnic groups.
>
> *(107)*

This passage is clearly reminiscent of Xu Shen's description, in the postface to the *Shuowen jiezi* (說文解字), of the origins of language:

> In antiquity, as Paoxi ruled the world as king, looking up, he observed celestial phenomena in the heavens; looking down, he observed regularities on the earth. He saw suitable matches between the earth and the marking patterns on birds and wild animals. From nearby he took such marking patterns from various parts of his own body, from afar he took them from various parts of things, and thereby created the eight trigrams [in the *Book of Changes*] in order to hand down normative representations. . . .
>
> The Scribe of the Yellow Emperor, Cang Jie, observing the traces of the footprints and tracks of birds and wild animals, understood that their linear structures could be distinguished from one another by the differences between them. When he first created writing by carving in wood, the hundred officials became regulated, the myriad things became discriminated.[11]

Seeking out the essence of graphic representation, Ah Banban observed animals and plants in the rain forest, which is quite similar to the way that, in ancient China, Paoxi (a.k.a. Fu Xi) and Cang Jie are said to have established images and created characters. This is not a random comparison. Based on early sources, in the lives of the primitive people the function of all markings and engravings, including tattoos, did not lie in their aesthetic effects but rather in an element that had characteristics of religious ritual and was perceived to be the source of civilization.

It is particularly noteworthy that the *Shuowen jiezi* defines *wen* 文 as "a set of intersecting lines (*cuohua* 錯畫), resembling a crisscross pattern (*wen* 文). All characters relating to writing/markings (*wen* 文) are derived from this 文 graph." Based on oracle bone inscriptions, the original form of the character *wen* 文 was actually 𡥀, which represents an image of a man with tattoos on his chest. Therefore, many scholars have observed that the character's core meaning is "tattooed body" (*wenshen* 紋身), suggesting that this directly references the character's mimetic origins. The postface to the *Shuowen jiezi* also offers an additional explanation of the relationship between graphs (*wen*) and characters (*zi*):

> When Cang Jie first created writing, he probably relied on the variety of things and made pictographs (*xiangxing* 象形). Therefore, he referred to such written words as *wen* 文 (written units of a cultured pattern). After this, *xingsheng* 形聲 (classifier and phonetic elements) were added together; accordingly, he referred to them as *zi* 字 (offspring characters). *Wen* 文 serves as the basis of all things, and as for the word *zi* 字, this refers to gradual increase through reproduction and multiplication.[12]

This passage explains that "graphs" (*wen*) originally relied on "pictographs" (*xiangxing* 象形), and their nature approached that of "pictures" (*tuhua* 圖畫), which came to serve as "the basis of all things." Characters (*zi*), meanwhile, were reproduced and multiplied for this express purpose, while the process of "combining classifier and phonetic elements" was key in this same process of reproduction and multiplication. This explanation foregrounds the significance of pronunciation – which is to say, the sound produced when language is spoken aloud, which is the key connection between graphs and characters. "Characters" (*zi*) were originally merely "a set of intersecting lines"; only after they were given sound did they become characters. Characters, accordingly, are the material signifiers of sound, and in practice, if the sound is the same, it can produce different characters that can be interchanged with one another (like the "di" in the name Fadiya in the preceding passage, which could be written as 蒂, 帝, or 娣). This, in turn, facilitates the characters' circulation and transformation. In addition, the following definition from the *Zuozhuan* 左傳 (Duke Xi of Lu, Year twenty-four) is particularly noteworthy: "Voice: writing of the body."[13] This definition takes the ornamental nature of the concept of "tattoo" (*wenshen* 紋身) (which is to say, "body markings" – *shen zhi wen* 身之文), and extends it to rhetorical speech. The line also regards speech as the basis of an individual's self-expression, which creates an internal convergence of "graphs" (*wen* 文), "speech" (*yan* 言), and "self" (*zishen/ziwo* 自身/自我).

Returning to *Monkey Cup*, an important element of the novel involves devotion not only to tattoos but also to different sorts of "linguistic/verbal" inscription. Compared to the relative stability of the form of Chinese characters, their pronunciation is constantly changing. This is particularly true in the case of the multitude of languages spoken in Borneo, which includes not only many different dialects of Chinese but also languages from other language families, including English, Malay, and Dayak. Within this heteroglossic environment, the first person we see is the taxi driver who drives Zhi back to his hometown:

> The driver, whose face was windblown and covered in frost, was of unclear ethnicity, appearing to be either Malay, Dayak, Indian, or the descendent

of one of the Indonesians who came to Malaysia after its economy took off. However, the driver introduced himself as Chinese, and in order to earn Zhi's trust, he spoke in fluent Hakka and Cantonese.

(32)

After this, we also observe the following dialogue between Zhi's grandfather and great-grandfather:

> The grandfather had even forgotten what language he had used the last time he spoke to the great-grandfather. Was it Hakka? Cantonese? Fujianese? Mandarin? . . . Or maybe it was English, Malay, or Dayak.
>
> *(217)*

Of course, when Zhi interacts with individuals of Dayak ethnicity, there are even more opportunities for linguistic confrontation:

> Badu . . . resembled a mosquito that was left uneasy by the questions, and buzzingly launched into a rapid explanation in Dayak. Zhi, Badu, and others were different species of lizards, and with their half-Chinese, half-English mother tongue, they were unable to grasp even half a word of this flying-mosquito language. That authentic and strangely accented orthodox Dayak could only be spit out by girls and boys from the inner mountains.
>
> *(114)*

> . . .

> When (Yanini) spoke Dayak, her speech meandered like a serpent, but when she spoke English, it was as meticulously chiseled and decorated as her pendant earrings.
>
> *(89)*

> . . .

> (Yanini's speaking style) remained multifarious and elusive. Using a speaking style that was as meandering as a serpent, as lithe as a monkey, as shelled as a bird, and as damp as a fetus, she slowly described the family home she was going to visit, which was her destination.
>
> *(306)*

Commentators have observed that an ethnic group's spiritual culture is always manifested in the group's language and writing system.[14] Borneo's heteroglossic environment reflects the hybrid quality of the local spiritual culture. On this point, the novel suggests a loosening and deconstruction of a misogynistic attitude foregrounding China and the Chinese language, and represents a natural development of language's localism. It also comprehensively embodies the power of literary governance that is opened up in a context where different ethnic groups have historically lived side by side.

However, does the work's setting also have an even deeper significance? Given that Sinophone literature is located at the interstices of Chineseness and localism, this so-called Chineseness is not a phenomenon that can be observed directly, but rather is an internal schema embedded within all sensory experience and cognitive concepts while also including life practice and cultural imagination, smoothly infiltrating people's life ethics and literary representations. Based on the preliminary differentiation of "characters/forms" (*zi* 字/*xiang* 象) and "graphs/marks" (*wen*文/*wen* 紋) offered above, careful readers will notice that whether it is the inking of "characters" in *Elephant Tropes*, the attention to "culture" in *Monkey Cup*, or the two works' abundant use of analogous terms such as *like, resembles, as,* and *as if,* these various elements all clearly reveal that in Zhang Guixing's novels notions of Chineseness and divisive processes of observation and representation are located not solely at the level of visible phenomena, but rather at the work's intersecting uses of "characters" and "graphs." From the perspective of inner spirit, plot construction, character development, and language use, Zhang's novels develop a dialectical engagement with the concept of Chineseness. Therefore, as we develop an understanding of the internal perceptual and conceptual qualities that the concepts of "characters" and "graphs" originally carried in Chinese culture, this will provide a basis for further analysis of related cultural imagination and representational strategies.

The origins of characters and the genealogy of graphs: the construction schema underlying the Chinese cultural imaginary

Unlike alphabetic writing systems, Chinese characters originated from "pictographs" (*xiangxing* 象形) and "ideographs" (*xiangyi* 象意), and therefore have characteristics of both "characters" (*zi* 字) and "forms" (*xiang* 象). For instance, as noted above, the character for "female," 女, resembles "a woman bowing and kneeling," while the character for "male," 男, signifies the notion that "man labors, plowing the fields." This is why the basic nature of a character not only lies in its pictographic origins but also includes a narrative or conceptual component, such that characters may function as a miniature cultural field, projecting primitive people's life experience and modes of thinking. The practice of a "deep examination of names" that began in the Qin and Han dynasties, together with countless exegeses on naming that have been produced since then, all rely on this basic principle.[15]

In addition, as discussed above, the original forms of characters (*zi* 字) are graphs (*wen* 文) possessing pictographic and pictorial qualities. In the Chinese cultural tradition, numerous words and concepts have developed out of this notion of *wen* – including *wenzi* 文字 (writing), *renwen* 人文 (human culture), *wenzhi* 文治 (statecraft), *liwen* 禮文 (ritual text), *wenci* 文辭 (diction), *wenxue* 文學 (rhetoric), *wenhua* 文化 (culture), *wenming* 文明 (civilization), and so forth. These concepts have penetrated deeply into Chinese life and thought, and therefore it is taken for granted that *wen* 文, together with the cultural imaginary that is projected out of it, is an important element of Chineseness. The genealogy of the concept of *wen* is long and variegated, but it actually has a very distinct trajectory. If we turn to its origins, accordingly, we can grasp the concept's essence.

The *Shuowen jiezi* explains that the character *wen* 文 is "a set of intersecting lines." From this image we can derive the meanings of "pattern" (*wenli* 文理) and "order" (*zhixu* 秩序). Based on a variety of inherited materials and unearthed documents, it is clear that in the pre-Qin period the character *wen* had three main uses: *wenzhi* 文治 (statecraft), *liwen* 禮文 (ritual text), and *wenxue* 文學 (rhetoric).[16] Of these, the *wen* in *wenzhi* (statecraft) was the most important core concept in pre-Qin China, and literally meant "governance based on following the *wen*." What is being "followed," here, is "the *wen* of heaven and earth" (*tiandi zhiwen* 天地之文), which is to say, the order of the cosmos. This point is clearly explained in the "Great Treatise" (*Xici* 繫辭) of the *Book of Changes* (周易):

> The Yi was made on a principle of accordance with heaven and earth, and shows us therefore, without rent or confusion, the course (of things) in heaven and earth. (The sage), in accordance with (the Yi), looking up, contemplates the brilliant phenomena of the heavens, and, looking down, examines the definite arrangements of the earth; – thus he knows the causes of darkness and light. . . . There is a similarity between him and heaven and earth, and hence there is no contrariety in him to them.[17]
>
> . . .
>
> In antiquity, as Paoxi ruled the world as king, looking up, he observed celestial phenomena in the heavens; looking down, he observed regularities on the earth. He saw suitable matches between the earth and the marking patterns on birds and wild animals. From nearby he took such marking patterns from various parts of his own body, from afar he took them from various parts of things, and thereby created the eight trigrams in the *Book of Changes* in order to show fully the attributes of the spiritlike and intelligent, and to classify the qualities of the myriads of things.[18]

This latter passage from the "Great Preface" is actually the origin of the passage from Xu Shen's postface to the *Shuowen jiezi*, cited above. Accordingly, the legendary figure of Fuxi, after observing the various "graphs/marks" (*wen/wen* 文/紋) that appear on the surface of the myriad things on heaven and earth, was able to discern the order hidden behind these physical images (which is to say, their internal "spiritual shape"), and furthermore, through the induction of this order, he was able to create the eight trigrams, which became the standard on which the *Book of Changes* was established. Later, the legend developed that King Wen, who allegedly composed the *Book of Changes*, was named Wen 文 not only because he could grasp the order behind heaven and earth but also, more importantly, because he was a manifestation of the practice, in "statecraft" (*wenzhi* 文治), of following the *wen* in governing the world. When the Duke of Zhou "instituted the rites and composed music," he did so in order to use a spirit of statecraft to implement a specific political practice. Confucius inherited the quintessence of the *wen* of ritual and music, and pronounced, "Poetry rouses us, we stand upon courtesy, and music is our crown" – and in this way he transferred the culture of ritual and music from political practice to personal life practice. Laozi also inherited the essence of King Wen's principle of "governing on the basis of following the *wen* of heaven and earth," and pronounced, "The Dao does nothing, and there is nothing it does not do."

Both "ritual text" (*liwen* 禮文) and "rhetoric" (*wenxue* 文學) are products of human culture, but also have their origins in the cosmological order. Zhou-dynasty ritual was closely related to "ornamentation" (*wenshi* 紋飾), which is to say, patterns of dress, and it was common to use fabric patterns to symbolize the patriarchal system and the order of heaven and earth – and in this way the patterns possessed a quality of "virtue comparison" (*bide* 比德) (likening character-istics in nature to human virtues) and functioned as a mark of "subalternation" (*chadeng* 差等). In pre-Qin texts, one often sees phrases such as *fufu wenzhang* 黼黻文章 (embroidered prose) and *jinxiu wencai* 錦綉文采 (brocade writings) – both of which refer to fabric patterns and not to the later literary meaning of "articles" (*wenzhang* 文章). This type of usage was common in Zhou-dynasty ritual records. For instance, in the "Records of the Examinations of Crafts-men" (Kaogongji 考工記) chapter of the *Rituals of Zhou* (周禮), it is written that "Green set beside red, this we call *wen*; red set beside white, this we call *zhang* 章 [seal]; white set beside black, this we call *fu* 黼 [embroidered black and white axes]; black set next to green, this we call *fu* 黻 [embroidered blue and black undulations]; the five colors are all prepared such that they refer to different types of embroidery."

Meanwhile, in the "Second Year of the Duke of Huang" chapter of the *Zuozhuan*, we find references to "robes, ceremonial caps, leathern aprons, and jade tablets," as well as to "weaves of fire, dragons, black and white axes, and blue and black undulations"[19] – all of which refer to the "nine *wen*" (namely, mountains, dragons, flowers, insects, seaweed, fire, powder rice, black and white axes, and blue and black undulations) that the "true ruler" has painted on the clothing he wears, symbolizing the fact that he has attained a virtue of "nine *wen*." However, in the "Twenty-Fifth Year of the Duke of Zhao" chapter of the *Zuozhuan*, in the exchange between Duanzi and Zhao Jianzi, there is an even clearer example of how all phenomena and ethics of the human cultural world are concealed within the cosmological order.[20] From this it can be observed that compared to the early Zhou notion of "statecraft" (*wenzhi*), which was predicated on a principle of "governance based on following the pattern (*wen*)," this period's "ritual text" (*liwen*) had already proceeded toward formalization and institutionalization based on "following the pattern (*wen*)," thereby becoming a custom-made human order. This is not merely a process of following a cosmological pattern (*wen*); it also involves taking all of the mortal world's phenomena and incorporating them into a cosmological pattern. In fact, through a process of analogy and symbolism, the ritual-legal system not only possesses a normative human order but furthermore is itself is a manifestation of that order. In this way, the cosmos, politics, and ritual law become an inseparable trinity.

Aside from this, the *wen* in *wenxue* (rhetoric) refers to *wenci* 文辭 (diction) and *wenxian dianji* 文獻典籍 (documents and classics). As for the contemporary meaning of *wenxue* as "literature," this did not begin to develop until the Wei-Jin and Six Dynasties periods. Not coincidentally, the essence of this *wen-xue* ("the study of the *wen*"), together with the path that it forms, similarly developed out of the concept of a "cosmological *wen*" (*tiande zhi wen* 天地之文). The "Originating in the Way" (*Yuandao* 原道) chapter of Liu Xie's 劉勰 *Wenxin diaolong* 文心雕龍 (The literary mind and the carving of dragons) builds on *The Book of Changes* and comes straight to the point:

> The power of the pattern (*wen*) as a power is great. It is born together with heaven and earth, and why is it so? With the black [of heaven] and the yellow [of the earth], the myriad colors are compounded. With the squareness [of the earth] and the roundness [of heaven], all forms are distinguished. The sun and the moon overlap each other like two jade disks, manifesting to those below the magnificent image of heaven. Rivers and mountains are brilliantly adorned to display the orderly configurations of the earth. These are the patterns of the Tao. As man looked up to see the radiance above and looked down to observe the inner loveliness below, the positions of high and low were determined and the two primary forms [heaven and earth] came into being. Only human beings, endowed with intelligence, can integrate with them. Together they are called the Triad. Human beings are the efflorescence of the Five Agents and are, in fact, the mind of heaven and earth. When mind came into being, language was formed. When language was formed, the pattern became manifest. This is the Dao, the natural course of things.[21]

The relation of *wen* 文 to *ren* 人 (human) is similar to the relationship among the sun, moon, mountains, and rivers and "(the Way of) the cosmos" (*tiandi [zhidao]* 天地 [之道]), in that they are both manifestations of a quality of "as-it-isness" (*ziran* 自然). This is an important discourse that emerged in China in the Wei-Jin period and is particularly associated with Liu Xie. This discourse, moreover, resonates closely with the assertion in the *Zuozhuan* that "voice [is] writing of the body," in that they both suggest that language and diction are manifestations of the individual self. Interestingly, this literary perspective of "as-it-isness" actually derives from a similar analogical principle as the discursive trinity of "cosmos, politics, and ritual law." Namely, the category of "human *wen*" (*ren zhi wen* 人之文) is analogous to the category of "heavenly *wen*" (*tian zhi wen* 天之文), and therefore the state of "as-it-isness" characteristic of heavenly *wen* guarantees a similar state as it pertains to human *wen*. The only difference is that the *wen* in *wenxue* ("rhetoric") is an activity initiated by humans and is based on the workings of one's mental state. It involves articulating one's will based on one's perception of reality (感物吟志). Given that every individual's talent and learning are different, they therefore produce literary works with different styles and features.

In sum, regardless of whether the concept of *wen* is found in the notions of *wenzhi* (statecraft), *liwen* (ritual text), or *wenci* (diction), the concept's origin and development is precisely the set of human ideals and modes of practice that constitute "human culture" (*renwen huacheng*). It refines an inner spiritual schema based on the changes of natural images, and from this it forms culture and displays civilization. Although these three notions do not constitute the entirety of "cultural imagination," they have undoubtedly long been its core elements. From the principle of creating "characters" (*zi*) to the development of the concept of graphs (*wen*), mimicry (*nixiang* 擬象) and analogy (*leibi* 類比) have long been important rules behind the formation and development of Chinese culture. Compared to Western culture's emphasis on conceptual analysis and precise definition, the perceptual experience and modes of thinking associated with Chinese culture have always emphasized a process of "adopting metaphors and associating categories" (*yinpi lianlei* 引譬連類) and "reasoning by analogy" (*chulei pangtong* 觸類旁通). Therefore, when applied to writing literature, so-called processes of "affective image" (*bixing* 比興), "metaphor" (*biyu* 比喻), and "symbolism" (*xiangzheng* 象徵) are not purely rhetorical techniques; they also carry deep cultural connotations.

However, precisely because mimicry and analogy were characterized by a quality of arbitrariness and contingency in the way they allowed one thing to serve as an analogy for another, it was common from the beginning for Chinese characters to have one sound that can correspond to multiple different characters and one character to have multiple different meanings, not to mention the way processes of borrowing and transference helped spawn more complicated usages. More specifically, whether it is a question of identifying a character's form, sound, and meaning or the relationship between a graph and its referent, or the way that diction and poetry rely on metaphor and symbolism to express specific meaning and grand significance, it is impossible to avoid internalizing many free-flowing random elements.

Accordingly, when we return to Zhang Guixing's novels, we notice that from the characters in *Elephant Tropes* to the graphs in *Monkey Cup*, there is precisely this sort of free flow that develops in dialogue with – or even deconstruction of – a sense of Chineseness/cultural imaginary. Below, I will develop this point through a process of textual analysis.

Explaining "graphs" and analyzing "characters": strategies of representation and internal tensions in *Elephant Tropes* and *Monkey Cup*

"Both character and form," "similar yet not similar," and "hunting elephants with form" – the hunt for language in Elephant Tropes *and its attendant paradoxes*

Elephant Tropes revolves around the ethnically Chinese boy Shi Shicai and his journey hunting elephants and searching for people in Borneo's rain forest, from which the novel presents a family history of how Shi Shicai's parents' families originally immigrated to Borneo, together with their complicated entanglements with local colonizers, Japanese soldiers, Communists, and aborigines. The most critical term in Zhang's novel is obviously the character *xiang* 象. As discussed above, because *xiangxing* 象形 (pictograph) is a key principle behind the construction of Chinese characters, the resulting characters all have a pictographic quality and represent a combination of "both character (*zi* 字) and form (*xiang* 象)." However, the paradox is that, in becoming characters, pictographs must thereby leave behind their former status as form, meaning that pictographic characters are fundamentally "similar yet not similar." Furthermore, in the process of writing, everything is a function of "imagery" (*yixiang* 意象) and symbolism (*xiangzheng* 象徵), meaning that characters are, as the *Book of Changes* puts it, a product of the process whereby "[the sage] simulates the shapes that different things may take, and calls them each an image" (擬諸其形容，象其物宜). That is to say, they are also an example of the principle of "similar yet not similar."

Interestingly, just as in the novel *Elephant Tropes* the character *xiang* 象 refers both to what in the real world are called "elephants" (*daxiang* 大象) and also more abstractly to the "real appearance" (*zhenxiang* 真象/相) of things, the novel's plot about hunting elephants and pursuing people becomes a chronicle of using *xiang* 象 (which is to say, writing) to hunt *xiang* 象 (elephants/forms). The character "*xiang*" 象 in the phrase *liexiang* 獵象 ("hunting elephants") includes, at the very least, the use of characters for the purpose of narration and symbolism. Its secret can perhaps be found in the novel's description of the origins and evolution of Borneo's elephants and other species, which is hinted at in the volume *Notes on Elephant Hunting*, written by the boy's uncle, Yu Jiatong.

First, let's turn to the work's discussion of actual elephants. The novel offers two legends about the origins of Borneo's elephants. The first is that in the year 326 the Indian Kong Porus gave six war elephants to the king of Brunei as a symbol of the friendship between the two countries, and the king of Brunei gave him countless rare birds and animals in return. The king of Brunei couldn't bear to keep the war elephants in confinement, and therefore set them free in

Borneo's rain forest. The six elephants were inseparable, and quickly reproduced to yield a large herd that has survived up to the present day (31–32). The second legend, meanwhile, is related to the Ming dynasty court eunuch Zheng He, and contends that the tributary gifts Zheng He brought back from his expeditions to East Africa included numerous lions and elephants, leopards and rhinoceroses . . . and when he stopped in Borneo, he exchanged some of his extra elephants for some local peacocks, guinea fowl, wildcats, and other indigenous birds and animals. Because the elephants were difficult to domesticate, however, the locals released them into the rain forest, where they reproduced until they yielded a large herd (32).

However, the narrative also notes that "regardless of whether they were Indian war elephants, wild African elephants, or elephants from somewhere else," the most interesting thing is:

> This herd was very intelligent and had a strong sense of exclusion. The enormous tusks that grew next to their trunks, however, became tempting valuables, and in the late seventeenth century, a British hunting expedition carried out an elephant slaughter. . . . In the early eighteenth century, a Dutch hunting expedition carried out another slaughter. . . . In the beginning of this century, there are still many hunting expeditions pursuing and killing these elephants. . . . After being hunted for several centuries, these elephants developed many techniques for protecting themselves and avoiding humanity. They developed this knowledge in response to their local conditions and passed it down from one generation to the next, such that they came to resemble hermits in the rain forest, completely isolated from the outside world. Humans only heard about them, but rarely saw them. They could only be found in some unknown location deep in the mountains, surrounded by clouds, where they enjoyed simple meals while reciting poems about the wind and moon.
>
> *(32–33)*

Although this passage is clearly describing elephants, the final line draws on language commonly used to describe human hermits. Furthermore, when the boy looks up documents in the library, he discovers that "elephants, which have a similar life expectancy as humans, also share similar behaviors and emotions with humans" (95). Is this above passage using elephants to represent humans, or as a symbol of a particular group of humans (perhaps Chinese)? Or is it an allusion to how ethnically Chinese Malaysians remember Chinese culture and are united in pursuing it? Or perhaps it is simply using elephants as a symbol of Borneo's natural resources, which have been continually exploited by outsiders? Throughout the novel, elephants flicker in and out of sight – and at one point they are trampling the boy's grandmother to death, while at another point they are rescuing the boy himself from the brink of death. The last time they are glimpsed by humans, they are either dead or dying, and they leave behind a multitude of priceless and highly coveted tusks. In this ambiguity, there are numerous spaces for discussion.

In addition, *Elephant Tropes* has many narrative lines that speak to the species' origins and subsequent evolution. One theme that runs through these various narrative lines concerns how, over time, both humans and animals were continually migrating and adapting to their new surroundings, such that their eventual relationship with their ancestors became one of being "similar yet not similar." Outsiders who move into the region, together with the lifestyles that they bring with them, may also change the local environment and lifestyle, such that the two become inextricably mixed. An example of the former phenomenon can be found in the African elephants that Zheng He allegedly brought to Borneo, where "the environment and food led them to evolve, over the course of the following centuries, until they were smaller than their African ancestors. The density of the rain forest and river system made it such that their ability to dissipate heat via their ears was not as important as it had been, and consequently their ears also became smaller than those of their ancestors" (32). An example of the latter phenomenon, meanwhile, is how "[traces of] China could be found everywhere in Borneo's long houses" and how "the local way of planting rice was handed down from the Tang dynasty" (90).

The aboriginal girl Fadiya is described as having "black hair, black eyes, and high cheekbones," and she "looked Chinese." Her appearance might be the result of human migration, though it was difficult to identify her ancestors with certainty:

> Peking Man . . . Java Man . . . our Asian ancestors. Four million years ago, Homo erectus migrated from Africa to the Asian continent. One million years ago, Java Man Java Man was active in the Southeast Asian landmass of Sundaland (which extended from what is now the Malay Peninsula to Java, and from Borneo to the Philippines' Palawan Island). Eight hundred thousand years ago, Java Man migrated north and reached southern China, becoming Lantian Man. Six hundred thousand years ago, Lantian Man migrated even further north, becoming Peking Man. Meanwhile, in 1900 members of the Shi clan migrated south from southern China, and settled in Borneo, thereby returning to the homeland of their Java Man ancestors.
>
> *(91)*

This is indeed a factual account of the course of human evolution and migration, but if we compare it to the great Chinese migration to Southeast Asia, it is hard to avoid seeing this as a symbolic commentary that conveys deep meaning with few words. In this respect, Teacher Shao's discussion, in his course on Chinese culture, of the migration and evolution of crocodiles is particularly thought-provoking. According to a paleometeorologist cited by Teacher Shao:

> Before the Xia and Shang dynasties, the climate of China's central plains region had been similar to that of the tropics, and this was particularly true

of the middle and lower regions of the Yellow River and the corresponding alluvial fan region, which were full of swamp and wetlands, with high humidity and heavy rainfall, and dense forests that were conducive to both herbivores and carnivores – thereby providing crocodiles with ideal living conditions.

(19–21)

. . . .

During the Xia and Shang dynasties, the climate and ecology of the Central Plains region underwent a significant transformation. The region became colder, droughts became common, lakes dried up, and crocodile populations declined until they disappeared entirely from northern China. Eventually, all that was left was the relatively small Chinese alligator – also known as the Yangtze alligator, which can be found in the middle and lower regions of the Yangtze River. From the Qin and Han dynasties forward, the central plains became increasingly cold, and the Chinese alligator almost went extinct. Eventually all that was left were legends. These legends were gradually replaced by myths, whereby the crocodiles became a primitive form of dragons. They became the mystification of dragons, the animalization of dragons, and the secularization of crocodiles.

(21)

Teacher Shao then emphasizes in a loud voice: "The central plains dragons were indeed terrifying; they were man-eating crocodiles" (21).

The Chinese often call themselves the descendants of dragons. In traditional culture, dragons occupy a mysterious, sublime position, and are often compared to emperors. In the past, scholars often believed that the imagination of dragons developed out of the worship of snake totems in the ancient central plains region. However, *Elephant Tropes* tells us, "The central plains dragons were indeed terrifying; they were man-eating crocodiles." Here, not only is the dragon's sublimity and sacredness stripped away, the central plains terrestrial snakes that were originally the object of totem worship are replaced by aquatic crocodiles. Moreover, these man-eating giant crocodiles originally developed in the central plains region, but because of climate change they could no longer survive there and migrated south. Accordingly, does not the crocodile stand as a metaphor for Chinese migrants to the South Seas region, which in reality are actually the original authentic ethnic Chinese?

In returning from the mythical dragon to the primeval, secular, and terrifying crocodile, another layer of meaning that emerges is that once the layer "humanism" (*renwenxing* 人文性) that develops out of culture and civilization is stripped away, what is revealed is the phenomenon's "animalistic" natural appearance. Critics have already noted that Zhang Guixing's novels have a "bestiary" quality, in which many human characters display animalistic tendencies.[22] This tendency runs parallel with a process of negating the dragon as crocodile, and involves a dismantling and displacement of a corresponding concept of Chineseness. That is to say, if a concept of *wen* – together with the various cultural ideals and practices that develop out of it – serves as the core of a sense of Chineseness, then a return to the animality of primitive species is precisely a return to the primal state of a "cosmological *wen*" (*tiandi zhi wen* 天地之文).

With respect to the *Notes on Hunting Elephants* left behind by Yu Jiatong, the text uses a halting "wild language" to record both real life elephant-hunting experiences as well as an astonishing family secret: namely, that Japanese invaders castrated Shicai's father and raped his mother, after which his mother gave birth to Shicai's elder brother, Shinong. Moreover, all of Shicai's other siblings were then born as a result of his father's repeatedly using his mother's body to pay off his own gambling debts. The next generation of the Yu clan, accordingly, all had the same mother but different fathers, and in this way the clan's bloodline became completely hybridized.

This sort of "true appearance" is, of course, completely astonishing, and the boy's reading experience was like diving into a river until he almost drowned:

> Uncle's handwriting was messy and his characters were as large as buckets. Every character resembled a leech full of blood occupying the text, which was like a metal box used to scoop parasites and algae out of the river. Withered characters, succulent parasites. Skeletal sentences, tangled algae. The murky and entangled first-person narrative resembled a tombstone inscription at the bottom of a river. The boy had sunk down to the river-bed and his breath had become as thin as a filament, and after catching a glimpse of a sentence fragment he frantically swam back up to the surface.
>
> *(217)*

In this description of how the boy, as a result of his "elephant/text hunt," found his spiritual breath becoming as thin as a filament, the textual violence inherent in his use of imagery is very clear. Coincidentally, in real life the boy's father died as a result of consuming text. That is to say, his father, his mind already addled by age,

> ate with chickens and ducks, slept with dogs and cats, and would mistake calendars, newspapers, and books for delicacies, eating them whenever he saw them. . . . He consumed Yu Dafu's "Sinking," Lu Xun's "Diary of a Madman," and Sartre's *Nausea*, as well as *The Pagan Tribes of Borneo*, *A History of Magic*, and *Tropical Flora*, among other literary classics.
>
> *(141–142).*

In the end, the father dies:

> Father sat motionless in the corner, his legs stretched out and his hands dangling down. His throat, esophagus, and stomach were stuffed full of

all sorts of chewed-up multicolored paper, and his stomach protruded to the point that it looked like he had swallowed an entire boar. He was facing upward, his eyes appeared half-closed, and he had a colored scrap of a map in his mouth. That was an octavo map of Borneo, and the hot and humid southeastern portion had already entered Father's stomach, while the northwestern portion, which abutted the southern China Sea, was soaked in saliva.

(195–196)

As everyone knows, the theme of cannibalism in Lu Xun's "Diary of a Madman" has both a realistic and a symbolic component, and obviously the father's book consumption has a similar function. It is a real-life symptom of an illness while also symbolizing the crazed enthusiasm that South Seas Chinese have for Chinese "graphs" and "characters," and for literary and cultural knowledge – though in this case what the father is pursuing is no longer a pure "Chinese" culture.

From this it can be observed that the foundation of the account of "elephant" (*xiang* 象) hunting in *Elephant Tropes* is grounded on the polysemic value of the Chinese character *xiang* 象. From notions of "both character and form" (*jizi jixiang* 即字即象) to "similar yet not similar," and from narrative to symbol, the character *xiang* 象 plays a paradoxical role of both construction and deconstruction throughout the entire novel. It originates as a pictographic Chinese character that is used to pursue and hunt elephants (*xiang* 象), with the result that it deviates from the notion of China/Chineseness that is nominally its source and objective.

The rewriting of "graphs" – body "graphs" (wen 文) or body "markings" (wen 紋)? The construction of human culture, or the weak being consumed by the strong?

In addition to "characters" (*zi* 字), *Elephant Tropes* is also very attentive to "pictures" (*tuhua* 圖畫). The map of Borneo and the Chinese landscape painting titled *Landscape of Wind and Rain* mutually reflect on each other, even as they anticipate the speculation on and rewriting of the traditional concept of *wen* 文 that we subsequently see in *Elephant Cup*. This part of the work's narrative strategy features qualities of both simile and analogy found in the notion of "similar yet not similar," as well as the quality of mimicry found in the notion of "not similar yet similar."

In *Elephant Tropes* the map of Borneo is first mentioned in the context of a discussion of a map of China, which reveals the protagonists' sense of national identification:

When Yu Jiatong was attending his middle school geography class, his politically leftist, ethnically Chinese instructor would often fold a map of Borneo into the shape of a begonia, saying, "If Mongolia had not secured

independence, look how similar China and Borneo would have been!"
The instructor would refer to Sarawak's longest river, the Rejang, as the
Yangtze, and would refer to its second-longest river, the Baram, as the Yel-
low River. Later, when Yu Jiatong assumed personal command over the
Rejang River, this came to be the origin of his phrase "Yangtze Brigade."

(85)

The *Landscape of Wind and Rain* painting, meanwhile, is a work by the
Southern Song painter Wu Jian, and is also Teacher Shao's family treasure.
In his Chinese culture class, Teacher Shao solemnly introduces it and adds:
Every time I see it, I can't help but think of the magnificent mountains
and rivers or our homeland. . . . Whichever of you turns out to be most
successful in life, I will give you this painting.

(120)

However, the irony is that, in the end, this latter painting follows Yu Jiatong
back to the base camp of the "Yangtze Brigade," and as the troops' ideals collapse and they fail to attain their original goals, the painting undergoes a subtle
transformation:

Under the light of the oil lamp, *Landscape of Wind and Rain* revealed a different charm, mimicking a hot and humid tropical landscape. . . . With
long houses and stilt houses replacing the painting's original brocade pavil-
ions, and the painting's literati students traveling through mountains and
streams being transformed into half-naked Iban girls playing in water,
the entire Southern Song landscape painting became instead a batik print
depicting South Seas sentiments. The light from the oil lamp revealed
Teacher Shao's handwriting on the blackboard, which included some
characters that were so misshapen that they were difficult to recognize,
while others still revealed their indistinct strokes. They were like a pile of
bones, like a tomb filled with bones that has been exposed by the wind and
rain. Geckos were crawling around through the bones like a nest of snakes
crawling through a chicken grave.

(149–150)

Particularly noteworthy here is the use of the word *mimicry* (*nitai* 擬態). This
term is borrowed from evolutionary biology, where it refers to how a species acquires qualities similar to those of another, in order to prevent other
animals (particularly predators) from recognizing it. In this way, the species
goes from "nonsemblance" (*buxiang* 不像) to "semblance" (*xiang* 像). Here,
the implicit significance of the Southern Song landscape painting that mim-
ics a batik print depicting South Seas sentiments, or the Chinese characters
appearing misshapen or indistinct, like character bones or character graves,
is obvious.

Fundamentally, both the operations of simile and analogy contained in the notion of "similar yet not similar" and the mimicry contained in the notion of "not similar yet similar" share a quality of deceptiveness. However, the former, which derives its meaning from the *Book of Changes*, is an important channel in construction of the cultural world, while the latter, which is derived from biology, refers to the phenomenon of evolution in the natural world. The difference between the two is manifested in the different narrative strategies adopted by *Elephant Tropes* and *Monkey Cup*. In *Elephant Tropes*, there is no lack of examples of the use of mimicry as a rhetorical device, though the work primarily emphasizes the mimetic quality of Chinese characters, and by using the evolutionary trajectory of a single species it reflects on the position of Malaysian Chinese at the interstices of Chineseness and locality. The narrative strategy of *Monkey Cup*, meanwhile, involves a return to origins. The work begins by foregrounding humanity's "animality," then uses a variety of different "deceptive" rhetorical operations to establish a dialogue with a traditional notion of *wen*, thereby fundamentally displacing and rewriting a cultural imaginary grounded on an idea of human culture that emphasizes statecraft and ritual.

Monkey Cup describes a teacher from Malaysia, named Zhi, who in Taiwan sleeps with a prostitute who turns out to be his student, as a result of which he is forced to quit his job and return to Borneo. At home, he discovers that his "sister," Limei, has disappeared after giving birth to a deformed child, whereupon Zhi goes into the rain forest to search for her; from this he lays out a chronicle of his clan history. At first glance, the structural mode of "entering the forest" and "pursuit" would appear to be quite similar to that of *Elephant Tropes*. However, unlike *Elephant Tropes*, which emphasizes the clan's underlying hybridity and uses the Sarawak Communist Party's resistance efforts, together with the plot line that offers elephant hunting as a metaphor for the imagination of and disillusionment with Chinese culture, *Monkey Cup* focuses on describing how the protagonist's Yu clan, after migrating to the South Seas and setting up a local industry in Borneo, developed a complicated administrative relationship with the colonized subjects, the aborigines, and even the local Chinese. From this the novel develops its various different reflections on – and rewritings of – the concept of *wen*. The concept's "deceptive" rhetorical operation is first revealed in the ambiguity in the types of name. For instance, the work's protagonist is named Zhi (literally, "pheasant") and his younger brother is named Ling ("wagtail lark"); by contrast, in Borneo, the rhinoceros that Zhi's grandfather has been raising in captivity for many years is called Viceroy. In other words, human characters are given animalistic names, while actual animals are given names that carry human characteristics.

Moreover, the novel often uses animalistic descriptions of human characters. For instance, Zhi is described as "resembling a small insect, creeping shamefully in a tree" (26), and the narrative adds that "[the girl] seemed to view Zhi as that nocturnal beast, and through her mother's explanations, she recognized and remembered him" (28). Zhi's female student in Taiwan is similarly described in animalistic terms:

> Zhi emerged from the wholesale store, and as he was crossing an overpass on his way to school he encountered a group of small animals. . . . Zhi's steps were relatively large, and as he walked in front of that group of animals, he didn't dare to turn around and look back.
>
> *(28–29)*

Later, "the following semester, it turned out that the wild rabbit he had pursued more than a month earlier could become his student" (61). Conversely, actual birds and animals are anthropomorphized and frequently display human characteristics. For instance, "the pigs resembled charming girls, the ducks had the expression of boudoir blues, while the chickens were like monks cultivating *zen*" (121), and "the rooster paced back and forth through the bare room, enduring hardships in order to realize its ambition, and worrying about the country and the people" (203–204). This personification is particularly evident in the reference to the rhinoceros as Viceroy, and every time an anthropomorphic conceit appears in the novel, it confuses the readers' understanding of the text. For instance, Viceroy is first introduced in the following scene:

> Zhi still remembered that time when he was fifteen and was walking under the rambutan bridge with Viceroy, and how at dusk his grandfather crossed over a single-plank bridge while leading the nine-year-old Limei by the hand. Zhi opened a wooden fence, passed through the Yu clan pineapple orchard and pepper garden, then proceeded through the wild grass and noisy birds to enter the Yu family home.
>
> *(34)*

At first glance, in this description of Zhi and Viceroy taking a stroll at dusk while Zhi's grandfather is leading Limei home, readers might assume that "Viceroy" is either a member of the Yu family or a close friend. Only after the narrative specifies that "in the animal pen, Viceroy's calls were like drumbeats and its hoofs resembled claps of thunder" does it become clear that Viceroy is not human, but rather an animal.

There is obviously no deep meaning behind why this particular member of one of Borneo's endangered species came to be called Viceroy. As everyone knows, Borneo had previously been colonized by the British, and the highest-ranking local official was the viceroy. Therefore, when it comes to the experiences of the rhinoceros, the novel describes how, after the animal reached maturity,

> its horn swayed back and forth, its hoofs circled around, it sliced and smashed its enemies, appearing very casual, with a king-like air. More than half a year later, it was given the title of Viceroy . . . as if announcing

to the world that it was ruling this wilderness just like the English viceroy
ruled over Britain's colonial territories.

(73)

The Yu family is able to own such a large plantation beside the Baram River
because Zhi's great-grandfather and grandfather preemptively fenced in a
large piece of land, "and in this way, a large amount of undeveloped or semi-
developed land had come under the control of the Yu family" (85). Also, the
great-grandfather, after repeatedly going in and out of the governor's house,
ultimately emerged "carrying a copy of the colonial government's development
certificate and a reclamation treaty directing workers to exploit the land" (162).
After the rhinoceros was captured by Zhi's great-grandfather and grandfather, it
became a member of the Yu household; "Grandfather, Viceroy, and four dogs"
became close allies, and together "they defended this chaotic and ambiguous
home" (53).

Here it is easy to see that in giving the wild-born rhinoceros the British
imperial title of viceroy, the novel is commenting on how in the wilds of Borneo, both the rhinoceros and the administrator occupied a "colonial" position. The Yu family's vast horticultural business is a result of cronyism and
a process of currying favor, meaning that these two "viceroys" of the world
of men and the world of beasts mirror each other. In fact, eventually Zhi's
great-grandfather himself becomes a "viceroy." It is particularly significant
that in order to expand its own assets, the Yu family is clever and unscrupulous, and its business administration completely abandons the ritual-legal
governance previously promoted with Chinese culture and instead comes to
rely on an animalistic logic of "survival of the fittest." Zhi recounts how his
grandfather

> purchased the coffee and tobacco plantations that the colonial govern-
> ment had entrusted him to operate, and inside the plantations he opened a
> casino, opium house, and brothel. Then he reclaimed a second plantation
> further down the Bantam River. . . . He spent ten years using a combina-
> tion of bribes and threats, combined with practices of sowing discord and
> using foreigners against each other, as he attempted to appease, control,
> and eliminate the locals.

Most significant, however, is that

> the relationship between the plantation and the locals resembled that
> between bears and bee hives, orangutans and wild durians, and cobras and
> macaques – it was a complex evolutionary lesson in survival of the fittest
> and a food chain debate, with the key element being who is the predator
> and who is the prey.

(180–181)

Zhi's great-grandfather is sinister and diabolical, and in order to expand his family's land he massacres the locals, not sparing even his fellow immigrant Chinese. Zhi's grandfather inherits the family business and is in no way inferior to his predecessors. This is precisely an example of using a predatory approach to managing the wilderness. From the preceding summary of the development of the ideas of *wen* 文 and *wenzhi* 文治 (statecraft) from the Qin dynasty forward, it is clear that this is another example of "governance based on following the *wen*" – though the *wen* that is being followed here is no longer the internal spiritual form of the cosmos, nor is it a culturally constructed human order; instead it is an animalistic order of survival. With this, China's traditional idea of statecraft has been completely inverted and rewritten.

At the same time, we must return to the novel's theme of tattoos and its dialogue with the concept of ritual. As discussed above, ritual text (*liwen* 禮文) was originally correlated with fabric markings (*wen* 紋), and the markings on clothing would frequently symbolize a cosmic order and patriarchal system. *Monkey Cup* focuses not on apparel but rather on extravagant local tattoos; and it does not discuss a ritual-legal patriarchal system but rather emphasizes a set of interpersonal flows of desire and ethical upheavals. Both Zhi, who is himself a teacher, and Borneo's famous Chinese instructor, Teacher Luo, have inappropriate sexual relations with their female students. Similarly, when Zhi's grandfather was younger, he fell in love with a girl named Xiaohuayin ("little flower print") who had been sold into the Yu family to settle her father's debt, but after he was stopped by Zhi's great-grandfather, the girl was sexually assaulted by the great-grandfather and immediately transferred to a brothel. Several decades later, Zhi's grandfather sexually assaults Xiaohuayin's daughter – Limei, who is also his own granddaughter – as compensation, which results in her becoming pregnant and having a child, and with a wounded body and spirit she crawls around on the ground like a lizard. Countless other women are set to brothels, where they are assaulted day and night, most because their fathers gambled and smoked opium at the encouragement of the Yu family and therefore feel they have no choice but to sacrifice their daughters in order to repay their debts.

However, when the girl suffers paternal/patriarchal domination, is this not another side of the patriarchal system? We can see why, after the Japanese invade and establish the plantations, the thirty-odd women in the brothel decide to run away together – "they hated the plantation, and didn't want to return to the parents who had sold them off, and furthermore were afraid that the Japanese devils would force them to become comfort women." The women eat and sleep out in the open, and follow the Rajang River deep into the rain forest. They "ate raw fruit discarded by bats, birds, and monkeys, as well as rotten fruit that had been masticated by long-haired boars and howling deer. They ate potentially poisonous mushrooms and drank water out of nepenthes pitchers. . . . When food was scarce or unreliable, they relied entirely on this water from nepenthes pitchers to slake their thirst." Ultimately,

after more than a hundred days, they were taken in by several Dayak families living in long houses, finally bringing to an end their terrifying flight.
From that point on, the girls spoke Dayak, and their language and behavior
became just like that of the Dayak. They were strong and industrious, and
accepted their fate of hard work, and never again had tender, white skin.
They married Dayak men, and gave birth to a passel of children. In order
to commemorate the day of their mothers' escape, the children all had an
image of a nepenthes pitcher tattooed on their arms.

(277)

The description brings us back to the title of *Monkey Cup*, together with the
symbolic meaning of the novel's tattoos. "Monkey cup" refers to nepenthes, a
type of carnivorous plant that traps its food with a pitcher-shaped growth resembling a vagina. In the novel, the two largest species of local nepenthes plants
include what white people call noble nepenthes and raffles nepenthes. The former name comes from Governor James Brooke, who was among the first generation of white people to arrive in Sarawak, while the latter comes from Stamford
Raffles, the British imperialist who is recognized as the father of modern Singapore (23). The liquid inside the pitchers could slake people's thirst, and although
it originated as a way of trapping insects, it was often eaten as carrion. According
to Teacher Luo, the women's reliance on nepenthes pitchers "resembled someone
cultivating a barren field, and the poorer the soil, the more it thrived" (177).

The nepenthes tattoos, accordingly, are not merely peculiar images, they
also function as a defense of an earlier notion of "ritual text" (*liwen*). This is
not merely a case of discarding clothing in favor of the body or of transforming fabric patterns into corporeal tattoos; more importantly, it involves taking
nepenthes pitchers – natural objects indigenous to the Asian tropics, not fabric
markings from Chinese clothing – and using them for a process of "virtue
comparison" or as marks of "subalternation." The tattoos commemorate the
women's escape and mark the disgrace and humiliation the women endured at
the hands of both foreign colonizers and patriarchal domination, together with
their subsequent hybridity and rebirth after being integrated into their new life
in the rain forest.

This analysis can then be extended to the question of language in *Monkey
Cup*. As mentioned above, the *Zuozhuan* states that "voice [is] writing of the
body." "Voice," accordingly, is like the fabric markings on clothing – or even
tattoo marks on the body – thereby becoming a marker of self-identity. Badu, the
grandson of the tattoo master Ah Banban, has countless tattoos intermixed with
his birthmarks. The hybrid origin of these bodily markings seems to suggest that
they function as a sort of corporeal language, and the source of their composition
is also different. The languages of Borneo are hybrids, and the novel uses different sorts of analogies to describe the various languages, which is evident in the
descriptions of mixed diction. For instance:

> Yanini used English, Chinese, Dayak, and sign language interchangeably, producing a linguistic situation that only Zhi could understand. It had glimmers of weirdness and a bright red beauty, as though like a mixed-race child with four different lineages. Just as a hybrid child may be infected by its mother via vertical transmission, or by nursing and licking her saliva, grammar and intonation function almost exactly the same way, in that they are chewed up like quadruplets. Or, more accurately, they are the product of a process whereby Zhi and Yanini mutually infected each other in a ping-pong fashion as a result of repeated coupling, after which Yanini gave birth to a bastard child with no name or nationality, and who was already destitute even as his mother's vagina was still bleeding.
>
> *(314–315)*

Language is a conduit by which people communicate with one another, and also a medium for expressing emotion. It appears as something that is originally unstructured and is formed through convention. However, in the process of development language already contains, from early on, the spiritual connotations and perceptual and conceptual modes that are specific to the local ethnic group's language family. When languages from different language families are used together, the spiritual connotations and perceptual and conceptual modes of the corresponding ethnic groups also become intermixed.

Yanini is a Dayak girl with a nepenthes pitcher tattoo on her arm, signifying that her maternal ancestors were women who escaped from the plantation, and after she accompanies Zhi into the rain forest to search for Limei, she falls in love with him. In order to protect Zhi from Badu – who will try to kill him to prevent him from becoming a fellow clansman – she repeatedly devotes herself to him. Meanwhile, the novel concludes with Zhi affirming his intention to marry Yanini: "I will marry you, Yanini. In my heart, you are already my wife" (317). In order to integrate with the Dayak community, Zhi learns the Dayak language while Yanini uses a combination of different languages to communicate with Zhi and his grandfather. Although there are always some things that they find difficult to communicate, nevertheless a new language and mode of expression is gradually formed. If we can say that Zhi's marriage vow to Yanini signifies that the physically and mentally exhausted protagonist has decided to seek a new life with this local girl, then their "new life" emerges precisely out of this hybrid language – while the language's transformation naturally also connotes a renewal at the level of spiritual connotations and modes of perception and cognition.

Conclusion

As a kind of "linguaphone," Sinophone literature's fundamental characteristic lies in how, in treating Chinese as both a spoken and a written language, it continually reflects on the indeterminate relationship between Chinese and corresponding notions of both Chineseness and locality – and from this it develops a local literary quality. Chinese-language literary works from different regions generally share the same Chinese characters, and therefore the characters' structural characteristics, implicit modes of perception and cognition, and earliest form – namely, *wen* 文, together with the various concepts derived from it, including "statecraft" (*wenzhi*), "ritual text" (*liwen*), and "rhetoric/diction/speech" (*wenxue/wenci/yanshuo*) – collectively become an important component of the resulting notion of Chineseness. All cultural imagination develops out of this.

Zhang Guixing's *Elephant Tropes*, meanwhile, focuses on "characters" (*zi*) and, starting from the multiple meanings of the character *xiang* 象, it uses techniques of mimicry and symbolism, and by means of textual form (*xiang*) it pursues and hunts form/elephants (*xiang*) while reflecting on the changes that species undergo as a result of migration. The result, however, is that the narrative departs from the China/Chineseness that nominally served as both the work's point of origin and the object of its search. *Monkey Cup*, meanwhile, focuses on the concept of *wen* 文, taking as its entry point the bodily tattoos of the Borneo aborigines, then expanding to consider the dialogue among concepts of "statecraft," "ritual text," and "rhetoric/diction/speech" within Chinese culture. The novel reflects on the multilayered oscillation and dialectics between corporeal "marks" (*wen* 紋) and corporeal "graphs" (*wen* 文). It replaces "humanity" with a more primitive "animality," and replaces an ideal of "human cultural formation" with a reality of "survival of the fittest." Given that Borneo's tropical setting is already different from China's landscapes, the resulting linguistic hybridity metaphorically expresses a change in individuals' spiritual beliefs and modes of perception and cognition.

As a result, Zhang Guixing's novels – under the combined influence of the space of the rain forest, the reclamation system, and the communist utopia's multiple historico-geographical influences – ultimately yields a distinct style characterized by a deep localism. Even so, media that feature textual representation continue to rely on Chinese characters, and the tension between them is continually manifested in Sinophone literature's self-dialectics. However, after the self-dialectics is formalized as a system of interconnected meanings, how will the resulting literary formation establish a dialogue or connection between its own localism and literatures from other language regions? This is a question that requires further investigation.

Carlos Rojas, trans.

Notes

1 Shu-mei Shih, *Visuality and Identity: Sinophone Articulations across the Pacific* (Berkeley: University of California Press, 2007); David Der-wei Wang 王德威, *Huayifeng: Huayu yuxi wenxue sanlun* 華夷風：華語語系文學三論 [When the Wind of the Sinophone Blows: Three Essays on Sinophone Literature] (Gaoxiong: Zhongshan daxue wenxueyuan, 2015); Jing Tsu, *Sound and Script in Chinese Diaspora* (Cambridge: Harvard University Press, 2010). Other works that address Sinophone literature include Andrea Bachner, *Beyond Sinology: Chinese Writing and Scripts of Cultures* (New York: Columbia

University Press, 2013); E. K. Tan, *Rethinking Chineseness: Transnational Sinophone Identities in the Nanyang Literary World* (Amherst, NY: Cambria Press, 2013); Alison Groppe, *Sinophone Malaysian Literature: Not Made in China* (Amherst, NY: Cambria Press, 2014); and Brian Bernards, *Writing the South Seas: Imagining the Nanyang in Chinese and Southeast Asian Postcolonial Literature* (Seattle: University of Washington Press, 2018).

2 See Hou Jiping 侯紀萍, *Yulin de Fuchou–Zhang Guixing xiaoshuo yuanxiang yishi yanjiu* 雨林的復仇－張貴興小說原鄉意識研究 (The Rainforest's Revenge–A Study of Native Consciousness in Zhang Guixing's Novels), MA thesis, Dongwu University, 2009; Chen Huiling 陳惠齡, "Lun Zhang Guixing *Qunxiang* zhong yulin kongjianzhanyan" 論張貴興《群象》中雨林空間的展演 (Discussing the Presentation of Rainforests in Zhang Guixing's *Elephant Tropes*), *Gaoxiong shida xuebao* 高雄師大學報 16 (2004).

3 Yun-Hong Lin 林運鴻, "Bangguo tiancui yihou, yuli haiyou shenme?–Shilun Zhang Guixing de qinshou daguanyuan" 邦國殄瘁以後，雨裡還有什麼—試論張貴興的禽獸大觀園 (What Is Left in the Rainforest Besides Nationalism? The Anthropoid Beasts in Zhang Guixing's Fiction), *Zhongwai wenxue* 中外文學 32, no. 8 (January 2004): 5–33.

4 Tee Kim Tong 張錦忠, "Wenziyuan zhi jinchu" 文字圍城之進出 (Entering and Leaving the Besieged City of Language), *Jiaofeng* 蕉風 (May 1989).

5 Li Youcheng 李有成, "Huangwen yezi" 荒文野字 (Desolate Writing and Wild Characters), in Li Youcheng, *Shi de huiyi ji qita* 詩的回憶及其它 (Recollections on Poetry and Other Matters) (Kuala Lumpur: Youren, 2016), 102–104.

6 Ng Kim Chew 黃錦樹, "Ci de liuwang–Zhang Guixing de xiezuo daolu" 詞的流亡—張貴興的寫作道路 (Words in Exile: Zhang Guixing's Literary Path), in Ng Kim Chew, *Mahua wenxue yu Zhongguoxing* 馬華文學與中國性 (Mahua Literature and Chineseness) (Taipei: Maitian, 2012), 297–317; and Zhang Guixing 張貴興, "Cong geren de tiyan dao hei'an zhi xin – Lun Zhang Guixing de yulin sanbuqu yu Dama Huaren de ziwo lijie" 從個人的體驗到黑暗之心—論張貴興的雨林三部曲與大馬華人的自我理解 (From Individual Experience to a Dark Heart–Discussing Zhang Guixing's Rainforest Trilogy and the Self-Understanding of Malaysian Chinese), in Zhang Guixing, *Wo sinian de changmin zhong de nanguo gongzhu* 我思念的長眠中的南國公主 (My South Seas Sleeping Beauty) (Taipei: Maitian, 2001), 249–266.

7 See Tee Kim Tong, "Mahua wenxue de dingyi ji shuxing" 馬華文學的定義及屬性 (The Definition and Attributes of Mahua Literature), in Tee Kim Tong, *Malaixiya huayu yuxi wenxue* 馬來西亞華語語系文學 (Malaysian Sinophone Literature) (Kuala Lumpur: Youren, 2011), 16–29; and Ng Kim Chew, "Dongnanya Huaren shaoshuminzu de Huawen wenxue 東南亞華人少數民族的華文文學 (The Chinese-Language Literature of Ethnic Chinese in Southeast Asia), in *Chongxie Mahua wenxueshi lunweji* 重寫馬華文學史論文集 (Collected Essays on Rewriting Chinese-Language Literature), ed. Tee Kim Tong (Natou: Jinan daxue dongnanya yanjiuzhongxin, 2004), 115–132.

8 Zhang Guixing, *Wanpi jiazu* 頑皮家族 (Rogue Clan) (Taipei: Lianhe wenxue, 1996), 10–11.

9 Zhang Guixing, *Qunxiang* 群象 (Elephant Tropes) (Taipei: Shibao chuban, 1998), 16–19.

10 Zhang Guixing, *Houbei* 猴杯 (Monkey Cup) (Taipei: Lianhe wenxue, 2000), 25.

11 Xu Shen 許慎, "Shuowen jiezi xu" 說文解字敘 (Explaining Graphs and Analyzing Characters, Postface), in *Shuowen jiezi zhu* 說文解字注 (Explaining Graphs and Analyzing Characters, Annotated), ed. Xu Shen, annotations by Duan Yucai 段玉裁 (Taipei: Yiwen yinshuguan, 1955), 761.

12 Xu Shen 許慎, "Shuowen jiezi xu," 8.

13 Ruan Yuanxiao 阮元校, *Zuozhuan* 左傳 (Taipei: Yiwen, 1981), 225.

14 See Wilhelm von Humboldt, *On Language: On the Diversity of Human Language Construction and its Influence on the Mental Development of the Human Species*, ed. Michael Losonsky (Cambridge: Cambridge University Press), 1999.

15 See Gong Pengcheng 龔鵬程, *Wenhua fuhaoxue* 文化符號學 (Cultural Semiotics) (Taipei: Xuesheng shuju, 1992).

16 See Lin Shujuan 林淑娟, *Wen de puxi* 文的譜系 (The Literary Pedigree), PhD diss., Qinghua University, 2016.

17 Ruan Yuanxiao 阮元校, ed. *Zhou yi* 周易 (Book of Changes) (Taipei: Wenyi, 1981), 143–164. Translation adapted from James Legge, trans., *The I Ching: The Book of Changes* (New York: Dover, 1963), 353.

18 Ruan Yuanxiao, *Zhou yi*, 165–181. Translation adapted from James Legge, trans., *The I Ching: The Book of Changes*, 383.

19 "Huangong ernian" 桓公二年, *Zuozhuan* (左傳), 92–94. Translation adapted from Stephen Durrant, Wai-yee Li, and David Schaberg, trans., *Zuo Tradition/Zuozhuan: Commentary on the "Spring and Autumn Annals"* (Seattle: University of Washington Press, 2016), 77.

20 "Zhaogong ershiwu nian" 昭公二十五年, *Zuozhuan* 左傳, 888–892.

21 Liu Xie 劉勰, *Wenxin diaolong zhu* 文心雕龍校注 (The Literary Mind and Carving of Dragons, Annotated), ed. Huang Shulin 黃叔琳 (Taipei: Kaiming shudian, 1959), 1. Translation adapted from Zong-qi Cai, ed., *A Chinese Literary Mind: Culture, Creativity and Rhetoric in Wenxin diaolong* (Stanford: Stanford University Press, 2002), 48.

22 Yun-Hong Lin, "Bangguo tiancui yihou."

Works cited

Bachner, Andrea. *Beyond Sinology: Chinese Writing and Scripts of Cultures*. New York: Columbia University Press, 2013.

Bernards, Brian. *Writing the South Seas: Imagining the Nanyang in Chinese and Southeast Asian Postcolonial Literature*. Seattle: University of Washington Press, 2018.

Cai, Zong-qi. *A Chinese Literary Mind: Culture, Creativity and Rhetoric in Wenxin Diaolong*, 48. Stanford: Stanford University Press, 2002.

Chen Huiling 陳惠齡. "Lun Zhang Guixing *Qunxiang* zhong yulin kongjianzhanyan." 論張貴興《群象》中雨林空間的展演 (Discussing the Presentation of Rainforests in Zhang Guixing's *Elephant Tropes*). *Gaoxiong shida xuebao* 高雄師大學報 16 (2004).

Durrant, Stephen, Wai-yee Li, and David Schaberg, trans. *Zuo Tradition/Zuozhuan: Commentary on the "Spring and Autumn Annals"*. Seattle: University of Washington Press, 2016.

Gong Pengcheng 龔鵬程. *Wenhua fuhaoxue* 文化符號學 (Cultural Semiotics). Taipei: Xuesheng shuju, 1992.

Groppe, Alison. *Sinophone: Malaysian Literature: Not Made in China*. Amherst, NY: Cambria Press, 2014.

Hou Jiping 侯紀萍. *Yulin de Fuchou – Zhang Guixing xiaoshuo yuanxiang yishi yanjiu* 雨林的復仇－張貴興小說原鄉意識研究 (The Rainforest's Revenge: A Study of Native Consciousness in Zhang Guixing's Novels). MA thesis, Dongwu University, 2009.

Humboldt, Wilhelm von. *On Language: On the Diversity of Human Language Construction and Its Influence on the Mental Development of the Human Species*. Ed. Michael Losonsky. Cambridge: Cambridge University Press, 1999.

Lin Shujuan 林淑娟. *Wen de puxi* 文的譜系 (The Literary Pedigree). PhD diss., Qinghua University, 2016.

Lin, Yun-Hong 林運鴻. "Bangguo tiancui yihou, yuli haiyou shenme? – Shilun Zhang Guixing de qinshou daguanyuan." 邦國殄瘁以後，雨裡還有什麼？一試論張貴興的禽獸大觀園 (What Is Left in the Rainforest besides Nationalism? The Anthropoid Beasts in Zhang Guixing's Fiction). *Zhongwai wenxue* 中外文學 32, no. 8 (January 2004): 5–33.

Liu Xie 劉勰. *Wenxin diaolong zhu* 文心雕龍校注 (The Literary Mind and Carving Dragons, Annotated). Ed. Huang Shulin 黃叔琳. Taipei: Kaiming shudian, 1959.

Li Youcheng 李有成. "Huangwen yezi" 荒文野字 (Desolate Writing and Wild Characters). In *Shi de huiyi ji qita* 詩的回憶及其它 (Recollections on Poetry and Other Matters), edited by Li Youcheng, 102–104. Kuala Lumpur: Youren, 2016.

Ng Kim Chew 黃錦樹. "Ci de liuwang – Zhang Guixing de xiezuo daolu." 詞的流亡—張貴興的寫作道路 (Words in Exile: Zhang Guixing's Literary Path). In *Mahua wenxue yu Zhongguoxing* 馬華文學與中國性 (Mahua Literature and Chineseness), edited by Ng Kim Chew, 297–317. Taipei: Rye Field Publishing.

———. "Dongnanya Huaren shaoshuminzu de Huawen wenxue 東南亞華人少數民族的華文文學 (The Chinese-Language Literature of Ethnic Chinese in Southeast Asia). In *Chongxie Mahua wenxueshi lunweji* 重寫馬華文學史論文集 (Collected Essays on Rewriting Chinese-Language Literature), edited by Tee Kim Tong, 115–132. Natou: Jinan daxue dongnanya yanjiuzhongxin, 2004.

Ruan Yuanxiao 阮元校, ed. *Zhou yi* 周易 (Book of Changes). Taipei: Wenyi, 1981.

———, ed. *Zuozhuan* 左傳. Taipei: Yiwen, 1981.

Shih, Shu-mei. *Visuality and Identity: Sinophone Articulations across the Pacific.* Berkeley: University of California Press, 2007.

Tan, E. K. *Rethinking Chineseness: Transnational Sinophone Identities in the Nanyang Literary World.* Amherst, NY: Cambria Press, 2013.

Tong, Tee Kim 張錦忠. "Mahua wenxue de dingyi ji shuxing." 馬華文學的定義及屬性 (The Definition and Attributes of Mahua Literature). In *Malaixiya huayu yuxi wenxue* 馬來西亞華語語系文學 (Malaysian Sinophone Literature), edited by Tee Kim Tong, 16–29. Kuala Lumpur: Youren, 2011.

———. "Wenziyuan zhi jinchu." 文字圍城之進出 (Entering and Leaving the Besieged City of Language). *Jiaofeng* 蕉風, May 1989.

Tsu, Jing. *Sound and Script in Chinese Diaspora.* Cambridge: Harvard University Press, 2010.

Wang, David Der-wei 王德威. *Huayifeng: Huayu yuxi wenxue sanlun.* 華夷風: 華語語系文學三論 (When the Wind of the Sinophone Blows: Three Essays on Sinophone Literature). Gaoxiong: Zhongshan daxue wenxueyuan, 2015.

Xu Shen 許慎, "Shuowen jiezi xu." 說文解字敘 (Explaining Graphs and Analyzing Characters, Postface). In *Shuowen jiezi zhu* 說文解字注 (Explaining Graphs and Analyzing Characters, Annotated), edited by Xu Shen, annotations by Duan Yucai 段玉裁, 761. Taipei: Yiwen yinshuguan, 1955.

Zhang Guixing 張貴興. "Cong geren de tiyan dao hei'an zhi xin – Lun Zhang Guixing de yulin sanbuqu yu Dama Huaren de ziwo lijie." 從個人的體驗到黑暗之心—論張貴興的雨林三部曲與大馬華人的自我理解 (From Individual Experience to a Dark Heart: Discussing Zhang Guixing's Rainforest Trilogy and the Self-Understanding of Malaysian Chinese). In *Wo sinian de changmin zhong de nanguo gongzhu* 我思念的長眠中的南國公主, edited by Zhang Guixing, 249–266. Taipei: Maitian, 2001.

———. *Houbei* 猴杯 (Monkey Cup). Taipei: Lianhe wenxue, 2000.

———. *Qunxiang* 群象 (Elephant Tropes). Taipei: Shibao chuban, 1998.

———. *Wanpi jiazu* 頑皮家族 (Rogue Clan). Taipei: Lianhe wenxue, 1996.

PART III
The global Chinese diaspora

9

TALES OUT OF SCHOOL

Campus fiction from Taiwan

Mary Goodwin

In the spring of 2017, the Taiwan media were riveted by the saga of Lin Yi-han 林奕含, a promising young writer who had just published her first novel, *Fang Siqi de chulian leyuan* 房思琪的初戀樂園 (Fang Ssu-chi's first love paradise).[1] The plot of the novel, centering on a young girl who had been seduced and raped by her cram school teacher, was said to mirror Lin's own experience as a teenager. Like her protagonist, Lin was an excellent student who had a special interest in Chinese literature and, lacking a close relationship with her parents, struck up a friendship with a cram school teacher. The book quickly became a best-seller, and Lin gave numerous interviews, in one of which she memorably said that the massacres of war were nothing compared to the rape of Fang Ssu-chi.[2] In April 2017, two months after the book came out, however, the twenty-six-year-old Lin was found by her husband of two years, dead in her apartment.

In the ensuing public uproar, commentators analyzed the novel for its roots in Lin's own experience, and for its critique of social mores and public awareness of sexual assault and mental health issues in Taiwan.[3] Lin's family tied her suicide to a depression that had engulfed her since the rape years earlier. Lin's supporters used the internet to identify and expose her former cram school teacher, whose own daughter tried to commit suicide following the bad publicity targeting their family.[4] Commentators focused on many aspects of Lin's personal life to "explain" the situation, including the possibility of neglect by her wealthy parents. Others pointed out the excessive dependence of Taiwan parents on cram schools to help students score well on the all-important entrance exams to high school and university. *Fang Ssu-chi* tells the story of a vulnerable young woman who lacks attention at home, as her parents occupy themselves with getting and staying rich. She loves literature and is susceptible to romance and flattery. Under pressure to do well in school, she takes extra classes at a cram school, as do so many Taiwan students, with charismatic, talented teachers sought after for their success in helping students get into good colleges. In a cynical bargain, such teachers have free rein because parents and students trust them, and because the school depends on them to earn money. In Taiwan, cram schools are commonplace and popular, in some cases supplanting regular school in their importance for a student's academic career. However, they are also seen as a pit of vice, bad habits, and bad comrades, and a breeding ground for disease and exhaustion. In Lin's novel it is gradually revealed to the reader that Fang Ssu-chi's Chinese literature teacher has a secret history of seducing young female students. In time he seduces Ssu-chi, blackmails her to keep her quiet, then dumps her for a younger conquest. Ssu-chi has a breakdown, and her diary detailing her experience is found.

While extreme in its depiction of assault and betrayal, Lin's novel has a place in a historical line of Taiwan fiction that depicts intimate relationships between teachers and students. A well-known earlier example is *Outside the Window* (Chuangwai 窗外) (1963), by the popular novelist Chiung Yao 琼瑶 (the pen name of Chen Che 陳喆), which tells the story of a Taiwan high school student who falls in love with her teacher.[5] Like Lin Yi-han's novel, *Outside the Window* has its roots in the real-life experience of the author, the child of mainland Chinese parents who came to Taiwan in 1949. Chiung Yao was a student at Chung Shan Girls' high school, one of Taiwan's top high schools, and published fiction while still a student. After failing the entrance exam to university, she started writing in earnest. Success came swiftly, as Chiung Yao's romance novels became best-sellers in Taiwan and later in China and around Asia. Her first novel, *Outside the Window*, was made into a popular movie in 1973, launching actor Brigitte Lin and others on long, successful acting careers.[6] By 2017 Chiung Yao's novels had been made into 100 films and TV series.

In her fiction, Chiung Yao frequently focuses on protagonists who are plain and ordinary girls who win the hearts of successful, good-looking men. Unlike the characters in Lin's work, the protagonists in Chiung Yao's *Outside the Window* seem to enjoy a mutual fascination, a "true love." In the novel, Jiang Yan-rong is a senior high student who has a strained relationship with her parents. She grows closer to her teacher, Nan Kang, a popular and respected member of the faculty. The attraction is mutual, and while the relationship remains chaste, they decide to separate, fearing social consequences. Yan-rong then tries to commit suicide but is found in time by her mother. She begs her mother to allow them to marry. The mother pretends to agree, but then goes to Nan Kang and accuses him of seducing her daughter. Nan Kang is fired by the school and forced to take a position at a mediocre school in a remote location. Eventually Yan-rong marries a man who abuses her, so she leaves him to look for Nan Kang. In the end, however, she finds a broken, unkempt, alcoholic old man who doesn't even recognize her.

The novels of Lin Yi-han and Chiung Yao focus on the emotional stresses experienced by young female students dealing with complex personal relationships, including strained family ties, amid the all-consuming pressure in Taiwan to do well on tests and get into good universities. In these novels, the students look for support elsewhere and find it with a trusted teacher. In recent decades there have emerged a number of works in English by long-term foreign residents in Taiwan that similarly take up the theme of relationships between teachers and students. Below, I consider *Under the Phoenix Tree* (1991) by Catherine Dai and *Lessons in Essence* (2006) by Dana Standridge, both of which were written in English and set in Taiwan.[7] While featuring taboo relationships between young students and older teachers, these "campus novels" also shed light on issues related to Taiwan's history and social and political relations, above all its changing relationship with China, and how these factors are manifested in Taiwan's education policy. These contemporary sociological elements create a contrast to the Taiwan campus novels by Lin and Chiung Yao, where political issues are hardly touched on. The novels by Dai and Standridge give insight into ongoing struggles in Taiwan between the old regime and new Taiwan, over reverence for the legacy of Chinese culture and respect for authority itself, and the way forward for Taiwan identity.

All four novels share a number of key features. As in the novels by Chiung Yao and Lin, the teacher figures in Dai's and Standridge's novels are male, while the students are female; the teachers are all close to retirement, while the students are decades younger, with Lin Yi-han's protagonist a teenager and the others in their early twenties. Moreover, all four male protagonists are authorities on classical Chinese culture: the teachers in *Fang Ssu-chi, Outside the Window,* and *Under the Phoenix Tree* are specialists in classical Chinese literature, and Teacher Li in *Lessons in Essence* specializes in classical Chinese music and painting. Their students, meanwhile, are young women whose classmates include firebrands who are fomenting rebellion and agitating for a new world order, resisting traditional authority in politics and society and most certainly in terms of education.

Under the Phoenix Tree is by Catherine Dai, the pen name of Catherine Diamond, an American professor of English and drama at Soochow University in Taiwan. In addition to her scholarly work on Southeast Asian theater and dance groups, Dai has written several books of fiction set in Taiwan, including a collection of short stories.[8] The plot of the novel centers on the relationship between Professor Bai, an elderly scholar of Chinese literature at a university in Taiwan, and Jin Hsiao-hwa, a student some forty years his junior. Hsiao-hwa is pursued by another student, Fan Lin-yu, who has fallen in with a radical political group. Although not overtly political, the novel was published only a few years after four decades of martial law ended in Taiwan in 1987, against a background of political upheaval and transitions between the mainland Chinese contingent, represented by the Nationalist Party (Kuomintang or KMT), and the opposition Democratic Progressive Party (DPP), whose members advocate Taiwan's independence from China, alongside the rise of multiparty democracy, new media freedom, and massive public demonstrations on a wide range of demands. The novel is filled with well-drawn depictions of Taipei in the period: city residents stuffed into the hot, sagging buses that crawled up and down the local roads before the Mass Rapid Transit system was built; decrepit landmarks and perpetual street food stands still visible below the window of my Taipei apartment; the slow bureaucratic nature of university literature departments. Indeed, given the local feel of the setting and the author's pen name, I initially assumed that Catherine Dai was a Taiwan native.[9]

Issues of Taiwan's political changes, its relationship with China, and the value of tradition in education and society are approached obliquely in this novel through a triangular love story. Taiwan's colonial history, starting with the Japanese occupation and moving on to the arrival of Chiang Kai-shek and his Nationalist army, is woven into the family background of the protagonist, Jin Hsiao-hwa, a young university student majoring in Chinese literature. Hsiao-hwa's mother comes from a mainland family whose father, an impoverished scholar of Chinese literature who devoted himself to preserving Chinese history, was "lost in the past" (5). Mrs. Jin finds in her daughter the same spirit, her father's soul "reincarnated in Hsiao-hwa's instinctual refinement," and she imagines them, heads bowed over ancient poems, "locked together so far away from the mundane world she herself inhabited" (3). Dreamy, beautiful, intellectual, trained in both Western and Eastern culture but preferring Eastern, Hsiao-hwa, called by her mother "Big Precious," has transferred from the foreign languages department in her university to the Chinese literature department. Her mother does not see this as a wise move, asking, "What is the use of Chinese literature?" (62). Mrs. Jin's second daughter, Hsiao-ping, is a talented athlete with physical strength "like a wild animal" (14). Burdened by the patriarchal family structure, Mrs. Jin accepts her humble place, but is firm in wanting her daughters not to depend on anyone, so as not to "feel the yoke of gratitude" (10).

Jin Hsiao-hwa is surrounded by young firebrands who want a new heaven and new earth for Taiwan, politically, socially, and economically. There is Lin Ron-hwa, a rich student returned from America and a success story in the making; he sees in Hsiao-hwa's "impractical" literature major the opportunity to teach Chinese to American businessmen who want to work in China. While Ron-hwa tells her she is not his type, her brilliant classmate, Fan Lin-yu, pursues her with prickly energy. Lin-yu, who "flaunts his rags," is a young man in the vanguard of political, social, and educational changes in Taiwan (212); he is an idealist, albeit one grown tough and calloused in sparring with the older generation accustomed to an authoritarian regime and the smothering overlay of Chinese culture.

In rejecting both of these young men, Hsiao-hwa seems to turn her back on the "Taiwan future." Instead she pines for the elderly Professor Bai in her department and the pure realms of art she imagines that he represents. The core of the novel is the pull of two cultural and political perspectives, past and future, and the clash of values that each represents. She "feels torn between two worlds . . . the world of words . . . [of] rarefied perception . . . and the world of the boy students around her, of their drives and ambitions" (65).

The professor and his student are aesthetes and romantic idealists. For them the modern world lacks grace and beauty; it is loud and hot and greedy, ambitious and industrial and political. This shared aesthetic response to the world is

the basis of Hsiao-hwa's attraction to Professor Bai rather than any physical passion, although she imagines touching "the marble coolness of his skin" (210). She
is convinced that with Bai, she can achieve the "sublime union of elderly man
and young woman," like Song dynasty poet Su Dongpo 蘇東坡 ("Su Deng-po")
and Wang Chaoyun 王朝雲 ("Wang Jao-yun"), the poet's much younger third
wife. Hsiao-hwa believes that like these legendary lovers, "she and Bai should
make a similar pledge of continence, to preserve his vital fluids sex was known
to exhaust" (210–211).

Like Hsiao-hwa, Bai has his own romantic vision for his future. Never married, Bai was born into a rich family in China and escaped death at the hands of
the Japanese when monks sheltered him in a monastery. He struggles with his
conscience over his growing attraction to Hsiao-hwa and his desire to return,
spiritually and physically, to a peaceful countryside setting as a Chinese scholar
of old might. Near retirement, he sees himself following in the footsteps of Laozi
("Lao Tsu") (143), and his dream of a rustic retreat is fired by meeting the farmer-
painter Liu (158).

By the end of the novel Bai has disappeared entirely, like the fisherman who
discovers utopia in "The Peach Blossom Spring" (桃花源記), by the early poet
and famous recluse Tao Yuanming 陶淵明. In a fairy-tale touch, Bai's house
is leveled right after he leaves; only the phoenix tree in the courtyard remains
(326). Reading Bai's farewell letter and poem, Hsiao-hwa imagines becoming
a legendary lover after death, when the tree she contemplates hanging herself
from would "become sacred to couples" (329). The cultural power derived from
her association with Bai is hinted at in Fan Lin-yu's pronouncement: Hsiao-hwa
"wants to be Bai, not his wife or mistress, but to have his privilege" (282).

Under the Phoenix Tree touches on many critical issues in the historical development of Taiwan's educational system. The novel is merciless in lampooning the
decaying educational bureaucracy of the era, Taiwan academics' slavish admiration of the West, and their habit of parroting Western intellectual trends. Professor Bai's colleagues in the Chinese department, Teachers Lu, Su, and Wu, are
comically drawn as ineffective, complacent bureaucrats, "beetly little men" (148)
with no passion for education, who gauge their success by how many students
they fail (290). In Lin-yu's estimation, students too are mostly useless, "so bright,
so hardworking, so materialistic, so boring" (171). Even Bai, more open to student opinion than his colleagues, finds that "the students kept insisting they had
no opinions" (291). With "Chinese literature at the bottom of the curriculum"
and his students just marking time until they can graduate, Bai has little hope for
future generations of Taiwan students: "the greatest works of the greatest men in
China are now read by no one but bored schoolgirls" (31).

However, the novel's most withering criticism is reserved not for the bureaucrats killing time at their desks but for those ambitious members of the department looking to hitch a ride on the currents of Western intellectual trends. In
one scene the department head invites a foreign scholar to speak. Brought in
at great expense to the department, the famous scholar is supercilious and slick
(90); Fan Lin-yu falls all over himself laughing at the spectacle, remarking that

"he's nothing but an academic whore who specializes in quickies" (93). No one in the department has read the foreign scholar's work with comprehension, and the scholar himself seems to assume that no one will challenge him. Interestingly, the only person in the audience to stand up to the speaker, taking aim with quotations from Chuang Tzu, is Professor Bai. As Lin-yu remarks, Bai may have been "born out of time" and have "no sense of reality," but he is also the only faculty member with the intellectual poise to challenge the foreign scholar (40).

This scene echoes moments in the history of Taiwan's educational development, in particular the ongoing debate about how Taiwan universities might become more competitive on the international stage. Facing market pressures following enormous investment in new universities in recent decades and a declining birth rate,[10] along with galloping globalization, Taiwan administrators have adopted Western standards for publication in internationally respected journals as necessary criteria for hiring, evaluating, and promoting university faculty. But this publish-or-perish approach, already well established in the West, has costs, partly in that extraordinary emphasis is placed on research quantity rather than teaching and service quality, resulting in a "less friendly environment for learning and instruction due to the market-driven educational policies," according to Brookings Institute research by Prudence Chou.[11]

The other great cost is in the emphasis on English as the dominant language of research, as papers deemed acceptable to the international journals in SSCI, SCI, and AHCI international citation indices must be written in English. Such an approach bows to Western intellectual discourse and devalues local diversity in the focus and application of Taiwan-centered research, as Chou and others have pointed out. Chou dubs this addiction of Taiwan educational administrators to the metric of international indices the "SSCI syndrome":

> The SSCI syndrome in Taiwan reinforces the privileged status of English in the international academic community. Ironically, while the vast majority of the Taiwanese researchers are non-English speakers, scholars in Taiwan have been encouraged by government and university to self-align with the privileged discourse and participate in the international academic community regardless of discipline and academic background. Taiwan's higher education policymakers still believe that the legitimacy of a hegemonic English-based knowledge industry will enable Taiwan's academia to bring about a diverse voice from the periphery and lead to a paradigm shift coming from within Taiwan's academic community.[12]

Under the Phoenix Tree anticipates these and other educational conundrums in Taiwan, in particular Taiwan's historical relationship with China, a political and social flashpoint that has smoldered for decades. If Professor Bai and others in *Under the Phoenix Tree* look backward to the glory of Chinese culture for the light it lends Taiwan's present, there are still many others who vehemently reject the identification of Taiwan with China. With respect to the traditional viewpoint on the purpose and content of education, Douglas C. Smith observes that "Taiwan education today focuses on ensuring the orderly transmission of the heritage of China and on developing attitudes that suggest that the group – family, siblings, peers, community, nation – is of paramount importance in the preparation of harmonious and prosperous living."[13] Nevertheless, protests against the content of Taiwan textbooks by students and academics are regular occurrences. Following the 2014 Sunflower Movement, in which thousands of students and others occupied the nation's Legislative Assembly in protest against a new trade agreement with China, there were protests the next year against textbooks perceived to be too pro-China:

> Hundreds of youths stormed the ministry of education compound . . . in a bid to repeal changes to history books likely to hit school shelves this week. Protests in Taiwan over textbook revisions which students say aim to brainwash them into accepting a "one China" view of history underscore the island's growing sense of independence from its vast neighbor and geopolitical foe.[14]

Even after the election of DPP leader Tsai Ing-wen as Taiwan's president in 2016, the textbook disputes have continued. Those who advocate reforming the content of history and social science textbooks ask, How far is Taiwan beholden to Chinese culture? How best should Taiwan's identity be presented, in balance with its historical connection with China, and who decides what message should be disseminated among future generations of Taiwan students? The academic response in recent years has been to call for greater emphasis in Taiwan educational texts on local work:

> In August 2017 the Association for Taiwan Literature called on the Ministry of Education to change the education curriculum in Taiwan to focus less on traditional Chinese classics and instead to draw on materials more suitable to contemporary Taiwan. . . . Taiwanese language learning materials still contain a large amount of classical Chinese, with 45% to 65% percent of class materials in classical Chinese despite [the fact] that classical Chinese is not in use in either Taiwan or China.[15]

The bittersweet message of Dai's novel is that dreamers don't hold up well under the real-world pressures that Taiwan faces and must overcome to survive. The present is crass, noisy with ambition and strivers, and the future is likely to be even more so, but looking backward is not a reasonable or effective option. The world must be dealt with on its own terms. In this novel, the idealists, in particular the cultural idealists, are stalled, even the most promising among them; the new movement of students promoting the cause of Taiwan identity and independence is similarly threatened by cynical and predatory onlookers who will use their naïve faith for criminal profit. The work ends on a tragic note for Hsiao-hwa, who is left contemplating suicide at the phoenix tree in the courtyard of the home her professor has abandoned. Her classmate Lin-yu has similarly made regrettable choices. First he sends an anonymous note to the university, accusing Bai of seducing a student. Next, Lin-yu falls into the grasp of a local hoodlum he had mistaken for a revolutionary leader in their political movement, and following the directives of this character, unwittingly serves as a drug mule. Just as Lin-yu belatedly realizes the part he has played in the melodrama, sirens are heard screaming in the background.

The novel does point the way to a solution, in a reconciliation through Hsiao-hwa of the Chinese past, represented by Bai, and Taiwan's future, represented by Fan Lin-yu, but Hsiao-hwa herself is pessimistic about this possibility, remarking that "her destiny lay not in choosing between them but in effecting their reconciliation . . . no, it was impossible" (65). In her final contemplation of suicide outside Bai's home, with Lin-yu in trouble with the law and Bai vanished, it would seem that this reconciliation is not a strong possibility in her future.

Indeed, the only character in this novel who moves forward, even if at a hobble, is Hsiao-hwa's younger sister, Hsiao-ping. After her dream of athletic superstardom is crushed, she moves on to the next plan, which is to make her way to the West for higher education. She sees a path forward to wealth and power: "They want women in math, can you believe it?" (318). Hsiao-ping has the discipline and stubbornness to persevere in chasing her dreams, and those dreams are obstinately material. Observing a luxury apartment complex on the side of a mountain on the outskirts of Taipei, she decides that "someday she would live there. She did not envy the people who lived there now, telling herself that she only needed to be patient; her time would come, of that she had no doubt" (245).

Hsiao-ping's practical and dogged response to adversity stands in contrast to that of the other characters, for whom escapism and self-destruction are the first resorts. Ironically, her talented and conventionally "Chinese" sister and her sister's brilliant suitor, Lin-yu, were everyone's first choice to go to the West for further education; both were brought down by emotional crises, questionable judgment, bad choices. Like her mother, Hsiao-ping is a survivor, but she refuses to submit to being merely "ordinary" (275). Hsiao-hwa says, "her aims were defined and she had all the necessary discipline and determination to accomplish them" (252). Indeed, there is much of Taiwan people's relentless determination and flexibility in Hsiao-ping's response to her situation.

The problems and solutions posed by Dana Standridge's *Lessons in Essence* are similar but not identical to those found in *Under the Phoenix Tree*. In *Lessons*, we encounter another elderly Taiwan scholar involved with a young female student, who similarly takes steps to remove himself from the noise and confusion of city life. Compared to *Under the Phoenix Tree*, however, *Lessons* has a much narrower focus not broken up among multiple important characters who represent different aspects of Taiwan. For the most part *Lessons* hews closely to the perspective of Teacher Li, and the number of characters is limited. On the periphery of Teacher Li's life are his wife, his daughter, some random students including his former lover, his mountain neighbor Professor Gao and his lover, and his best friend, Hero. But Teacher Li spends a great deal of time alone, brooding in his rotting house on the mountain.

Li, a specialist in the *qin*, an ancient Chinese musical instrument, seems to be having a nervous breakdown as the novel opens. While his wife and children are in New York, attempting to solve issues related to the family's emigration to the United States, he initiates an affair with Cai Hong Mei, a young family friend. His wife inevitably finds out, and Li immediately decides to retire from his teaching position, leave the city, and set up house alone in a ruin in the mountains. This is the very uncomfortable "room of one's own" that Teacher Li seems to need; the novel is very good on the points of uncomfortable camping. In addition to mold, rot, and plants growing on the inside steps, Teacher Li must contend with poisonous snakes, typhoons, and landslides in an affecting picture of general decay.

Teacher Li's retreat to the mountains in pursuit of a contemplative life is framed as an imitation of a similar exodus by Shi Wu 石屋 ("Stonehouse"), a Yuan dynasty poet. The novel's epigraph consists of lines from Stonehouse's homage to mountains: "I close my eyes and everything is fine / I open them again because I love mountains."[16] Li's retreat is stylized and theatrical, a personal struggle to cast aside the noisy world and find purity in a "noble scholarly retreat to the mountains" (81). The model for this quest is Chinese, as was Bai's. But herein lies the contradiction: Teacher Li, like his friend Hero, identifies politically as a "green" – as favoring Taiwan nationalism, rather than ties to mainland China – and is a member of the Democratic Progressive Party, not the nationalist KMT. He has nightmares about China invading Taiwan. He cannot, of course, retreat to a mountain in mainland China, although his models and life's work are culturally Chinese. Li does not seem aware of this contradiction.

Teacher Li is not an accomplished hermit. Instead, he is an accidental one, on the run from the women in his life angry enough to kill him for his indiscretions. He tells himself that he needs to remove himself from the social world to get something done, ostensibly to write a treatise on aesthetics: "When the tourists leave, Grass Mountain is divine. He does not yet know this, but in his landscapes as still-lifes, it is to this he is yearning" (93). He runs to the mountain because he thinks his wife is selling their Taipei house out from under him, but it turns out that she instead wants to sell their New York home because of the September 11 terrorist attack. In the mountains he attempts to make his ruin of a house habitable, but for this he needs the help of other people, namely the students who follow him up even as he tries to leave them behind (92). Even his affair with Cai Hong Mei is treated not as a true love connection but as a symptom of some greater unease in Teacher Li. Although Cai Hong Mei follows him to the mountain and commands other students to help him fix his house, he easily turns his back on her, and she disappears from the narrative as well. It is therefore ironic that the project Li has planned, his "last work," attempts "to try to understand how he once glimpsed humanity in aesthetic perfection. Or is it to find beauty in human imperfection?" (232). The narrative does not attempt to sort out Li's own human relations, which are very tangled. For all his ambitions as a hermit, he appears heavily dependent on human company to deal with even the smallest issues in his life.

Another curious aspect of the novel is Teacher Li's relationship to his profession. Unlike Bai, Hsiao-hwa, and Fan Lin-yu in *Under the Phoenix Tree*, Li is not by any stretch an idealist, neither with respect to his academic profession nor with respect to people in general. He is more of an artisan or skilled worker whose field is narrowing or producing fewer masters as time goes on. The image of Taiwan's education system that is presented in *Lessons* resonates with that found in *Under the Phoenix Tree*. In both works, the arts and classical Chinese study are similarly starved, and there is apparently no place for aesthetics in Taiwan education (53). There is no new generation to take over, as Li's own students seem to drift, lacking purpose or commitment (54) – they are, he reflects, "slop-hazard dogs, western music students, and ingenuous felines, private students made to study the *qin* by their fathers" (29). Teacher Li muses that teaching is a waste of time: "you can't really teach anyone anything" (171; 173). The Confucian tradition of a moral bond between teacher and student is frayed here, both in terms of the eroding authority of the teacher and his waning investment in the well-being and progress of his students, and with respect to inappropriate liaisons between teachers and students, such as those between Teacher Li and Hong Mei, and between Professor Gao, Li's neighbor on the mountain, and his dropout lover Mong Hua. The contrast with *Phoenix* is that in the earlier novel, general blame for the faults of the system lies in broader social and economic issues. Here, though, Li is a cantankerous burnout; the relationship between teachers and students is flawed and both parties are to blame, with the teachers unable to communicate effectively with the next generation. In *Lessons* everyone seems to be adrift, morally and intellectually; no one is a grownup; no one is in charge.

Although characters in *Lessons* seem superficially more aware of Taiwan politics and world politics – including the potential for a Chinese invasion, the real-life attempted assassination of presidential candidate Chen Shui-bian, and other events – than characters in *Under the Phoenix Tree*, they nevertheless seem more passive and less affected by politics than the student activists in the earlier novel: no one here risks anything, at least not to the extent that Fan Lin-yu does. Teacher Li holds himself at arm's length from daily Taiwan life, which is muddled, complex, noisy; he seems to relish cutting off communication. When portentous outside world events, such as the September 11 terrorist attacks in New York, intrude into the narrative, they end up being fairly peripheral to the characters' lives. For instance, following the attempted assassination of Chen Shui-bian, and his subsequent election, Teacher Li simply returns to the mountain house and continues his work.

Far more consequential issues in this novel concern the cultural resources of the past and their use or misuse by the generation of the present. Teacher Li's escape tactics differ from Professor Bai's in that Bai seems to want to run away and disappear into his intellectual and aesthetic paradise, without a backward glance. Teacher Li, on the other hand, has a project to accomplish in his self-imposed exile on the mountain. Echoing in his ears are the words of his friend Hero: "Just do something! Do! Do!" (232). In the last moments of the novel, he discovers what he needs to do and gets to work: "All right, I'll just write it down, get it out of my head," he says, pulling the rice paper down off the window to begin writing (232). But this is a circular endeavor: Who is his audience; for whom is he writing? Colleagues, students, even fame in his profession all seem to mean little to Teacher Li. Is this aesthetic exercise then undertaken only for himself? If so, his solitary and self-centered effort gives evidence of heightened individuality, which echoes the Zen hermit ideal (although Stonehouse wrote poetry and Li will write a treatise on aesthetics) yet seems to contradict what Taiwan scholar Huang Chun-chieh calls the "Confucian spirit [of] integral inter-subjective and cosmic involvement."[17] Huang argues that "Taiwanese modernity poses a danger and a promise" to the legacy of Confucianism (88). The lifting of martial law in 1987 "propelled the awakening of individuality in Taiwanese society, [representing] the most important milestone in the development of humanism in Chinese society and culture" (186). But the danger is "the ailment of egocentrism" in modern society, which Huang believes can be overcome by the "traditional Confucian values firmly rooted" deep in the consciousness of Taiwan people (187). Teacher Li seems to exactly represent the conundrum at the heart of the Confucian tradition: How does one pursue individual achievement while avoiding egocentrism and acknowledging one's place as a member of the social whole, which for a teacher would certainly include his students?

In *Literary Culture in Taiwan: Martial Law to Market Law*, Sung-sheng Yvonne Chang makes a similar point in relation to changes in Taiwan culture following martial law:

> Under martial law, cultural institutions in Taiwan were firmly under government control and political legitimacy generally overshadowed other principles of consecration. . . . The lifting of martial law in 1987 transformed Taiwan almost overnight into an open society consciously adapting to liberal democracy. The cultural sphere was likewise restructured.[18]

To return to a central feature in all four novels, the teacher figure is an older man who specializes in classical Chinese culture, while the young woman is his student. On one level, these novels offer a metaphor for the two sides of the Taiwan Strait and ongoing issues of cultural legacy, with the older generation as the gatekeepers to the cultural riches of China and the younger students as torn between this weighty legacy and their loyalty to Taiwan. Without a doubt, mastery of the arts of classical Chinese culture gives the older teachers the power to bedazzle and seduce their students. In Lin Yi-han's work this expertise is used cynically, as a tool for abuse. In *Under the Phoenix Tree* and *Lessons*, the classical arts represent a fast-receding, romanticized past in China that is losing force as a cultural standard in modern Taiwan. At the same time, however, the seducers are themselves seduced – the teachers appear to be under the sway of the ancient poets they admire, in choosing to retreat from the world. It may be significant as well that these teachers are near retirement, and perhaps are grasping at a last chance to establish a legacy after problematic or unsatisfying careers.

This seduction motif in these campus novels raises a final and unavoidable issue concerning the place of female students in a culture dominated, historically, by male teachers. In all four novels younger female students fall into relationships with older male teachers. In *Outside the Window* and *Fang Ssu-chi's First Love Paradise*, the student is neglected by her family and seeks comfort elsewhere, but the novels offer no happy endings for any of the female characters, who are abandoned, mentally broken, or contemplating suicide. Not all of the professors are predators, as in Lin Yi-han's novel, but the potential for abuse in the unequal power relationship between teacher and student remains strong. Unequal access to power may be, in some cases, the impetus for a closer relationship: As Fan Lin-yu observes with respect to Hsiao-hwa's crush on Professor Bai, Hsiao-hwa wants Bai's power and privilege, rather than the man himself. Bai himself reflects on the problematic role models offered the young by the assigned curriculum, and particularly the dead end that classical literature offers female students:

> No sooner did he close his notebooks when a high-pitched clamor would rise from the female students as if their spirits were being unleashed from the millennia of patriarchal restraint. Why, after all, should they be interested in works in which, if women appeared at all, it was as confined daughters, interfering mothers, overly ambitious concubines, and chaste widows?
>
> *(31–32)*

Commentary on Lin Yi-han's *Fang Ssu-chi* has also pointed to her naïveté and the lack of adequate sex education in Taiwan as factors in her victimization, in addition to general social and familial avoidance of frank sex discussions for young women in particular, in China as well as in Taiwan.[19] As numerous Taiwan feminist scholars have demonstrated, there are gender dynamics at work even in the reception of novels and other texts by female authors that speak to the unequal status of women in Taiwan and in Chinese culture generally. Taiwan scholar Lin Fang-mei explores not only the plot and contents of Chiung Yao's *Outside the Window* and other works but also the changing reception it received and the eventual place it was assigned in the cultural hierarchy dominated by what Lin calls the "Angry Young Men" authors, Taiwan intellectuals torn between support for nativist Taiwan literature and for mainland Chinese modern literature.[20] Miriam Lang similarly laments the devaluation of Chiung Yao's work over time: Initially, "several aspects of [*Outside the Window*] attracted critical attention. . . . [It was] read as a novel about the tensions and misunderstandings between generations and hailed as a depiction of the conflict of 'traditional' values with 'progressive' ones."[21] In Lang's view, Chiung Yao was savaged for her "prolific output, and commercial success," and significantly, because her "chief appeal is to women readers and not necessarily to those who possess the cultural capital of a tertiary education" (94). Lang points out that although *Outside the Window* was originally interpreted as "realism," this evaluation swiftly changed:

> Chiung Yao's status as a serious writer of modern realism was extremely short-lived. Before the end of the decade, the elements of "realism" in her work were apparently reclassified as the features of "melodrama," and her novels came to be considered formulaic, commercialized, and "popular": in short, "trash."
>
> *(93)*

Beginning even in the 1960s, with the publication of Chiung Yao's *Outside the Window*, Taiwan had begun reshaping itself politically and socially, with a growing number of young people and others questioning the role of the government's education ministry and curriculum selection, as well as the authority of teachers themselves. Added to this is greater Western cultural encroachment in Taiwan over time, bringing economic as well as political pressure, and the growing dominance of Western academic standards affecting universities and their faculties. Dai's and Standridge's novels revisit the Confucian model of the relationship between teachers and students as it has transformed over time with political, social, and economic changes in Taiwan. These novels address the "generation gap" between modern Taiwan and its cultural relationship with its own past and its Chinese cultural legacy, between an older generation of teachers and a modern, restless, impatient generation of students trying to shape their own future in a changing global landscape. As a mirror of Taiwan society and more specifically Taiwan attitudes toward education, these novels betray a longing for old China while also exposing the futility of that backward glance. In Lin Yi-han's novel, classical learning is used as a tool of abuse. In *Under the Phoenix Tree*, classical knowledge is a virtual dead end, an excuse for evasion and retreat for a teacher and an invitation to potential psychological crisis for some students. The novels also reveal a lack of confidence among Taiwan's intellectuals, anxiety over competition to produce world-class scholarship and over their relationship with the West. A similar concern has echoed through decades of criticism of creeping globalism: How can Taiwan take its place on the world stage while maintaining distinct features of its own culture? As Hsiao-hwa puts it, "How will we ever develop our own ideas if we just keep running after the West?" (91).

In challenging the traditional roles of teacher and student, as well as the test-based utilitarian culture of Taiwan, these novels offer a bracing vision of contemporary debate on the island over the function and methods of education, and how educational policy is created against a backdrop of uncertainty over Taiwan's identity and status on the world stage. The introduction of novels by Dai and Standridge also offers a challenge to an issue that confronts Taiwan outside the campus as well: the matter of Taiwan identity and what constitutes Taiwan literature. This essay began on the assumption that works about Taiwan, in any language, could be considered Taiwan literature, particularly if, like the novels by Dai and Standridge, they focus entirely on Taiwan characters, with few if any Western characters. Historically, language and even "racial identification" has not been an obstacle for inclusion of other work under the umbrella of Taiwan literature: Wu Zhuoliu's iconic Taiwan memoir *Orphan of Asia* (1945) was originally written in Japanese; in the Columbia University Press English translation series it falls in the category of "Modern Chinese Literature from Taiwan." The 2011 film *Seediq Bale* (dir. Wei Te-shing), which chronicles the conflicts between aboriginal groups and the occupying Japanese, features a script almost entirely in the aboriginal language Seediq, and is listed as a "Taiwanese historical drama." In recent years, Julie Wu, Francie Lin, Ed Lin, and Shawna Yang Ryan, Americans with ancestral ties to Taiwan, have all written novels in English that are set in Taiwan. In this writer's opinion, these examples demonstrate that there is neither a linguistic nor a "racial" standard for identifying a work as Taiwan literature.

However, authors Dai and Standridge do not as easily see their work as Taiwan literature. This perspective is complicated by both actual and perceived responses to their position as "outsiders" to Taiwan culture, although both have spent decades on the island. In an email interview, Dai describes a contentious discussion on *Under the Phoenix Tree* at a conference on Asian and North African literature:

> At a 1997 conference, I presented *Phoenix* as a novel written by an outsider of Taiwanese society, but not emphasizing outsider status, making it as transparent as possible. . . . I delivered the lecture without revealing that I was the author. [When I revealed this] the Taiwanese in the audience were outraged and insulted, saying it was not possible for an outsider to present/represent Taiwanese society.[22]

Dai said that "*Phoenix* strove to have no American or foreign connection, but to be a local story," and as such is "not appropriate for the general Western public – you need to know something of Chinese/Taiwanese society, and also there is no Western character for them to identify with." At the same time, however, Dai believes that "no Taiwanese reader/scholar has ever considered my books either as literarily worthy or as interesting views of Taiwanese society."

Dana Standridge, meanwhile, approaches the issue from the opposite direction. She says that *Lessons in Essence*, which was published in the United States, was "definitely written for a non-Taiwanese audience. From the opening pages, I'm trying to explain Taiwan politics, history, Chinese cultural traditions, you know, *everything*. It was my hope to interest Americans/Westerners in the Taiwan independence question." In her years in Taiwan as a radio journalist at International Community Radio Taipei (ICRT), Standridge became well aware of what she calls "semantic differences" in describing Taiwan identity:

Taiwan and *Taiwanese* are not synonymous because of the way people self-identify. This semantic difference is fairly ingrained in me, so I could never think of my novel as Taiwanese literature. Taiwan literature, maybe. Literature about Taiwan, sure. National Geographic used to have a website called the Ultimate Travel Library that listed my novel as Taiwan literature, and that was fine, especially because it was a list aimed at travelers and not natives. Would a Taiwanese person look at my book as Taiwan literature? I don't know.[23]

What is not disputed is that these works by Dai and Standridge sound new notes in a consideration of Taiwan, its education system, its relationship to the greater world (particularly to cultural forces of the West) and perhaps most significantly, gender relations and issues of authority (familial and scholarly) in Taiwan. In their deep consideration of what makes a scholar, what a scholar needs, and how he or she might find fulfillment, these Anglophone novels make a fascinating counterpoint to the works by Chiung Yao and Lin Yi-han, which likewise struck deep emotional chords in Taiwan readers with their own focus on campus relationships.

Notes

1 Lin Yi-han 林奕含, *Fang Siqi de chulian leyuan* 房思琪的初戀樂園 [Fang Ssu-chi's First Love Paradise] (Taipei: Guerrilla Publishing, 2017).
2 See interview with Lin published in May 2017: https://news.readmoo.com/2017/0/05/170505-interview-with-lin-02/.
3 See Jessie Yang, "What Suicide of Author Lin Yi-Han Can Teach Us about Mental Health," May 19, 2017, https://studybreaks.com/2017/05/19/lin-yi-han/.
4 See interview with Lin's cram school teacher: Sean Lin, "Teacher Accused of Sexual Assault Breaks His Silence," *Taipei Times*, May 11, 2017, www.taipeitimes.com/News/front/archives/2017/05/11/2003670351.
5 Chiung Yao 瓊瑤, *Chuangwai* 窗外 [Outside the Window] (Taipei: Crown Literature Publishing Co., 1963). Among the many examples of Taiwan fiction, TV programs, and films that depict campus relationships, particularly those between teachers and students, are *Liumang jiaoshou* 流氓教授 [Rogue Professor] by Lin Jianlong 林建隆 (Taipei: Ping An Culture Co., 2000); *Weixian xinling*危險心靈 (Dangerous Minds) by Hou Wen-yong 侯文詠 (Taipei: Crown Literature Publishing Co., 2003); *Laoshi, ni huibuhuilai*老師，你會不會回來 [Turn Around; or Literally, "Teacher, Are You Coming Back?"] by Wang Zhengzhong 王政忠 (Taipei: Times Publishing, 2011); and *Heaven Lake* by John Dalton (New York: Scribner's, 2004).
6 See Li Hongrui, "The Romance Novels by Chiung Yao That Launched Many Acting Careers," *China Daily*, April 12, 2017, http://wap.chinadaily.com.cn/2017-04/12/content_28878691.htm.
7 Catherine Dai, *Under the Phoenix Tree* (Taipei: Bookman, 1991); and Dana Standridge, *Lessons in Essence* (Emeryville, CA: Shoemaker and Hoard, 2006).
8 Catherine Dai, *Bound Feet: Stories of Contemporary Taiwan* (Taipei: Bookman, 1988).
9 "It's astonishing how under-rated and little-known Catherine Dai's work is; perhaps one day she will receive some much-deserved recognition as one of the best modern writers on Taiwan." Trista di Genova, *The Wild East*, June 23, 2012, www.thewildeast.net/2012/06/catherine-dais-under-the-phoenix-tree-book-review/.
10 A 2014 report notes that "Taiwan's Ministry of Education suggests that Taiwan's rapid social changes, overextended colleges and universities, and slower and

slower birth rate are creating a gap between educational training and careers." See Hao Chen and Hsin-hsien Fan, "Education in Taiwan: The Visions and Goals for the 12-Year Curriculum," November 11, 2014, www.brookings.edu/opinions/education-in-taiwan-the-vision-and-goals-of-the-12-year-curriculum/.

11 Chuing Prudence Chou, "Education in Taiwan: Taiwan's Colleges and Universities," November 12, 2014, www.brookings.edu/opinions/education-in-taiwan-taiwans-colleges-and-universities/.

12 C. P. Chou, "The SSCI Syndrome in Taiwan's Academia," *Education Policy Analysis Archives* 22, no. 29 (2014), http://dx.doi.org/10.14507/epaa.v22n29.2014.

13 Douglas C. Smith, "Foundations of Modern Chinese Education and the Taiwan Experience," in *The Confucius Continuum: Educational Modernization in Taiwan*, ed. Douglas C. Smith (New York: Praeger, 1991), 1–64.

14 See report on textbook protest in Michael Gold, "Taiwan School Textbook Row Highlights Antipathy to 'One China'," August 2, 2015, www.reuters.com/article/us-taiwan-politics-education/taiwan-school-textbook-row-highlights-antipathy-to-one-china-idUSKCN0Q806820150803.

15 See report on current textbook revision in Brian Hioe, "Recent Debates about Teaching Classical Chinese in Taiwan," *New Bloom*, August 27, 2017, https://newbloommag.net/2017/08/27/classical-chinese-taiwan/.

16 Standridge, *Lessons*, epigraph.

17 Chun-chieh Huang, *Taiwan in Transformation: Retrospect and Prospect* (NTU Press/New Brunswick: Transaction Publishers, 2014), 88.

18 Sun-sheng Yvonne Chang, *Literary Culture in Taiwan: Martial Law to Market Law* (New York: Columbia University Press, 2004), 6, 22.

19 For discussion of sex abuse of children in China in reference to Lin's suicide, see Zhang Xinyuan, "Tormented by the Past," *Global Times*, May 11, 2017, www.globaltimes.cn/content/1046452.shtml.

20 Lin Fang-mei, "Social Change and Romantic Ideology: The Impact of the Publishing Industry, Family Organization, and Gender Roles on the Reception and Interpretation of Romance Fiction in Taiwan, 1960–1990," PhD diss., University of Pennsylvania, 1992.

21 Miriam Lang, "Qiong Yao and San Mao: A Popular Pair," *Modern Chinese Literature and Culture* 15, no. 2 (Fall 2003): 93.

22 Email interview with the author.

23 Email interview with the author.

Works cited

Chang, Sun-sheng Yvonne. *Literary Culture in Taiwan: Martial Law to Market Law*. New York: Columbia University Press, 2004.

Chen, Hao, and Hsin-hsien Fan. "Education in Taiwan: The Visions and Goals for the 12-Year Curriculum." November 11, 2014. www.brookings.edu/opinions/educationin-taiwan-the-vision-and-goals-of-the-12-year-curriculum/. Accessed November 5, 2017.

Chiung Yao 琼瑶. *Chuangwai* 窗外 (Outside the Window). Taipei: Crown Literature Publishing Co., 1963.

Chou, Chuing Prudence. "Education in Taiwan: Taiwan's Colleges and Universities." November 2, 2014. www.brookings.edu/opinions/education-in-taiwan-taiwans-colleges-and-universities/. Accessed October 30, 2017.

———. "The SSCI Syndrome in Taiwan's Academia." *Education Policy Analysis Archives* 22, no. 29 (2014). dx.doi.org/10.14507/epaa.v22n29.2014. Accessed October 29, 2017.

Dai, Catherine. *Bound Feet: Stories of Contemporary Taiwan*. Taipei: Bookman, 1988.

————. Email interview. Conducted by Mary Goodwin, December 5, 2017.

————. *Under the Phoenix Tree.* Taipei: Bookman, 1991.

Gold, Michael. "Taiwan School Textbook Row Highlights Antipathy to 'One China'." August 2, 2015. www.reuters.com/article/us-taiwan-politics-education/taiwan-school-textbook-row-highlights-antipathy-to-one-china-idUSKCN0Q806820 150803. Accessed August 2, 2017.

Hioe, Brian. "Recent Debates about Teaching Classical Chinese in Taiwan." *New Bloom*, August 27, 2017. newbloommag.net/2017/08/27/classical-chinese-taiwan/. Accessed September 4, 2017.

Huang, Chun-chieh. *Taiwan in Transformation: Retrospect and Prospect.* NTU Press/New Brunswick: Transaction Publishers, 2014.

Lang, Miriam. "Qiong Yao and San Mao: A Popular Pair." *Modern Chinese Literature and Culture* 15, no. 2 (Fall 2003): 93.

Li, Hongrui. "The Romance Novels by Chiung Yao That Launched Many Acting Careers." *China Daily*, April 12, 2017. wap.chinadaily.com.cn/2017-04/12/content_28878691.htm. Accessed June 20, 2017.

Lin, Fang-mei. "Social Change and Romantic Ideology: The Impact of the Publishing Industry, Family Organization, and Gender Roles on the Reception and Interpretation of Romance Fiction in Taiwan, 1960–1990." PhD diss., University of Pennsylvania, 1992. repository.upenn.edu/dissertations/AAI9227710/. Accessed September 4, 2017.

Lin, Sean. "Teacher Accused of Sexual Assault Breaks His Silence." *Taipei Times*, May 11, 2017. www.taipeitimes.com/News/front/archives/2017/05/11/2003670351. Accessed August 4, 2017.

Lin Yi-han 林奕含. *Fang Siqi de chulian leyuan*房思琪的初戀樂園 (Fang Ssu-chi's First Love Paradise). Taipei: Guerrilla Publishing, 2017.

————. Interview. May 2017. www.news.readmoo.com/2017/0/05/170505-interview-with-lin-02/. Accessed July 7, 2017.

Seediq Bale. Directed by Wei Te-sheng, Vie Vision, 2011.

Smith, Douglas C. "Foundations of Modern Chinese Education and the Taiwan Experience." In *The Confucius Continuum: Educational Modernization in Taiwan*, edited by Douglas C. Smith. New York: Praeger, 1991.

Standridge, Dana. Email Interview. Conducted by Mary Goodwin, November 29, 2017.

————. *Lessons in Essence.* Emeryville, CA: Shoemaker and Hoard, 2006.

Wu Zhuoliu. *Orphan of Asia.* Trans Ioannis Mentzas. New York: Columbia University Press, 2006.

Yang, Jessie. "What Suicide of Author Lin Yi-Han Can Teach Us about Mental Health." May 19, 2017. www.studybreaks.com/2017/05/19/lin-yi-han/. Accessed June 5, 2017.

Zhang, Xinyuan. "Tormented by the Past." *Global Times*, May 11, 2017. www.globaltimes.cn/content/1046452.shtml. Accessed July 6, 2017.

10

THE PRACTICE OF ANNOTATION AND TRANSLATION IN QIU XIAOLONG'S INSPECTOR CHEN MYSTERIES

Charles Lowe

Although the US-based author Qiu Xiaolong is currently best known for his popular Inspector Chen mysteries, he began his literary career as a scholar and a translator. Having already translated T. S. Eliot's *The Waste Land*, *The Love Song of J. Alfred Prufrock*, and other works into Chinese, Qiu came to the United States in 1988 to continue his study of T. S. Eliot at Washington University in St. Louis. After the military crackdown on the Tiananmen Square democracy protesters the following year, he decided to remain, ultimately receiving his doctorate in comparative literature in 1995. In 2000, Qiu published his first Inspector Chen novel, *Death of a Red Heroine*, and he has since written eight more volumes. The novels, which Qiu writes in English, have been translated into Chinese and several other languages. The fiction has been adapted for radio broadcast,[1] and the film rights have been procured for seven Inspector Chen novels.[2]

Qiu Xiaolong's background as a translator, and specifically his interest in T. S. Eliot, informs his fiction in several respects. First and most obviously, the protagonist of Qiu's series, Inspector Chen, is himself a professional translator. Second, Eliot's well-known "impersonal theory" of literature resonates with the emphasis in the series on an abstract process of ratiocination, in that Qiu's protagonist adopts a detached attitude while attempting to maintain his focus on the physical evidence of the case.[3] Third, just as Qiu's translation of *The Waste Land* is characterized, as Tiziana Lioi has noted,[4] by his heavy use of footnotes to fill in the gaps that inevitably open up between the implicit source text and the translation, Qiu has similarly noted the challenge, in writing his Inspector Chen series, of capturing in English certain cultural nuances that could be expressed more directly in Chinese. Finally, and perhaps most intriguingly, there is an important respect in which Qiu's novels, despite being written in English, could be viewed as virtual translations in their own right – or, to be more precise, as works written as if composed directly in translation, with no prior source text.

Although translation is often associated with an inevitable loss of meaning, as deployed in the Inspector Chen series the trope of translation does not connote loss but rather contributes to the novels' appeal in two key respects. First, Qiu Xiaolong's fictional protagonist accrues implied expertise by virtue of being a translator, and second, in his paratextual writings, Qiu suggests an anxiety about the need to fill in the gaps in meaning between the novels and the implicit source text, thereby suggesting that the act of reading the novels functions as a sort of crime investigation in its own right. Similar questions of authority are also central to the fictional works themselves. As a minor public official, for instance, Inspector Chen recognizes that he may not have the authority and influence he needs in order to obtain all relevant information about the victim's death. As a professional translator, however, he feels obligated to present as complete an account of the case as possible – though he also understands his obligation to produce a report that is consistent with Party aims and directives. Furthermore, in *Death of a Red Heroine*, Chen is also self-conscious about how his reading of the female victim's body has been compromised by his questionable private conduct. His anxiety over his ethical authority culminates in a parallel between his own affair with a married colleague and the suspect's entanglement with the murdered "red heroine" – though with the caveat that the suspect was "only a little less lucky."[5]

Other novels in English by Chinese-born authors have similarly emphasized the practice of translation. For instance, Xiaolu Guo's first English-language novel, *A Concise Chinese-English Dictionary* (2008), consists of a (fictional) diary in English by a young Chinese woman who has recently arrived in England. Written in very broken English, the initial portions of the diary may be read as a virtual translation of a (nonexistent) Chinese original. Similarly, the protagonist of Guo's more recent novel *I Am China* is a professional translator who has been hired to translate a mysterious set of letters and diaries from Chinese into English. A more immediate parallel to Qiu Xiaolong's detective fiction, however, can be found in Robert van Gulik's Judge Dee series. Like Qiu, van Gulik initially worked as a translator and a scholar before becoming a novelist. Van Gulik began his Judge Dee series in 1949 with a translation of the anonymous eighteenth-century Chinese detective novel *Di Gong'an* (狄公案), which he published under the title *Dee Goong An: An Ancient Chinese Detective Story.*[6] After this translation, van Gulik proceeded to write and publish a series of original works inspired by the same protagonist, each of which innovates on the original Chinese source text by adding Westernized elements – including repositioning the solution of the mystery to the end of the novel and granting the eponymous judge more human qualities. Like Qiu's novels, van Gulik's mysteries feature a large number of literary and cultural allusions, and his prefaces and postscripts give the works the appearance of a scholarly study – with particular care being taken to explain the rationale for his modifications to the model provided by the Chinese source text, in order to accommodate the perceived needs of – as Donald Lach puts it in his introduction to one of the novels – "western readers."[7]

Another point of departure involves the way fictive translation becomes a frame for eroticized imagery. Van Gulik studied and translated Ming erotic handbooks, and he later drew on his interest in these texts in producing the highly sexualized representations of women in the Judge Dee mysteries. Van Gulik's stylized graphic drawings, with titles like "Judge Dee in the boudoir of a dead lady," create a sense of scholarly distance from which the presumptively Western readers of his detective fiction can safely observe the unclothed victim. The appearance of disengagement suggested by the frequent annotations, meanwhile, has a similar function in Qiu's novel, allowing his protagonist to adopt a mien of professional detachment throughout his graphic account of the naked body of the murder victim. The tone of studied disinterest filters through the narrator's documentation of the victim's appearance in the suspect's pornographic photographs.

In an interview with Jeffrey Wasserstrom, Qiu acknowledged having read van Gulik's novels before composing his own detective fiction and explained that he was particularly fascinated by the subversive connotations of the detective's official title:

> Dee is a Judge, not a cop or a detective, and in real life, he once served as a prime minister; for that matter, in other Judge stories as well — [as] the "judge," not in the ordinary sense of the word, but in reality a high ranking official. That in itself speaks about the fact that, lacking an established legal system, a detective could do so little, it has to take a resourceful well-connected official to make a difference. So the suspense comes not just in whodunit, but in the almost impossible mission to have the criminal punished against odds in the complicated power struggle.[8]

Qiu's emphasis on the significance of the judge's official title is relevant to the treatment of translation as a practice in his mystery. Qiu's inspector, like van Gulik's judge, is a well-connected official with keen political instincts. In this respect, Chen offers a sharp contrast to his subordinate, Detective Yu, who refuses to allow Party interests to interfere with the case and suffers the consequences of his insensitivity in his lack of career advancement.

Below, I examine a pattern of allusions in *Death of a Red Heroine* that grant Qiu's work the semblance of scholarly translation even as they underscore the author's own subjective positionality. In particular, the references undercut the author's pretense of objective detachment by suggesting his private and public agendas as a reader of the imaginary source text about the death of the female victim. The emphasis on the limited reliability of the narrator as a figurative translator, instead of implying loss, contributes to the work's thematic content.

"Cooking with words"

In the opening chapter of *Death of a Red Heroine*, we find an allusion to language and translation. A nuclear engineer by the name of Liu Guoliang has just been reunited with a former classmate named Gao Ziling, whom he has not seen for twenty years. Gao now works as the captain of a Shanghai patrol boat, and the two high school buddies proceed to go fishing in a canal off Shanghai's Suzhou River. Liu explains to Gao how much the taste of fish means to him, and the narrator remarks that

> Liu had worked for twenty years in a desert area, where the local peasants observed a time-honored tradition of serving a fish carved from wood in celebration of the Spring Festival since the Chinese character for "fish" can also mean "surplus," a lucky sign for the coming year. Its taste might be forgotten, but not the tradition.[9]

In this passage, the narrator refers elliptically to the fact that the Chinese character for "fish" (*yu* 魚) is homophonous with a different character meaning "surplus" (餘), and consequently is sometimes used in its place. Accordingly, like the practice of replacing the character for "fish" with the homophonic character for "surplus," the tradition of serving a wooden replica of a fish in place of a real fish gestures to the "surplus" that is embedded in both cultural tradition and individual meaning.

In his essay 2014 essay "Cooking with Words," Qiu uses another example involving fish to describe the challenges he encounters in attempting to convey the meaning of Chinese words in English. Discussing the Chinese character *chan* (饞), Qiu notes that the term does not have a precise equivalent in English:

> *Chan* is not hungry; rather, it means "a craving for something with its specific taste." *Chan* can be used as verb or as adjective. As a verb, it usually takes an object. There's even a well-known story about it. Zhang Jiying, a high-ranking official of the Jin dynasty (265–420), missed Songjiang river perch so much, he resigned his position in the capital for the sake of the precious fish.[10]

In this passage, Qiu alludes to a historical anecdote about river perch to explain the meaning of the phrase *chungeng lukuai* (蓴羹鱸膾), an intense craving for a specific dish, and in this context a craving for river perch. Qiu suggests that this set phrase captures the meaning of the Chinese word *chan* – though the term *chan* itself does not, in fact, appear in the phrase in question; nor does Qiu point to a specific word or phrase in his own novel that functions as a direct translation. Instead, Qiu's point seems be that the phrase *chungeng lukuai* and his own description of Inspector Chen in his novels both convey a sentiment associated with the word *chan*. In the beginning of Qiu's first novel, this sentiment is manifested in Liu Guoliang's hunger for a particular dish, which in turn leads him to a fishing spot where he discovers the body of the murder victim.

We find a similar use of literary and historical allusion in the novel's second chapter, in which Inspector Chen is hosting a housewarming party. His first guest is a young reporter named Wang Feng, and the narrative uses a Tang dynasty allusion to describe her attractive figure:

> In the afternoon light streaming through the plastic blinds, her complexion was matte porcelain. Her eyes were clear, almond-shaped, just long enough to be suggestive of a distinct character. Her black hair cascaded halfway down her back. She wore a white T-shirt and a pleated skirt, with a wide belt of alligator leather that clinched her "emancipated wasp" waist and accentuated her breasts.
>
> *Emancipated wasp.* An image invented by Li Yu, the last emperor of the South Tang dynasty, also a brilliant poet, who depicted his favorite imperial concubine's ravishing beauty in several celebrated poems. The poet-emperor was afraid that he might break her in two by holding her too tightly. It was said that the custom of foot-binding also started in Li Yu's reign. There was no accounting for taste, Chen reflected.[11]

Here, the narrator – evidently speaking in the voice of the protagonist – uses an antiquated metaphor to describe his guest, then proceeds to explain the metaphor's historical provenance.

Chen and Wang Feng reminisce about how they first met, and Wang Feng quotes a verse from one of Chen's own poems. The poem is about parting, and she speculates that it must have been inspired by the departure of someone dear to him. Chen prefers not to discuss this earlier relationship with her, remarking, "A poem does not have to be about something in the poet's life. Poetry is impersonal. As T. S. Eliot has said, it is not letting loose an emotional crisis – ."[12] Ironically, in cutting off this question about the personal significance of his poem, Chen alludes to Eliot's well-known theory of impersonal poetry (which contends that artistic creation is a process of depersonalization), which had considerable personal significance for the author Qiu Xiaolong himself.

At this moment Chen's friend Lu Tonghao barges in carrying an enormous "beggar's chicken" and asks what Chen and Wang Feng are talking about. Chen, however, sidesteps the question:

> He had a ready excuse in busily unwrapping the beggar's chicken. The recipe had supposedly originated when a beggar baked a soil-and-lotus leaf-wrapped chicken in a pile of ashes. The result was an astonishing success. It must have taken a long time to cook.[13]

Here, the narrative cites the traditional origin of the dish's name, but the allusion to begging embedded in the name also reflects Lu's underlying objective: to encourage Chen to lend him money for the purchase of a restaurant.

The preceding descriptions of the woman's "emancipated wasp" waist and Lu Tonghao's "beggar's chicken" are both assigned a detailed historical background that is ostensibly necessary for readers to understand the full significance of the phrases in question. In "Cooking with Words," Qiu discusses how he uses allusions to construct a realistic text that, in his view, resembles a translation, and cites the example of his attempt to translate the essence of the river-crab dish from Mandarin to English. Crab is an important motif in the novel, referenced dozens of times. The red heroine herself is compared to a hermit crab, in that "politics form her outer shell,"[14] and the act of solving the mystery of her death is compared to cracking that shell.

The river-crab banquet occurs near the midpoint in the novel. Peiqin, Detective Yu's wife, has invited Inspector Chen for a family meal to express her appreciation for Chen's intervention into her husband's workplace dispute with his supervisor, Commissar Zhang. Zhang adheres to a political perspective on the investigation while Detective Yu instead proposes a more technical approach. However, while respecting his subordinate's professionalism, Chen fears that the detective's lack of political skill may hobble an investigation that requires the cooperation of the authorities in order to ascertain the facts and to arrest the murderer. In "Cooking with Words," Qiu explains the challenge of conveying in English the specific connotations that crab-related terms carry in Chinese:

> For Shanghainese, the most scrumptious parts of the crab are *xiehuang* and *xiegao*. In the City God Temple Market, a dash of *xiehuang* on top of the mini soup bun could double or triple the price of the luscious snack. I had talked about *xiehuang* and *xiegao* in Chinese for so long without bothering to find out what exactly they are. For a possible clue, I could bring to mind only a phrase in connection with it, *jiucishixiong* (preferable with female crabs in the ninth lunar month, and male crabs in the tenth lunar month). So I had to open a dictionary. *Xiehuang* is the female crab ovary and digestive gland; *xiegao*, the male crab seminal collection of semen and organs. I drew in a deep breath, and double-checked. No mistake. But how could I represent the mouth-watering flavor by using the English dictionary definition?[15]

The description of the river crabs in *Death of the Red Heroine* follows the pattern found in Qiu's earlier allusions to beggar's chicken and to the woman reporter's emancipated wasp waist, in that it brackets the translation of the cuisine. These annotations express Qiu's intention to communicate the linguistic distinctions that would otherwise be lost in translation.

Befitting the banquet's central position in the novel, the description of it emphasizes its ceremonial function:

> It was an excellent meal, literally a crab banquet. On the cloth-covered table the crabs appeared rounded, red and white, in small bamboo steamers. The small brass hammer shone among the blue and white saucers. The rice wine was nicely warmed, displaying an amber color under the light. On the windowsill, a bouquet of chrysanthemums stood in a glass vase, perhaps two or three days old, thinner, but still exquisite.[16]

The table's colorful arrangement suggests a careful balance. The crab's red and white color connotes harmony, while the phallic hammer and the receptive saucer complete the eroticized pairings. The amber lighting and the exquisite bouquet of chrysanthemums suggest the dish's delicacy:

"I should have brought my Canon to photograph the table, the crabs, and the chrysanthemums," Chen said, rubbing his hands. "It could be an illustration torn from *The Dream of the Red Chamber*."

"You're talking about Chapter 28, aren't you? Baoyu and his 'sisters' composing poems over a crab banquet," Peiqin said, squeezing out the leg meat for Qinqin. "Alas, this is not a room in the Grand View Garden."

"Not even in Qingpu Grand View Garden." Yu was pleased that they had just visited the garden. "But our Chief Inspector Chen is a poet in his own right. He will read us his poems."

"Don't ask me to read anything," Chen said. "My mouth's full of crab. A crab beats a couplet."[17]

Here, Chen's allusion to *Dream of the Red Chamber* illustrates his expertise, thereby adding to the romantic aroma of the proceedings. Tellingly, the narrative describes this as an illustration "torn" from the classic Qing dynasty novel, suggesting that the reference has been taken out of context.

Chen's wish to use a camera to memorialize the ceremony adds to the violent connotations of the scene, in that within the novel, the camera is a motif associated with the pornographic record of a handcuffed actress and the documentation of violence on the murder victim's body.[18] Chen compares the act of consuming river crabs to the recitation of classical couplets, a gastronomical experience that climaxes with his consuming the "golden digestive glands of a female crab,"[19] which also carries erotically violent connotations.

Peiqin, the wife of Detective Yu, is also conversant in the classics and shows an attentiveness to the difference between a ceremony in its traditional and contemporary contexts, remarking, "Alas, this is not a room in the Grand View Garden."[20] However, her view of the ceremony is inflected by her sense of her maternal obligation, a dutifulness expressed by her "squeezing out the meat" for her son. The ceremony initiates foreplay for her, ultimately concluding in a romantic scene that brings out the crab's erotic connotations, with Detective Yu listening to the "bubbles of crab froth, bubbles with which they moistened each other in the dark."[21] These frothy bubbles further reinforce the dish's sexual connotations, which Chen misses in his English-language descriptions of the traditional Chinese dish.

The banquet scene in Qiu's narrative, accordingly, makes several literary allusions that collectively lend the narrative the appearance of a translation. In "Cooking with Words," Qiu explains that his uses of historical allusions are intended to convey the differences between English and Chinese culinary terms. Chen's attention to the erotic connotations of the dish suggests his anomalous position as a male detective tasked with recording an official account of the female victim's death. Peiqin's reading of the banquet further destabilizes his authority as a translator by suggesting that there is another reading of the cuisine embedded within a conventional moral framework.

One way the banquet scene differs from the other representations of cuisine in the novel is the inclusion of an embedded audience, the Yus' son:

"Su [Dongpo], the Song Dynasty poet, said on one occasion, 'O that I could have crabs without a wine-supervisor sitting beside me.'"

"A wine-supervisor of the Song Dynasty?" Qinqin spoke for the first time during the meal, showing his interest in history.

"A wine-supervisor was a low-ranking officer in the fifteenth century," Chen said, "like a medium rank police officer nowadays, responsible only for other officials' behavior at formal feasts and festivals."

(Ch. 19)

Chen's comparison of the wine supervisor to the police reflects both his ambivalence about being responsible for monitoring other officials' behaviors and an opposing desire to act outside the boundaries of official authority. But the detailed historical annotations make sense because they are not part of an interior monologue. Instead, this lecture directed to Qinqin, an inquisitive and dutiful son, appears reasonable in the context of his education in the Chinese classics.

Caroline Cummins (2003) observes a certain degree of awkwardness in Qiu's practice of embedding explanations within his novels to clarify the significance of his literary and historical allusions. She asks why "a Shanghai native [would] need to remind another Shanghai native that, 10 years previously, taxis had been scarce on the city's streets?"[22] A similar point could be made with respect to allusions contained within the narrative's interior monologue. To whom is Chen's narrative addressed? Why does a highly erudite translator require a full reference to the Song dynasty locus classicus to contextualize his reference of her "emancipated wasp" waist?

In Qiu's next novel after *Death of a Red Heroine*, *A Loyal Character Dancer* (2002), the question of the implied addressee is partly remedied by the inclusion of a foreign audience. Catherine Rohn, a US marshal who is fluent in Chinese but has only rudimentary familiarity with Chinese culture, poses questions that are most likely pressing Chen's readers. In this way, the author's explanations of the significance of the phrase "born under a peach tree"[23] or his contextualization of loyal dancer acquire meaningfulness as imperfectly formed translations in response to her inquiries.

This device only works, however, when there is a foreign listener present. In the introduction to *Shanghai Redemption* (2015), the most recent novel in the series, the narrator quotes a Tang dynasty quatrain while adding background on contemporary Party politics into his commentary. The information may offer the presumptive lay reader a useful crutch, though as a means of conveying Chen's ratiocination process it would appear to be unnecessary.

In Qiu's Inspector Chen series, accordingly, the trope of translation appears somewhat artificial, though it may serve as a useful instrument for a popular series seeking to achieve a wide readership. Judging from the English-language reviews, with a few possible exceptions such as the one by Cummins, Qiu's mysteries have been accepted as virtual translations. Furthermore, this view of the novels as works of virtual translation and political realism has enhanced the popularity of the series itself. For example, Andrea Kempf in *Contemporary Asian Culture* notes of his first novel:

> What raises the novel well above a typical police procedural is the quirky, erudite inspector. Chen is able to quote a Tang-dynasty poem appropriate to every situation; and when Chinese poetry fails, he quotes T. S. Eliot or Matthew Arnold. He delights in eating a good meal, and the many that he consumes are described along the way to the murder's solution.[24]

Similarly, in *Publishers Weekly* an anonymous reviewer writes, "the author, himself a poet and critic, peppers the story with allusions to classical Chinese literature, juxtaposing poignant poetry with a gruesome murder so that the novel reads *like the translation of an ancient text* [emphasis added] imposed over a modern tale of intrigue."[25] In noting that the novel resembles a translation, the reviewer indicates that the work is successful in presenting the illusion that it is based on a prior source text. Melanie Ho, a Hong Kong-based reviewer, singles out the references to Song dynasty poetry for particular praise in her review of *Enigma of China* (2013), noting that allusions to traditional literature mix "suspense with a pleasant charming tone" and add "comic sidebars involving descriptions of food – Chen asks for the recipe for an omelet-like dish called super crab meat and roe and gets told the story behind cross-bridge noodles."[26]

An anonymous customer on the website *Alibris* sums up the popular allure of the allusions to classical poetry and to Chinese culture in the Inspector Chen mystery:

> As Qiu unravels very convincing mysteries, he also instructs, but in a very involving, enjoyable way that is not at all heavy-handed, about Chinese culture. His detective is a poet and the poetry which interweaves each of the books is not intrusive but adds an intellectual level of emotion. A bonus for readers who like to eat: the food descriptions are enough to cause hunger pangs![27]

The supposed political realism of his translated mysteries has likewise been the subject of praise. *Kirkus Reviews* commends Qiu Xiaolong for "using mystery to focus a large and nuanced portrait of contemporary China."[28] Louisa Lim on National Public Radio titled her 2006 interview with Qiu Xiaolong "Shanghai Detective Fiction Reflects a Changing China," inviting her listeners to view his detective fiction as a "portrait of China in transition."[29] Similarly, Catherine Sampson ranks *Death of a Red Heroine* first in her list of "top 10 Asian crime fiction," citing the book as "a vivid description of present day Shanghai, and the satisfying ending is utterly believable."[30] Sampson created her list with the object of identifying crime fiction in China as a "small but growing genre," noting: "To write about crime in China – however fictional – is to advertise the fact that Chinese society is not an entirely harmonious and benign thing."[31]

The author of a popular work of detective fiction set in China, Sampson recognizes the marketability of a narrative that claims to both accurately depict a hidden society and maintain its popular appeal as crime fiction. A review by Stéphane Lagarde on Radio France International identifies the resonance of Qiu's political fiction in translation when he observes that the Inspector's growing "duplicity" through the evolution of his series reflects growing corruption in Chinese society.[32]

On the other hand, a *China Daily* review of the Chinese translation of *Death of a Red Heroine* contends that the realistic veneer of the Inspector Chen mystery undermines its scholarly merit. The article, titled "No Mystery in Qiu's Mastery," criticizes the work's use of literary allusion as detracting from its realism while only offering "reductive explanations of each and every poem." This reviewer emphasizes in his generally positive appraisal that the literariness of Qiu's first novel allows a "lyrical" escape from the realities of contemporary China,[33] an otherworldliness accentuated by the publisher's decision to erase Shanghai as the location for the mystery from its Mandarin translation. In a 2015 interview, Qiu expressed irritation about the decision to remove the references to its fictive location.[34] The elision, however, may be an inevitable result of a process in which a work that is a virtual translation from a (nonexistent) Chinese source text is translated back into Chinese.

Notes

1 Caroline Cummins, "Qiu Xiaolong and the China Enigma," *January Magazine*, January 2003.
2 Pip Bullbeck, "Qiu Xiaolong's Chief Inspector Chen' Books to be Adapted into Seven Feature Films," *Hollywood Reporter*, August 11, 2011.
3 Qiu Xiaolong, *Death of a Red Heroine* (New York: Soho Crime, 2000), 15.
4 Tiziana Lioi, "T. S. Eliot in China: A Cultural and Linguistic Study on the Translation of the Waste Land in Chinese," ed. Patrizia Dadò (Rome: Instituto Italiano di Studi Orientali, 2003).
5 Qiu Xiaolong, *Death of a Red Heroine*, 463.
6 Robert Van Gulik, *The Willow Pattern* (Chicago: University of Chicago Press, 1965), 4.
7 Van Gulik, *The Willow Pattern*, 4.
8 Jeffrey Wasserstrom, "Shanghai Mysteries: A Q&A with Qiu Xiaolong," *Los Angeles Review of Books*, September 30, 2015.
9 Qiu Xiaolong, *Death of a Red Heroine*, 3.
10 Qiu Xiaolong, "Cooking with Words: The Linguistically Modified Meals of the Redoubtable Inspector Chen," *The Common Reader: A Journal of the Essay*, October 1, 2014.
11 Qiu Xiaolong, *Death of a Red Heroine*, 13.
12 Qiu Xiaolong, *Death of a Red Heroine*, 15.
13 Qiu Xiaolong, *Death of a Red Heroine*, 9.
14 Qiu Xiaolong, *Death of a Red Heroine*, 149.

15 Qiu Xiaolong, "Cooking with Words."
16 Qiu Xiaolong, *Death of a Red Heroine*, 210.
17 Qiu Xiaolong, *Death of a Red Heroine*, 210.
18 Qiu Xiaolong, *Death of a Red Heroine*, 280.
19 Qiu Xiaolong, *Death of a Red Heroine*, 211.
20 Qiu Xiaolong, *Death of a Red Heroine*, 211.
21 Qiu Xiaolong, *Death of a Red Heroine*, 221.
22 Caroline Cummins, "Qiu Xiaolong and the China Enigma."
23 Qiu Xiaolong, *A Loyal Character Dancer* (New York: Minotaur Books, 2003), 79.
24 Andrea Kempf, "Book Review: Shanghai," *Library Papers and Presentations* (2001): 11.
25 "Death of a Red Heroine," *Publishers Weekly*, June 2001.
26 Melanie Ho, "*Enigma of China* by Qiu Xiaolong," *Asian Review*, August 9, 2013.
27 "Untitled Review," *Alibris*, July 26, 2007.
28 "Shanghai Redemption," *Kirkus Reviews*, July 1, 2015.
29 Louisa Lim, "Shanghai Detective Fiction Reflects a Changing China," *NPR Morning Edition*, September 29, 2006.
30 Catherine Sampson, "Catherine Sampson's Top 10 Asian Crime Fiction," *The Guardian*, August 26, 2007.
31 Sampson, "Catherine Sampson's Top 10 Asian Crime Fiction."
32 Stéphane Lagarde, "New Inspector Chen Novel Honored on RFI," *Radio France Internationale*, December 24, 2016.
33 "No Mystery in Qiu's Mastery," *China Daily*, December 31, 2003.
34 Layden Green, "International Thrills: An interview with Qiu Xiaolong by Layton Green," *The Big Thrill*, July 2015.

Works cited

Alter, Alexandra. "Fiction's Global Crime Wave." *The Wall Street Journal*, July 1, 2010.
Cummins, Caroline. "Qiu Xiaolong and the China Enigma." *January Magazine*, January, 2003.
"Death of a Red Heroine." *Publishers Weekly*, June, 2001. Furth, Charlotte. "Rethinking Van Gulik Again." *Men, Women & Gender in Early & Imperial China* 7, no. 1 (March 2005): 71–78.
Gilmour, Rachael. "Living between Languages: The Politics of Translation in Leila Aboulela's Minaret and Xiaolu Guo's a Concise Chinese-English Dictionary for Lovers." *Journal of Commonwealth Literature* 47, no. 2 (2012): 207–227.
Green, Layton. "International Thrills: An Interview with Qiu Xiaolong: Perceiving China Through a Poetry-Spouting Sleuth." *The Big Thrill: The Online Publication of International Thriller Writers*, July 30, 2015.
Guo, Xiaolu. *A Concise Chinese-English Dictionary for Lovers*. London: Vintage, 2007.
Ho, Melanie. "Enigma of China by Qiu Xiaolong." *Asian Review*, August 9, 2013.
Kempf, Andrea. "Book Review: Shanghai." *Library Papers and Presentations* 13 (2001): 13.
Lach, Donald. "Introduction." In *The Chinese Lake Murders*. Chicago: University of Chicago Press, 1960.
Lagarde, Stéphane. "New Inspector Chen Novel Honored on RFI." *Radio France Internationale*, December 24, 2016.
Lim, Louisa. "Shanghai Detective Fiction Reflects a Changing China." *NPR Morning Edition*, September 29, 2006.
Lioi, Tiziana. *T. S. Eliot in China: A Cultural and Linguistic Study on the Translation of the Waste Land in Chinese*. Ed. Patrizia Dadò. Rome: Instituto Italiano di Studi Orientali, 2003.

"No Mystery in Qiu's Mastery." *China Daily*, December 31, 2003.

Qiu Xiaolong. "Cooking with Words: The Linguistically Modified Meals of the Redoubtable Inspector Chen." *The Common Reader: A Journal of the Essay*, October 1, 2014.

———. *Death of a Red Heroine*. New York: Soho Crime, 2000.

———. *Enigma of China*. New York: Minotaur Books, 2013.

———. *A Loyal Character Dancer*. New York: Minotaur Books, 2003.

———. *Shanghai Redemption*. New York: Minotaur Books, 2015.

Sampson, Catherine. "Catherine Sampson's Top 10 Asian Crime Fiction." *The Guardian*, August 26, 2007.

"Shanghai Redemption." *Kirkus Reviews*, July 1, 2015.

Untitled Review. *Alibris*, July 26, 2007.

Van Gulik, Robert. *The Willow Pattern*. Chicago: University of Chicago Press, 1965.

Wasserstrom, Jeffrey. "Shanghai Mysteries: A Q&A with Qiu Xiaolong." *Los Angeles Review of Books*, September 30, 2015.

11

FROM *CHINESE DIASPORA* TO *SINOSPORE*

Multispecies Chineseness and transmemory in Larissa Lai's *Salt Fish Girl*

Belinda Kong

To trace the evolving meanings of the concept of diaspora is to trace its evolving contradictions. In contemporary Chinese literary and cultural studies, debates about the term have shifted dramatically in the past three decades, from apprehensions of essentialism and an insistence on hybridity to affirmations of globalization and the rise of Chinese capital. Rather than follow these models, this chapter charts an alternate course that reframes Chineseness in relation to human-nonhuman assemblages. It turns to speculative fiction in tandem with recent theories of multispecies ecology drawn from cultural anthropology and the new materialist studies in order to rethink the Chinese diaspora as *sinospore*. Through the sinospore framework, we may come to a vision of the Chinese diaspora that does not merely dispense with origin for the sake of difference, but rather stretches diasporic lineage beyond cultural postmemory into more radical imaginings of transincarnational, specieswide, and multispecies transmemory – forms of embodied remembrance that do not hollow out cultural and racial identity but connect it to planetary history and deep time.

The multispecies framework: from Chinese diaspora to Sinospore

For one prominent turning point in the history of theorizing diaspora in contemporary China studies, we can turn to Tu Wei-ming's early 1990s notion of "cultural China." In Tu's well-known formulation, cultural China encompasses three "symbolic universes," or sites of production for "the changing meaning of being Chinese today": the ethnic Chinese-majority societies of mainland China, Taiwan, Hong Kong, and Singapore; the diaspora as defined through racial descent and migration; and the broader discursive "international

communities of scholars, students, officials, journalists, and traders who provide a global forum for China-related matters."[1] By outlining this tripartite
model, Tu sought to decenter the authority of the mainland communist state as
the chief arbiter of meaning for contemporary Chineseness, and to recognize
the powerful role that the "periphery" can play in pluralizing cultural identity.
Though Tu did not employ these terms, we may view his model as dispersing
Chineseness along the three axes of geography, race, and discourse. Those in the
first symbolic universe who live in Chinese-majority countries are *geographically*
Chinese, or Chinese by virtue of residency or location; those in the second symbolic universe who live in non–Chinese-majority countries are *racially* Chinese,
or Chinese via the social production of racial difference; and those non-ethnic
Chinese communities in the third symbolic universe who shape global constructions of Chineseness are *discursively* Chinese, or Chinese by participation in
discourse production.[2]

Some critiques of Tu have centered precisely on his characterization of the
diaspora, especially his reification of its "sojourner mentality" and persistent
homeland nostalgia. "The diaspora Chinese," according to Tu, "cherish the
hope of returning to and being recognized by the homeland," so that even after
decades abroad or multiple remigrations to countries ever farther from China,
"the sojourner mentality lingers on."[3] It was in reaction to this cultural "cen-
trism" and "homogenization" of Tu's account that Ien Ang, for example, argued
against essentializing Chineseness in *On Not Speaking Chinese*, and later, against
diaspora altogether as a theoretical paradigm.[4] Under the conceptual shadow
cast by Tu, Ang has come to see *all* invocations of diaspora as possessing an
"inevitable tendency to stress its internal coherence and unity," and as ultimately
reinstating the exclusivity of the very category of the nation it attempts to displace. Diasporic thinking, Ang concludes, is "proto-nationalist in its outlook."[5]
Post-Tu, the word *diaspora* in China studies carries a particular discursive residue.
Whereas it is typically aligned with deconstructive and poststructuralist tenets in
literary and cultural studies at large, within China studies it additionally retains
sharp echoes of essentialism and origin-centrism.

In recent years, though, another origin story has arisen for the term *Chinese
diaspora* that links it specifically to globalization. Hong Liu and Els van Dongen,
for instance, suggest that the term came into widespread use within China studies when theories of globalization emerged as a dominant critical paradigm in
the 1990s, after which the study of Chinese migration came to be reframed with
"an emphasis on mobility, networks, and flexible identities."[6] Their formulation
in turn carries strong traces of Aihwa Ong's notion of "flexible citizenship,"
which positions transnational Chinese subjects within circuits of global capital
and regimes of nation-state governance rather than as homeland-nostalgic emigrants or postnational cosmopolitans. If diaspora studies as an academic field
was first consolidated in the early 1990s under the sway of deconstruction and
postcolonialism and their respective political energies of decentering and subversive critiques, invocations of diaspora now – perhaps especially of the Chinese

diaspora in the era of mainland China's global economic power – are much more likely to get absorbed into analyses of global capital.

Coincidentally, around the same millennial moment when Ong's framework gained traction, one of the pioneer scholars of Chinese diaspora studies emphatically rejected *diaspora* as an umbrella term precisely for its association with the fluidity model of transnational capital. In a 2001 interview, Wang Gungwu called attention not to the recent waves of transnational entrepreneurs so exemplary for Ong but to labor migrants past and present. "For the last two hundred years," he observed, "the Chinese who left China by the millions were not, for most of them, traders or businessmen. They were poor, and very much in the situation of the journeymen [leaving] today the countryside for urban areas in hope of a better future. Those migrants were far from wealthy, rather the opposite." For Wang, *diaspora* remains tied to connotations of "business acumen and wealth" as well as an assumption of inviolable social "cohesion," both of which have "little relevance with the realities."[7] Wang's rejection of the word is as much political as empirical. On one hand, he dismisses the cohesion principle by underscoring that overseas Chinese are highly adaptive, so that a Chinese community in one country can drastically differ from that in another. More fervently, though, he objects to the word for being easily coopted by a renewed racist discourse in the new millennium:

> The word "diaspora" is in itself an oversimplification and I find personally very alarming that people talk commonly of a Jewish diaspora, an Indian diaspora or a Chinese one, as if the world consists of [a] few "leagues." It is simply not true, but unscrupulous people can use such description to build up the image of a new yellow peril. Some people are even going further, saying that China is behind it, sending out people and contacting people all around, acting like an enormous octopus, spreading its tentacles and building-up its network. Such nonsense is bound to be believed when one is using out-of-context words like "diaspora."[8]

The danger, Wang implies, is especially salient in the period of mainland China's economic rise, when the specter of a Chinese leviathan looms large again, "some kind of international conspiracy or network of Chinese all over the place acting as one force . . . all these people acting as if they were responding with very sensitive antenna to each other against the rest of the world, with China behind it."[9] In this ventriloquized portrait of the Chinese as a dehumanized race with buglike antennae scheming to take over the world, Wang clearly invokes classic yellow peril tropes of the late nineteenth and early twentieth century, only too easily revived in the contemporary era.

Thus, the debates no longer turn so heatedly on accusations of essentialism or origin nostalgia, nor do they ride so heavily on utopian appeals to hybridity and multiplicity as liberatory, subversive forces. Not just globalization but also China's economic ascent have shifted the terrain for theorizing diaspora and its attendant promises and pitfalls. Even as scholars from various quarters attempt to reconfigure, expand, or pluralize Chineseness by being ever more inclusive of diasporic subjects under alternative rubrics such as *global China* or the *Sinophone*, the term *diaspora* itself has become further dispersed, no longer signifying that for which it is hailed *or* censured. Against the assumed dominance of a transnational capitalist template, though, how might we reimagine diaspora?

This chapter experiments with rethinking the Chinese diaspora as sinospore by drawing on recent theories of multispecies ecology. One proposition here is that diaspora as a concept, although initially conceived as a theoretical model of dispersal and diffusion and hence of scale, nonetheless often comes up against its own limit because of its dialectical and supplemental relation to notions of origin. And so, articulations of the Chinese diaspora are often counterposed to Chineseness at the sites of origin rather than to Chineseness as situated in more expansive networks. The concept of the sinospore may offer a more capacious understanding of Chineseness within mixed assemblages of culture and nature, the human and the nonhuman – an approach that retains a concern with latitudinal dispersal on a planetary scale but also probes longitudinal descent through attention to deep time.

Of particular conceptual importance here is the work of Anna Lowenhaupt Tsing, whose focus on the matsutake mushroom acutely brings to our attention the ecological interconnectivity between humans and nonhumans. As she emphasizes, the matsutake is a variety that cannot be cultivated but grows only in "blasted landscapes" such as the post-atomic ruins of Hiroshima. Hence, it symbolizes the ecological entanglements of human and nonhuman life in the wake of environmental catastrophes. Tsing tracks the matsutake's routes from numerous foraging sites to its delivery to global commodity chains as a prized delicacy, chiefly in Japan but also increasingly elsewhere in the world. Fortuitously, one of her first landscapes is southwestern China, the prime supplier and producer of matsutake consumed in Japan. In the young forests of Yunnan province, wild mushroom picking, Tsing is astounded to learn, officially supports an economy of at least six hundred thousand people, including "women and children [who] are out every morning scouring the woods . . . because mushroom picking is especially appealing to those without other resources."[10] Expensive mushrooms are separated out for private companies to sell abroad while the rest are dried and typically sold in local markets. When told by a mycologist about the poisonous varieties, one woman forager cheerfully replies, "Yes, I know. . . . I wouldn't sell them to you. But if I sell them to a company, where they are mixed with other mushrooms, it doesn't matter."[11] A nation-based and globalization-oriented analysis would likely focus on these rural mushroom pickers as the lowest rung of a predatory global capitalist system of exotic food production. Such a reading would position them as neocolonial subalterns, perhaps also trickster figures, but nonetheless subsisting on the dark underside of China's neoliberal development. The line of critique would then proceed to target Chinese urban entrepreneurs for profiting from rural labor as well as the communist government for prioritizing national wealth over social equity, before ending perhaps with a reproach of first-world middle-class consumers who remain complicitously ignorant of these remote sites of their foods' production.

In Tsing's analysis, however, these nation- and humancentric critiques may and sometimes do make an appearance, but they are conceptual stopovers rather than endpoints. The post–Great Leap, post–Great Famine forests of Yunnan constitute just one "damaged landscape" that is then linked to other sites of matsutake production across other continents, from the post–World War II industrial ruins of Oregon's Cascades to the glaciated and post-Chernobyl forests of Finland to the satoyama nostalgia gardens of post–atom bomb Japan. In this intercontinental saga, China's Maoist legacy is connected to the histories of world wars, nuclearism, industrialization, environmentalism, and globalization. Chinese peasants and entrepreneurs are considered alongside American loggers and conservationists, Laotian and Cambodian refugees in the US Pacific Northwest, Finnish foresters and television producers, and several generations of citizen groups and park reconstructionists in Japan. At the same time, from the perspective of multispecies ecology, all these human groups make up but one set of actors alongside crucial nonhuman ones, such as the soil and the forests and the many species of trees and mushrooms the forests are composed of, both those preserved and those cleared away. For Tsing, the significance of such an enlarged analytical frame involves the ethics of living in our time: "In these times of mass destruction, appreciating the forms of life that populate disturbed landscapes is particularly important," as "varied disturbance regimes . . . have become places to live for humans and nonhumans around the world."[12] In this regard, matsutake mushrooms are especially inspiring, for they cannot be cultivated in artificial environs but can grow only in the wake of "histories of radical disturbance." They thus remind us that at least some "trajectories of destruction and disturbance" can make "ecologically viable" certain "species mixes."[13] As Tsing concludes, "to follow matsutake guides us to possibilities of coexistence within environmental disturbance," to "one kind of collaborative survival" and "an exemplification of precarious livelihood."[14] The matsutake extends a model of "*disturbance-based ecologies in which many species sometimes live together without either harmony or conquest.*"[15]

This is not a simple reprisal of postmodernism's exaltation of hybridity and mixture, for it asks us to attend much more closely to material and anthropogenic histories whose devastation effects linger all over the planet. Yet such an approach can also be adapted for cultural projects, particularly those that try to think beyond discrete identities and isolated inheritances toward complex networks, contingent alliances, and human-nonhuman assemblages. Tsing herself arrives at her multispecies perspective partly via Bruno Latour's actor-network theory, his well-known response to the limits of critique and the cooptation of postmodern science by climate change deniers, and his effort to recuperate something beyond human social constructions by attending to interfaces between culture and nature. It is perhaps not wholly out of frivolity, then, that

Tsing titles her essay on Latour "Worlding the Matsutake Diaspora" – with the suggestion that humans too can be reconceived beyond binary relations of origin versus diaspora, authenticity versus hybridity, nostalgia versus assimilation. Nonhuman diasporas such as that of the matsutake compel us to recall kinship ties not just in cultural practices or linguistic knowledge but "in the flesh," in the dynamic symbioses between bodies and environments, and they invite us to envision temporality not in terms of singular national or ethnic histories but on "eon-stretching time scales."[16] What would a transfer of this matsutake diaspora model look like for human beings?

For one answer, I turn to Chinese Canadian writer Larissa Lai's second novel, *Salt Fish Girl* (2002),[17] which develops the model that I am calling the *sinospore*. If multispecies ecology emphasizes entanglements of materiality and culture on the one hand and embodied histories on the other – the unique species pathways by which lifeforms interact with each other in shared environments – for Lai, human fleshiness takes form most acutely as race, on which terrain social constructions of value, biological histories of racial difference, and cultural mythology and memory collide. Just as it matters for Tsing that there is no single generic human or mushroom history, that the anthropocenic narrative retain varied but nontransferable stopovers in post-Mao China, post-Chernobyl Ukraine, and postbomb Japan, and that the species story of the matsutake *not* be used as a propulsion device toward the genus story of every mushroom, it similarly matters for Lai that her novel routes the imagination of diaspora through specifically Chinese racialized bodies and their own reconstructed cultural histories. Racial embodiment and racial memory become Lai's techniques for resisting the idea of a generically human diaspora, where all dispersal paths converge under one theoretical formula.

Conceptually, then, the sinospore does not imply a universal and deracinated category of *diaspore* that simply displaces *diaspora*. If, following Ang and Wang, we note the impulsion toward singularity, cohesion, and closure within the latter term, we may also note its intimations of a generic Jew, a generic Indian, a generic Chinese, and so on, as so many prototypes of the generic human. By the same logic, while a generalized principle of the diaspore is conceivable here, I would resist the temptation to pose the sinospore as a sufficient prototype for it: the impulse to slide from *sino-* to *dia-* without routing through any other racialized or multispecies history replicates only too readily the putative foreclosure of the diaspora concept. If there is a semiticspore, an afrospore, or another similar assemblage to be had, its relation to the sinospore would be radically heterotopic rather than comfortably analogical, and the telos would certainly not be a macro taxonomy that subsumes all spores as commensurable units. The sinospore, hence, delineates a more modest scope: it retains a commitment to specific cultural genealogy and racial difference as structures that internally divide and diversify the human; it marks its difference from either a generic diaspora or diaspore by insisting on its own relation to Chineseness, even as it continually subdivides this latter category from within by amplifying traces of broken lineages and forecasting ever more mixed species assemblages in our planetary future.

The multispecies novel: from origin myth to posthuman future

Larissa Lai's *Salt Fish Girl* anticipates many of the themes raised by more recent dystopian novels by Asian Anglophone writers such as Kazuo Ishiguro's *Never Let Me Go* (2005) and Chang-rae Lee's *On Such a Full Sea* (2014).[18] Part mythological fantasy, part historical romance, and part dystopic science fiction, Lai's novel opens on the bank of the Yellow River in pre-Shang dynasty China and features the goddess Nu Wa as its protagonist. Reworking the traditional image of Nu Wa as the repairer of heaven, the restorer of cosmic order, and the savior of humankind from calamity, the novel's first chapter focuses instead on the goddess's role in Chinese myths of human creation, but mixed with Christian biblical echoes so as to highlight the cultural hybridity of this diasporic origin tale. "In the beginning there was me," Lai's Nu Wa narrates, "the river and a rotten-egg smell . . . the stink of beginnings and endings." Out of loneliness, she molds a fistful of mud into her own snakelike image, the first man, also serpentine, but with "a stubby little tail so it wouldn't think itself better than me" (2). Later, endowing her humans with the capacity for procreation, she decides to make "the strong ones into women and the weak ones into men" (5). But unlike both the Christian God and the mythological Nu Wa, Lai's goddess comes to resent her own creations and envy their pleasure and passion – so much so that she gives up her divinity to be reincarnated in a human body, whereupon she promptly falls in love with another woman who looks uncannily like herself (a figure later hinted to be Fu Xi, the legendary brother/husband of Nu Wa and co-creator of humans). Lai's is a self-ironic creation myth, one that undercuts the genre's religious and political theology even as it rewrites both its Christian and Chinese source texts in queer feminist terms.

Thereafter, in alternating chapters, the novel traces Nu Wa's two successive incarnations as a human, first in late-nineteenth- and early twentieth-century south China, then in mid-twenty-first-century North America. Lai's temporal and spatial narrative canvas thus anticipates Anna Tsing's, in both its "eon-stretching time scales" and its cross-continental scope. Moreover, with its focus on the interbreeding of future Asians with plants and animals in "blasted landscapes" haunted by human wars and environmental wreckage, Lai's text offers one imaginative vision of what Tsing calls "disturbance-based ecologies," where mixed-species human life and genetically modified nonhuman life vitally depend on each other for "collaborative survival." And whereas Tsing spotlights the matsutake and devotes an entire chapter to capturing its signature pungent odor, variously a source of disgust and delight for her, Lai places center stage in her ecological fable one smelly fruit: the durian.

To set up her critique of contemporary global capitalism and its ecological impact, Lai makes use of her 1800s story line to establish the historical traffic of humans and goods between south China and North America. Here, Nu Wa is reborn into a village near Canton, and at fifteen she falls in love with the Salt

Fish Girl, the daughter of a coastal migrant merchant who specializes in salt fish. To avoid an arranged marriage to a farmer's son, she runs away with the Salt Fish Girl to the city, where they survive on the streets by picking pockets, fending off repeated sexual assaults, and once resorting to killing in self-defense. Blackmailed into working at a wind-up toy factory by a man who witnessed the · murder, but also wanting to redeem herself by living "an honest life" (121), the Salt Fish Girl trades thievery for slave-wage labor, rapidly losing her eyesight as she pieces together small tin animals. Meanwhile, Nu Wa continues to pick pockets until she is seduced one day by a foreign woman, who magically leads her through a thick fog to the city of Hope on the Island of Mist and Forgetfulness, a thinly veiled allegory for America but also a dystopian inverse of the Peach Blossom Spring. There, Nu Wa too is blackmailed, for supposed illegal immigration, into working as a maid at a luxury hotel. After escaping from a hotel fire but without a means of support in the strange land, she briefly becomes a scam artist with a telemarketing firm that targets old Chinese folks before being tricked again into trafficking heroin without her knowledge. Arrested for illegal immigration and drug smuggling, she spends five years in a women's prison. Upon release, she finally succeeds in returning to China, only to discover that fifty years have passed there. Turned away by a now wizened Salt Fish Girl, who feels embittered by a lifetime of betrayal and abandonment, Nu Wa winds her way back to her home village and is accepted into the fold of family, only to be married off as tribal recompense to the Salt Fish Girl's cousin, a frail old man who has inherited his father's fortune importing tobacco from San Francisco. Under pressure to produce a son, she is compelled by her new husband to find a mate elsewhere but gets caught in the act of adultery. As she is hunted down by her fellow villagers to be drowned in punishment, she decides to jump into the river and drown herself instead.

In just this half of the novel, Lai manages to weave in themes of Chinese patriarchy and lesbian romance, urban industrialization and female labor exploitation, transnational capital and human trafficking, immigration and racism. From echoes of Maxine Hong Kingston's *The Woman Warrior* (1976), especially the "No Name Woman" chapter, to prefigurations of Paolo Bacigalupi's *The Windup Girl* (2009), Lai's novel brings to bear on its historical sketch of Chinese migration not only classic concerns of Asian American literature but also much more recent ones from contemporary Chinese fictions of capitalism and migrant labor as well as biopunk science fiction. The text's second plot line in particular plays out the biopunk genre's futuristic apprehensions.

Multispecies life: durians and fish at the end (and rebirth) of the world

In her next incarnation, Nu Wa is reborn in the year 2044 as Miranda Ching, in a walled city called Serendipity somewhere on the West Coast of North America. In her new avatar, Miranda carries the smell of durian from birth, "the reek of cat pee tinged with the smell of hot peppers that have not been dried and are on the verge of going off . . . so sour and acrid that no amount of roll-on deodorant, however liberally applied, could take the odour away" (15). The mystery of this body odor will pervade the novel. First, we learn that Miranda's mother, a retired cabaret starlet named Aimee Ling who had built a glamorous career by performing self-exoticizing musical numbers, miraculously conceived Miranda in her early sixties after eating a "wild" durian. As a girl, Aimee had tasted the fruit when "her grandmother smuggled one in from Hong Kong," but now, a handful of corporations rule the continent as all-powerful governing bodies, and they strictly regulate the food economy by forbidding "wild things" that grow outside the gated communities (14). Despite the risks, however, Miranda's father brings home a durian from the "Unregulated Zone" one day to satisfy his wife's craving, and the surprising gift briefly reignites their marriage – long enough for Miranda to be conceived, born, and raised with love as a "reeking bundle" (15).

The secret behind this postmenopausal conception and its unwelcome olfactory trail is not revealed until the novel's final two chapters, in the year 2062. The strange durian tree that Miranda's parents spotted almost two decades ago, blooming near a North Pacific beach in an out-of-place climate, turns out to be not wild at all but carefully cultivated by a group of renegade female clones called the Sonias. Nor is the tree the natural product of a genetically autonomous species history. As the character Evie Xin – the reincarnation of Salt Fish Girl and herself a human-fish hybrid clone with .03% freshwater carp DNA – tells Miranda:

> "It's all conjecture, but Sonia 14 says it started a century ago. They were implanting human genes into fruit as fertility therapy for women who could not conceive. And of course the pollen blew every which way and could not be contained. And fertilized the fruit of trees bred for other purposes – trees bred to withstand cold climates, trees bred to produce fruit that would strengthen the blood. Perhaps some natural mutations were also involved. What we learned was that the fruit of certain trees could make women pregnant without any need for insemination."
>
> *(258)*

Rather than primal nature or originary divinity, the durian tree's secret history traces multispecies entanglements and environmental assemblages. Human agriculture and bioengineering play as crucial a role in the tree's development as wind pollination and natural mutation. After a century of these combined interactions, what Tsing would call "radical disturbances," the tree bears fruit that has the capacity for human fertilization, leaving an olfactory imprint on the human offspring's body, as with Miranda. In effect, genetically modified durians can replace men as reproductive partners for women, and it is for this purpose that the Sonias painstakingly cultivate and protect their special durian tree. Its fruit allows them to reproduce or clone themselves, indeed, to erase the difference between natural and unnatural reproduction, and thereby frees them from their corporate owners and paternal creator, the villainous and ironically named Dr. Flowers.

As the stock evil scientist, Dr. Flowers considers his creations property rather than persons, to be used purely for corporate profit or human pleasure. Hence, he sells off the clones as wage-free factory workers to a designer shoes company while keeping two for himself, "one for a wife and one for a daughter," with Evie being the latter (252). The unruly products of fertility trees, however, he deems "monstrosities . . . neither natural nor controllable," and "too dangerous" (256). His language of "neither natural nor controllable" echoes Tsing's definition of "gaps" – those "invisible, and sometimes illegitimate zones" that exist in the cracks of "universal knowledge projects" and their binary categories.[19] By chance, Tsing similarly pauses on the durian in her meditations here, for the durian tree, she notes, is an example of life that thrives in gap landscapes, "maintained in part by those human-fruit tree interactions that fall somewhere in the gap between cultivation and the wild" (178). Lai's durian tree is just such a product, sustained in the gap between cultivated and wild, as are its genetic human offspring and clone tenders. And it is precisely these mixed species that she allies as heralding new forms of planetary life in a posthuman future.

In the novel's most resonant passage, Miranda muses:

> We are the new children of the earth, of the earth's revenge. Once we stepped out of mud, now we step out of moist earth, out of DNA both new and old, an imprint of what has gone before, but also a variation. By our difference we mark how ancient the alphabet of our bodies. By our strangeness we write our bodies into the future.
>
> *(259)*

As "new children of the earth," Miranda and Evie are figured as multispecies assemblages – composed of "DNA both new and old," neither singularly human nor reproductively autonomous, yet existing in a zone between nature and biotechnology that they help carve out from the ruins of capitalist science. They are both Chinese, but Chinese as defined not by nation or ethnicity, culture or language, so much as a combination of genetic inheritance and incarnational past. Evie herself has no biological human parents who can lay claim to a notion of Chineseness, and the novel's playfully extended prospect of showing us a glimpse of her "point zero three per cent" carp "mom" turns out to be an unfulfilled narrative red herring (261). Instead, throughout the text, she and Miranda are presented as being Chinese mainly by virtue of being Asian bodies within various systems of racialized power: of global capitalist labor, national citizenship, and science and technology. As Evie explains at one point, the Sonias do not know their human genetic "source," but they do have rumors and a "nice origin story" about "a woman called Ai, a Chinese woman who married a Japanese man and was interned in the Rockies during the Second World War," both of whose bodies were "sold to science" after their deaths. She hypothesizes too about the Sonias' ties to a corporate-owned "Diverse Genome Project," which might have consolidated the genetic information of "peoples of the so-called Third World, Aboriginal peoples, and peoples in danger of extinction" into blueprints for worker clones (160). These speculations intimate that the clones may be direct genetic heirs to several racial histories: of the Chinese diaspora, for one, but also, perhaps more widely, of other Asians in North America as well as other non-white peoples across the planet. For a being like Evie – who is also a reincarnation, we suspect, of the gender-fluid Fu Xi – origin is not limited to China or her previous avatars as a Chinese woman or deity but can encompass multiple races, continents, and species. The orbit of her lineage may pass through Chinese mythology and nineteenth-century Canton as well as precolonial indigenous communities, Japanese Canadian internment camps, freshwater rivers and ponds in Europe or Asia, and corporate biolabs.

As Lai's exemplary sinospore subjects, Evie and Miranda descend from numerous potential ancestries, homelands, and habitats. While fabricating origin myths is existentially motivating and politically advantageous in providing "a perfect focus for revolt" (160), what drives them is not nostalgia for a true home country. Indeed, Nu Wa's China story line dispels any faith in a messianic homecoming to biological family and ancestral village. Rather, theirs is a tale of salvage survival on a damaged earth, of open-ended evolving lifeforms making the most out of capitalism's ecological debris, not just to be "an imprint of what has gone before, but also a variation." To adapt in new planetary conditions, they will not simply shed as obsolete the nonhuman components of their genes. In lieu of a march toward another humancentric destiny as represented by Flowers and his corporate partners, Lai's spirited protagonists will continue to rely on the altered fruits of historical assemblages. So, even after Flowers massacres most of the rebel Sonias and has their durian tree cut down and burned, the remaining clones manage to save "three large fruits and a basket of radishes" (250), another plant that can "support and strengthen the [clone] fetuses" (258). For future collaborative livelihood, animal- and plant-hybrid humans as well as human-hybrid vegetation are needed.

In her ecocritical analysis of Lai's novel, Cheryl Lousley views Miranda, Evie, and the durian as constituting a "re-assembly," and it is these narratives of "interconnection" as well as readings "responsible and *responsive*" to entanglements, she suggests, that help us forge better "ecocritical futures."[20] Similarly, Michelle Huang reads Lai's novel through the lens of "symbiogenesis," whereby the "driving force of life and creative evolution is bodily contamination and radical intersubjectivity, *not* oversimplifications of interspecies competition."[21] Such a model, she argues, "dismantles the autonomous narrative of anthropocentric progress" and can foster "an understanding that humankind and our stories have been posthuman all along."[22] These critics aptly bring out the utopian dimension of *Salt Fish Girl*.

Yet the novel's concluding fantasy of a future multispecies ecology is far from assured. Aside from the slaughtered Sonias and the burnt durian tree, what conspicuously drops out of the narrative is the animal, especially the aquatic life gestured to by the title. In the frantic last chapter, Miranda and Evie make a quick detour to the Zodiac Aquarium, run by the Chinese geneticist Chang, who collated Evie's genes and is a kind of alter-father figure to her. As if to remind us of the biodiversity left behind even by her heroines, Lai dwells in some detail on the range of life held captive in this aquatic zoo, from the "beautiful . . . yellow, blue and orange fish" to the "vibrant, translucent corals that shivered with a strange, barely animate life" (261–262). In one tank is a giant octopus, its "brown bulbous body pulsing with a visceral, membranous sort of intelligence," its "white suction cups pushed against the glass, not at all the slimy stuff of horror movies, but something infinitely more delicate and lovely." Its loveliness goes unrecognized by its keepers, however, as its label highlights only that its eyes are "very similar in their construction and functioning" to human ones, its worth measured solely by its proximity to human anatomy. In another tank are human-size lungfish, described as "beautiful, covered in large, rectangular scales, silver tinged with pink," their "fins rippl[ing] with the precise sensitivity that many of the underwater creatures . . . seemed to share." And finally, there is an arboretum with an artificial pond "teeming with flapping carp, golden and white, black, orange and spotted" (262–263). Evie feeds the fish a crumpled biscuit, but in a missed rendezvous, she is not able to identify her carp mother before she and Miranda must escape again, leaving both her mother and Chang behind. Likewise, they cannot save the many species detained here, eyes "glazed and stunned" (262), as human spectacle and experimental gene pool. If Miranda's initial reaction that the aquarium is a "terrible, sad place" is countered by Evie's retort that "many lives begin here" (261), our final sight of it is decidedly one of horror, as Miranda spies a storage room "where many fish lay in glass cases, trapped under ice," and "several human beings as well, frozen in blocks and perched upright" (264). Against the protagonists' prospect of a utopian multispecies freedom, there lingers this other dystopic image of a multispecies living tomb/lab/museum. Whereas durians augur expansive possibility, fish haunt as utterly biopoliticized captured life.

Multispecies Chineseness: from broken lineages to racial genealogies

In a 2002 talk given at Fu-Jen Catholic University in Taipei, subsequently published as the essay "Future Asians" in the Canadian journal *West Coast Line*, Lai outlines the myriad strands of *Salt Fish Girl*'s critical engagements. She explains that she started the novel before 9/11, and it grew out of a moment in international politics when it seemed "the massive corporatization of everything and anything would become the new hegemony," with nation-states "so enfeebled by free trade policies" that they would "more or less cease to matter." Her thinking shifted after 9/11, however, after she witnessed the resurgence of nationalism and fascism around the world, so that the nation, she now believes, "will remain in place to feed the war machine and various fundamentalisms."[23] *Salt Fish Girl,* though, captures her earlier vision of a denationalized, deterritorialized capitalist world order, where all-powerful corporations have become authoritarian states and banks control the populace with simulated video games and real police forces. If Miranda's repeated lapse into complicity with these industrial-military regimes reflects the intense ideological hold of neoliberalism and its promise of the good life for "law-abiding corporate citizens" (14), Evie, by contrast, represents Lai's "attempt to play with the figure of the cyborg Asian, and at the same time . . . of the exploited factory worker."[24] Lai's projection of global capital's effect on future diasporic Chinese, then, unlike Aihwa Ong's but akin to Wang Gungwu's, spotlights the persistence of racial and gendered hierarchies in transnational labor. Far from a jet-setting entrepreneur with flexible citizenship, Evie is patented goods rather than a person with "legal existence" (249). She is life killable with impunity by anyone and thus recalls Giorgio Agamben's concept of *homo sacer*, just as the mass grave of the dismembered Sonias signals their biopolitical condition of bare life.[25]

Yet Lai refrains from rendering Evie a mere trope of the victimized subhuman for the sake of biopolitical critique. On the contrary, though "abused, [and] repeatedly reproduced, she emerges as a sort of damaged superhero figure, but one seething with spite and fury . . . a murderer and a traitor . . . vindictive, brimming over with anger."[26] Lai's implicit homage to Donna Haraway is clearly discernable here. Evie, evocative of Haraway's cyborg, is a "creature[ ] simultaneously animal and machine, who populate[s] worlds ambiguously natural and crafted"; she appears "precisely where the boundary between human and animal is transgressed"; and more than any other character, she is "oppositional, utopian, and completely without innocence."[27] Further following Haraway but playfully revising the latter's final declaration that "I would rather be a cyborg than a goddess,"[28] Lai variously rescripts the Judeo-Christian creation myth and its structural role in narratives of Western science by displacing the biblical God with Nu Wa, by queering Adam and Eve as Nu Wa/Miranda and Fu Xi/Evie, and by substituting smelly, sensuous durians for the forbidden apple. Instead of Western patriarchal origin tales, the novel gives us snake-woman goddesses from Chinese mythology, but a mythology that is itself hybridized, with "many more traditions . . . inflected with Western literary references."[29] And against a normative heterosexuality and the criminalization of woman in an imagined paradise at the beginning of human time, the novel dreams of transincarnational female partnership, a matriarchal community of rebellious cyborgs, and genetically modified life salvaged out of capitalist ruins.

As many scholars have observed, *Salt Fish Girl* is deeply concerned with origins and their rewriting. For most, the significance of this motif in Lai's novel fundamentally lies in destabilizing Eurocentric, patriarchal, and heteronormative epistemologies, whether by interrogating white patriarchal constructions of the human,[30] warning against masculine science's instrumentalizing of body technologies,[31] critiquing Canada's national myths of home,[32] or challenging multiculturalism's discourses of oriental exoticism.[33] Some also see Lai as thereby building more positive political visions, whether by delinking Asian American racial subjectivity from the ancestral Asian homeland,[34] facilitating coalition politics across identity lines,[35] or broadening transfeminism beyond the terms of trans identities alone.[36] Lai herself has repeatedly elaborated on the theme of origins. As an academic and a literary scholar, she often offers explications of her own fiction in her essays, a rather extensive body of writing that one critic dubs the "paratextual 'tail'" of her fictional texts.[37] So in "Future Asians," for instance, Lai details how *Salt Fish Girl* is her attempt to rethink "the whole question of origins," to "create a myth of origins for girls that travel, girls who come from many places at once," those who represent "people like me."[38] In "Corrupted Lineage," she again professes that, though culturally "rootless," she is nonetheless "obsessed with stories of rooting."[39] And in an earlier essay titled "Political Animals and the Body of History," she frames her fiction as partly an effort to answer the question, "How do we diasporized types make a homespace for ourselves given all the disjunctures and discontinuities of our histories, and for that matter, the co-temporalities of some of them?"[40] The model of multispecies origins in *Salt Fish Girl*, then, stems from Lai's keen awareness of being a diasporic subject, of belonging to a history of migration and remigration and "a lineage broken by language and travel."[41]

In fact, we can piece together much extended biographical information on Lai from her paratexts: that she was born in La Jolla, California, but grew up in St. John's, Newfoundland; that her parents were raised in small apartments in Hong Kong that have since been torn down; and that no one she knows has ever been to their ancestral village in China.[42] We also learn that she cannot read Chinese – "the result," she remarks candidly, "of an unfortunate combination of [her] own childhood foolishness and the pressures of assimilation" – so that her "readings of history are bleached,"[43] and her research into Chinese mythology must come "second or third hand from translators and compilers."[44] Regarding her first novel's use of the fox myth, she comments, "Let me be very clear. I got this story from library books. I don't read Chinese. I read it in English translation." She adds, "I am fine with that," because she does not want to feed "those old colonial tropes of the 'authentic.'"[45] By the time of *Salt Fish Girl*, though, this motif of linguistic loss and alienation surfaces with less bravado and greater melancholy and self-harm, from the potion Nu Wa drinks in the City of Hope that makes her "old language gush away . . . liquid, yellow and irretrievable" (126) to the child Miranda's frightened reaction to seeing Chinese signs for the first time, the characters not only illegible but "cryptic," "strange," "ominous and heavy" (30). If the discourse of diaspora by first-generation emigrants can still invoke firsthand knowledge of a home country and its language and culture as well as an experience of personal loss, Lai's emphasis on the next generation of diasporic subjects like herself, born abroad and growing up "in the assimilationist/multiculturalist era" of 1980s–1990s Canada, is precise in its historical and social reference. It is for this assimilated generation that the notion of origin becomes most frayed, if also most yearned for:

> There is no primal moment of break from some comfortable, homey root.
> There is no singular violent event or tragedy from which the present is
> a recovery. For some, history shatters under the quotidian pressures of
> identity and politics, leaving only the ghosts of an idyllic past in which the
> other (racialized people) is imagined, ironically, as being in full possession
> of language, culture, and being.[46]

In short, "there are no red shoes to click to return to China"; instead, there is
"only a perception of the past from the position of a subject who longs for it in
order not just to validate, but in fact, to produce the present."[47] Under the weight
of this notion of diaspora – which for Lai is propagated not so much by migrants
themselves as by the assimilationist state – the diasporic subject cannot lay claim
even to his or her own present. *Salt Fish Girl* subtly alludes to this sense of an
ongoing dispossession of the settled homeland with the city of Serendipity: "Ser-
endib" is an ancient name of Arabic origins for Sri Lanka,[48] and "serendipity"
is an eighteenth-century British neologism, coined by Horace Walpole in his
version of a Persian fairy tale. Thus for Miranda, the home of her birth is itself
named after a hyperreal orientalist palimpsest, and not even one for China. Lai's
novel, insofar as it emerges from these acute grapplings with diasporic histories,
may be read as a proto-diasporic text, but one that endeavors to recode identity
and Chineseness beyond a narrowly root-seeking restoration model.

What is rarely highlighted in the scholarship on *Salt Fish Girl*, though, is
that Lai's understanding of diaspora is not wholly deconstructive or poststructuralist. Tellingly, however distanced from Chinese culture and language the
novel's futuristic protagonists may be, they do not epitomize forms of diasporic
hybridity that have outstripped all roots in Chineseness. They are not generic
posthuman bodies with radically hollowed-out centers. The very premise of
the novel's two intertwined story lines – that Miranda and Evie are reincarnations of Nu Wa and Fu Xi/Salt Fish Girl – underscores that, for Lai, it remains
important to preserve genealogies of Chineseness, albeit in an eons-long time
frame. She elucidates this point in a recent essay. The concept of "the unstable
subject," she observes, "comes to us via poststructuralism as genealogically
produced on the one hand (Foucault) and differing within itself on the other
(Derrida)," and this European philosophical lineage now dominates critical
discourses in North America, so that many scholars tend to "simply leave the
subject on the curb."

> But for racialized people who have never taken the coherence of subjectiv-
> ity for granted, that the historical moment of a still-Eurocentric rejection
> of the subject should coincide with racialized entry into the possibility
> of an articulated subjectivity (on the Western critical record) for the first
> time, the move away from the subject seemed just the latest white act of
> denying racialized others in the long series of colonial gestures in Western
> philosophy and criticism.[49]

Here, Lai historicizes theories of subjectlessness not just as products of a Euro-centric tradition but also, more crucially, as part of a discourse that disavows its own hegemonic racial lineage exactly at the moment when other racialized sub-jects are first gaining a voice to articulate their own subjecthood. In the context of this inequity of discursive power, rather than making any a priori objection to poststructuralism, she rejects a totalizing rejection of the subject – and by extension, of origins. But instead of a return to or a reconstitution of origins in some idealized form, she advocates for the recovery of suppressed histories: "we must be careful not to imagine the subject as an affective illusion: otherwise how can we understand racialized trauma – the Chinese Head Tax and Exclu-sion Act, the Japanese Canadian uprooting, the Komogata Maru incident?" And instead of the regathering of an isolated racial or national past, she calls for a "relational" paradigm, with appeals to "all settlers – white, Asian and Black – for respect and relation, understood as human to human, certainly, but also human to nonhuman."[50] Lai's recent plea effectively outlines a model of multispecies politics where subjects retain rather than hollow out their specific histories and subjecthood, even as they acknowledge their connections to other human and nonhuman life in a shared environment.

Multispecies memory: from postmemory to transmemory

To be part of a multispecies ecology, then, is to maintain some species identity and cultural descent line, however entangled or corrupted. But if protracted dis-persal poses the problem of personal memory for postemigrant generations, for whom firsthand access to cultural knowledge and historical rupture is denied, what recourse do they have to recover even "racialized trauma"? This is a situa-tion that Marianne Hirsch, writing in the context of Holocaust survivors' chil-dren, addresses through the framework of postmemory, or "the response of the second generation to the trauma of the first."[51] For Hirsch, one of the most pow-erful mediating vehicles of postmemory is the photographic image, especially the family photograph. In *Salt Fish Girl*, Lai raises the additional possibility of other embodied forms of postmemory, not just familial or cultural but transin-carnational, specieswide, and even trans-species.

Among Lai's critics, Malissa Phung is exceptional in arguing that, far from having shed all traces of nostalgia for origins, Lai's novels in fact draw atten-tion to "homing desires" that continue to shape the postgeneration. Drawing on Hirsch, Phung proposes that these "homing desires compel the postgenera-tion to turn to postmemory, to radically re-envision the ways in which they can reconnect with their diasporic origins," so that those ways "stretch[ ] postmem-ory's empathetic possibilities."[52] Phung then follows several other critics in fore-grounding the sense of smell as Lai's key vehicle for "bodily inscribed memories" rather than "linguistic memories gleaned from the historical record."[53] Paul Lai, for instance, first zeroes in on smell in *Salt Fish Girl* as a "disruptive quality . . . that destabilizes liberal humanist conceptions of progress and modernity," for "modern societies," he notes, "have undergone a process of deodorization, banishing the stench of effluvia and body odor with sewage systems, deodorants, and cleansing products" to sites deemed "primitive and . . . outside of civilization."[54] Likewise, Stephanie Oliver focuses on olfactory experiences in *Salt Fish Girl* as a force that shapes diasporic memories of former homelands but also complicates that relationship through "smell-based discrimination."[55] On this score, Lai again precedes her critics. In "Future Asians," she explains her various motivations for concentrating on smell:

> In the novel, I use smell because it is the most evocative of the senses. Smell is linked to memory in a very emotional, intimate kind of way, so I use it to mine a history that has been largely unwritten and is in the process of being forgotten. I also use smell because it is such a powerful means by which the mainstream denigrates its others, particularly racialized and sexualized others. . . . Using this trope, I want to question the disgust we feel for those who are afflicted by history, those who carry the memories we were meant to forget at the moment of assimilation. By calling up such odours as those of salt fish and durian, I wanted to tap in to a visceral, bodily sense of memory, that kind of immediate connection one gets to a moment in the past when one is confronted by a scent. I want to call up its sensual, sexual aspects, its feminine aspects, its connection to the moment of birth. I wanted to point ever further back beyond the moment of birth to those moments in the past experienced by those who have gone before us. I do sometimes think we can touch those moments.[56]

At once a source of discrimination and resistance, repressed history and reclaimed memory, smell for Lai is both personal and transincarnational. As such, it offers an imaginative solution to the dilemma of the diasporic postgenerations by connecting individual bodies not just to familial histories but also to larger-scale transcultural experiences. Lai foreshadows Tsing here, who also dwells on smell as a site of what she calls "indeterminacies," where "all the cultural-and-natural histories [are] condensed together" to prompt a "tiger's leap into history."[57] And fortuitously, Tsing too mentions the durian as a forerunner to the matsutake for her, "that marvelously stinky tropical fruit" that made her want to vomit the first time she encountered it but that later "thrilled" her and came to smell "like joy."[58] For both writers, odor is a paradoxical conduit to multispecies ecologies: the more intense one's initial disgust in response to a scent, the richer its possible underlying interconnectivity with oneself.

And so, in *Salt Fish Girl*, both durians and salt fish are associated with cannibalism. Having grown up with the durian stench on her body, Miranda makes a point of never eating the fruit, for the very thought "disgusted" her as "something cannibalistic" (82, 224). Drawn to the durians on the Sonias' tree, she sees them as uncannily human, "flushed pink at the ends of their spikes . . . as though blood flowed from the inside to the pointed tips." Holding one in her hands, she feels as if she is holding "a small corpse" (221). When she tastes a durian for the first time, however, she finds it "delicious," though with a "very peculiar sensation," as though she had "bitten [her] own tongue" (224). This language echoes an earlier passage when Nu Wa dreams of eating a human-size salt fish: "It tasted like my own tongue. Its human taste shocked and horrified me" (144). Besides being plant-induced, Miranda, as the reincarnation of Nu Wa, is part fish, and she, like Evie, has a "fistula" on either ear that is an inheritance from her mother. Though useless, these fistulas ooze "a thin stream of briny-smelling fluid when rubbed," and Miranda speculates that they serve "the function of memory, recalling a time when we were more closely related to fish, a time when the body glistened with scales and turned in the dark, muscled easily through water" (107–108). If cannibalism names a human taboo that differentiates the species self as inedible body from the species other as edible meat, Lai's reworking of the trope calls attention to the human-constructed boundaries of our food economy. With a more multispecies perspective, the novel implies, we too, like Miranda/Nu Wa, might react viscerally to consuming other lifeforms on earth that not only sustain but also compose us. Disgust thus lies at the cusp of this species self/other divide, at once the gut emotion we feel "for those who are afflicted by history" and the instinctive recoiling we feel at the idea of devouring bodies we isolate as our own. A sentiment of cross-species cannibalism, by contrast, can represent a mode of multispecies memory, reminding us that we are not just human but planetary life. Multispecies transmemory allows us to recover from planetary anamnesis.

Yet, as with the tension between durians and fish, Lai again opposes this utopian promise of multispecies transmemory to a more dystopic one. Nu Wa in her original serpentine form has no feet and Miranda's transincarnational memory of herself depends on the vestigial anatomy of fistulas and scales, so feet come to function instead as a portal to specifically human varieties of traumatic transmemory. In the novel's future plot line, a mysterious "dreaming disease" plagues the human population of North America. Aside from a range of foul body odors, victims suffer from "terrible dreams with historical content" that "compulsive[ly] drive them to commit suicide by drowning" (100). Miranda first hears the case of "a girl who smelled of cooking oil, who remembered all the wars ever fought": "She could recall and recount every death, every rape, every wound, every moment of suffering that had ever been inflicted by a member of her ancestral lineage" (85). Later, Miranda comes to work with other patients, from "a man who smelled of milk and could remember all the famines that had ever been caused by war" to "a girl who smelled of stainless steel and could recite the lives of everyone who had ever died of tuberculosis" (101–102). The disease, it turns out, is a product of the anthropocene: a new "strange hybrid" that combines plant and animal infections and emerges from soil contaminated by genetically modified agriculture (102). The virus spreads through the soles of people's feet, giving them the "memory structures of other animals – fish maybe, or elephants" (103). Nonetheless, the contents of their dreams are specifically humancentric: the memories may or may not trace a person's family lineage, but they always encompass human atrocities or anthropogenic disasters. The disease is what Miranda later calls "the earth's revenge" (259), "the land itself fighting back" (244). She herself suffers a mild version of the contagion, but the destitute bear the brunt of it. In the poorest parts of the Unregulated Zone, children who cannot afford shoes or socks wear plastic bags over their feet to protect themselves from infection. But those who cannot afford even plastic bags roam the streets barefoot, "spewing memories of genocides and smallpox, smart bombs and slow starvation" (230–231), "their eyes swimming with grief and history" (244), glazed and stunned like those of the fish in the aquarium. If Hirsch designates by postmemory a "familial inheritance and the transmission of cultural trauma" (9), Lai here imagines an even broader form of human memory that is transfamilial and transcultural, a specieswide anthropocenic post-traumatic stress disorder that neither heals nor repairs.

Yet the novel leaves us with one other form of somatic transmemory, one that is not anthropocentrically self-destructive but culturally grounding, and personally as well as transincarnationally individualizing. Before ever hearing the story of Nu Wa, and with no conscious knowledge of her previous incarnation as the goddess, Miranda at eighteen begins to remember Nu Wa through drawing. After her mother's death, she begins to draw pictures of a woman with Aimee's face but a snake's "coiled body," at first "green and delicate," then redrafted with a rounder face and "a belly big enough to swim in" (186). Miranda's father identifies the drawings and tells her the myth of human creation by Nu Wa and Fu Xi, whereupon she begins to sketch the very scenes that Lai details in the novel's first chapter: of Nu Wa staring at her own reflection and molding the first humans. Miranda draws Fu Xi as a woman, overwriting her father's gendering of him, and instead of making them incestuous siblings, she twins Fu Xi and Nu Wa, rendering their faces "androgynous and almost identical," their "tails interlocked" (187). As an assimilated diasporic subject growing up in Serendipity, however, Miranda associates her drawings primarily with the Little Mermaid, and at one point, she sells her artwork to the designer shoes company as promotional advertisements. But even then, her drawings take on a life of their own, as if having "the last laugh" in a "wicked sheen of parody" (236). If the traumatic memories of the dreaming disease call up horrific past experiences, Miranda's drawings offer something else, something at once proleptic and primordial, rewriting beginnings and inaugurating alternate futures. And again, tellingly, this tunnel into origin is distinctively sinosporic. Miranda – as a surrogate for Lai here – may not be able to read Chinese with its "cryptic" sinoscript, but that does not prevent her from remembering Chinese through her hands, as sinograph. This transmemory is also a clairvoyant forecasting, for sure enough, in the novel's final paragraph, Miranda and Evie magically resume their serpentine forms, not according to the myths of tradition but as Miranda's drawings would have them, their bodies feminine and their coils interlocking – and a "little baby girl" birthed between them (269). With this closing and reopening of a metatextual loop, Lai gives us her novel as sinosporic transmemory, shot through with multispecies mixtures and multiracial genealogies, but ultimately threaded together with iconic bodies that come from no other lineage.

Notes

1 Tu Wei-ming, "Preface to the Standard Edition," in *The Living Tree: The Changing Meaning of Being Chinese Today*, ed. Tu Wei-ming (Stanford: Stanford University Press, 1994), viii.
2 Daniel Bell's recent argument in "Why Anyone Can Be Chinese" – that Chinese identity should be defined culturally rather than racially – is hence already anticipated by Tu's third prong, and without the need to legitimize Chineseness via claims to longtime residency, linguistic knowledge, or professional credentials. See Daniel A. Bell, "Why Anyone Can Be Chinese," *Wall Street Journal*, July 14, 2017, www.wsj.com/articles/can-anyone-be-chinese-1500045078.
3 Tu Wei-ming, "Cultural China," in *The Living Tree: The Changing Meaning of Being Chinese Today*, ed. Tu Wei-ming (Stanford: Stanford University Press, 1994), 19 and 24.
4 Ien Ang, *On Not Speaking Chinese: Living Between Asia and the West* (London: Routledge, 2001), 42–43; see also Ien Ang, "Together-in-Difference: Beyond Diaspora, into Hybridity," *Asian Studies Review* 27, no. 2 (2003): 141–154.
5 Ien Ang, "Together-in-Difference," 142 and 144. In *Tiananmen Fictions Beyond the Square*, I discuss Tu and his critics at greater length, with particular emphasis on the 1989 Tiananmen massacre as a historical spur for post-Tiananmen theoretical articulations of diasporic Chineseness by scholars outside of China. See Belinda Kong, *Tiananmen Fictions Outside the Square: The Chinese Literary Diaspora and the Politics of Global Culture* (Philadelphia: Temple University Press, 2012), 128–131.
6 Hong Liu and Els van Dongen, "Introduction," in *The Chinese Diaspora* (New York: Oxford University Press, 2013), retrieved from *Oxford Bibliographies*, www.oxfordbibliographies.com/view/ document/obo-9780199920082/obo-9780199920082–0070.xml.
7 Wang Gungwu, "Diaspora, A Much Abused Word," interview with Laurent Malvezin, *Asian Affairs*, 2001, www.asian-affairs.com/Diasporas/wanggungwu.html.
8 Wang Gungwu, "Diaspora, A Much Abused Word."
9 Wang Gungwu, "Diaspora, A Much Abused Word."
10 Anna Lowenhaupt Tsing, "Blasted Landscapes (and the Gentle Arts of Mushroom Picking)," in *The Multispecies Salon*, ed. Eben Kirksey (Durham, NC: Duke University Press, 2014), 94.
11 Tsing, "Blasted Landscapes," 94.
12 Tsing, "Blasted Landscapes," 107.
13 Tsing, "Blasted Landscapes," 88–89.
14 Anna Lowenhaupt Tsing, *The Mushroom at the End of the World: On the Possibility of Life in Capitalist Ruins* (Princeton: Princeton University Press, 2015), 4.
15 Tsing, *The Mushroom at the End of the World*, 5.
16 Anna Lowenhaupt Tsing, "Worlding the Matsutake Diaspora: Or, Can Actor-Network Theory Experiment with Holism?" in *Experiments in Holism: Theory and Practice in Contemporary Anthropology*, ed. Ton Otto and Nils Bubandt (Oxford: Wiley-Blackwell, 2010), 52.
17 I would like to acknowledge Michelle O'Brien, whose paper "Architectures of Life in Asian North American Texts: Convergences of Racial Bodies and the Nonhuman" at the 2014 ACLA conference first introduced me to Larissa Lai's work, and to *Salt Fish Girl* in particular. See Michelle O'Brien, "Architectures of Life in Asian North American Texts: Convergences of Racial Bodies and the Nonhuman," unpublished paper presented at the American Comparative Literature Association Annual Meeting, March 2014, New York.

18 Larissa Lai, *Salt Fish Girl* (Toronto: Thomas Allen, 2002). All references to this novel are cited in-text.

19 Anna Lowenhaupt Tsing, *Friction: An Ethnography of Global Connection* (Princeton: Princeton University Press, 2005), 172.

20 Cheryl Lousley, "Ecocriticism in the Unregulated Zone," in *Critical Collaborations: Indigeneity, Diaspora, and Ecology in Canadian Literary Studies*, ed. Smaro Kamboureli and Christl Verduyn (Waterloo, ON: Wilfrid Laurier University Press, 2014), 159–160.

21 Michelle N. Huang, "Creative Evolution: Narrative Symbiogenesis in Larissa Lai's *Salt Fish Girl*," *Amerasia Journal* 42, no. 2 (2016): 121.

22 Huang, "Creative Evolution," 134.

23 Larissa Lai, "Future Asians: Migrant Speculations, Repressed History, and Cyborg Hope," *West Coast Line* 38, no. 2 (2004): 169–170.

24 Larissa Lai, "Future Asians," 175. Numerous critics of this novel have focused on Lai's critiques of neoliberalism and/or capitalist science. See for example Rita Wong, "Troubling Domestic Limits: Reading Border Fictions Alongside Larissa Lai's *Salt Fish Girl*," *B.C. Studies* 140 (2003–04): 109–124; Tara Lee, "Mutant Bodies in Larissa Lai's *Salt Fish Girl*: Challenging the Alliance between Science and Capital," *West Coast Line* 38, no. 2 (2004): 94–109; Aimee Bahng, "Specters of the Pacific: Salt Fish Drag and Atomic Hauntologies in the Era of Genetic Modification," *Journal of American Studies* 49, no. 4 (2015): 663–683; and Christopher B. Patterson and Y-Dang Troeung, "The Psyche of Neoliberal Multiculturalism: Queering Memory and Reproduction in Larissa Lai's *Salt Fish Girl* and Chang-rae Lee's *On Such a Full Sea*," *Concentric: Literary and Cultural Studies* 42, no. 1 (2016): 73–98.

25 In an article on Stephen Frears's 2002 film *Dirty Pretty Things*, Lai demonstrates her fluency with and influence by Agamben's theory of biopower, which she sees as readily applicable to numerous Asian North American contexts, from the treatment of Chinese railroad workers in Canada at the turn of the twentieth century to the World War II internment of Japanese Canadians and Americans to contemporary Chinese migrants seeking to enter Canada without papers. "There is a battery of extranational subjects without rights or papers upon whom the state is built," she writes, "and whose violation and restricted movement is a necessary condition for the flow of international capital." See Larissa Lai, "Neither Hand, nor Foot, nor Kidney: Biopower, Body Parts and Human Flows in Stephen Frears' *Dirty Pretty Things*," *CineAction* 80 (2012): 70. By this definition, the early 1900s Nu Wa as much as Evie would be considered bare life in capitalist states of exception.

26 Larissa Lai, "Future Asians," 175.

27 Donna Haraway, "A Manifesto for Cyborgs: Science, Technology, and Socialist Feminism in the 1980s," in *Feminism/Postmodernism*, ed. Linda J. Nicholson (New York: Routledge, 1990), 191–192.

28 Haraway, "A Manifesto for Cyborgs," 223.

29 Larissa Lai, "Future Asians," 171.

30 See Robyn L. Morris, "What Does It Mean to Be Human?: Racing Monsters, Clones, and Replicants," *Foundation: The International Review of Science Fiction* 33, no. 91 (2004): 81–96.

31 See Sonia Villegas-López, "Body Technologies: Posthuman Figurations in Larissa Lai's *Salt Fish Girl* and Jeanette Winterson's *The Stone Gods*," *Critique: Studies in Contemporary Fiction* 56, no. 1 (2015): 26–41.

32 See Joanna Mansbridge, "Abject Origins: Uncanny Strangers and Figures of Fetishism in Larissa Lai's *Salt Fish Girl*," *West Coast Line* 38, no. 2 (2004): 121–133.

33 See Kate Chiwen Liu, "Hybridization as the Postcolonial-Anti-Exotic in Larissa Lai's *Salt Fish Girl*," *Concentric: Literacy and Cultural Studies* 35, no. 2 (2009): 309–336.

34 See Hee-Jung Serenity Joo, "Reproduction, Reincarnation, and Human Cloning: Literary and Racial Forms in Larissa Lai's *Salt Fish Girl*," *Critique: Studies in Contemporary Fiction* 55, no. 1 (2014): 46–59.

35 See Sharlee Reimer, "Troubling Origins: Cyborg Politics in Larissa Lai's *Salt Fish Girl*," *Atlantis* 35, no. 1 (2010): 4–14.

36 See Nicolas Birns, "'The Earth's Revenge': Nature, Diaspora, and Transfeminism in Larissa Lai's *Salt Fish Girl*," *Australian Critical Race and Whiteness Studies Association e-Journal* 2, no. 2 (2006): 1–15.
37 Susanne Wegener, "Forget Modesty–Here Comes the Tail: Abject Bodies, Post-Humanistic Philosophy and Larissa Lai's *Salt Fish Girl*," *Assuming Gender* 2, no. 1 (2011): 15.
38 Larissa Lai, "Future Asians," 171, 173, and 170.
39 Larissa Lai, "Corrupted Lineage: Narrative in the Gaps of History," *West Coast Line* 34 (2001): 50.
40 Larissa Lai, "Political Animals and the Body of History," *Canadian Literature* 163 (1999): 149.
41 Larissa Lai, "Corrupted Lineage," 50.
42 Larissa Lai, "Future Asians," 171.
43 Larissa Lai, "Political Animals and the Body of History," 149.
44 Larissa Lai, "Corrupted Lineage," 49.
45 Larissa Lai, "Afterword," in *When Fox Is a Thousand* (Vancouver, BC: Arsenal Pulp Press, 2004), 257.
46 Larissa Lai, "Corrupted Lineage," 45.
47 Larissa Lai, "Corrupted Lineage," 52 and 45.
48 Nicolas Birns, "'The Earth's Revenge,'" 4.
49 Larissa Lai, "Can Asian Am?: Knowing, Being, and Timing Asian Canadian Through and Across the 49th Parallel," *The Global South* 9, no. 1 (2015): 11.
50 Larissa Lai, "Can Asian Am?" 12.
51 Marianne Hirsch, "Surviving Images: Holocaust Photographs and the Work of Post-memory," *The Yale Journal of Criticism* 14, no. 1 (2001): 8.
52 Malissa Phung, "The Diasporic Inheritance of Postmemory and Immigrant Shame in the Novels of Larissa Lai," *Postcolonial Text* 7, no. 3 (2012): 12 and 5.
53 Phung., "The Diasporic Inheritance of Postmemory and Immigrant Shame," 6.
54 Paul Lai, "Stinky Bodies: Mythological Futures and the Olfactory Sense in Larissa Lai's *Salt Fish Girl*," *MELUS* 33, no. 4 (2008): 183.
55 Stephanie Oliver, "Diffuse Connections: Smell and Diasporic Subjectivity in Larissa Lai's *Salt Fish Girl*," *Canadian Literature* 208 (2011): 86.
56 Lai, "Future Asians," 172–173.
57 Tsing, *The Mushroom at the End of the World*, 52.
58 Tsing, *The Mushroom at the End of the World*, 48.

Works cited

Agamben, Giorgio. *Homo Sacer: Sovereign Power and Bare Life.* Trans. Daniel Heller-Roazen. Stanford: Stanford University Press, 1998.

Ang, Ien. *On Not Speaking Chinese: Living between Asia and the West.* London: Routledge, 2001.

———. "Together-in-Difference: Beyond Diaspora, Into Hybridity." *Asian Studies Review* 27, no. 2 (2003): 141–154.

Bahng, Aimee. "Specters of the Pacific: Salt Fish Drag and Atomic Hauntologies in the Era of Genetic Modification." *Journal of American Studies* 49, no. 4 (2015): 663–683.

Bell, Daniel A. "Why Anyone Can Be Chinese." *Wall Street Journal*, July 14, 2017. www.wsj.com/articles/can-anyone-be-chinese-1500045078.

Birns, Nicolas. "'The Earth's Revenge': Nature, Diaspora, and Transfeminism in Larissa Lai's *Salt Fish Girl*." *Australian Critical Race and Whiteness Studies Association e-Journal* 2, no. 2 (2006): 1–15.

Haraway, Donna. "A Manifesto for Cyborgs: Science, Technology, and Socialist Feminism in the 1980s." In *Feminism/Postmodernism*, edited by Linda J. Nicholson, 190–233. New York: Routledge, 1990.

Hirsch, Marianne. "Surviving Images: Holocaust Photographs and the Work of Post-memory." *The Yale Journal of Criticism* 14, no. 1 (2001): 5–37.

Huang, Michelle N. "Creative Evolution: Narrative Symbiogenesis in Larissa Lai's *Salt Fish Girl*." *Amerasia Journal* 42, no. 2 (2016): 118–138.

Joo, Hee-Jung Serenity. "Reproduction, Reincarnation, and Human Cloning: Literary and Racial Forms in Larissa Lai's *Salt Fish Girl*." *Critique: Studies in Contemporary Fiction* 55, no. 1 (2014): 46–59.

Kong, Belinda. *Tiananmen Fictions Outside the Square: The Chinese Literary Diaspora and the Politics of Global Culture*. Philadelphia: Temple University Press, 2012.

Lai, Larissa. "Afterword." In *When Fox Is a Thousand*. Vancouver: Arsenal Pulp Press, 2004.

———. "Can Asian Am?: Knowing, Being, and Timing Asian Canadian through and across the 49th Parallel." *The Global South* 9, no. 1 (2015): 10–17.

———. "Corrupted Lineage: Narrative in the Gaps of History." *West Coast Line* 34 (2001): 40–53.

———. "Future Asians: Migrant Speculations, Repressed History, and Cyborg Hope." *West Coast Line* 38, no. 2 (2004): 168–175.

———. "Neither Hand, Nor Foot, Nor Kidney: Biopower, Body Parts and Human Flows in Stephen Frears' *Dirty Pretty Things*." *CineAction* 80 (2012): 68–72.

———. "Political Animals and the Body of History." *Canadian Literature* 163 (1999): 145–154.

———. *Salt Fish Girl*. Toronto: Thomas Allen, 2002.

Lai, Paul. "Stinky Bodies: Mythological Futures and the Olfactory Sense in Larissa Lai's *Salt Fish Girl*." *MELUS* 33, no. 4 (2008): 167–187.

Lee, Tara. "Mutant Bodies in Larissa Lai's *Salt Fish Girl*: Challenging the Alliance between Science and Capital." *West Coast Line* 38, no. 2 (2004): 94–109.

Liu, Hong, and Els van Dongen. "Introduction." *The Chinese Diaspora*. New York: Oxford University Press, 2013. *Oxford Bibliographies*. www.oxfordbibliographies.com/view/document/obo-9780199920082/obo-9780199920082-0070.xml.

Liu, Kate Chiwen. "Hybridization as the Postcolonial-Anti-Exotic in Larissa Lai's *Salt Fish Girl*." *Concentric: Literacy and Cultural Studies* 35, no. 2 (2009): 309–336.

Lousley, Cheryl. "Ecocriticism in the Unregulated Zone." In *Critical Collaborations: Indigeneity, Diaspora, and Ecology in Canadian Literary Studies*, edited by Smaro Kamboureli and Christl Verduyn, 143–160. Waterloo: Wilfrid Laurier University Press, 2014.

Mansbridge, Joanna. "Abject Origins: Uncanny Strangers and Figures of Fetishism in Larissa Lai's *Salt Fish Girl*." *West Coast Line* 38, no. 2 (2004): 121–133.

Morris, Robyn L. "What Does It Mean to Be Human?: Racing Monsters, Clones, and Replicants." *Foundation: The International Review of Science Fiction* 33, no. 91 (2004): 81–96.

O'Brien, Michelle. "Architectures of Life in Asian North American Texts: Convergences of Racial Bodies and the Nonhuman." Paper presented at American Comparative Literature Association Annual Meeting, New York, March, 2014.

Oliver, Stephanie. "Diffuse Connections: Smell and Diasporic Subjectivity in Larissa Lai's *Salt Fish Girl*." *Canadian Literature* 208 (2011): 85–107.

Ong, Aihwa. *Flexible Citizenship: The Cultural Logics of Transnationality*. Durham: Duke University Press, 1999.

Patterson, Christopher B., and Y-Dang Troeung. "The Psyche of Neoliberal Multiculturalism: Queering Memory and Reproduction in Larissa Lai's *Salt Fish Girl* and Chang-rae Lee's *On Such a Full Sea*." *Concentric: Literary and Cultural Studies* 42, no. 1 (2016): 73–98.

Phung, Malissa. "The Diasporic Inheritance of Postmemory and Immigrant Shame in the Novels of Larissa Lai." *Postcolonial Text* 7, no. 3 (2012): 1–19.

Reimer, Sharlee. "Troubling Origins: Cyborg Politics in Larissa Lai's *Salt Fish Girl.*" *Atlantis* 35, no. 1 (2010): 4–14.

Tsing, Anna Lowenhaupt. "Blasted Landscapes (and the Gentle Arts of Mushroom Picking)." In *The Multispecies Salon*, edited by Eben Kirksey. Durham: Duke University Press, 2014.

———. *Friction: An Ethnography of Global Connection*. Princeton: Princeton University Press, 2005.

———. *The Mushroom at the End of the World: On the Possibility of Life in Capitalist Ruins*. Princeton: Princeton University Press, 2015.

———. "Worlding the Matsutake Diaspora: Or, Can Actor-Network Theory Experiment with Holism?" In *Experiments in Holism: Theory and Practice in Contemporary Anthropology*, edited by Ton Otto and Nils Bubandt, 47–66. Oxford: Wiley-Blackwell, 2010.

Tu Wei-ming. "Cultural China." In *The Living Tree: The Changing Meaning of Being Chinese Today*, edited by Tu Wei-ming, 1–34. Stanford: Stanford University Press, 1994.

———. Preface to the Standard Edition. In *The Living Tree: The Changing Meaning of Being Chinese Today*, edited by Tu Wei-ming, v–x. Stanford: Stanford University Press, 1994.

Villegas-López, Sonia. "Body Technologies: Posthuman Figurations in Larissa Lai's *Salt Fish Girl* and Jeanette Winterson's *The Stone Gods.*" *Critique: Studies in Contemporary Fiction* 56, no. 1 (2015): 26–41.

Wang Gungwu. "Diaspora: A Much Abused Word." Interview with Laurent Malvezin. *Asian Affairs*, 2001. www.asian-affairs.com/Diasporas/wanggungwu.html.

Wegener, Susanne. "Forget Modesty: Here Comes the Tail: Abject Bodies, Post-Humanistic Philosophy and Larissa Lai's *Salt Fish Girl.*" *Assuming Gender* 2, no. 1 (2011): 2–18.

Wong, Rita. "Troubling Domestic Limits: Reading Border Fictions Alongside Larissa Lai's *Salt Fish Girl.*" *B.C. Studies* 140 (2003–2004): 109–124.

12

XIAOLU GUO'S *I AM CHINA*

On copulas and copulation

Carlos Rojas

I Am China, the title of Xiaolu Guo's 2014 novel, hinges on a grammatical copula – the linking verb *to be*. The word *am* in Guo's succinct yet elliptical title posits an equivalence between the subject, *I*, and the subject complement, *China*, foregrounding questions of identity, reference, and representation. Embedded within this title statement, meanwhile, are two more sets of referential relationships. First, the pronoun *I* is what is known in linguistic terms as a deictic or a shifter, because it derives its meaning from a contextually determined relationship with its referent. Without additional context, accordingly, it is not clear in whose voice the title phrase is being spoken, and consequently to whom the pronoun *I* corresponds. Second, *China* is a proper noun, and therefore its link to its referent would appear to be straightforward. In fact, however, the precise relationship between a proper name and its referent can be very complicated. What, precisely, is the referent of the name *China*? Is *China* referring here to a political entity, a geographic region, a cultural nexus, or an idealized abstraction? Is it a singular entity or a plural one? Is it really equivalent to the referent of the pronoun *I*, whoever or whatever that may be?

At the same time, the novel itself revolves around a focus on copulation. In fact, the work opens with a description of the protagonist, a young Scottish woman named Iona Kirkpatrick, getting dressed after a one-night stand:

> Behind her in the background gloom of her flat, a nameless man finishes dressing, putting on his shirt and trousers. He gazes at Iona's bare back, her boyish bottom, her bony and compact features. He betrays a certain awkwardness. Iona doesn't ask him to stay for breakfast, or make the simple offer of a morning coffee. Since they woke up she has offered him nothing. Yet last night she had been so receptive, the way she had opened her body for him.[1]

The remainder of the novel details a series of Iona's sexual encounters, through which she appears to use hookups with virtual strangers as a substitute for a committed romantic relationship. Although these encounters are not the novel's primary focus, they nevertheless offer a suggestive counterpoint to the work's central narrative line, which involves the translation of a collection of personal documents belonging to a separated Chinese couple. The imbrication of intimacy and estrangement in these descriptions of Iona's sexual encounters offers an oddly powerful metaphor for the act of translation itself.

Even as Iona is pursuing these casual encounters as a means of indefinitely deferring the possibility of romantic and emotional intimacy, her translation project brings her into a displaced romantic relationship with the separated Chinese couple whom she initially only knows through the documents that have come into her possession. A professional Chinese-English translator, Iona has been given a collection of personal letters and diary entries by her publisher and been asked to translate them. Her editor has reason to believe that the documents may be of interest, but he doesn't read Chinese and consequently has no real idea what they might contain. As Iona works her way through the material, it becomes clear that the documents were composed by a young Chinese couple named Kublai Jian and Deng Mu, who were separated after Jian left China to live abroad. Iona becomes increasingly invested in the couple's relationship, alternately identifying with both Jian and Mu.

Translation is not merely the subject of Guo's novel; it is also the work's primary conceptual locus. Written by an expatriate author for whom English is her second language, *I Am China* derives from – and simultaneously reflects on – processes of translation and transposition. In the following discussion, I will use the twin figures of the copula and copulation to consider the novel's understanding of translation, as well as its broader implications for questions of reference and identity. In particular, I am interested in how translation comes to function as a metonym for political community.

"The axle"

Xiaolu Guo is a writer and filmmaker from China who published two novels in Chinese before relocating to London in 2002, when she began writing in English. Her first English-language novel, the 2007 volume *A Concise Chinese-English Dictionary for Lovers*, is composed in the form of a diary in the voice of a twenty-three-year-old Chinese woman who visits England for a year to learn English.[2] The diary begins on the day the protagonist – who goes by the initial Z, because she finds that foreigners have a hard time pronouncing her surname, Zhuang – first arrives in London, and it concludes when she returns to China twelve months later. The structural conceit of the novel is that each diary entry is preserved as it was originally written, and consequently the succession of entries offers a compelling record not only of the protagonist's impressions and experiences during her year in Britain but also of her gradual mastery of the English language – from the first few entries, which are composed in very rudimentary and ungrammatical English, to the impressively eloquent English prose in the final entries.

One feature of *A Concise Chinese-English Dictionary for Lovers* that partly undermines this structural conceit is the fact that the narrative repeatedly includes embedded explanations of Chinese terms and phrases. Although it is not surprising that the Chinese-speaking protagonist would occasionally use Chinese terms and phrases while trying to write in her diary in English, it is harder to understand why she would then add *English-language explanations* of these same terms in a private text that she is ostensibly writing for herself.[3] While these explanations are obviously provided for the benefit of the work's prospective English-language readers, they nevertheless undermine the novel's fictional premise.

This translation gap is even evident in the relationship between the work's title and its content. The novel's title refers to a Chinese-English dictionary, which is to say a dictionary in which Chinese terms are defined in English. The novel does explicitly incorporate a dictionary format into its narrative struc-ture (each diary entry is preceded by a word and its corresponding definition), but the dictionary entries in the novel proper are actually from a conventional English-language dictionary in which the terms being defined and the defini-tions themselves are both in English. Given the premise of the novel, it would arguably have made more sense to have structured it as an *English-Chinese* dic-tionary (the sort of dictionary that would be most useful to a Chinese speaker with minimal English skills), and to open each chapter with a dictionary-like entry in which the word being defined appears in English and the correspond-ing definition is in Chinese. This option, however, would have required leaving large chunks of the text in Chinese – which either the author or the publisher evidently was reluctant to do.

The result of these apparent concessions to the realities of the English-language publishing environment (in which it would be very unusual to see significant amounts of untranslated Chinese text in a work published by a major English-language publisher) is that embedded within the very structure of this work is a silent conversation between the work and ourselves, its presumptive readers. We are, accordingly, placed in the position of the diarist's two "ideal" readers: herself and her English lover (who is addressed as "you in future" in the novel's first diary entry, before the diarist has even met him, and whom she addresses again in the final entry after they have already separated, remarking, "I think I have received your last letter. The last.").[4]

After *A Concise Chinese-English Dictionary for Lovers*, Xiaolu Guo published several more novels in English, including *I Am China* in 2014. This novel simi-larly revolves around a series of diary entries, but in a way that more explicitly foregrounds issues of translation. In particular, *I Am China* details Iona's efforts to translate and make sense of the tranche of documents that her publisher gives her in April 2013. The documents include copies of both Mu's and Jian's diaries, as well as letters they wrote to each other. When Iona first contacts her editor in May 2013, he tells her, via e-mail, that when he was in Beijing "a few months ago" for an international literary festival, Mu had sought him out and, appearing very agitated, had given him photocopies of the diaries and the letters, explaining that her boyfriend, Jian, "was missing in Europe and they had lost contact two months ago" (98).[5] Iona spends the next several months organizing and translating the documents, periodically searching the internet for additional information about Jian and Mu.

Guo's novel includes numerous excerpts from Iona's translations of Jian's and Mu's documents – accompanied, in many instances, by copies of portions of the original handwritten Chinese versions. The narrative emphasizes Iona's struggles to decipher Jian's messy handwriting and his occasional use of local dialect. For example, one early letter contains some textual elements that are virtually unintelligible:

> The page she is holding with one dry hand is covered with doodles, black ink mixed with blue. Large characters. She recognises Kublai Jian's scrawl. Here and there the words have been furiously crossed out.
>
> It's a difficult text. Iona strains to understand. Jian seems very angry, and she doesn't totally comprehend some of the idiom he uses. She feels stressed. The Chinese seem to love using old, formal idiom, even when a young person is writing. But there is also masses of text written in a very colloquial way, as if it were a blog or an email dashed off in a rush.
>
> *(70–71)*

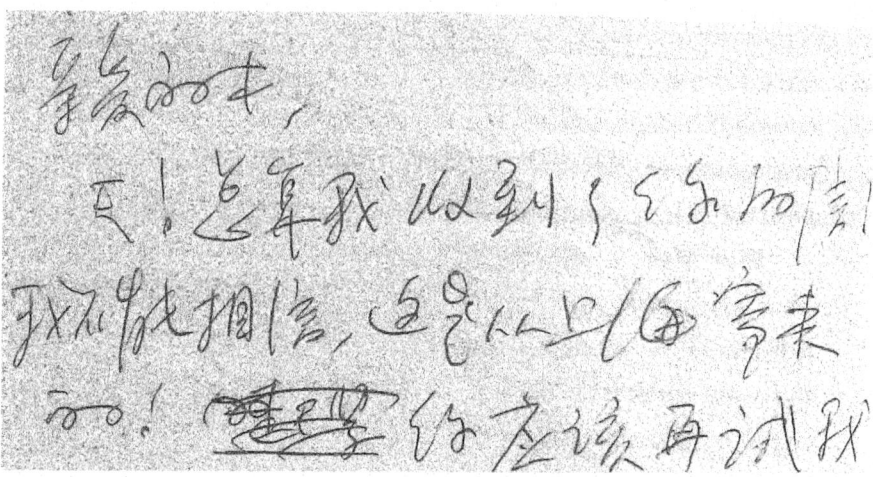

FIGURE 12.1 Reproduced from Xiaolu Guo, *I Am China.*

After another page of narrative, the novel includes a translation of the letter itself, but the translation diverges from the original handwritten version in several respects (See figure 12.1). Not only does the English translation fail to reference the crossed-out Chinese characters mentioned in the preceding narrative (which are reproduced in the copy of the original handwritten letter included in the novel), it also includes a "translator's note" in brackets, which explains that in that particular passage Jian is using a dialectal expression with which Iona is not familiar:

> *Thinking of you makes me "zhou* – 轴*."* [Translator's note: not sure what this means. It's a new colloquial expression not heard before.] *It's hard thinking about you and our life together, with me here in this brown-brick world.*
>
> (72)

The character *zhou* 轴 not only is marked as an element that resists translation but also is ultimately left untranslated in the text. In contrast to *A Concise Chinese-English Dictionary for Lovers*, in which all of the Chinese elements in the text are either translated into or explained in English, *I Am China* contains several other Chinese elements that, like *zhou*, are left untranslated.

Zhou literally means "axle" or "shaft," as in the rod to which the wheels of a cart are attached. In Beijing slang, however, it has come to mean stubborn or recalcitrant. Even as the untranslated term explicitly marks Jian's own stubbornness, it simultaneously functions as an indexical trace of a stubborn resistance to translation in this novel that is itself explicitly predicated on translation. In fact, to play on the double meaning of *zhou*, one could even say that this stubborn resistance to translation serves as the figurative axle around which the work itself revolves.

At one point the novel even includes an explicit reflection on this question of the limit of translation. Iona is sitting at a café in London working on her translation, waiting for her former professor to meet her. He shows up and asks her what she is working on, and after she tells him a bit about her project, he remarks, "You know what, Iona? There is one thing from all your classes with me that you ever wanted to learn: untranslatability" (214). Iona and her teacher proceed to have a back-and-forth in which her teacher insists on the importance of acknowledging the inherent limits of translation, while Iona instead prefers to think in terms of "the technical devices, the tricks of language – metaphors, paraphrase, adaptation" that can be used to address translational challenges (215). Eventually, however, she acknowledges,

> "I seem to be failing here. I spend my days grappling with the real people, trying to get them to come out. But I feel like I'm not making contact with them. It's like, despite all of my efforts to make them speak, they remain silent. Or won't speak to me. What can I do? What am I doing? What's the point with that connection?"

Her teacher responds, "I think, my dear, you're talking about something else here. I don't think it's about translation at all. I think it's more about you" (214–215).

Casual copulation

While working on translating Mu's and Jian's writings, Iona also has a series of casual sexual encounters. These are presented as being independent from – but at the same time apparently a displaced projection of – her translation work.

For instance, early on, in May 2013, Iona is working on one of Jian's letters to Mu, and she

> has an image of two rebels in love. Their strong emotions colour her mind with shades of red and shimmering blue. Mu and Jian, separated by their beliefs, and now separated by space, dropped on different alien planets. Both of them grappling with their own reality. Both of them trying to build a bridge on which to meet. And it's like Iona is building this bridge again, through her reading, her translation. Building a bridge of meaning from their letters, and she has to choose the right words to keep the structure standing.
>
> *(78)*

Later in the same passage, perhaps as a result of the strain of trying to build a bridge between two separated lovers, Iona herself begins to feel a sense of yearning:

> Iona sinks back into her chair. Her body feels lonely, although her mind is full. A longing, a need, a swoon is rising between her loins and mounting to her chest. She can't help but lower her hand. Her fingers find their way into her underwear – it's warm and damp there. She presses her pubic region. Her body begins to recede into a realm of pure sensation, delicate and enticing. She rests her head on the back of the chair. For a while she remains in that position, as if lying back on a man's chest, her head resting on the warm skin covering a pulsing heart. Away, away . . . in some drowsy mix of pleasure and sunlight, she falls slowly, and sinks into oblivion.
>
> *(81)*

A few days after this masturbatory scene, Iona visits a man she met over the internet:

> They barely speak to each other. She has come here for one simple reason: the unsaid sex in their brief but obvious Internet communication. Tony is muscular and tall, not at all unattractive. She feels her loins becoming wet as he is unzipping her lilac dress. He tries to kiss her, from her cheeks to her neck, then on the mouth, but Iona feels disgusted when his lips get close to

hers. She can't do it. There's something repulsive about the idea of their lips and tongues colliding. Instead, she commands him: "Lick me."

(94)

Just as Iona's masturbation in the preceding scene is presented as a displaced expression of her attempt to create a translational bridge between Jian and Mu, in this latter encounter, after Iona's disgust at the prospect of direct oral contact with the stranger and demand that he kiss her "lower lips" (95), her genital labia function as a displaced substitute for her momentarily silenced mouth.

When Iona first meets her editor, Jonathan, a few weeks after she begins work on the translation, the encounter is fraught with sexual tension as they speculatively eye each other:

> As Jonathan orders the coffee, Iona discreetly observes him. He is lean, wearing a close-fitting black suit and a pair of polished shoes that tap on the wooden floor as he waits for the coffees. His wavy, dark hair betrays hints of the dandy and bounces gently on his shoulders while he leans on the counter and turns to Iona. His voice is a warm, smoky baritone. . . .
>
> Iona feels his eyes on her breasts. She is wearing a low-cut pink blouse.
>
> *(103)*

Eventually Iona develops an extramarital affair with Jonathan (he is ten years older than she and has two children, but as she is completing the translation his wife runs off to India with her yoga instructor). In this way, Jonathan's status shifts from being an intermediary between Iona and the documents she obtains from Mu and Jian to being an object of mediation in his own right.

In addition to Iona's masturbatory episodes, her one-night stands, and her romance with her editor, her most intriguing sexual engagement is perhaps the one she develops with Mu and Jian in the process of translating their respective works. At one point in June 2013, for instance, Iona reflects that

> If you spend enough time reading someone ELSE's thoughts, after a while their thoughts begin to infect you. Your grasp on yourself becomes tenuous. Or you begin to see that you never were the essential you in the first place, Iona thinks to herself as she takes the bus back to Angel. To be a person is to imagine being someone, and the someone you imagine most of the time is what people call "you." How strange to be in time and space with something called a "character." Jian is separated from Iona by time and space. But there is something about his sadness, his strength, that emboldens her. It makes her long for some other self, some ability to reach outside herself and be brave.
>
> *(159–160)*

Iona then uses the metaphor of an oyster to describe the relationship that she feels she has developed with Jian and Mu, wherein she feels like a Tiresias figure – vicariously experiencing sexual desire from both a male and a female perspective:

> Iona feels her body is like an oyster, in its dark, cold sealed shell. In the first year of its life, a young oyster spills its sperm into the water. During the next two years it grows larger and then releases eggs. Then the water surrounding it does the rest of the work. An oyster shifts from being male to female. It plays both roles. That's how Iona feels as she walks around, confined to her oyster-shell flat – sometimes like Jian, sometimes like Mu, sometimes both.
>
> *(160)*

In this fascinating passage, Iona uses a fantasy of molluscan sex to explain the relationship she feels she has developed to the two individuals whose texts she is translating, while at the same time implicitly referring to the earlier reference to her own onanism. In particular, although the description of the oysters' sex switch is biologically accurate, her truncated summation that "then the water surrounding it does the rest of the work" seems to imply that the oyster's eggs are then fertilized by the sperm that *the same oyster* had released into the water a year or two earlier – which is to say, that the oyster is having "sex" with itself.

Moreover, the same oyster metaphor could be used to describe the act of translation itself. Just as the disseminative process of oyster copulation described above stands in stark contrast to the way (human) sexual relations are often viewed as expressions of physical and emotional intimacy, Iona's translation process (which is conducted almost entirely at a distance, with no direct contact with her subjects) similarly stands in direct contrast to the way that, say, diary or letter writing is conventionally viewed as a direct expression of the subject's views and feelings. In other words, (molluscan) copulation and translation, under this reading, are operations grounded not in abstract ideals of presence and identity but rather in processes of mediation, displacement, and dissemination.

The bluest sea

The preceding concerns with copulas, copulation, and issues of untranslatability come together in the title of Guo's novel – or, more specifically, in the work's *alternate* title. Although the novel was initially written and published in English and the cover contains only the English-language title, the title page nevertheless features a double, bilingual title:

I Am China | 最蔚藍的海
A NOVEL

Contrary to what readers might expect, the Chinese phrase that appears here is not a translation of the English title but a completely different phrase that literally means "the bluest sea." Curiously, however, although it ultimately comes to occupy a crucial position in the narrative, at no point does the novel ever provide an explicit link between the phrase as it appears in this (alternate) title and the corresponding English translation that eventually appears in the text itself.

The Chinese phrase first appears near the end of the novel, where Iona finds it in the final entry of Jian's diary (See figure 12.2). The chapter in question opens with an English translation of the penultimate page of the diary, which concludes with the line "And this morning I woke up with a single image in my head. I dreamed of the bluest sea I will ever see." Next, Iona turns to the final page of the diary:

> She is on the last page, there are no more photocopies in his file. On the white sheet, there are only two lines, scribbled with big characters. But the characters are sprawling out every which way and so messily written that they are nearly unrecognisable.
>
> It takes her a while to make out each character and she has to hold the page at odd angles to try and decipher the words. Eventually she has a rough translation of Jian's final two sentences:
>
> *The sea there is the bluest and purest. It's the last blue I will see.*
>
> *(312)*

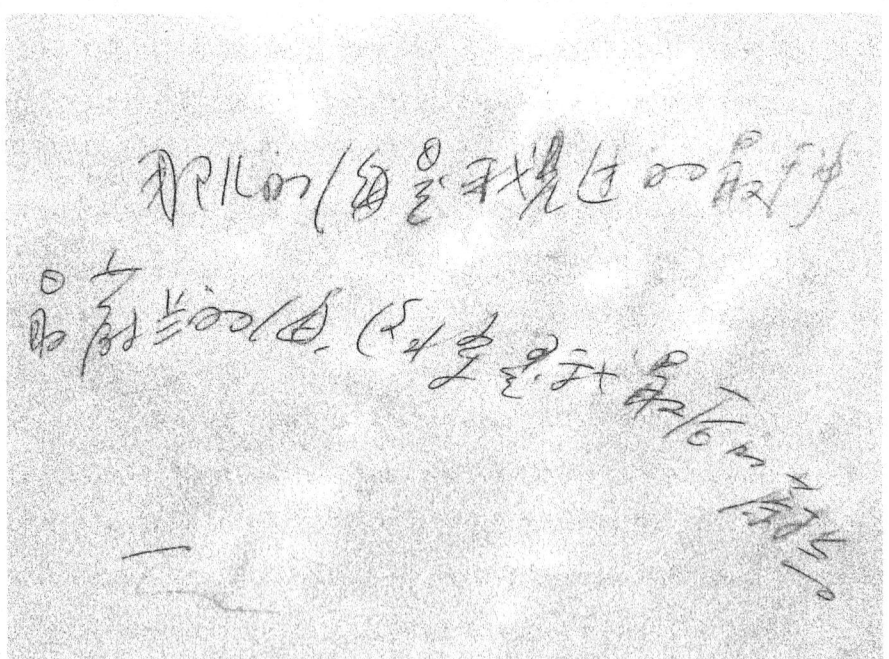

FIGURE 12.2 Reproduced from Xiaolu Guo, *I Am China*.

Compounding the difficulty of making out Jian's almost illegible handwriting, Iona is also challenged by the syntax of this final line, given that in translating the line into English it is necessary to specify certain syntactic elements – such as verb tense – that are indeterminate in the original Chinese. Iona experiments with several different translations, all of which are syntactically defensible readings of the Chinese phrase, but they nevertheless suggest significantly different understandings:

> The sea there is the bluest and purest. And this is the last blue I can see.
> The sea there was the bluest and purest. It was the last blue I have ever seen.
> There, that see, the bluest and purest sea. It will be the last blue I shall ever see.
>
> (313)

Although the novel's conclusion suggests that the final interpretation is likely the most accurate, this fascinating passage underscores the interpretive gap inherent in translation – and how the act of translation can help illuminate ambiguities present in the original text.

From this final diary entry, as well as other references made earlier in the diary, Iona develops a hunch that Jian may have traveled to Crete. She immediately purchases a plane ticket there, but shortly after arriving she learns that a Chinese man has recently committed suicide by jumping into the Mediterranean. Telling the police that she is related to the victim, Iona is taken to see his body and shown some of his possessions, including an unmailed letter to Mu:

> Under the gaze of two police officers and a secretary, Iona silently reads the first four lines of the letter. Then she stops. She can't bring herself to believe what she is reading.
>
> *To the ones in this world who will eventually read my words:*
>
> *And to Mu:*
> *The sea here is the bluest and purest I have ever seen. It's the last blue I will see. They say planet Earth is a blue planet when you see it from space. So I want to go out with the blue.*
>
> (342)

Iona is shocked to realize that if only she had succeeded in locating Jian a few days earlier, she might have been able to try to intervene. Like an arrow arcing toward a moving target, her translation project had been incrementally and inexorably closing in on Jian's and Mu's present-day lives, but she has arrived just a shade too late to save Jian's.

Although the conclusion of the novel revolves around the phrase "the bluest sea," as it appears in Jian's handwritten diary and suicide note, the work never provides a *printed* version of the corresponding Chinese characters (as it does, for instance, for the character *zhou* 轴). Moreover, although the Chinese characters for the phrase "the bluest sea" do appear (in various permutations) in the body of

answer. Her face becomes rigid. "When we were upstairs you told me you were this man's friend, you were his translator."

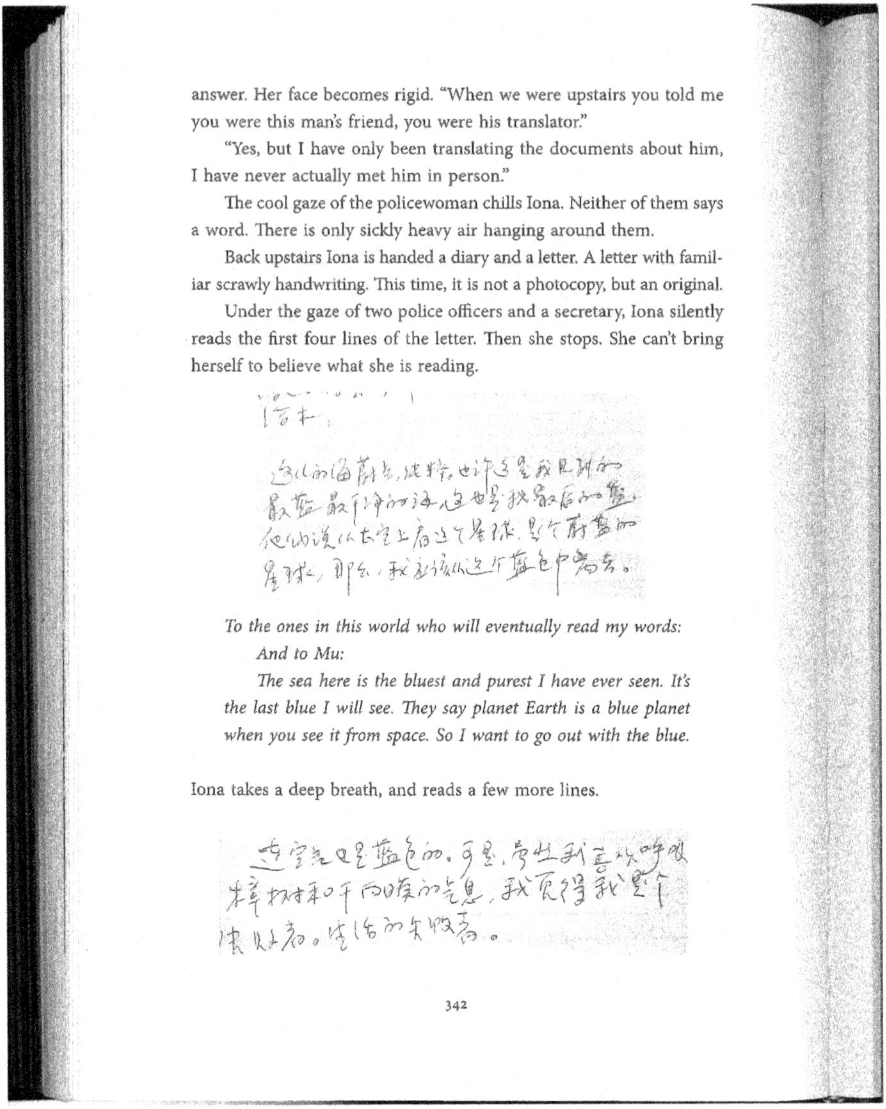

"Yes, but I have only been translating the documents about him, I have never actually met him in person."

The cool gaze of the policewoman chills Iona. Neither of them says a word. There is only sickly heavy air hanging around them.

Back upstairs Iona is handed a diary and a letter. A letter with familiar scrawly handwriting. This time, it is not a photocopy, but an original.

Under the gaze of two police officers and a secretary, Iona silently reads the first four lines of the letter. Then she stops. She can't bring herself to believe what she is reading.

To the ones in this world who will eventually read my words:
And to Mu:
The sea here is the bluest and purest I have ever seen. It's the last blue I will see. They say planet Earth is a blue planet when you see it from space. So I want to go out with the blue.

Iona takes a deep breath, and reads a few more lines.

342

FIGURE 12.3 Reproduced from Xiaolu Guo, *I Am China.*

the novel, they do so only in reproductions of Jian's handwritten documents (in which his handwriting is the typical messy "scrawl") (See figure 12.3). Moreover, in Jian's diary, he uses the extrasimplified version of the character for "blue" (*lan*), 兰, which is visually quite different from the alternate version, 藍, that appears in both his suicide note and the novel's Chinese title. For readers who do not already know Chinese, it would be very difficult to determine, based on the information provided within the novel itself, the meaning of the Chinese-language title on the work's title page. Consequently, this alternate title opens up a critical gap between the work's presumptive English-language audience and those readers who can also read Chinese.[6]

For instance, while it is true that the first time the novel's alternate Chinese title appears in the work *in Chinese* is at the end of Jian's diary, which was presumably written in 2013 and is translated and partly reproduced at the end of Guo's novel, a version of the same phrase also appears *in translation* in an early 1993 entry in the same diary, which is translated and discussed near the beginning of the novel. This 1993 diary entry, which is what led Iona to conclude, in late 2013, that Jian had decided to fly to Crete, was written just after Jian first met Mu. In it, Jian includes a sketch of Mu and describes a conversation they had about leaving China:

> *"Where would you go, if you could choose just one island?"*
>
> *"I don't know," I shrugged. "How are we to know anything if we have never been outside of China?"*
>
> *"Come on . . . just imagine. Imagine that one day you wake up and find yourself on a quiet and beautiful island in the middle of a very blue sea. Where would it be?" She nudged me.*
>
> *Then she covered my eyes with her palm, lifted my hand and let my finger land at random on the map. Then she removed her hand from my eyes and in an excited voice said: "Here it is. Crete." A Greek island in the middle of the Mediterranean. That's where my finger had found its place.*
>
> *(38)*

Although bilingual readers will undoubtedly notice that this early diary entry contains a version of the (Chinese) title phrase and be able to surmise that the entry is somehow important, readers who know only English will not realize this until the end of the novel, when the narrative explicitly establishes the link between the 1993 diary entry and Jian's final entry from 2013.

Irrespective of the reason Guo herself cites for including the alternate Chinese title on the title page of the English novel (see discussion in endnote 6), one obvious effect of the decision is that it invites *both* English-only readers and English/ Chinese bilingual readers to reflect on how they are positioned within the imagined community of the work's general readership. As a result, even as the work is exploring the constitution and fragmentation of miniature communities – including the fractured couple Jian and Mu, Iona's relationship with Jonathan and her vicarious relationship with both Jian and Mu, and Mu and Iona's eventual in-person rendezvous – it is simultaneously reflecting in a subtle fashion on the ways the novel's readers are positioned with respect to the work itself and to one another.

"I am China"

After Iona returns to London from Crete, she receives a letter from Mu, who obtained Iona's name and address from the publisher. In the letter, Mu says that she knows Iona has been translating the documents she, Mu, had given Jonathan earlier that year. Mu would very much like to meet Iona in person and invites her to attend her first poetry performance in the United Kingdom. Finally, Mu mentions that she has an additional document – a copy of a handwritten manifesto that Jian handed out at his last concert – that she would like to give to Iona.

The novel then includes a translation of that document, which opens with a section explicitly based on the famous discussion, in the *Zhuangzi* (庄子), of Zhuang Zhou's dream of being a butterfly. Whereas in the *Zhuangzi* passage Zhuang Zhou famously wonders aloud whether he just dreamed of being a butterfly or he was instead now a butterfly dreaming of being the philosopher Zhuang Zhou, Jian's manifesto opens with the premise that the narrator, "I," was dreaming of being not a butterfly but rather China itself:

Dream:

I had a dream. I dreamed I was a great nation. I was a state. My power stretched over the land and its peoples. I felt power running through my veins, and felt it strong in my heart. I was China.

Then I woke up. I wondered: was I a man waking from a dream of being China, or was China dreaming of being a man?

If I am a man dreaming I am China, I want to rule the world. To be a great state, with power over the people like small animals beneath me.

If China dreams of being a man, then I am just that man living out the myth of a great state. My thoughts and desires are not my own, but are taken from the state. China rules my heart.

(360)

The document contains several additional short sections and concludes with a final one-line section:

Break the spell:

I am China. We are China. The People. Not the state.

Here, in this manifesto reproduced in translation near the very end of the novel, is the first explicit allusion to the work's title line, "I am China." Despite the seemingly straightforward nature of this statement, its significance is deeply ambiguous, raising interesting questions of the nature of both identity and political community.

To begin with, the allusion to Zhuangzi's butterfly conundrum in the "Dream" section of the manifesto introduces an element of asymmetry and indeterminacy into the relationship between the subject and the subject complement or predicate, such that the predicate (the butterfly or China) may in fact prove to have a determining influence over what was otherwise assumed to be the subject ("I" or "we"). Moreover, in shifting from a singular "I" to a plural "we," the "Break the

Spell" section of the manifesto suggests that the referent of the original subject "I" is actually not an individual, but an individual speaking on behalf of a collective – just as the following two clauses suggest that the referent of the subject complement "China" is actually not a singular entity but a collective designated as "the people."

Following the translation of Jian's document, Xiaolu Guo's novel concludes with a description of Mu's London poetry performance. Iona arrives late and misses Mu's first reading, but is in time for her second and final one. The latter is a rendition of Allen Ginsberg's 1956 poem "America," but each reference to America has been replaced with the word "China." Mu begins by noting that the reading is dedicated to the memory of Kublai Jian, then recites:

China

China I've given you all and now I'm nothing.
China two dollars and twenty-seven cents.
I can't stand my own mind.
China when will we end the human war?
Go fuck yourself with your atom bomb.
I don't feel good don't bother me.
I won't write my poem till I'm in my right mind.

Mu's recitation continues for several more stanzas,[7] the last of which reads:

China I'm addressing you.
Are you going to let our emotional life be run by Time Magazine?
I'm obsessed with Time Magazine.
I read it every week.
Its cover stares at me every time I slink past the corner candystore.
I read it in the basement of the Berkeley Public Library.
It's always telling me about responsibility. Businessmen are serious, movie
    producers are serious. Everyone's serious but me.
It occurs to me that I am China.
I am talking to myself again.

The chapter ends on this reference to talking to oneself, as does the novel as a whole (though the work is then capped by a two-page postscript).[8] Ironically, however, in context the reading in question could not be farther from talking to oneself, insofar as Mu is engaged in a public performance directed in particular to Iona, expressly invited to attend. Moreover, Mu specifies that the performance is in memory of Kublai Jian, suggesting that he is also an addressee, as is the late Ginsberg, with whom Mu is figuratively in dialogue.

Although Mu's version of Ginsberg's poem concludes with the line "I am talking to myself again," the original poem continues for much longer. In fact, the very next two lines of Ginsberg's "America" resonate in a surprisingly suggestive manner with Mu's reinterpreted version:

> Asia is rising against me.
> I haven't got a chinaman's chance.

In Ginsberg's poem, these two lines are curiously in tension with each other. The reference to "Asia . . . rising" is presumably partly an allusion to the growing geopolitical power of Communist China (and, as such, it uncannily anticipates contemporary discourses celebrating "China's rise"), even as the subsequent reference to "a chinaman's chance" is grounded on a set of racist, anti-Chinese discourses that remain pervasive even today. Taken together, the two lines suggest that "I" (America) don't/doesn't have a "chinaman's chance" of resisting the growing geopolitical power of Asia, while in Mu's transposed version the "I" is equated not with America but with China itself, meaning that the elided two lines would have suggested that "I" (China) don't/doesn't have a "chinaman's chance" of resisting the growing geopolitical power of Asia (China).

Ginsberg's original poem is dated January 17, 1956, and its reference to *Time* magazine covers staring back at the author may have been an allusion to the January 16, 1956, issue, which featured a portrait of Israel's premier, Ben Gurion – whom the accompanying cover story calls a "prophet with a gun."[9] Ginsberg, who was born into a Jewish family but as an adult became a practicing Buddhist and was vocally antimilitary, would presumably have felt an oddly alienated relationship with the face on this cover – a figure who represented a very different worldview from his own.

Although Ginsberg's original reference may have been partly to the Ben Gurion cover, Deng Mu's subsequent performance of "China" presumably has little relationship to that issue of the magazine published more than half a century earlier. Instead, Mu's contemporary reinterpretation of Ginsberg's poem may contain a tacit allusion to the cover image of the international edition of *Time*'s December 2, 2013, issue, which features an oversized pair of hands holding a small child accompanied by a caption referring to the proposed lifting of China's one-child policy.[10] As we learn earlier in the novel, Mu and Jian actually had a son in late 2005, while they were still in China, but the child died six months later, and the experience was so devastating for both of them that they separated shortly afterward. However, although Mu's London performance of "China" takes place in December 2013, we are previously told that it was in May 2012 that Mu came up with the idea of transposing the Ginsberg poem into a poem about China (129–130) – meaning that her original reinterpretation could not have been informed by the *Time* issue on China's one-child policy, which was not published until a year later.

Given the specific focus of Mu's London performance – and indeed of Guo's entire novel – on concerns with migration and assimilation, Mu's ventriloquistic allusion to the *Time* covers in her adaptation of the poem may instead be in reference to a famous cover from almost precisely twenty years earlier. On November 18, 1993, *Time* published a special issue titled "The New Face of America: How Immigrants are Shaping the World's First Multicultural Society."

The cover for that week features the face of an attractive young woman, and a caption that reads:

> Take a good look at this woman. She was created by a computer from a mix of several different races. What you see is a remarkable preview of . . . The New Face of America.

This 1993 cover story underscores the role played by immigration in shaping American demographics. Previously, race-based restrictions on immigration (in particular, the Chinese Exclusion Act of 1882) and an array of antimiscegenation laws significantly restricted interracial marriage, and even sex, in many US states and territories until after World War II. During the latter half of the twentieth century and the first decades of the twenty-first, however, the percentage of ethnic minorities (including mixed-race individuals) has increased rapidly, to the point that it is projected that within another fifty years no single ethno-racial group will account for a majority of the population.[11] If we were to transpose the subject of Jian's earlier manifesto from China to America (the same way that Mu transposes Ginsberg's poem from America to China), then the 1993 *Time* cover offers a compelling (prophetic) illustration of the postulate "I am [America]. We are [America]."

Whether or not Mu (or Guo, for that matter) was alluding to the 1993 "multi-ethnic America" cover, the sentiment that underlies the cover story is very consonant with that of *I Am China*. The *Time* story emphasizes the fact that a nation's identity is not fixed but rather is a product of its people – who are themselves shaped by the process of immigration and reproduction. In *I Am China*, meanwhile, the novel's interest in the function of the copula *am* directly parallels its exploration of a variety of different forms of literal and metaphorical copulation. These parallel themes come together most evocatively in Iona's comparison of her status as a translator to the process of oyster reproduction – wherein copulation becomes literally a process of disembodied dissemination. Just as the oyster's relationship to its own offspring is fundamentally distanced and mediated by the sea, the identity of the nation is not an autonomous ideal but rather necessarily resides in the constantly shifting makeup of its citizens and residents. To borrow a coinage by postcolonial theorist Homi Bhabha, the nation is, ultimately, the product of a continual process of "dissemiNation."[12]

Finally, to the extent that *I Am China* is ultimately a reflection on – and a product of – processes of translation, we may also find embedded in the figure of the oyster a useful metaphorical commentary on translation itself. Oysters are, of course, commonly associated with pearls, which are produced when an irritant is introduced between an oyster's shell and its mantle and as a result of being covered in multiple layers of nacre eventually becomes a beautiful pearl. Similarly, in a translation, nodes of untranslatability (like the character *zhou* in Guo's novel) function as irritants that may generate compelling literary products. At the level of the nation, meanwhile, the parallel to these figurative irritants would be elements that on the surface appear to be at odds with idealized understandings of national identity, but which, through a process of adaptation and transformation, may help generate new modes of identity and belonging.

Notes

1 Xiaolu Guo, *I Am China: A Novel* (New York: Doubleday, 2014), 9. Subsequent citations from this work will be referenced parenthetically in the main body of the chapter.
2 Xiaolu Guo, *A Concise Chinese-English Dictionary for Lovers* (New York: Anchor, 2008).
3 For instance, at one point she writes, "All the work is called '讨生活' – scavenge the living. Making shoes, making tofus, making plastic bags, making switches. . . . All these works rely on our bodies. And bodies earn our living back" (122). Here, the addition of the English-language phrase "scavenge the living" seems odd, in that it serves no obvious function other than to parse the meaning of "讨生活" for English readers. Similarly, on the following page, she writes,

> Intellectual: 知识分子 (*zhi shi fen zi*)
>
> "知识" mean knowledge, "分子" mean molecule. Numerous molecules of knowledge will make up man knowledgeable.
>
> *(123)*

Here, there is more of an attempt to incorporate the explanation of the Chinese term into the narrative, but it still feels somewhat artificial (particularly the inclusion of the pinyin romanization, which a native Chinese speaker writing for herself presumably would not need).

4 Xiaolu Guo, *A Concise Chinese-English Dictionary for Lovers*, 3, 282.
5 The literary festival in question was presumably the Beijing Bookworm International Literary Festival, which in 2013 ran from March 8 to 22. http://bookwormfestival.com.
6 In a recent interview, Guo replied to a remark that the novel's Chinese title is very different from its English title by explaining,

> The book is not published in Chinese nor in China. I gave the English version a Chinese title as well so that I could have control over it and stop anyone giving it the wrong Chinese title. I hate literal translations – although it's called "I Am China" in English, in Chinese it's called "The Bluest Sea" or "The Most Blue Sea." I did this because I was worried that someday a crazy translator would decide on "Wo Shi Zhongguo" which is nonsense in Chinese. I feel I will enter a dark place when it's mistranslated, so I had to prevent that. (Xiaolu Guo, in conversation with Ralf Hertel, "Writing China Across the Globe," *Aglistentag 2016 Hamburg: Proceedings*, ed. Ute Berns and Jolene Mathieson [Trier: WVT Wissenschaftlicher Verlag Trier, 2017], 8)

This explanation is rather curious. Given that the entire novel revolves around Iona's attempts to translate and make sense of Mu's and Jian's writings *outside of their control*, it is odd that the author would make such an explicit gesture of attempting to *retain control* over her own text in anticipation of the possibility that it might be translated into Chinese.

7 Although Ginsberg's original poem is not divided into stanzas, the version of Mu's reinterpretation of the poem that appears in Guo's novel is divided into stanzas of seven or eight lines each. The original poem can be found in Allen Ginsberg, *Collected Poems 1947–1980* (New York: Harper & Row, 1984).

8 Guo's explanation, in the interview cited above, that in supplying the novel with an alternate Chinese title she was trying to preempt "some crazy translator" from using a literal translation ignores the fact that "Wo shi Zhongguo" is arguably no odder in Chinese than "I am China" is in English. Moreover, given that the English phrase appears within the main body of the novel, even if a Chinese translator were to use Guo's alternate Chinese title for the work, he or she would still need to translate the line "I am China" as it appears in Mu's transmuted version of Ginsberg's poem. A published Chinese translation of the original poem renders the corresponding line "I am America" as "*wo jiu shi Meiguo*" (我就是美国) – precisely the translation that Guo rejects as "nonsense," except for the "*jiu*" (就), which is added for emphasis. See http://blog.sina.com.cn/s/blog_621757f301015efn.html.

9 Although the official publication date of the Ben Gurion issue of *Time* was January 17, 1956, one day before Ginsberg wrote "America," the magazine would have been available on newsstands up to a week before that date.

10 *Time* frequently uses different cover images for the domestic and international versions of the magazine, and for the week of December 2, 2013, the US edition featured a cover about the problems facing "Obamacare" (i.e., the domestic health care reform that President Obama helped implement), while all of the magazine's international editions featured the image from the article on China's one-child policy.

11 D'Vera Cohn, "Future Immigration Will Change the Face of America by 2065," *Fact Tank: News in the Numbers* (October 15, 2015). www.pewresearch.org/fact-tank/2015/10/05/future-immigration-will-change-the-face-of-america-by-2065/.

12 Homi Bhabha, "DissemiNation: Time, Narrative and the Margins of the Modern Nation," in *Nation and Narration*, ed. Homi Bhabha (New York: Routledge, 1990), 139–170.

Works cited

Bhabha, Homi. "DissemiNation: Time, Narrative and the Margins of the Modern Nation." In *Nation and Narration*, edited by Homi Bhabha, 139–170. New York: Routledge, 1990.

Ginsberg, Allen. *Collected Poems 1947–1980*. New York: Harper & Row, 1984.

Guo, Xiaolu. *A Concise Chinese-English Dictionary for Lovers*. New York: Anchor, 2008.

———. *I Am China: A Novel*. New York: Doubleday, 2014.

Guo, Xiaolu, in conversation with Ralf Hertel. "Writing China across the Globe." In *Aglistentag 2016 Hamburg: Proceedings*, edited by Ute Berns and Jolene Mathieson. Trier: WVT Wissenschaftlicher Verlag Trier, 2017.

INDEX

Note: Page numbers in *italic* indicate an illustration on the corresponding page.

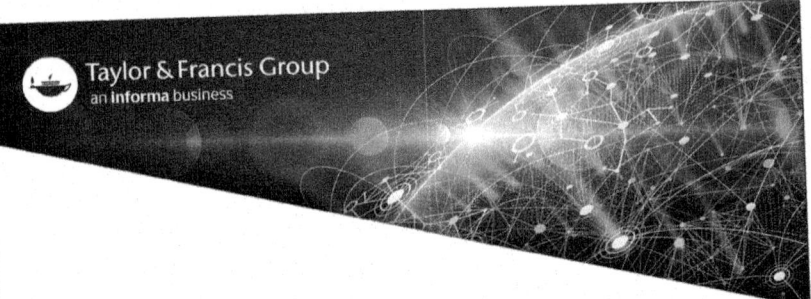